MORE PRAISE FOR
A SURVIVAL GUIDE
FOR NEW SPECIAL EDUCATORS

"An excellent, hands-on approach for any special education teacher. Very appropriate examples and a terrific sense of what a special education teacher does each day makes this book a MUST HAVE resource!"

—Elizabeth LeClear, Ph.D.,
Principal, Santa Fe High School,
Gainesville, Florida

"Comprehensive yet reader friendly, *A Survival Guide for New Special Educators* is an excellent go-to resource for the busy beginning special education teacher. From finding the right job, to internalizing the skills to do the job, to mastering the profession with a high degree of excellence, this book is a must have for educators who work with students with special needs. Go ahead and write your name in it, because you will not be giving this one away!"

—Rachella Prince,
Special Education Curriculum and Instruction Administrative Assistant,
Raleigh County Schools, West Virginia

JOSSEY-BASS™
A Wiley Brand

A Survival Guide for
New Special Educators

BONNIE S. BILLINGSLEY
MARY T. BROWNELL
MAYA ISRAEL
MARGARET L. KAMMAN

WILEY

Cover design: Michael Cook
Cover photo: ©Rob Lewine/Getty

Published by Jossey-Bass
A Wiley Imprint
One Montgomery Street, Suite 1200, San Francisco, CA 94104-4594—www.josseybass.com

Jossey-Bass books and products are available through most bookstores. To contact Jossey-Bass directly call our Customer Care Department within the U.S. at 800-956-7739, outside the U.S. at 317-572-3986, or fax 317-572-4002.

Wiley publishes in a variety of print and electronic formats and by print-on-demand. Some material included with standard print versions of this book may not be included in e-books or in print-on-demand. If this book refers to media such as a CD or DVD that is not included in the version you purchased, you may download this material at http://booksupport.wiley.com. For more information about Wiley products, visit www.wiley.com.

Bonnie Billingsley was employed at Virginia Tech and subsequently at the University of North Carolina at Greensboro during the period that this book was written.

Library of Congress Cataloging-in-Publication Data

Billingsley, Bonnie S.
    A survival guide for new special educators / Bonnie S. Billingsley, Mary T. Brownell, Maya Israel, Margaret L. Kamman.
        pages cm
    Includes bibliographical references and index.
    ISBN 978-1-118-09568-3 (pbk.)
    ISBN 978-1-118-26193-4 (ebk.)
    ISBN 978-1-118-22357-4 (ebk.)
    ISBN 978-1-118-23692-5 (ebk.)
        1. First year teachers—United States. 2. Special education—United States. I. Brownell, Mary T. II. Israel, Maya.
    III. Kamman, Margaret L. IV. Title.
    LB2844.1.N4B55 2013
    371.90973—dc23

                                                                                2012048512

Printed in the United States of America
FIRST EDITION

PB Printing   10 9 8 7 6 5 4 3 2

The Authors

Bonnie S. Billingsley, a former special education teacher and administrator of special education, is a professor at Virginia Tech. Her research interests include special education teacher quality, retention, and teacher induction. Billingsley is the author of the book *Cultivating and Keeping Committed Special Education Teachers* as well as numerous articles in publications such as *Exceptional Children, The Journal of Special Education,* and the *Journal of Learning Disabilities.* She has consulted with numerous educational agencies about special education teacher development and support.

Mary T. Brownell, a former special education teacher, is a professor at the University of Florida and is the director of the Center on Collaboration for Effective Educator Development, Accountability and Reform. She has had numerous grants related to special education teachers and has published extensively in the areas of teacher preparation, quality, retention, and professional development, including articles in *Exceptional Children, The Journal of Special Education,* and *Learning Disability Quarterly.* Brownell is lead author of *Inclusive Instruction: Evidence-Based Practices for Teaching Students with Disabilities.*

Maya Israel, a former special education teacher, is an assistant professor of special education at the University of Illinois. Her primary areas of specialization include using technologies to mentor new teachers and supporting student access to science, technology, engineering, and mathematics (STEM) learning through instructional strategies and technologies. She is involved in several research and development projects supported through the US Department of Education and the National Science Foundation that investigate student digital and print literacies as well as teacher use of instructional strategies and technologies to enhance STEM learning.

Margaret L. Kamman is an assistant scholar and project coordinator at the National Center to Inform Policy and Practice in Special Education at the University of Florida. The purpose of the center is to inform educational agencies of policies and practices that improve the retention and quality of beginning special education teachers. She also teaches graduate classes on language and literacy interventions and assessment for general and special education teachers. She served for a decade in the public schools teaching students with disabilities in K–12 and serving as a special education specialist.

Acknowledgments

The authors are especially grateful to Emily Rex from the University of North Carolina, who worked diligently with the authors to edit this book. We also extend our appreciation to LaQuinta Clark and Courtney Fischer, who helped compile the appendixes.

We express our sincere appreciation to the following individuals who reviewed one or more chapters of this book. They made numerous suggestions that helped make this work stronger.

Susan Asselin, Virginia Tech

Tammy L. Barron, University of North Carolina at Greensboro

Elizabeth Bettini, University of Florida

Pamela W. Carter, University of North Carolina at Greensboro

Jean Crockett, University of Florida

Jeff Diedrich, Michigan Integrated Technology Supports (MITS)

Dimple Malik Flesner, University of Florida

Jessica Gerdes, Illinois State Board of Education

Susan A. Gregson, University of Cincinnati

Matthew Hoge, University of Arizona

Kara Battin Holden, University of North Carolina at Greensboro

Bree A. Jimenez, University of North Carolina at Greensboro

Megan Kemmery, University of North Carolina at Greensboro

Michael Kennedy, University of Virginia

Mary Theresa Kiely, St. John's University

Jenna Kimerling, University of Florida

Richard Lemke, Durham Public Schools' Duke Hospital School

Erica McCray, University of Florida

Emily Rex, University of North Carolina at Greensboro

Lisa Hess Rice, George Washington University

Fred Spooner, University of North Carolina at Charlotte

We'd also like to thank the following educators and colleagues, who contributed their expert advice in the form of textboxes throughout the manuscript:

Tammy L. Barron

Elizabeth Bettini

Carol M. Bland

William Bursuck

Nicole Dobbins

Dimple Malik Flesner

Theresa Forte

Stephanie Gardiner-Walsh

Kara Battin Holden

Aleksandra Hollingshead

Angela Jones

Megan Kemmery

Teresa Little

Yujeong Park

Emily Rex

Stacey Rice

Wenonoa Spivak

Rachel Thomas

Kristin Zimmerman

Contents

Chapter Seventeen: Teaching Students with Limited to Pervasive Intellectual Disability   303
Bree A. Jimenez and Pamela J. Mims

PART FOUR: ADDITIONAL CONSIDERATIONS

Chapter Eighteen: Managing Student Health Needs   325
Pamela W. Carter

PART FIVE: APPENDIXES

Appendix A: Definitions and Resources about Disability   345

Tables, Figures, and Exhibits

TABLES

FIGURES

EXHIBITS

Introduction

Most special educators enter teaching with the desire to help students learn, but being a great special education teacher is also about successfully handling all the tasks that are a part of meeting the needs of students with disabilities. To succeed in this profession you will need knowledge and strategies for teaching students with disabilities effectively, tools for communicating successfully with others, ways of efficiently handling varied work activities, and the ability to take charge of your own growth and well-being.

The primary goal of this book is to provide relevant and practical information and identify resources that will assist you in establishing a productive and satisfying career as a special education teacher. The authors know what you're going through; we have all been beginning teachers and we still remember the enthusiasm and feelings of anxiety we had on the first day of our jobs. Since that day, collectively, we have accumulated more than ninety years of experience as special education teachers, administrators, teacher educators, and researchers. We have also conducted research on new teachers, learning about what their needs are, the types of support they find helpful, and what more and less accomplished special educators do as they begin their careers in schools. We draw from all of these prior experiences to provide a handbook that is designed to help you navigate your first years in the classroom. Other experienced contributors have added valuable ideas to the book as well.

All of us made it through that first year successfully and so can you with the strategies and ideas contained in this survival guide. The major purposes of this book are the following:

- ▶ Provide a big picture of what it means to be an accomplished and committed special education teacher
- ▶ Provide specific guidelines for effective teaching, emphasizing key evidence-based practices
- ▶ Outline strategies for managing your varied roles and nonteaching responsibilities
- ▶ Suggest key print and online resources relevant to special educators' work

OVERVIEW OF THE CHAPTERS

Part One, "The Basics," provides an overview of steps you can take to have a great start in your career. In chapter 1 we outline how to search and interview for jobs that match your preparation and skills. A careful job search is important because teachers who find good matches are more likely to be successful and stay in their positions. In chapter 2 we provide a snapshot of what it's like to be a new special educator, the top challenges new teachers face, and ways to find the support you need. In addition, we also outline ten actions that new special educators can take to become accomplished and effective teachers. These ten actions provide the foundation for your work as a special educator.

Chapter 3 provides communication guidelines for working with adults, including specific suggestions for interacting with colleagues, paraeducators, parents, mentors, and administrators. The relationships you form are critical in developing a team approach for supporting students with disabilities. In chapter 4 we provide guidance for legal questions you may have and tips for ensuring that the key principles of the Individuals with Disabilities Education Act (IDEA) are met. Chapter 5 specifies guidelines for working with others to develop individualized education programs (IEPs) that meet the needs of students, including how to align the goals of the IEP with the academic standards required of all students.

Once you've learned the basics, Part Two, "Becoming an Accomplished Educator," will help you learn the finer points of working as a special educator. Chapter 6 outlines strategies for organizing your work, time, and space, which will help you balance the multiple tasks of teaching special education and preserve as much time as possible for instruction. Chapter 7 highlights goals and major approaches to collaboration, including tips for forging more successful interactions with your colleagues. In chapter 8 you will learn about the importance of a positive approach to behavior management and many strategies for helping your students. Chapter 9 builds on the behavior management chapter by providing you with strategies for building positive relationships with students, establishing high expectations for their learning and behavior, and motivating them to persist even in the face of challenges.

Chapters 10 and 11 will guide you in designing instruction with your general education colleagues. Chapter 10 reviews information about the importance of assessment for guiding instruction in content area and intervention instruction. Without solid assessment data, you and your general education colleagues cannot meet the fundamental requirement of IDEA: an appropriate education that is specially designed to meet the needs of students with disabilities. Chapter 11 provides you with frameworks for planning instruction that can be helpful for coordinating your efforts with your general education colleagues. Additionally, you will read about major approaches to instruction that are based on research.

Part Three, "Mastering Effective Practices," discusses information you can use to improve your instruction. Chapters 12 through 16 provide frameworks for approaching instruction in the content areas. These chapters outline key instructional ideas for reading, writing, mathematics, social studies, and science. You will also learn about evidence-based strategies in these areas. Practical examples are used to help you with implementing these strategies. Chapter 17 offers specific information about how you can apply knowledge of evidence-based instruction to the instruction of students with severe disabilities.

Chapter 18 provides the information you need to know when working with students who have significant health problems and receive either IDEA services as a result of their issues or require services to participate in the general education curriculum.

Learning to implement the strategies in this book will help you to become an accomplished special education teacher; work effectively with general education colleagues, related service personnel, and families; and fulfill your professional responsibilities under IDEA. Additionally, careful study of the ideas in this book puts you on the path to becoming a lifelong learner, a mind-set that will allow you to become an expert in special education.

> A number of the tools in this book can be downloaded for free from the publisher's website. See Appendix E for more information.

 **PART ONE**

THE BASICS

CHAPTER ONE

Getting the Right Job

In this chapter you will learn about:

- How to find a job that is a good match for your skills and interests
- How to prepare for your first job interviews
- Tips for putting together a résumé

Dory received the dreaded letter—she didn't get the job she really wanted. She plans to search for several different positions and is thinking about how to prepare better for the interviews. Dory wishes they had provided more guidelines for this in her preparation program.

Great beginnings are no accident. We hope, as part of your teacher preparation, you developed critical knowledge about how to teach students with disabilities and started putting what you learned into action through field experiences in schools. Yet learning to teach is a lifelong process and the steps that you take at the beginning of your career are critical to a great start. The first step is to find a job that is a great match.

AN INITIAL PRIORITY: FIND A GOOD JOB MATCH

Special education teachers wanted: well-prepared, enthusiastic, intelligent, energetic, and personable individuals—intrinsic rewards unlimited[1]

Finding a good job match is perhaps the most important step you can take toward having a great beginning to your teaching career. Your ability to find a good match may be difficult or easy depending on the job market in which you live or the one in which you hope to relocate. Although some new teachers have multiple offers, others struggle, and the lack of available jobs in some areas is a significant source of stress for new teachers.

It is also important to know that central office personnel and principals may be constrained in whom they hire and when they can hire. For example, they may be required to hire employees who have been laid off before considering anyone else. Sometimes the reassignment of teachers creates delays in hiring, with offers coming later in July or even in August.

If you are applying in an area where there are few special education jobs, keep in mind that it is often easier to find jobs in rural or high-need schools. For example, in one geographical region, it is almost impossible to get a job in a preferred school system. However, it is relatively easy to get jobs in the surrounding areas. If the job market is tight in your preferred school district, you will want to be vigilant about learning about the school system, its needs, and what the administration is looking for in applicants.

A thoughtful and systematic approach to your job search should increase the odds of finding a position that is a good match for your qualifications and interests. If you are not in a hurry and if you have options about where you live, you can afford more time in looking for a good match. Some teachers take the first position that is offered even when it is not a very good match for their interests, skills, and abilities. Those who are not well matched to their jobs are more likely to leave their positions.[2]

STEPS IN YOUR JOB SEARCH

Once you decide on your priorities, take time to get the most out of the job search process. Following are specific considerations when searching for a position that is a good match.

Identify Your Priorities

Consider what is important in a job for you. The clearer you are about what you want, the easier it will be to find positions that match your interests and abilities. Take ten minutes to write a description of your ideal position. For example, consider the following:

- ▶ Is it at the elementary or secondary level?
- ▶ Would you be as comfortable working in a large versus small school or a suburban versus urban environment?
- ▶ Do you want to spend most of your time co-teaching?
- ▶ Are you interested in teaching a particular subject(s)?
- ▶ What certifications do you hold? What additional certifications are you willing to acquire?
- ▶ Do you have more experience with some kinds of students with disabilities than with others?
- ▶ Where do you want to live?
- ▶ How far are you willing to commute?

Of course, you probably won't find the perfect fit, but by identifying your priorities, you will help focus your attention on finding a pretty good match. Even better, make a list of must-haves, should-haves, and nice-to-haves. Evaluate each job according to these priorities. Karen, a new graduate with a master's degree, describes the job she wants:

I hope to find a job in an elementary school that is fully inclusive. Because I have worked mainly with students with emotional and behavioral disabilities, I want to make sure I have opportunities to work with these students. I want to work close to home so working in one of several specific counties is important to me. Having materials as well as support from administration and mentors are priorities.

Investigate a Range of Options

Perhaps you know exactly where you want to work; if so, skip to the next point. Most prospective teachers will want to search a range of possibilities. Fortunately, there are many different websites for teachers interested in learning about special education positions (e.g., Council for Exceptional Children—Career Center, Recruiting New Teachers, and the National Association of State Directors of Special Education). If you are interested in a particular state, district or school, you can contact it through its website or through the district personnel office.

Develop Your Résumé

A well-crafted résumé highlights the most important aspects of your teaching work. You should take copies to teacher job fairs and your interviews. You should also send it as part of your application. You may want to revise your résumé for specific positions, highlighting those aspects of your preparation and experience that are consistent with the position you are seeking. For example, if the job announcement includes references to specific skills, such as co-teaching or tiered instruction, highlight those relevant experiences on your résumé.

Those who interview you may look at your résumé very quickly, so make sure you highlight the most important information. Here are some specific tips to consider when developing your résumé. An example is shown in exhibit 1.1.

> ► Emphasize your strengths and your specific knowledge and skills.
> ► Highlight your work with students with disabilities and your specific skills.
> ► Create a focused, concise, and readable résumé (12-point font such as Times New Roman).
> ► Use a high-quality printer and good paper.
> ► Use bullets, not sentences or paragraphs.
> ► Proof carefully and have other professionals read and make suggestions.

Complete Your Application and Follow Up

After you have narrowed your search, you will need to complete the application process. This usually includes providing a written or online application, securing transcripts and references, and providing teacher exam scores. Be sure to follow the instructions exactly. Don't leave anything out. You should follow up to make sure the district has received all parts of your application. If you do not hear anything after a period of time, call the district to let them know you are still interested.

THE INTERVIEW PROCESS

Be prepared for the interview. In particular, read the job announcement carefully and prepare for any aspects of the position that are highlighted in the interview (e.g., help students prepare for postsecondary settings, co-teaching). Here are some key tips to increasing your chance of getting an offer.

Exhibit 1.1   Résumé Example

ALTHEA POLSNEY

948 Deerfield Drive   (123) 456–7891

Anytown, NY 12345   apolsney@gmail.com

Education

University of Brightsville	May 2012
Master of Education in Special Education	GPA: 3.9
University of Highrock College	May 2009
Bachelor of Psychology/Spanish minor (fluent)	GPA: 3.8

Student Teaching Jan.–May 2012

Dominion Elementary School, Anytown, NY

- ► Co-taught lessons in reading and mathematics in fourth- and fifth-grade classrooms
- ► Managed a caseload of twenty-two students with high-incidence disabilities
- ► Developed IEPs and implemented curriculum-based measurement
- ► Participated in the schoolwide improvement committee
- ► Presented a professional development session on positive behavioral supports

Employment

Graduate assistant, Department of Special Education	Aug. 2010–Jan. 2012
Assisted faculty in research, teaching, and service	
Preschool paraeducator at Lilly Park Preschool	Aug. 2009–June 2010
Provided assistance to three students in a fourth-grade classroom	
Summer camp counselor for students with autism	June 2010–Aug. 2010
Assisted primary-age children at a summer camp full time	

Volunteer and Leadership Activities

President, student chapter, Council for Exceptional Children	Sept. 2010–Aug. 2011
After-school tutor, Monterey Elementary, Anytown, NY	Aug. 2007–Dec. 2009
Volunteer coach, Special Olympics, Anytown, NY	Jan. 2006–Dec. 2006
Highrock College Spanish Club	Aug. 2007–Aug. 2009

Before the Interview

► Review the job announcement carefully.

► Learn about the district and the school.

► Visit the school. Some school districts have centralized interviews at the district office, others hold them at the school, and still others offer district and school interviews. If possible, visit the school or schools that have openings. In addition, try to talk with other teachers and administrators at the school: they have insights that will help you better understand the job.

Preparing for Interview Questions

► Interviewers will likely ask a range of questions about numerous aspects of your experiences and your knowledge and skills as a teacher. Thinking through possible questions and practicing your responses is an excellent way to prepare for your interview. Exhibit 1.2 provides examples of questions that you might be asked. You may want to outline a few of the key points you would make for each of the questions in the column on the right-hand side of the exhibit. You will likely make a better impression if you concentrate on several well-thought-out points than to try and share everything you know about a topic. Also, include specific examples, especially things that worked well.

► If you have difficulty with any of the practice questions, review the specific chapters in this handbook that address that material. Use the additional resources listed in each chapter if you need more information.

► If you are applying for a position for students with a specific disability (e.g., students with autism or students who are hard of hearing), customize the questions by rewording them to apply to a specific population. For example, what are characteristics of effective instructional environments for students with autism?

► Be ready with a written list of your own questions (e.g., mentoring support, student–teacher ratio).

The Interview Itself

► Dress professionally for the interview.

► Arrive on time.

► Make eye contact with everyone who is present.

► Bring a portfolio or examples of lessons (ask if they are interested in looking at them).

► Don't ask about salary until an offer is made (this information is often available on the district website).

After the Interview

► Thank each individual for taking the time to interview you.

► Express your interest in the position.

► Follow up with a handwritten note or at least an e-mail indicating your interest.

Exhibit 1.2   Job Interview Questions[3]

Areas	Possible Questions	Highlight Key Points You Want to Make
Experience and preparation for position	Tell us about yourself and your preparation for this position.	
State requirements: (1) Licensure (2) Required teacher tests (3) College program accreditation	Tell us about your preparation for this position and your current licensure status in this or other states.	
Teacher dispositions	How would your students describe you? Tell us about yourself and what you bring to this position. What was your biggest challenge in your last job (or internship) and how did you address this challenge?	
Teacher roles	Describe your ideal teaching position. How would you describe the role of the special educator in the school? What concerns do you have about filling this role?	
View of special education	What are characteristics of effective instructional environments for students with disabilities?	
Understanding students with disabilities	Describe the needs of a student with disabilities whom you have worked with over a period of time.	
Understanding diversity and working with families	Describe considerations that you have made in addressing the needs of students (and families) from diverse backgrounds. How do you communicate with parents?	

A Survival Guide for New Special Educators, by Billingsley, Brownell, Israel, and Kamman. Copyright © 2013 by John Wiley & Sons, Inc.

Exhibit 1.2 Continued

Areas	Possible Questions	Highlight Key Points You Want to Make
Assessment and monitoring of learning	Describe specific strategies that you have used to assess student learning. How do you prepare students for state assessments?	
Collaboration and co-teaching	Tell us about your experiences collaborating with general educators. Please give an example of a situation that worked well and any challenges you encountered. What are various ways that you might collaborate and co-teach with general educators?	
Knowledge of content and state standards	How do you teach to state standards? What content area(s) do you feel best prepared to teach and at what levels? For the area you selected, outline some considerations that are important to teaching that specific content.	
Instructional strategies	What types of teaching strategies have you used in your teaching? How do you decide which teaching strategies to use?	
Individualized education programs (IEPs) Transition planning	Describe how you would facilitate an IEP meeting. How would you incorporate transition planning in the IEP?	
Student behavior	How would you approach working with a student who regularly disrupted a class and refused to cooperate?	
Paraprofessionals	Describe how you would establish a positive working relationship with paraprofessionals.	
Assistive technology	Describe any experiences or training that you have had using assistive technology.	

CONSIDER THE OFFER

Congratulations, you received an offer! Before accepting on the spot, write down the specifics of the offer. Ask how much time you have to make a decision. Usually they will give you at least a couple of days. Take time and review the written description that you outlined. How well does this specific job match your abilities, experiences, and interests?

One note of caution: some districts make offers and later assign you to positions. If the district is unable to tell you what position you will have at the time they extend an offer, ask if they can ensure you a particular level (e.g., elementary) or type of position (co-teaching). At this time, you may also ask about any incentives such as signing bonuses, paying for course work, and so on. Although some districts do not offer special incentives, others do.

TO SUM UP

▶ Know the kind of job you really want and systematically search for that job.

▶ Prepare a well-crafted and readable résumé that emphasizes your strengths and abilities.

▶ Prepare for the interview and practice with specific questions.

▶ If you have difficulty with any of the questions, try to review the material in this book before the interview.

▶ Consider your offers carefully, weighing the extent to which the job is a good match for you.

WHAT'S NEXT?

In chapter 2 we will cover some of the things you might expect in your first few years based on what we know about new special education teachers. We will also cover ten actions that you can use to have a great start. In addition, we address how to take advantage of available support systems and resources that will help you in your professional learning.

CHAPTER TWO

Great Beginnings

> **In this chapter you will learn about:**
>
> - What to expect in the first years as a special education teacher
> - Ten actions that will help you become an accomplished and committed teacher
> - How to create a network of support
> - Online professional learning resources

Miguel made it through his first year. Yes, the job was overwhelming at first but he knew what steps to take and he planned carefully and then made sure he took just one day at a time. He felt grateful that his mentor was so helpful and he also made sure to find other sources of support when he needed them. He shared with his friends, "It has been worth it because my principal and mentor really focus on the children and they've helped me figure out what I need to know to do a good job of teaching."

You got the job—congratulations! This is an exciting time. You will have exhilarating and challenging times throughout the first year. It helps to understand what new special education teachers experience so you will know that you are not alone in what you go through. More important, it is essential that you take specific actions to have a great start to becoming an accomplished and committed special educator.

REALITY 101: WHAT TO EXPECT IN THE FIRST YEARS

Even the best prepared teachers can be overwhelmed with new demands as they try to figure out how to apply what they know to new teaching situations. One brand-new teacher captured the sentiments of many beginning special education teachers when she said, "Although I learned much of what I needed to know in college, I had difficulty figuring out how to put it into practice in my new setting."[1]

If you are like many new teachers, you will feel great about your work on some days, excited to be contributing to the growth of your students. On other days you may be discouraged or even question your career choice. This is typical for many teachers. Consider these teachers' experiences:

▶ Althea, a co-teacher in third grade, was frustrated because she couldn't find time to work with general education teachers. She stated, "I don't know what the teachers are going to do each day and I'm walking in having to try to figure out what to do at the last minute. So I got a little mad at them and then it got even worse."

▶ Kevin complained that the students wouldn't pay attention and were "so noisy that I couldn't even teach. The others were sitting there . . . just staring at me like I didn't know what I was doing."

▶ Patrice struggled because she didn't have books for her science and history classes. She stated, "The other teachers got their books but mine never came in. It has been hard to try to figure this out on my own. I had to borrow books but then I didn't have them when I needed them."

We hope you will have opportunities to solve these kinds of challenges with your mentor and we discuss sources of support at the end of this chapter. As you get started, try not to just focus on the problems—rather, concentrate on the things that are going well. Teaching life is not ideal—for many new teachers, idealism collides with the reality of the life of teaching. The mismatch between what they expect and what a teaching life is really like can be a major stressor.

It is also important to know that you will no doubt have your hands full as you learn about your school and district, develop teaching routines, and manage various dimensions of your work. New teachers often underestimate how long it will take to complete tasks and overestimate what they can accomplish. Today's teachers must be concerned about accountability requirements with an emphasis on standards-based outcomes for students. New teachers must deal with these work challenges, sometimes without well-established systems of support.

Across studies, new special educators report needing to continue to learn about key aspects of teaching and how to manage varied work tasks. They need assistance with continuing to develop their own content knowledge, teaching to standards to students with disabilities in general education classrooms, managing key aspects of the job—including scheduling—and dealing with stress.

Table 2.1 shows areas in which special education teachers typically request help. Remember, even very well-prepared teachers struggle but many of them grow over time into highly skilled teachers.

Table 2.1 You Are Not Alone: Percentage of Special Educators' Requiring Assistance[2]

Needs	Percent
Paperwork and IEPs	84
Referral, placement, and evaluation	75
Materials	70
Getting acclimated to the school	66
Behavior management	60
Instructional strategies	58
Assessments	54
Collaboration with general educators	54
Parent–family conferences	48
Learning and using the curriculum	46

Working through your struggles now will pay off in the long run as you develop the skills to offer your students an excellent education. Throughout the chapters in this guide, we provide many suggestions for managing these struggles so that you will be able to fulfill your varied teaching roles.

> The quality of work experience depends at least to some extent on what you focus on, so try to keep a positive attitude about your work and the people you work with and remind yourself of your accomplishments, even when things are not going well. Create a folder for thank-you notes and inspiring ideas—notice those things that are improving and track your accomplishments. You could also save sweet notes given to you by your students.

YOUR CHALLENGE: BECOME AN ACCOMPLISHED AND COMMITTED SPECIAL EDUCATOR

Teachers today have a lot to juggle, of course; it takes time to learn the ropes and master effective teaching practices. In the following we identify ten actions that you can take to become an effective and committed special education teacher. Yes, these actions take a great deal of effort but those who work to become first-rate teachers realize the satisfaction of making a difference in their students' lives. Each of the ten actions is discussed briefly in this chapter and then elaborated on throughout this book.

Ten Actions toward Becoming an Accomplished and Committed Special Educator

- ▶ Reflect on the moral purpose that guides your work.
- ▶ Develop knowledge about the professional standards and ethics of the profession.
- ▶ Learn about the community and key policies and guidelines.
- ▶ Learn more about the content standards for subjects you teach.
- ▶ Use and refine your knowledge about evidence-based practices.
- ▶ Know your students and systematically monitor their learning.
- ▶ Collaborate effectively with administrators, colleagues, and parents.
- ▶ Protect instructional time and balance your responsibilities.
- ▶ Develop resilience and manage stress.
- ▶ Take initiative for your own professional learning.

REFLECT ON THE MORAL PURPOSE THAT GUIDES YOUR WORK

Most special education teachers enter the field because they want to make a difference in students' lives. Elizabeth Stein, a special educator for nearly two decades now, was told initially by other teachers that she was excited about teaching because she was new. Two decades later, she is a national-board-certified special education teacher and still has great energy and enthusiasm for teaching. What is her secret? Elizabeth has a well-articulated core vision and set of values. Every day she asks herself, "What can I do for children?" Elizabeth stated, "This question keeps me in the mode of turning my passion into performance. I'm talking about purposeful performance that links my core values with an empathetic awareness of the views of those around me."[3] Like Elizabeth, taking time to find a way of stating your core vision or even writing a mission statement can help you stay focused when things get difficult.

Special education teachers often serve in advocacy roles and try to ensure that others understand and respond to the learning needs of students with disabilities. In inclusive environments, administrators, teachers, and staff throughout the school all work toward making sure that the needs of students with disabilities are met. However, when this is not the case, special education teachers often must take on advocacy roles for their students. Teachers also need to be committed to the learning of all students and work to ensure that students from diverse and culturally different backgrounds have equitable opportunities to learn. In chapter 3, we provide some tips for how you can be an effective advocate and still maintain positive relations with your colleagues and principal.

> The committed professional thinks of his or her job more as a calling. "I'm not just a therapist; I'm an advocate for persons with developmental disabilities."[4]

DEVELOP KNOWLEDGE ABOUT PROFESSIONAL STANDARDS AND ETHICS

Accomplished special educators should know the professional standards for their career. The following are some of the teaching standards that guide the work of special education teachers. If you take time to become familiar with at least one of these sets of standards, you will have a better understanding of how to act professionally and appropriately in your new roles.

State Standards

All states have requirements that teachers must achieve in order to be licensed in that state. Some states have reciprocity, meaning that they recognize licenses earned in other states. In special education, licenses may be categorical (e.g., a specific license in learning disabilities) or noncategorical (teachers may be approved to teach students across varied categorical groups). Some states also have professional ethics that teachers need to know.

Council for Exceptional Children (CEC)

The Council for Exceptional Children (CEC) is an international professional organization concerned with improving education for students with disabilities as well as students with special gifts and talents. CEC also has initial and advanced professional content standards for special education teachers. CEC also advocates for appropriate policies, provides professional development, and works to improve conditions for professional practice.

The Council for Exceptional Children also has ethical principles and practice standards that set a benchmark for respecting diversity and meeting the needs of individuals with exceptionalities and their families. It is important to be familiar with the following ethical principles:

▶ CEC Ethical Principles for Special Education Professionals
▶ Maintaining challenging expectations for individuals with exceptionalities to develop the highest possible learning outcomes and quality of life potential in ways that respect their dignity, culture, language, and background

- ▶ Maintaining a high level of professional competence and integrity and exercising professional judgment to benefit individuals with exceptionalities and their families
- ▶ Promoting meaningful and inclusive participation of individuals with exceptionalities in their schools and communities
- ▶ Practicing collegially with others who are providing services to individuals with exceptionalities
- ▶ Developing relationships with families based on mutual respect and actively involving families and individuals with exceptionalities in educational decision making
- ▶ Using evidence, instructional data, research, and professional knowledge to inform practice
- ▶ Protecting and supporting the physical and psychological safety of individuals with exceptionalities
- ▶ Neither engaging in nor tolerating any practice that harms individuals with exceptionalities
- ▶ Practicing within the professional ethics, standards, and policies of CEC; upholding laws, regulations, and policies that influence professional practice; and advocating improvements in laws, regulations, and policies
- ▶ Advocating for professional conditions and resources that will improve learning outcomes of individuals with exceptionalities
- ▶ Engaging in the improvement of the profession through active participation in professional organizations
- ▶ Participating in the growth and dissemination of professional knowledge and skills[5]

National Board for Professional Teaching Standards (NBPTS)

NBPTS (www.nbpts.org) is an independent, nonprofit, nonpartisan, and nongovernmental organization that seeks to advance the quality of teaching and learning by developing professional standards for accomplished teaching, creating a voluntary system to certify teachers who meet those standards, and integrating certified teachers into educational reform efforts. Teachers who complete this advanced certification in exceptional need may become leaders in their schools and districts. (See more about this in the professional learning section later in this chapter.)

LEARN ABOUT THE COMMUNITY AND KEY POLICIES AND GUIDELINES

Professionals are expected to be knowledgeable about the communities in which they work and the various policies and guidelines developed by states, districts, and schools. Teacher orientations, online websites, and written handbooks are often sources for this information. It is helpful to keep copies of key policies and guidelines handy so you can refer to them as questions arise. The following sections describe several major areas to consider.

District and School Community

Take time to learn about your school community, the makeup of the student body, and the community that you serve. What pressing challenges face the district, school, and the special education program? How diverse is the student body in your school? What do you know about the needs of the students in your school and on your caseload?

District, School, and Local Policies

Your school and district will have guidelines in any number of areas, including hiring, teacher evaluation, student discipline, and student assessments. Usually relevant policies are reviewed during initial meetings and orientation. Often clarifications are needed, so ask questions and seek assistance as the need arises.

Special Education Policies and Guidelines

Federal laws govern the provision of special education (see chapters 4 and 5) and this is an area in which special educators often need assistance. Learning to use these guidelines in daily work is often challenging. Reviewing procedures with your mentor or observing an IEP meeting in the district can be helpful.

Confidentiality

IDEA and the Family Educational Rights and Privacy Act (FERPA) require that students' privacy must be protected and their records must be handled in a secure and confidential manner. Special education professionals need to protect student privacy and follow local policies and procedures for the collection, use, and storage of student information. Professionals must also exercise care to ensure that discussions about students occur only as necessary in professional settings.

Protecting the Privacy Interests of Students: The Family Educational Rights and Privacy Act (FERPA)

The Family Educational Rights and Privacy Act (FERPA) is a federal law that protects the privacy interests of students. It affords parents the right to access and amend their children's education records and gives them some control over the disclosure of the information in these records. As employees of a school and education institution, you will have access to individual student records in performing your official duties. You are legally and ethically obliged to safeguard their confidentiality. This applies to any education agency or institution that receives funds under a program administered by the US Department of Education. In addition, for students who attend a public school district, all records pertaining to services provided under IDEA are considered education records under FERPA. As such, they are subject to the confidentiality provisions of both acts (see chapter 4 for more information).

LEARN MORE ABOUT THE CONTENT STANDARDS FOR SUBJECTS YOU TEACH

All students with disabilities are, by law, supposed to have access to the general education curriculum, and it is incumbent on special education teachers to ensure that they have this access. Helping students with disabilities achieve content area standards is one important way of providing access. Each state has content area standards listed on its department of education website. Many states are now implementing the Common Core State Standards (CCSS) (see www.corestandards.org), which are being developed nationally to guide curriculum and instruction in their states. Beginning teachers need to know these standards because they will be expected to address them in their instruction; however, beginning teachers should also be aware that knowing about the standards and implementing them are two entirely different matters.

Teachers are required to help all students achieve content area standards according to the No Child Left Behind (NCLB) Act but this outcome is not easy to achieve. Students with disabilities often have difficulties in language, thinking, communication, and social skills that create some hurdles for achieving these standards. Beginning special education teachers will need to work closely with their general education colleagues to determine how they can help students with disabilities meet these standards. A plan for the types of accommodations, assistive technology, assessments, and interventions that students with disabilities need results from the collaborative efforts of special and general education teachers working together.

USE AND REFINE YOUR KNOWLEDGE ABOUT EVIDENCE-BASED PRACTICES

Students with disabilities have learning or behavioral problems that make learning difficult; however, they can learn when teachers use evidence-based practices. We know, from decades of research, that some teaching and behavior management practices are more effective than others. When you and your general education colleagues use organized, explicit instruction that engages students academically, you can help many students with disabilities learn more effectively. Explicit instruction can accomplish the following:

- ▶ Helps students focus on the main concepts they are to learn and helps them make connections between concepts
- ▶ Involves making expectations clear for students
- ▶ Provides modeling for what you want students to learn
- ▶ Provides sufficient practice so students can learn new material
- ▶ Provides students with corrective feedback that helps them understand what they did well and what they need to do differently

Students need to learn in caring and productive environments where they feel safe and develop self-confidence. Teaching students how to follow the rules they need to get along with others and manage their own behavior will be imperative. In parts two and three of this book we describe numerous research-based strategies. However, you will also need to make it a top priority to learn and practice these strategies. Fortunately, there are many excellent online resources that we identify throughout this book such as IRIS, Connect, the RTI Action Network, the Center for Applied Special Technology (CAST), and LD OnLine, to name a few.

KNOW YOUR STUDENTS AND SYSTEMATICALLY MONITOR THEIR LEARNING

Effective teachers know a lot about their students—not just academically but also about who they are as people. They know what is important in their students' lives and what motivates them. They know about each student's disability and the impact it has on learning (see appendix A for an overview of disability areas and related resources).

Accomplished teachers also monitor the progress their students are making toward identified learning goals. They assess progress as they teach and make adjustments to their instruction based on how their students are advancing. There is a difference between assessing students' mastery of the content taught (e.g., using tests and quizzes on specific material) and progress monitoring. In the latter, teachers identify the goals that a student must meet by the end of the year and the identified rate of progress students must make to meet annual goals. The teacher regularly monitors how students are progressing toward these goals using probes that sample from the entire range of material to be learned throughout the year. Examples of appropriate assessments and progress monitoring strategies are provided throughout this book.

COLLABORATE EFFECTIVELY WITH ADMINISTRATORS, COLLEAGUES, AND PARENTS

Students with disabilities have complex needs that cannot be met by any one individual. This is why the Individuals with Disabilities Education Act (IDEA; 2004), the law governing the education of students with disabilities, demands that these students be served by a multidisciplinary team and that schools involve parents as partners in the educational process. To be successful in working with colleagues and parents, you will need strong communication skills, an understanding of the needs of diverse populations, and a collaborative ethic. Chapters 3 and 8 provide guidelines and strategies for facilitating good communication and collaboration with colleagues, administrators, and parents.

PROTECT INSTRUCTIONAL TIME AND BALANCE YOUR RESPONSIBILITIES

Special education teaching is a rewarding career but it is also a demanding one. As a special education teacher, you will have many responsibilities, including teaching students, developing IEPs, developing and managing instructional resources, completing paperwork, collecting student assessment data, keeping up with the growing professional knowledge base, and communicating with teachers and families. These responsibilities can take a toll if you do not set priorities for each day and week and manage your time. It is particularly important to protect instructional time because the amount of time students are engaged in instruction is critical to their achievement. In chapter 6 we provide information and strategies about how you can develop clarity about your role, better manage your time, and meet the various responsibilities in front of you.

DEVELOP RESILIENCE AND MANAGE STRESS

Teaching is not easy but many find it rewarding. Take a long view of your career and remember why you chose teaching as a profession. The quality of your teaching experience will function at least to some degree on what you choose to focus on each day. Pay attention to your daily successes and take care of your health and overall well-being. Keep learning. When difficulties arise, problem solve (don't blame) and try not to take things personally. Learning to deal with stress is part of many jobs, so practice these stress busters:

▶ *Develop an awareness of your stress levels and the specific things that you find particularly stressful.* If you develop an awareness of specific situations that trigger stress, you can better recognize when you are stressed and take actions to reduce stress (e.g., leave the situation, take ten deep breaths).

▶ *Remember that self-care is particularly important when dealing with stress.* Taking time for the four pillars of health will help reduce stress: exercise, a healthy diet, adequate rest, and relaxation.[6]

▶ *Develop realistic expectations of yourself and others.* Expecting too much of yourself and others can add to stress levels. Setting priorities, setting realistic goals, and managing your schedule to meet these goals can help reduce stress levels.

▶ *Develop supportive relationships with others.* Supportive colleagues can help buffer stress. Having others in your life who will listen and problem solve with you is a valuable source of support. Scheduling social activities outside of work is also important to your overall well-being.

▶ *Look for solutions—don't blame.* Blaming others for things that go wrong can actually make stress worse. Instead, assume that the other person has good intentions and try to generate solutions.

What All Special Educators Should Know about the Common Core State Standards

Emily Rex, University of North Carolina at Greensboro

What are the common core state standards (CCSS) and what is the purpose of the standards?

▶ The CCSS are educational standards of what students are expected to achieve at each grade level in English language arts and mathematics (adopted by forty-five states and Washington, DC).

▶ The standards provide teachers and parents with a clear understanding of what students are expected to learn at each grade level.

▶ They are designed to prepare students for success in college and the workplace and to compete in the global economy.[7]

How can educators help all students achieve using CCSS?

▶ Use response-to-intervention (RTI). By responding early to children's academic challenges, educators can focus on helping all students achieve grade-level CCSS (RTI is addressed in chapter 10).[8]

▶ Use universal design for learning (UDL). By creating lessons and materials that allow all students to access and engage with the general curriculum, teachers increase the likelihood of each student's success (chapter 11).[9]

▶ Collaborate with other educators. By engaging the collective expertise of a variety of educators, students are more likely to receive the resources and instruction they need to succeed (chapter 8).[10]

▶ Write standards-based IEPs that incorporate CCSS to create high expectations for students with disabilities.[11]

How will students with disabilities be affected?

▶ Students with disabilities will need teachers who deliver high-quality, evidence-based, and individualized instruction on CCSS.[12]

▶ Students with disabilities may require additional instructional supports and services to access the general curriculum.[13]

TAKE INITIATIVE FOR YOUR OWN PROFESSIONAL LEARNING

Accomplished teachers are adept at figuring out what they need to know and finding resources. Effective professionals are committed to their own learning and call on colleagues, former professors, and online sources to obtain needed information. Peer observations and feedback, course work, reading journals, and interactions with colleagues are potential ways of continuing to learn.

MAKING IT HAPPEN: CREATE A NETWORK OF SUPPORTS

Adequate supports can help you avoid "turbulent landings"[14] as you begin your career. We hope you will be in a district and school that provides a range of supports, such as induction and mentoring programs. Yet, these programs are sometimes designed without special educators in mind and may not fully meet your needs. Another challenge is that, often, there are fewer special educators in schools to serve as mentors; therefore, sometimes assistance must be provided outside the school, through e-mail or through online supports. This may be particularly true for teachers of students with low-incidence disabilities.

The good news is that, in addition to using available supports, you can create your own support network. There are many potential sources of support, from assigned mentors and professional development sessions to former professors, colleagues, and paraprofessionals. Consider the four major types of support[15] outlined in the following sections.

Emotional Support

New teachers indicate they most value emotional support.[16] Emotional support stems from relationships in which people feel accepted, liked, and respected. When there is a great deal of trust, people feel they can share openly with each other without feeling judged. Emotional support is particularly important when things are stressful—teachers need to talk with others about their concerns. Emotional support can be provided in and out of school but finding the right people is important.

Feedback Support

New teachers want to know what is expected of them and often desire feedback about how they are doing. However, expectations are not always clear and teachers often receive little specific feedback about their teaching. Think about appraisal as providing two types of support: standards that guide professional behavior and the formal and informal feedback that you receive.

Standards to Guide Your Professional Behavior

Standards are important because they provide guidance for what teachers do in their work. The standards, ethics, and actions outlined previously and discussed in more detail throughout this book can guide your work. It is also important to know of any specific standards for teacher evaluation that are used in your district and school. For example, Charlotte Danielson's framework for teaching[17] is one of the systems used across many districts in the United States. If you don't already know what the teacher evaluation standards are, please check with your mentor or principal. In addition, the following professional guidelines are expected of teachers:

BASICS

▶ Arrive on time

▶ Dress professionally

▶ Follow school policies

▶ Ensure confidentiality

▶ Maintain accurate records

MANAGE YOUR WORK

▶ Organize your work

▶ Be goal directed

▶ Work hard and use your time well

INTERACT POSITIVELY WITH OTHERS

▶ Be approachable and friendly

▶ Treat everyone with courtesy and respect

▶ Be impartial in dealing with others

▶ Say thank-you and express your appreciation to others

BE A TEAM PLAYER

▶ Be committed to school goals

▶ Maintain an optimistic attitude

▶ Network with others

▶ Expect the best from others

▶ Show flexibility in working with others

▶ Support your colleagues, students, and parents

▶ Do what you say you will do

▶ Listen to others before making important decisions

Formal and Informal Feedback You Receive about Your Work

New teachers usually want more feedback, observation, and coaching than they receive.[18] Be sure to seek out informal feedback and understand the processes for formal evaluation. Whether formal or informal, try to keep in mind that everyone needs constructive feedback. Try to listen and keep an open mind and listen without getting defensive. See appendix D for more about teacher evaluation.

Professional Learning Supports

The best teachers continue to improve their knowledge and skills throughout their careers. They develop an awareness of their own strengths and weaknesses and model lifelong learning for their students.

Your school and district will probably provide a number of different learning supports, some of which are outlined in the following sections. However, you may need specific types of assistance that are not provided through local professional learning activities. Taking responsibility for learning what you need to know is a hallmark of a professional so use high-quality online resources (see table 2.2), talk with a former professor, or ask a colleague. In addition, listen carefully to feedback from mentors and administrators because they have received special preparation to help you identify areas for additional learning.

The following sections describe formal and informal professional learning supports to consider in your first years.

Induction and Mentoring

In the first years, professional learning opportunities are often structured for you. Take advantage of new teacher induction and mentoring programs that include orientations, professional development learning sessions, and meetings with other new teachers and assigned mentors. New teachers who work with their mentors, plan with their colleagues, and participate in external communities (e.g., through professional organizations or online communities) are more likely to remain in the profession.[19]

Professional Learning Communities (PLCs)

Today there is an emphasis on PLCs. Teachers within schools work together on an ongoing basis, review results of assessments, plan lessons, and problem-solve together. Some teams read books related to larger schoolwide goals. PLCs are important not only to improving schools and student learning but also as an important form of collective professional development.

Professional Organizations and Conferences

Professional organizations provide another way of staying current with the principles and practices of the field. Be sure to become familiar with the goals of these organizations and check out their membership benefits (e.g., conferences, journals, newsletters, access to websites). These organizations may also sponsor state and national conferences, which are a great way for you to connect with other teachers in your field.

Online Learning Resources and Learning Communities

There are many online professional learning resources that are free for special and general educators. Table 2.2 lists high-quality websites about new teachers' needs.[20] Vanderbilt University's IRIS site and the University of Kansas's Special Connections are examples of high-quality web-based resources designed for teachers seeking to learn more about effective instructional practices for students with disabilities. New special educators may also find online interactive resources helpful, such as CEC's "Reality 101" (www.cecreality101.org), where experienced and new teachers can interact through online discussions.

National Board Certification

Although not available to teachers in their first three years, the NBPTS is an avenue you may eventually want to consider for advanced certification. The NBPTS recognizes accomplished teachers and uses the certification as a method of developing teacher leaders. Special educators who have earned the exceptional needs certificate identify it as one of the most valuable professional learning experiences they have had.[21] Some states and districts encourage teachers to participate by supporting the costs of the program.

Specific Support Needs

New teachers often need assistance with specific tasks, such as writing IEPs, developing a schedule, and ordering materials. You may also need assistance in solving specific problems (e.g., dealing with a conflict or a legal concern). In some districts, support may be provided through district-level facilitators, coordinators, or supervisors. If you aren't sure of the best source of support, ask your mentor, principal, or another teacher in your school.

Table 2.2 Online Resources for New Teachers

Key Special Education Websites	Examples of Modules or Resources
4Teachers.org (www.4teachers.org)	**Effective Instruction** • Assistive technology web resources **Assessment** • RubiStar for quality rubrics • QuizStar for online quizzes • Assessment web resources (e.g., for managing assessments, alternate assessments, authentic assessments, portfolios)
Beach Center on Disability (www.beachcenter.org)	**Collaboration with Others** • Family-related resources
CAST (www.cast.org)	**Effective Instruction** • Universal design for learning resources
Council for Exceptional Children (www.cec.sped.org /am/template.cfm?section=Home)	**Managing the Job and Dealing with Others** • Reality 101: CEC's blog for new teachers
Intervention Central (www.interventioncentral.org)	**Assessment** • CBM warehouse
IRIS (http://iris.peabody.vanderbilt.edu)	**Content Knowledge and Standards** • CSR: A reading comprehensive strategy • PALS: A reading strategy for high school • Improving writing performance: A strategy for writing expository essays • Applying learning strategies to beginning algebra (part 1) • Cultural and linguistic differences: What teachers should know • Teaching and learning in New Mexico: Considerations for diverse student populations • Effective instruction • Differentiated instruction module • Five RTI modules **Assessment** • Classroom assessment (part 1): An introduction to monitoring academic achievement in the classroom • Classroom assessment (part 2): Evaluating reading progress **Behavior Management** • Addressing disruptive and noncompliant behaviors (part 1): Understanding the acting-out cycle • Who's in charge? Addressing disruptive and noncompliant behaviors (part 2) • Behavioral interventions: A comprehensive behavior management system **Collaboration with Others** • Collaborating with families

(Continued)

Table 2.2   Continued

Key Special Education Websites	**Examples of Modules or Resources**
	Managing the Job and Dealing with Stress • The prereferral process: Procedures for supporting students with academic and behavioral concerns • Supporting beginning special educators: Tips for school leaders
LD Online (www.ldonline.org)	**Content Knowledge and Standards** • The clarifying routine: Elaborating vocabulary instruction • Vocabulary assessment and instruction
National Center for Response to Intervention (www.rti4success.org)	**Effective Instruction** • RTI in middle schools webinar **Assessment** • Introduction: CBM for progress monitoring • Using CBM for progress monitoring in reading • Using CBM for progress monitoring in math • Using CBM for progress monitoring in writing and spelling • Using CBM to determine response to instruction
Special Connections (www.specialconnections.ku.edu)	**Content Knowledge and Standards** • Strategies for accessing the science curriculum for special needs students • Strategies for accessing the social studies curriculum for special needs students **Effective Instruction** • Direct instruction • Universal design for learning • Instructional accommodations **Assessment** • Curriculum-based measurement • Data-based decision making • Quality test construction • Grading • Assessment accommodations **Behavior Management** • Functional behavior assessment • Positive behavior support planning • Positive behavior support interventions • Classroom and group support **Collaboration with Others** • An introduction to cooperative teaching • Keys to successful paraeducator supervision Online, this is called "Working Effectively with Paraeducators" **Managing the Job and Dealing with Stress** • Creating a schedule

TO SUM UP

▶ Expect to have exciting and challenging times in your first years. Most teachers do, and it is part of the experience of learning to teach.

▶ Make the ten key actions a priority—yes, they require a great deal of effort. The reward of mastery is becoming a first-rate teacher and seeing your students succeed.

▶ Assess your own effectiveness and use the chapters and tools in this book to build your skills.

▶ Take advantage of the support and professional learning opportunities that are provided for new teachers

▶ Ask for help from mentors, colleagues, former faculty, and external networks.

WHAT'S NEXT?

Now that you have a picture of ten actions that will help you become an effective and committed teacher, we will move on to tools for effective communication—these are absolutely critical to your day-to-day work in schools.

ADDITIONAL RESOURCES

▶ CEC. (2009). *What every special educator must know: Ethics, standards, and guidelines* (6th ed.). Retrieved from www.cec.sped.org/Content/NavigationMenu/ProfessionalDevelopment/Professional Standards/What_Every_Special_Educator_Should_Know_6th_Ed_revised_2009.pdf

▶ National Board for Professional Teaching Standards. *Exceptional needs standards.* Retrieved from www.nbpts.org

CHAPTER THREE

Working with Others

In this chapter you will learn about:

- Engaging in work and relationships in a professional and energizing way
- Elements of effective communication
- How to problem solve and address conflicts
- How to have a great start with the parents of your students
- How to schedule, plan, and lead parent conferences and other meetings
- Tips for e-mail, working effectively with administrators, general educators, and paraeducators

Jewel felt exasperated. It started with the fourth-grade teacher telling her that he didn't have time to make the accommodations listed in the IEP. "Well, I told him we could do it together, but he just ignored me. I've had two parent complaints and it is only the first week of school. Before I started teaching, I just didn't think much about working with all of these adults—now it is always on my mind."

Accomplished special educators realize the importance of becoming part of the school community to advocate effectively for their students' needs. They realize they must work across the boundaries of general and special education and communicate effectively with general education teachers, related services personnel, administrators, and parents. They are also networkers: they figure out with whom they need to coordinate to accomplish important work goals and they work to develop positive relationships with others.

Learning to interact in a positive and productive manner with other adults is a critically important part of your work as a teacher. However, many new special education teachers indicate that they have questions about interacting with parents, administrators, teachers, and paraeducators.[1] For example, new special educators struggle with specific types of problems, such as the following:

▶ How do you work with a colleague who does not want to include your students?

▶ What do you say when the paraeducator keeps disagreeing with your decisions?

- ▶ How do you respond to an angry parent?
- ▶ What do you do when the principal tells you to do one thing and the special education director asks you to do another?

New teachers must deal with these types of problems while they are still getting to know parents, coworkers, and administrators. Taking time to build relationships with others from the moment you begin interacting with them in the district is important. Strong relationships are important to helping students meet their goals and allow you to solve problems more easily. Teachers who establish positive relationships will also be less stressed and more satisfied with their work, and those who experience chronic interpersonal problems have greater stress, withdraw, and will likely be less effective in their work.

BE AN ENERGIZER

Your colleagues will be attracted to those who bring energy and a can-do attitude toward their work. Like Tigger in the Winnie-the-Pooh books by Milne, energizers—individuals who work toward compelling goals and are highly engaged in their work—exude energy and optimism and see possibilities in every turn. In contrast, deenergizers tend to have a negative and cynical focus, emphasizing problems and constraints, like Eeyore. Following are eight specific behaviors that are characteristic of energizers:[2]

"1. Do you make an effort to weave relationship development into work and day-to-day interactions?

2. Do you do what you say you are going to do?

3. Do you address tough issues with integrity and sincerity?

4. Do you look for possibilities or identify only constraints? Do you critique ideas without venturing alternatives or revealing your own thinking?

5. When you disagree with someone, do you focus attention on the issue and not on the value of that person's contributions?

6. Are you mentally and physically engaged in meetings and conversations?

7. Are you flexible or do you force others to come to your way of thinking?

8. Do you use your own expertise appropriately and not too aggressively?"

BE AN EFFECTIVE COMMUNICATOR

Many excellent books have addressed good communication. *The 7 Habits of Highly Effective People* by Stephen Covey is a favorite of ours.[3] When you consider your own communication skills, think about your strengths as well as areas for self-improvement. The following sections offer some specific recommendations that are important to communicating effectively with others and for establishing strong professional relationships. These are important to professional relationships in general. Of course, simply reading and thinking about communication isn't sufficient; it is important to put effective communication skills into practice. For example, if you tend to talk more than listen, practice specific listening skills each day for a week in every conversation.

Show Courtesy and Respect and Acknowledge Others' Efforts

Treating others with care and respect, listening, and showing genuine appreciation for their efforts are ways of letting them know that you value them and your interactions with them. Later in this chapter

Kara Battin Holden, a special education teacher, describes how she communicates with others and expresses communication to her colleagues. Over time, consistent and genuine efforts to treat your colleagues well will help contribute to trusting relationships.

It's the Nonverbal, Unspoken Things That Say the Most

Experts suggest that nonverbal behaviors communicate far more than what you say. Small nonverbal behaviors, such as being distracted during conversations, can hinder relationships. Your facial expressions, body language, tone of voice, and demeanor matter and it is important to be aware of verbal and nonverbal messages.

Take Time to Listen

It is important to listen well to understand the needs and perspectives of others. This is especially important in high-stakes situations or in situations when conflict occurs. Listening requires effort. Here are tips for improving your listening skills:

- ▶ Establish intent to listen.
- ▶ Truly listen versus thinking about what you plan to say next.
- ▶ Give your full attention to the speaker.
- ▶ Establish and maintain eye contact.
- ▶ Sit still and lean slightly toward the other individual.
- ▶ Avoid checking your watch, clock, or cell phone.
- ▶ Do not interrupt.
- ▶ Show understanding (e.g., nod to indicate agreement).
- ▶ Ask for clarifications and elaborations if you are confused or have questions.
- ▶ Do not assume anything.
- ▶ If the conversation is sensitive, consider hanging a do-not-disturb sign on the door.

Quit Taking It Personally

You will have a great deal of contact with a variety of individuals through face-to-face conferences, e-mail, telephone, and written notes. A great stress reliever is to quit taking it personally. It is easy to read too much into communication. For example, reread an e-mail from a parent in a friendly tone versus the one you ascribed to it. If you take all communication at face value instead of reading into it, you can prevent needless worry, anxiety, and refrain from giving an unproductive response. Even if an individual is disrespectful, try not to take that personally either. It is a reflection on them, not you, and you can model professional and respectful behavior. Of course, you should not put up with abuse. Talk with your principal if abusive behavior occurs.

Problem Solve, Don't Blame

When things go wrong on the job (and they will), take a problem-solving approach. Instead of pointing fingers or blaming, consider these questions: What needs to happen? What is the goal? What needs to be accomplished? Who is going to take responsibility for varied tasks?

Advice about Communication and Expressions of Gratitude

Kara Battin Holden, University of North Carolina at Greensboro

ADMINISTRATION AND OFFICE STAFF

► Administrators have different preferences for communicating. Some even change their preference from year to year. For example, some prefer that I just walk into their office and start a conversation but others prefer e-mail. At the beginning of every year, I ask each administrator (and office staff) what type of communication he or she prefers.

► Initially, I communicated with administrators only to ask them something specific, such as about attending an IEP meeting or figuring out a weekly schedule. Over time, I realized I had much to learn from them; for example, how to communicate better with students' parents. The more time I spent with my administrators, the more comfortable I felt asking their advice about specific situations.

► It brightens my day to have a casual conversation with office staff. It provides a break from my busy day and allows me to build a relationship with the people who are crucial to the functioning of the school.

PARENTS

► During my first year of teaching I learned that some parents communicate easily with teachers and others may not be as comfortable doing so. I work hard to create and maintain relationships with all of the parents. I keep a daily communication log and hold a monthly parent support group.

► *Communication log:* I ask parents whether they would like to communicate by e-mail or a notebook that we send back and forth in the student's backpack. This regular communication helps parents feel connected to the classroom, learn about their child's day, and be informed of any difficulty that arose. I also use e-mail and notebooks to send reminders about field trips, days off, or make requests. Parents appreciate these communications and they also serve as documentation if any issues arise.

► *Parent support group:* Once a month I host an after-school informal parent support group in my classroom for any parent of my students. Parents ask advice or share their thoughts with other parents who are in similar situations. Conversations range from "Where do I take my child to the dentist?" to sharing local sibling support groups for siblings with special needs. I sometimes offer my advice but mostly let parents interact with one another and only assist with conversation when needed.

TEACHERS AND PARAEDUCATORS

► I survived my first years of teaching because of the outstanding teachers and paraeducators I worked with on a daily basis. I learned just as much from them as I did during my preteaching classes.

► I leave thank-you notes and flowers for colleagues to communicate my gratitude to them for their efforts. Other times, I just leave a piece of candy or a Kudos bar on their desk to let them know what a great job they were doing and how much I appreciated them not only helping the students but helping me as well.

► I also give flowers or a note to my administrators during teacher appreciation week. Students may not always perceive administrators as teachers but they deserve appreciation during these times as well.

WORKING THROUGH CONFLICTS

Taking steps to establish positive and productive relationships with others is the best way to avoid problems. However, sometimes disagreements will emerge and you will need to try to address them. It is important to distinguish between what are often minor differences (e.g., disagreement with a grade on a specific assignment) and more significant disputes (e.g., parents are unhappy with the education their child is receiving). However, even minor disputes can become major ones, so they deserve care as well.

In addressing problems with parents, be sure to keep your administrator and mentor aware of any issue that is not quickly resolved. It is important to note that questions about placement, services, and IEPs must be addressed by committees and you cannot make changes without convening an IEP meeting and sometimes an eligibility meeting (see chapter 4 on the laws and chapter 5 on IEPs). When legal issues are involved, you or the principal may want to discuss the situation with the director of special education, but follow the organizational chart and speak with your principal first unless it is clearly OK to proceed otherwise.

Consider the following guidelines as you work with others to address conflict. In general, try to address conflicts early. If there are disagreements, it may be helpful for school personnel and parents to take some time to think about the situation. However, allowing unresolved problems to fester over extended periods sometimes leads to more serious conflicts.

Be Aware of Your Own Reactions First

In difficult situations, it is easy to lose sight of the big picture and get caught up in emotions, especially if a colleague or parent says something derogatory. Monitor your own emotional responses to difficult situations so you can remain calm and professional when interacting with others. When things are especially difficult, ask yourself, what is the goal of this communication? Focus on your goal (e.g., working toward a solution, clarifying expectations).

Never Respond in Anger

There may be situations that arise in your work with others that are upsetting or make you feel angry. In these situations, postpone your response, especially if you are feeling a lot of emotion, such as frustration. Take a day before you respond to an upsetting e-mail or think through how you want to respond to a comment that you perceive as unkind. This requires that you keep your own emotional reaction in check and establish your goal for communication before proceeding.

Listen and Make Sure You Understand the Problem

Sometimes there is a misunderstanding of what is being requested. Although it may be difficult, listening to others is an important step in resolving conflict. Allow the other person to fully state what is on his or her mind before sharing your perspective. Begin with, "I would like to know how you see the situation." You may find out information that you did not know and it may help you resolve the problem.

Describe Behaviors Rather Than Make Judgments

State the facts (the behavior) and remain calm. Instead of "Louis was angry and completely out of control," specifically describe what happened in a calm manner: "After Louis was told he had to stay in class to finish his homework, he got up from his desk, threw his book against the wall, and walked out of the room." The latter communicates what Louis did and the context in which it happened. Always avoid value judgments and putting someone down.

Focus on the Goal of Communication

Blaming others is rarely a good strategy and can end a relationship. Don't get caught up in finding fault with others; rather, try to focus on the task or problem at hand. There are several ways to do this:

▶ State the problem as a goal: "I think our goal is to discuss how to help Mabel interact positively with others during recess."

▶ Once the purpose is agreed on and clear, ask, "Could we take a few minutes to discuss . . . ?" (e.g., some possible ways to coordinate our responsibilities).

Consider Multiple Ways of Addressing a Problem

Communication often breaks down when individuals focus on a single solution rather than considering a range of possibilities. Brainstorm a list of solutions and then consider a few options.

Admit When You Do Not Know

Teachers cannot be expected to be able to answer every question. If you do not know something that a parent or colleague asks about, demonstrate honesty by admitting you do not know and show willingness to seek more information.

Apologize

If you forget to do something or act thoughtlessly, offering an apology may help get a relationship back on track.

A GREAT START WITH PARENTS

Parents are experts on their children. It is in everyone's best interest if you work to develop respectful, cooperative, and supportive relationships early in the year. Special educators may work with parents over a several-year period, so taking time at the beginning to establish strong relationships can have long-term payoffs. New teachers may be concerned about the following:

▶ Not knowing how much they should communicate or interact with parents

▶ Low parent involvement

▶ Experiencing anxiety in their interactions with parents

▶ Need help planning and leading meetings with parents[4]

Table 3.1   Attitudes and Behaviors to Promote Positive Relationships with Parents[5]

Theme	Indicator
Communication: Enabling effective and efficient coordination and understanding among all parties	• Frequent, open, and clear communication • Listening • Respectful, positive, tactful, and honest interactions • Sharing resources and coordinating information
Commitment: Having sense of devotion and loyalty to the child and family; believing in goals for child and family	• Demonstrating commitment to child and family and showing that work is more than a job • Being sensitive, encouraging, accessible, and committed
Equality: Having a perception of equity in how decisions are made and implemented; displaying reciprocity among all involved	• Acting equal; validating and empowering others • Showing a willingness to explore all options • Fostering harmony among all partners
Skills: Having a perception that others are competent and able to fill roles and use recommended practices	• Showing competence, acting on behalf of child to meet individual needs, and considering the whole family • Being willing to learn new skills
Trust: Sensing that others are dependable (e.g., have character, strength, ability, and are truthful)	• Acting reliably and keeping children safe • Showing discretion and respecting confidentiality
Respect: Viewing each other with esteem through communication and action	• Being nonjudgmental, exercising nondiscrimination, being courteous, and avoiding intrusion

Adapted from Blue-Banning, M., Summers, J. A., Frankland, H. C., Nelson, L. L., & Beegle, G. (2004). Dimensions of family and professional partnerships: Constructive guidelines for collaboration, *Exceptional Children*, 70(2), 167–184.

The development of strong partnerships can help teachers, principals, service providers, and parents and families work together on behalf of the child's needs. Parents want to know that you care about their child, that he or she is safe with you, and that you have the skills to teach them. Parents are more likely to respond positively to relationships based on effective communication, commitment, equality, skill, trust, and respect. Table 3.1 presents examples of each of these attitudes and behaviors.

TEN ACTIONS TO DEVELOP POSITIVE RELATIONSHIPS WITH PARENTS

New teachers sometimes find it challenging to work with parents, especially if interactions lead to misunderstandings, problems, or conflicts. It is important to make sure you review all local policies related to communication (e.g., about e-mail, confidentiality, parent conferences, and frequency of feedback). Review these policies with your mentor and ask for advice if you have questions or concerns. It is also important to avoid a one-size-fits-all approach to family relationships. Also, monitor the language you use to ensure that you are respectful of cultural, language, and family differences. In this section we address how to have a great beginning with your parents and strategies for dealing with difficulties should they arise.

Start Your Relationship on a Positive Note

▶ In your first communication with parents, emphasize that you care about their child and that you look forward to helping their child meet his or her educational goals (see exhibit 3.1). Let the parents know that you look forward to working with them and that you value their input.

▶ Early in the year, call or send a note to the parent(s) with a positive message about their child (see exhibit 3.2).

Exhibit 3.1   Sample: Beginning-of-Year Letter from Special Education Teacher

Dear Parent,

I am so pleased to be part of your child's educational program this year. I look forward to getting to know your child.

I am happy to be at Five Forks Elementary and am enjoying getting to know all of the people who work here. Last year, I finished my master's degree in special education and taught in an elementary and middle school. I have reviewed your child's IEP and I am collaborating with the general education teachers so that we can work together to meet your child's needs.

Next week is our open house at Five Forks Elementary. It is scheduled on Thursday from 4 to 7 PM. I hope you are able to visit the school. I can also be reached through e-mail (kvalentine@ FFE.edu) or through phone (540-238-8555).

Today your child brought home a blue folder that will be sent home every day from our fifth-grade classroom. The left-hand side is labeled "Review, sign, and return." The right-hand side is labeled "Things to keep," including examples of work that your child has completed. Please add any notes that you would like either the fifth-grade teacher or me to read. In the left-hand side of the folder is a form for sharing information about your child. Please send this back with your child, mail it to school, or bring it to the open house.

Sincerely,

Karen Valentine, special education teacher, fifth grade

Exhibit 3.2   Encouraging Note to Parents about Their Child

KUDOS!

_____ deserves a big "bravo" for _____

_____.

Sincerely,
Karen Valentine

▶ Try to begin each conversation or conference with a parent on a positive note, perhaps commenting on specific areas in which the child is improving or show examples of their child's work.

▶ Write positive notes on each child's paper in addition to corrections.

Show Respect and Appreciation

▶ Let parents know that you appreciate the opportunity to talk with them and that you value their input.

▶ Avoid judging parents; rather, accept them as they are.

▶ Demonstrate respect by being on time for meetings and acknowledge parents' efforts with their child.

▶ Listen to parents' concerns about their child's safety and well-being. Parents will be anxious and sometimes difficult if they are not sure that their child is safe and well cared for while at school or on the bus.

▶ Let the parent know you hear them by paraphrasing. For example, "I understand that you are concerned about the homework requirement in science . . ."

View Parents as Experts on Their Child

▶ Parents are experts on their child and know their child in ways that you cannot. You can learn a lot about the child and the parent by listening; taking time to listen is a great way to begin your relationship. As the following quote from a parent of a child with a disability shows, equality and reciprocity are important to parent–child partnerships: "The first thing is to listen to us . . . because we know our kids better than anybody . . . I think some of these people have preconceived notions about everything . . . So if I tried to say, to tell them [professionals something], it'd be *listen to me.*"[6]

Remember That Parents Have Specific Legal Rights

▶ Parents have special rights under IDEA, including the right to participate in educational decisions that affect their child.

▶ Be sure to follow all policies related to parents' rights (these are reviewed in chapter 4 of this book).

▶ Avoid education jargon.

▶ Special education has many different legal terms (e.g., *IEP, free appropriate public education [FAPE]*), so take time to explain and invite parents to ask for help with any terms or documents.

Make Accommodations for Parents of Students Who Do Not Speak English

▶ If an interpreter is not provided, the child or an older sibling might be able to help with some basic communication. However, it is important to have a translator or interpreter available for eligibility and IEP meetings and parent conferences.

▶ Use online tools to help you translate written material from English into other languages.

Communicate Frequently and Follow Through

▶ Keep parents updated about their child's progress.

▶ Use checklists and forms to communicate on a weekly or even daily basis as needed.

▶ Let parents know that you are willing to answer any questions they have.

▶ Parents may ask questions and it is OK not to have the answers. They appreciate when you follow through to get answers.

Share Resources with Parents

▶ There are many high-quality special education websites that may be helpful to parents who have a child with a disability or your colleagues who teach their children and some are listed at the end of this chapter. You may want to share these links through a web page or a print copy of links.

▶ Create a parent shelf with books and resources (e.g., state department resources, books about understanding IEPs).

Document Communication with Parents and Keep Copies of Correspondence

▶ Keep a basic log of parent phone calls, important notes, and meetings. These do not need to be extensive, just a basic record (see exhibit 3.3).

▶ Consider copying yourself on all parent e-mails so you have a record of all correspondence.

▶ Consider using miniscanners that can be attached to your computer to scan correspondence in a matter of seconds.

Respect Confidentiality

▶ Understand confidentiality and follow guidelines.

▶ Parents also appreciate discretion when they share personal information.[7]

Exercise Care When Using E-mail and Social Networking

▶ Review your district and school policy about e-mail communication (e.g., time frame to respond to parents, what can and cannot be shared, suggested wording).

▶ For difficult situations, have a face-to-face conversation so parents can hear your tone.

▶ Do not post any information about your students, parents, or colleagues or your feelings about your job on social network sites such as Facebook or Twitter.

A GREAT START WITH ADMINISTRATORS

During your interview, orientations, and the first days of school, district and school leaders and mentors will likely begin sharing information about the school and district. With any luck they will provide explicit information about how the organization operates and your responsibilities within the organization. For example, they may share an organizational chart showing who in the organization is responsible for particular responsibilities and who are the contacts in various areas (e.g., assessment, personnel, technology).

Exhibit 3.3   Teacher–Parent Communication Log

Date	To	Type of Communication	Notes
		___phone ___note ___meeting ___e-mail	
		___phone ___note ___meeting ___e-mail	
		___phone ___note ___meeting ___e-mail	
		___phone ___note ___meeting ___e-mail	
		___phone ___note ___meeting ___e-mail	

A Survival Guide for New Special Educators, by Billingsley, Brownell, Israel, and Kamman. Copyright © 2013 by John Wiley & Sons, Inc.

Seek Clarification about Expectations and Responsibilities

Special education teachers have varied responsibilities beyond teaching. If your responsibilities are not clear, please seek clarification from mentors and supervisors. It is important to have a grasp of your responsibilities. Try to discuss the full range of your responsibilities with your principal, district supervisor, and mentor.

Determine if You Have One or Multiple Supervisors

In some districts, special education teachers work with principals and central office administrators. Your primary supervisor is likely to be a principal, assistant principal, or department chair, although district personnel will likely supervise some aspects of your work (e.g., compliance with IEPs). Be sure to ask for clarification if you are confused about expectations or if you receive conflicting messages from your principal and special education supervisor. For example, "I am not sure what to do since the director told me that the supplies are to be ordered through the school. Could you help me figure this out?"

Working with Parents from Varied Cultural Backgrounds

Nicole Dobbins, University of North Carolina at Greensboro

In order to communicate effectively and establish positive relationships with parents and students from varied cultural backgrounds, teachers must develop an open and accepting atmosphere when they work with parents. Consider the following actions when you work with parents from cultural backgrounds that differ from your own.

REFLECT ON YOUR OWN EXPECTATIONS AND VALUES AND THAT OF OTHERS

► Develop an awareness of how your own background and experiences influence your behaviors and value systems.

► Embrace your own cultural identity and learn about and accept the diversity of the families you work with.

► Demonstrate respect toward parents and realize that there will be differences between parent perspectives and the dominant school culture.

► Avoid making judgments or drawing conclusions based on stereotypes.

LEARN ABOUT PARENTS' CULTURES AND NEEDS

► Use surveys early in the year to provide families with opportunities to share information about their backgrounds with you.

► Listen to parents to learn about how they perceive education, discipline, schoolwork, and decision-making roles.

► Invite parents and students to present and discuss their backgrounds as they relates to curriculum topics.

CREATE A WELCOMING ENVIRONMENT

► Create an inviting classroom and welcome parents.

► Provide a parent bookshelf with materials in Spanish or other languages (see National Dissemination Center for Children with Disabilities [NICHCY; www.nichcy.org] for free materials).

► Let parents know that you value their input and that you are willing to hear their thoughts and concerns at any time.

► Invite parents to share their thoughts and concerns during conferences and IEP meetings.

PLAN SCHOOL EVENTS IN YOUR STUDENTS' COMMUNITIES THAT INVOLVE IMMEDIATE AND EXTENDED FAMILY MEMBERS SUCH AS GRANDPARENTS, AUNTS, UNCLES, AND COUSINS

► Participate in community events.

► Organize field trips that explore and introduce neighboring communities.

Understand the Chain of Command

The concept of a chain of command refers to the order in which you approach supervisors if you have a problem or concern. Generally, you work with those closest to you in the organization first. If you are not sure about whom to contact, begin with your mentor or department chair (if you have one) and then your principal. Even if you eventually talk with your district supervisor, you will want to keep the school administrator in the loop.

Become Familiar with Teacher Evaluation Processes

Today, teacher evaluation systems are under increased scrutiny and districts around the country are establishing more formal expectations for teachers. Understanding the expectations, schedule, and activities surrounding teacher evaluation will help you communicate more effectively with your administrators (see appendix D).

Seek Solutions

Teachers often need to share concerns or needs with their principals. It is often more effective to state the need as a problem to be solved rather than blaming others. For example, think about your goal (e.g., need to create more opportunities for my students in general education settings) rather than finding fault with colleagues who may not be cooperating with you.

Listen to Feedback

If an administrator comes to you with a concern, asks for you to do something differently, or criticizes some aspects of your behavior, listen carefully. Try to fully understand what the person is saying (e.g., asking him or her to elaborate until you understand) and provide any needed clarifications. One part of becoming an effective teacher is your willingness to consider feedback from others without getting defensive.

A GREAT START WITH YOUR MENTOR(S)

Mentors can guide you to becoming an accomplished and committed teacher. Your mentors may be assigned and part of a formal program or a colleague who provides guidance on an as-needed basis. With luck you will have multiple mentors, perhaps previous professors or a teacher who works across the hall from you.

If you are involved in a formal mentoring program, there may be specific requirements, a schedule of meetings and observations, and assessments. In less formal arrangements, it may be up to you and your mentor to make these decisions. In general new teachers who communicate more frequently with their mentors are more satisfied than those who have less communication.[8] The following actions can create a positive mentor–mentee relationship:

▶ Review written expectations about the mentor program.
▶ Discuss expectations for the mentor–mentee relationship (e.g., frequency of meeting, preparation for meeting).

A Great Start with Your Paraeducator

Teresa Little, University of North Carolina at Greensboro

New teachers often indicate that they have insufficient preparation to work with paraeducators and may be reluctant to provide direction to individuals who are older and perhaps have more experience than they do. Yet, it is the responsibility of special education teachers to make sure that paraeducators are engaged in ways that are productive and benefit students with disabilities. Following are strategies and tips that will assist with making the school year run smoothly for you and your paraeducator.

SCHEDULE A MEETING BEFORE THE SCHOOL YEAR BEGINS

Before the school year begins, meet with your paraeducator to discuss duties, responsibilities, and their schedules (see exhibit 3.4 for an example schedule).[9] You should emphasize your expectations and priorities, discuss annual evaluation procedures, and provide specific guidelines that reflect how you will each make the year successful. Consider the following possible responsibilities for paraeducators:

- ▶ Assist in supporting students through reinforcing instruction or assisting with behavior
- ▶ Help with monitoring student learning
- ▶ Assist with monitoring of behavior management plans
- ▶ Help with school responsibilities, such as monitoring hallways or bus duty
- ▶ Provide assistance to students in a range of ways, including helping with personal care

DETERMINE INTERESTS AND SKILLS

Because you will spend an enormous amount of time working side by side with your paraeducator, you should have a discussion regarding each other's skills and talents.[10] Being aware of one another's strengths will ensure the best possible outcomes for students and will allow each of you to showcase your talents. Consider the following questions as you get to know paraeducators:

- ▶ How has their work been structured in the past?
- ▶ What has worked well in the past?
- ▶ What do they feel are their strengths?
- ▶ In what areas are they interested in learning more?

MEET WITH YOUR PARAEDUCATOR ON A REGULAR BASIS

Schedule a weekly meeting with paraeducators to discuss specific plans for their work. These meetings can also be used to provide specific and constructive feedback so paraeducators will know what they are doing correctly and in which areas they can improve.[11] Avoid criticism and offer specific, constructive feedback so paraprofessionals know what they are doing correctly and how they might improve. Instead of saying, "You didn't redirect Mark back to his writing assignment," you might say, "When Mark is off task, please be sure to redirect him back to his writing assignment."

(Continued)

Exhibit 3.4 Paraeducator Schedule Form

Time	Place and Student(s)	Specific Activities	Supervising Teacher
8:30 AM			
9:00			
9:30			
10:00			
10:30			
11:00			
11:30			
12:00 PM			
12:30			
1:00			
1:30			
2:30			
3:00			

A Survival Guide for New Special Educators, by Billingsley, Brownell, Israel, and Kamman. Copyright © 2013 by John Wiley & Sons, Inc.

INVOLVE PARAEDUCATORS IN IEPS

Discuss the purpose of the IEP by highlighting goals and objectives as well as reviewing accommodations and modifications.[12] By sharing each student's IEP with paraeducators, they will gain a better understanding of academic and social areas to address.

ENSURE THAT PARAEDUCATORS DO NOT LIMIT STUDENTS' ACCESS TO THEIR CLASSMATES

In some settings paraeducators may inadvertently isolate a student with a disability by restricting their interactions with others. When possible seat students with disabilities in a central place and let paraeducators know that they should encourage (not get in the way of) student interactions with others.

PREPARE YOUR PARAEDUCATOR TO COLLECT DATA

Documenting student progress is an essential component of teaching that requires a team approach, and your paraeducator can be an excellent contributing team member. When asking him or her to collect data, explain the importance of this task and provide opportunities to model procedures and maintain paperwork.[13]

ASK FOR INPUT

When determining your students' strengths and needs, ask for input from the paraeducator. Just like you, they work with the students on a daily basis, can help with solving ongoing problems, and can brainstorm ways to improve teaching strategies.[14] Additionally, when conducting IEP meetings and parent–teacher conferences, invite paraeducators to attend so they can contribute their valuable ideas.

PROVIDE ONGOING LEARNING OPPORTUNITIES

Not only will you provide training at the beginning of the year, but you should also continue to provide opportunities for the paraeducator to learn throughout the school year. Inviting your paraeducator to participate in professional learning opportunities; sharing information you learn from training sessions, webinars, websites, and books; and developing professional learning goals with your paraeducator are all excellent ways to encourage ongoing learning and development.

DISCUSS KEY SCHOOL AND CLASSROOM POLICIES

In particular, be sure to stress the importance of policies, procedures, and professional behavior, including the following:

- ▶ Confidentiality and FERPA (see chapter 4)
- ▶ School rules
- ▶ School discipline policy
- ▶ School safety procedures
- ▶ Working with diverse learners
- ▶ School and classroom resources
- ▶ Class rules and established procedures for homework, dismissal, and so on

(Continued)

▶ Be on time for meetings.

▶ If possible, meet frequently with your mentor.

▶ Ask for what you need. For example, keep a list of things to discuss with your mentor so you can make the most of your meetings:

- Ask to observe your mentor teach a lesson in an area in which you struggle
- Ask your mentor to observe you and give you feedback on an IEP
- Ask for assistance with a parent meeting

▶ Try not to be defensive if the mentor gives you suggestions. Try to understand by listening carefully. Ask clarifying questions as needed.

▶ Keep track of all meetings and observations so you can show your participation.

▶ Participate in any evaluation(s) of the mentor-induction program.

▶ Don't expect your mentor to solve all of your challenges.

▶ Express appreciation to your mentor and let him or her know what you find particularly helpful.

A GREAT START WITH COLLEAGUES

Take time in your daily activities to build relationships with your colleagues. The use of strong communications skills (discussed earlier in this chapter) is essential to developing relationships with your colleagues. The benefits of good relationships are especially helpful to new teachers because colleagues can help to buffer the stress and difficulties of getting started in a new job. As one teacher stated, "Getting to know other teachers reduced the initial isolation that I felt. Their interest and concern made me want to hang in there and sometimes a good laugh was what I needed when I felt overwhelmed." As you think about working with your colleagues, ask yourself the following questions:

▶ Do I avoid saying negative things about those with whom I work?

▶ Can they count on me to do what I said I would do?

▶ Am I flexible and open to their viewpoints about teaching?

▶ Do I avoid trying to win at all costs?

Strong partnerships with other teachers should lead to productive meetings and better teaching. Being part of an elementary or secondary team of general educators can help to promote ongoing collaboration. For example, in some elementary schools, a special education teacher is assigned to a particular grade and meets with teachers in that grade to understand the curriculum, assessments, and collaboratively plan for students with disabilities. In secondary schools, you may be assigned to a team of teachers who teach in a specific content area.

Teachers who communicate regularly with individuals or teams of general education teachers have greater opportunities to do the following:

▶ Discuss student goals, curricula, and resources
▶ Discuss student groupings
▶ Learn from each other
▶ Problem-solve about student needs
▶ Assess which students are learning and which ones need reteaching and greater support

Perhaps one of the most difficult situations for new teachers is to deal with resistance from general education teachers as they try to work with them to address the needs of students with disabilities in their classrooms.

Avoid Blame and Power Struggles

If you accept that individuals have differing beliefs because of their experiences and educational background you may be more effective at soliciting the cooperation of others. Individuals may resist including students for varied reasons, such as lack of awareness about why inclusion is important, other demands on their time, or a difficult experience with a particular student. Try not to blame others for seeing things differently than you see them, even if you feel they are wrong.

Involve Others in Determining Effective Solutions

Instead of saying, "I need for you to modify Althea's tests to what her IEP states," try, "Althea is struggling with the tests in this class. I think she knows more than she is showing on these assessments. Could we brainstorm other ways to assess what she knows?"

Clarify Responsibilities

General educators may be concerned that they will not have adequate support for addressing the needs of students with disabilities. Clarify your students' support needs and mutually determine how responsibilities will be shared among all involved with the student.

Request Professional Development (PD)

It may be that administrators, teachers, or parents have had limited information about inclusion. In this case you may want to discuss the need for PD about inclusion with your principal or director. Chapter 8 addresses teacher collaboration and co-teaching.

LEADING EFFECTIVE PROFESSIONAL MEETINGS

Teachers in schools often complain about meetings because they believe they take away from their instructional responsibilities. Yet, meetings are a necessary part of professional life and you will likely be expected to organize and lead a variety of professional meetings (e.g., conferences with parents or collaborative meetings with other teachers). Learning to lead these meetings in an efficient way is essential because time is a precious resource.

Meetings are also a necessary vehicle for accomplishing important goals and tasks, such as discussing a student's behavioral plan or writing an IEP. In the first years, you will likely participate in IEP meetings, parent–teacher conferences, and co-teaching and collaborative meetings. Whether or not you lead meetings, knowing about what makes an effective meeting can help you be a productive participant.

Meetings require scheduling, thinking about what needs to be accomplished, and sometimes follow-up after the meeting. Table 3.2 provides specific guidance for these tasks. New teachers describe that leading meetings can be a stressful experience.

Table 3.2 Tips for Planning and Leading an Effective Professional Meeting

Meeting Tasks	Tips
Specify a Goal(s) for the Meeting • Identify the major goal to be accomplished (e.g., develop a behavioral plan for Althea, complete Jason's IEP). • Identify other goals for the meeting (e.g., schedule follow-up meeting with Jason's team in one month).	• If you cannot think of a goal for the meeting, you probably do not need to meet. • The purpose of the meeting will make it clear who should attend.
Schedule Your Meeting • Schedule a date, begin and end times, and a place for the meeting so others will know how much time to allow. • Schedule sufficient time, especially when addressing complex tasks such as IEPs. • Make sure you consider everyone who should be invited or notified about the meeting. • When inviting others, share goals for the meeting and any materials relevant to preparing for the meeting. • Record each meeting date in your calendar so you do not forget. • Record dates and times in your calendar for you to send reminders. • Select a place that is appropriate given the size and purpose of the meeting (round tables give the message that collaboration is expected).	• Give appropriate notice for the meeting (preferably at least a week). • Decide who needs to be at the meeting. • Use doodle or other web programs to check others' availability. • Be sure to contact those without e-mail by phone or letter. • If key people cannot attend, you will probably want to wait until later. • For parent meetings, you can send home a list of available dates and times and ask parents to indicate their top four preferences. • Copy forms to save time. • Save templates for scheduling letters in your e-mail so you can avoid writing out the information each time.
Prepare for Meeting • Write out the agenda for the meeting and prioritize items from the most important at the beginning to items that can wait at the end. • Distribute an agenda to all participants prior to the meeting if needed. • Ask those who cannot attend if there is anything they would like shared.	• Applications, such as Agenda, are available for download on an iPad or computer and can be used to keep track of what you plan to discuss (some of these can be linked to your calendar). • A meeting file or bin can be used to place materials prior to your meetings (particularly helpful if you have successive meetings).

Table 3.2 Continued

Meeting Tasks	Tips
• Put all materials needed for the meeting in a folder (e.g., student portfolio, assessment data). • Request that an attendee take notes during the meeting.	• Send out premeeting material (e.g., detailed agenda, PowerPoints, reading material) at least forty-eight hours in advance.
Lead the Meeting • Welcome each person to the meeting and thank all for attending. • Early on review the goals and agenda for the meeting and state when it will end. • Use the agenda as your framework for the meeting. • Try to involve all participants. Parents may need direction invitations to participate ("I'm wondering if you have any thoughts about this idea"). • Keep the meeting moving along (say, "We have fifteen minutes left to discuss this issue and then we need to move to the next agenda item"). • Use your judgment: sometimes you cannot postpone discussion, particularly if there is emotion involved.	• As appropriate, develop rapport with participants. • If a meeting evolves into a complaint session or becomes unproductive, gently remind the group of the goals of the meeting (e.g., "It is understandable that we may want to discuss this further at another time; however, today we need to . . ."). • If a member resorts to blaming others, refocus on the goal and problem solve (e.g., "How can we address this need? Can we brainstorm ways to solve this problem?").
Summarize • In the last five minutes, summarize (e.g., review any agreements, such as specific action items, who will complete each, due dates). • Plan a follow-up meeting if necessary. • Try to end on time (it will depend on the circumstances and what is acceptable in your school) and thank others for attending.	• If you have time, you may want to ask others to summarize the main points. • If you have planned too much, say so: "It looks like we won't have time for everything so we should probably reschedule a time to talk about…"
Follow-up • In some situations you may want to send a thank-you note to a parent for attending. • Distribute meeting notes via e-mail.	• Forms can be used to make follow-up easier.

Here are several tips for getting started to lead meetings:

▶ Observe others lead meetings early in the year.

▶ Use table 3.2 as a planning guide for your first meetings; consider each tip item on the list.

▶ Because you will likely not know parents and teachers, allow extra time in your first meetings for getting to know others.

▶ If you do not feel confident, write out what you plan to say.

▶ If you are dealing with a potentially difficult situation, ask your mentor or another teacher to attend.

▶ Ask another teacher to observe how you lead the meeting and to give you feedback or, alternatively, at the end of the meeting ask participants what was effective and ineffective about the meeting.

TO SUM UP

▶ Be an energizer and work on relationship development throughout your day.

▶ Consider your own communication skills—what do you do well, what do you need to work on?

▶ Be a person your colleagues and administrators can trust to follow through, act with integrity, and see possibilities.

▶ Take time to show your appreciation to others who help and assist you.

▶ Handle conflicts carefully, listen to understand others' perspectives, and take a problem-solving versus blaming approach.

▶ Communicate with parents, emphasizing what is going well before what needs improvement.

▶ Work with paraeducators to structure their roles and clarify expectations.

▶ Learn to listen to feedback objectively.

WHAT'S NEXT?

We hope you now have an understanding of specific actions you can take to communicate effectively with administrators, colleagues, parents, paraeducators, and mentors. Next we will move on to key laws that you need to be aware of, particularly IDEA.

ADDITIONAL RESOURCES

COMMUNICATION

▶ Patterson, K., Grenny, J., McMillan, R., & Switzler, A. (2002). *Crucial conversations: Tools for talking when stakes are high.* New York: McGraw-Hill.

WORKING WITH PARENTS

▶ Brown, M. (2009). A new multicultural population: Creating effective partnerships with multiracial families. *Intervention in School and Clinic, 45*(2), 124–136.

▶ National Dissemination Center for Children with Disabilities: www.nichcy.org

▶ Beach Center on Disability: www.beachcenter.org

▶ LD OnLine: www.ldonline.org

▶ PACER Center: www.pacer.org

WORKING WITH PARAEDUCATORS

▶ Iowa Department of Education. (nd). *Guide to effective paraeducator practices.* Retrieved from www.aea267.k12.ia.us/paraeducators/index.php?page=guidelines

▶ National Clearinghouse for Paraeducator Resources: www.usc.edu/dept/education/CMMR/Clearinghouse.html

▶ National Resource Center for Paraeducators: www.nrcpara.org

CHAPTER FOUR

Special Education Law

In this chapter you will learn about:

- Laws that apply to special education and why they are important
- Key principles and requirements of special education law
- Practical tips for managing legal requirements
- What to do when presented with legal challenges

Christine was nervous about her meeting with her mentor today because the topic of their conversation was compliance. Although Christine learned about pertinent laws in her preparation program, she was concerned about forgetting details and that she might do something wrong. She hoped meeting with her mentor could help her confidence in complying with district and federal regulations.

New special education teachers often worry about meeting the legal requirements of their jobs. You might wonder about how to complete a referral, evaluation, or IEP form given to you during orientation. You are not alone.

KEY LAWS RELATED TO STUDENTS WITH DISABILITIES

Teachers who know and understand the law undoubtedly provide a more sound education to all students.
Dr. Elizabeth LeClear, former special education teacher and current principal

Laws help us to define terminology and set a foundation and provide guidance for procedures, services, and implementation in special education. Even something as basic as a definition of special education is critical: "*Special education* means specially designed instruction, at no cost to the parents, to meet the unique needs of a child with a disability."[1] Let's start by reviewing the four most important laws related to educating students with disabilities. Table 4.1 provides an overview.

Table 4.1 Laws Related to Special Education

Provisions	Importance	Implications for Special Education Teachers
Education for All Handicapped Children Act (EAHCA) of 1975	• Children with disabilities have a right to a free and appropriate public education (FAPE). • Included IEPs, parental rights, education in the least restrictive environment (LRE), and nondiscriminatory assessment.	• Required training for general and special education teachers to communicate with parents about student placement, and various instructional program options. • Emphasis on testing and evaluation as nondiscriminatory as well as multidisciplinary collaboration in IEP teams.
IDEA of 1990, 1997, and 2004	• The EAHCA was amended and reauthorized as IDEA in 1990. • IDEA 1997 and 2004 aimed to increase the academic achievement of students with disabilities through FAPE and LRE with an emphasis on accountability and assessment.	• Emphasis on obtaining highly qualified teachers and improving teacher quality. • Teachers now must prepare all students for inclusion in state assessments to work toward a school's adequate yearly progress (AYP). • IEP goals must be tied to the general education curriculum.
Section 504 of the Rehabilitation Act of 1973	• Civil rights law. • No individual shall be excluded from any program receiving federal financial assistance based on his or her disability. • Students with disabilities are to be provided with a comparable education to students without disabilities.	• Flexibility in teacher practices and expectations. • Modifications, accommodations, and adjustments to environments or strategies. • Assessment of student progress and effective communication with parents.
ADA of 1990, 2008	• Civil rights law. • Guarantees equal opportunity for individuals with disabilities in employment, public accommodations, transportation, state and local government services, and telecommunications.	• Any physical barrier in any environment must be removed to allow students with disabilities equal access. • Students with disabilities have the right to full and equal enjoyment of goods, services, facilities, and accommodations.

EDUCATION FOR ALL HANDICAPPED CHILDREN ACT

In 1975, Congress enacted landmark legislation, the Education for All Handicapped Children Act (EAHCA), when for the first time "all children with disabilities have available to them a free appropriate public education, which emphasizes special education and related services designed to meet their unique needs."[2] Moreover, the act made provisions so the rights of parents were protected. Specifically, the EAHCA asserted six main principles.

Zero Reject

States and local education agencies are required to locate, identify, and provide services to students with disabilities deemed eligible. Examples include the following:

- ▶ Screening students for speech and language, hearing, and vision
- ▶ Identifying students who are not achieving in the general education classroom
- ▶ Providing information about disabilities to parents through advertising, websites, and meetings

Protection in Evaluation

An assessment must be conducted to determine if a student has an eligible disability through the following:

- ▶ In all of the suspected areas of disability
- ▶ By a team of knowledgeable evaluators trained in the use of assessment materials
- ▶ Using a variety of techniques and procedures that are nondiscriminatory
- ▶ Including information from a variety of sources
- ▶ Using information that is instructionally useful in planning for student education needs

Free Appropriate Public Education (FAPE)

Once a student is determined eligible for special education services, a team must develop an individualized education program (IEP) to benefit the student. The IEP team determines what FAPE means for each student. The team uses current levels of performance to make decisions about appropriate goals, educational and related services, and the extent to which the student will be educated in general education settings. It is the responsibility of the district to ensure that this plan is implemented as described in the IEP.

Least Restrictive Environment

Students with disabilities must be educated with their nondisabled peers to the maximum extent appropriate.

Procedural Safeguards

Parents must be provided with rights and responsibilities for the special education process (see exhibit 4.1).

Parental Participation

Procedures must be in place for schools and parents to collaborate in eligibility decisions and to participate in the development of the child's plan for special education services (see chapter 5).

These six principles set the foundation for special education services. Since the passage of the original law, significant progress has been made in improving the educational landscape for programs and services in early intervention, special education, and related services.

Tips for Determining
Least Restrictive Environment (LRE)

The IEP team determines what constitutes the least restrictive environment for each student. The extent to which students with disabilities are educated in general education classrooms varies greatly across states and districts. In some districts, almost all students are educated in general education classrooms, whereas other districts maintain resource and full-time classrooms as well as special schools. Therefore depending on local expectations, some committees may be more or less inclined to recommend general education settings.

It is critical to emphasize that the LRE principle requires that students be educated with their nondisabled peers to the maximum extent appropriate. Following are some tips to assist the team in making the LRE determination.[3]

START WITH REVIEWING GOALS AND SERVICES

The student goals and services are central to the IEP and should be the focus of placement decisions. For example, if the goal is for the student to receive speech instruction in a small group, these services may be more appropriate in a separate setting where there are fewer distractions and where it is more likely the student will be able to hear the differences in sounds.

DISCUSS THE ENVIRONMENT NECESSARY TO SUPPORT PROGRESS ON GOALS

The IEP team discusses what type of environment can help to facilitate success on goals. These questions may help:

► What type of instruction is necessary? (small or large group? direct instruction?)
► What level of teacher-to-student interaction is needed?
► Are peer interactions necessary for meeting specific goals in speech, social emotional, or engagement?

DISCUSS PLACEMENT OPTIONS

The team begins by discussing the current placement and appropriateness. Then they consider each placement option with the benefits or potential harm including possible accommodations and consider supplementary aids and services that might be helpful in the setting. According to IEP requirements, the team must provide a rationale if the placement is not in a general education classroom and setting.

COME TO A CONSENSUS

Using the list created when discussing placement options, the team decides on the scenario that will meet the student's needs in the least restrictive environment. These placements should not be considered permanent because the student can move from one environment to another as needs change.

Exhibit 4.1   Procedural Safeguards: Parent Rights Summarized[4]

Parents have the right to the following:

▶ Receive a complete explanation of all the procedural safeguards available under IDEA and the procedures in the state for presenting complaints

▶ Expect confidentiality and the ability to inspect and review the educational records of their child

▶ Participate in meetings related to the identification, evaluation, and placement of their child and the provision of FAPE to their child

▶ Obtain an independent educational evaluation of their child

▶ Receive prior written notice on matters relating to the identification, evaluation, or placement of their child and the provision of FAPE to their child

▶ Give or deny their consent before the school may take certain action with respect to their child

▶ Disagree with decisions made by the school system on those issues

▶ Use mechanisms for resolving disputes including the right to appeal determinations

INDIVIDUALS WITH DISABILITIES EDUCATION ACT

The Individuals with Disabilities Education Act (IDEA; 1990, 1997) is an amendment renaming the EAHCA (1975). In 2004, it was renamed again to the Individuals with Disabilities Education Improvement Act (IDEIA).[5] You will still hear most people refer to the law as IDEA. In each of the reauthorizations, new regulations were added that affect you directly as a special education teacher.

Meeting IDEA Requirements: From Identifying Children to Finding Placement

IDEA is very specific about nearly every detail of special education. The major provisions of IDEA can be broken down into ten steps:[6]

A Child Is Identified as Potentially Needing Special Education or Related Services

▶ Each state is required to identify, locate, and evaluate children suspected of having a disability. This is called the child-find provision. A parent, friend, doctor, or teacher may ask for the child to be evaluated.

▶ Parent consent is required for evaluation and the subsequent evaluation must occur within sixty days of consent.

The Child Is Evaluated

▶ The evaluation must be comprehensive, individual, and nondiscriminatory. The evaluation must assess all the areas that may be related to the suspected disability.

▶ The results will serve as the basis to determine eligibility for special education and related services as well as assisting in determining programming and appropriate placement.

Eligibility Is Determined

▶ A team of professionals and parents collaborate to decide if the child meets disability criteria as defined by IDEA.

▶ If the parents do not agree, they may challenge the decision.

The Child Is Eligible for Services

▶ If the team determines the child has a disability and needs the support of specially designed instruction, then he or she is eligible for special education–related services.

▶ Within thirty days, the team must meet to write an IEP for the child.

IEP Meeting Is Scheduled (See Details in Chapter 5)

▶ Usually the school schedules and holds the IEP meeting.

▶ The following must occur:
  • Notify the parents early enough so they can attend.
  • Schedule the meeting at a time and place that is agreeable to the parents and school.
  • Tell the parents the purpose, time, and location of meeting.
  • Alert the parents so they may invite other people who may have knowledge about the child.

IEP Meeting Is Held and IEP Completed

▶ The team meets to discuss the child and write the IEP.

▶ LRE is determined.

▶ Parents and students (when appropriate) participate in the process.

▶ Parents receive a copy of the IEP.

▶ Parents must give consent before a child receives services the first time.

▶ If the parents disagree, the team should discuss differences and work for consensus.

▶ If parents and the school disagree, parents can ask for mediation, file a state complaint, or file a due process complaint.

After the IEP Is Completed, Services Begin

▶ The school is then responsible for making certain the IEP is implemented as specified.

▶ Each of the teachers and service providers has access to the IEP and should know his or her specific responsibilities in implementing the program.

Progress Is Monitored and Reported

▶ The child's progress in meeting annual IEP goals is assessed and reported on the IEP.

▶ Parents are regularly informed about their child's progress at least as frequently as general education peers are informed of progress.

IEP Is Revisited

▶ At least once a year, and perhaps more often, the IEP is reviewed and revised.

▶ Parents are always invited to the IEP meetings and participate with the team.

▶ At least every three years the child must be reevaluated.

▶ The purpose of the reevaluation is to determine if the student continues to have a disability as defined by IDEA.

As a special education teacher, you have many responsibilities related to implementing IDEA. States take the federal law and apply it in different ways. For example, all states require the use of IEPs but the paperwork is different in every state and often varies even by district (IEPs are discussed in more detail in chapter 5). Duties of a special education teacher will vary by your assignment.

Common Tasks for Special Education Teachers in Implementing IDEA

▶ Planning and facilitating IEP meetings

▶ Writing IEPs with the input of the team

▶ Serving as a case manager for students and monitoring implementation of the IEP by all providers

▶ Assessing students and reporting progress to parents

▶ Conducting manifestation determinations

▶ Providing instruction consistent with the goals on the IEP

It is important that you discuss your role with your administrator so you are clear about your specific responsibilities. You may face situations in which you are not sure how to interpret the legal requirements. In these cases, seek out a knowledgeable colleague or administrators who can help you maintain compliance with IDEA.

IDEA Disability and Related Services Terms

See appendix A for a definition of each disability and a discussion of resources.

▶ Attention deficit hyperactivity disorder (ADHD)

▶ Autism spectrum disorders

▶ Deaf and hearing loss

▶ Developmental delay

▶ Emotional disturbance

▶ Hearing impairment

▶ Intellectual disability

▶ Other health impairment

▶ Specific learning disability

▶ Speech and language disorders

▶ Traumatic brain injury

▶ Visual impairment including blindness

The Basics on Disciplinary Procedures and Students with Disabilities

TEN-DAY REMOVAL

► School personnel can remove a student for no more than ten days in a row. During these ten days, students with disabilities do not have to be provided with educational services.

► Beginning on the eleventh cumulative day of suspension the school system must provide education services so the student can continue to participate in the general education curriculum and progress toward meeting IEP goals.

CHANGE OF PLACEMENT

► After ten cumulative days of suspension in one school year, the school must determine if the removal is a change of placement.

► A change of placement occurs if the removal is more than ten consecutive school days or the student removals constitute a pattern (removals are for similar actions).

CASE-BY-CASE DETERMINATION

► School personnel consider whether a removal from school that constitutes a change of placement is appropriate on a case-by-case basis.

► This allows schools to consider factors such as a student's ability to understand consequences, expression of remorse, or if supports were provided to the student prior to the disciplinary violation.

PARENT NOTIFICATION

► When the school decides that the student's removal is a change of placement, the school must notify the parent of the decision and provide procedural safeguards.

MANIFESTATION DETERMINATIONS

► When a change of placement is made because of disciplinary actions, then a manifestation determination must be conducted within ten days of the decision.

► At this meeting, the team decides if the behavior that caused the suspension had a direct and substantial relationship to the disability.

► If the team decides the student's misconduct was a direct result of the disability, then the student will be returned to the original placement and a functional behavior assessment must be conducted immediately followed by enacting a behavior intervention plan (see chapter 7 for more information).

► If the team decides the student's misconduct was not a direct result of the disability, then the student can have the same disciplinary procedures as would be applied to a student without disabilities.

SPECIAL CIRCUMSTANCES

► Schools can unilaterally remove students to an interim alternative education setting (IAES) for up to forty-five school days for offenses including drugs, weapons, or inflicting serious bodily injury even if it is a manifestation of the disability.

► When students are placed in an IAES they are still entitled to receive services necessary to continue to participate in the general education curriculum and progress toward meeting their goals on the IEP.

Additional IDEA Requirements

TRANSITION SERVICES

▶ This provision requires assistance for students with disabilities as they transition from school to postschool activities (see chapter 5 for a description of transition services).

HIGHLY QUALIFIED SPECIAL EDUCATION TEACHERS

▶ This provision specifies requirements for a highly qualified status in general, when teaching a core academic subject, when teaching to alternative standards, and when teaching multiple subjects.

EARLY INTERVENTION SERVICES

▶ This is referred to as part C and designates supports for infants and toddlers, from birth to age three.

▶ This provision ensures coordination across agencies to implement a comprehensive early intervention system, including child find, evaluation, identification, service delivery, and parent rights.

CHILDREN WITH DISABILITIES IN PRIVATE SCHOOLS

▶ The provision describes obligations of the state in providing services to students with disabilities in private school settings.

DISPROPORTIONALITY

▶ This provision requires states to monitor the policies and procedures for identification to prevent overidentification or disproportionate representation by race or ethnicity. States collect and disaggregate data by race and ethnicity on identification, placement, and incidence, duration, and type of disciplinary action.

▶ When necessary, states must create a plan for remedying disproportionality.

INCORPORATION OF RTI IN IDENTIFICATION

▶ This provision does not use the language of RTI but opens the door for use of the RTI process in identifying students with disabilities:

- First, students are screened to identify those who are at risk for poor learning outcomes or challenging behavior.

- Second, support is provided to students by linking assessment and instruction to inform educator's decisions about teaching. This includes three levels of intervention (commonly called *tiers*) focusing on using research-based curricula and evidence-based interventions.

- Finally, if the student fails to respond to interventions, further evaluation may be necessary to identify a disability. The progress-monitoring data used in the RTI process can assist in making the disability determination (see chapter 10 for more details).

► IDEA specifies how schools can respond to behavioral infractions of children with disabilities.

SECTION 504

Section 504 is often considered as being the legislation that levels the playing field for individuals with disabilities.[7] Section 504 is different from IDEA in that it is civil rights legislation and uses a broader definition of disability. As such, students with Section 504 plans are typically students with disabilities who do not require special education. As a special education teacher you will not typically provide direct services to these students. However, because you might be regarded as an expert on disabilities, general education teachers may look to you for guidance in providing educational accommodations.

Some examples of students who may be protected by Section 504 include students with the following conditions:

► Allergies
► Asthma
► Temporary disability caused by an accident
► Hepatitis or AIDS
► ADD or ADHD
► Cancer
► Those who are addicted to drugs or alcohol

Teachers must implement a 504 plan to provide a student with access to equal educational opportunities. These are just a few of the typical accommodations that may be provided in 504 plans:

► Adjusting classroom schedule
► Preferential seating
► Extra time to complete work
► Adaptions to exams (e.g., give orally, take-home test, frequent short quizzes)
► Daily notes home
► Adult supervision on bus
► Enlarged copies of text
► Providing visual cues
► Frequent reassurance

You may interact with this population of students and provide services to special education students in the general education classroom environment. Every district has someone designated to coordinate efforts concerning Section 504. If you or your colleagues have questions, locate the person in your district with this designated role.

AMERICANS WITH DISABILITIES ACT

President G. H. W. Bush signed the Americans with Disabilities Act (ADA) into law in 1990 and it was amended in 2009.[8] It is the most comprehensive civil rights law providing rights for millions of Americans with disabilities. ADA protects people with a disability in the following areas:

EMPLOYMENT

► Requires employers with fifteen or more employees to provide qualified individuals with disabilities equal opportunity and prohibits discrimination in recruitment, hiring, promotions, training, pay, social activities, or any other privilege. Businesses must provide reasonable accommodations.

PUBLIC TRANSPORTATION

► Must be accessible to people with disabilities. You cannot deny people with disabilities participation in programs or activities that are available to people without disabilities.

PRIVATE ENTITIES AND PUBLIC ACCOMMODATIONS

► Must comply with basic nondiscrimination requirements that prohibit exclusion, segregation, and unequal treatment (e.g., movie theaters, private schools, doctor's offices).

TELECOMMUNICATIONS

► Telephone companies offering services to the public must have a relay system for individuals who are deaf.

You will have limited direct responsibilities regarding ADA. However, there may be situations when you must advocate or help your students advocate for protections under ADA. Consider the following scenarios that may apply to your students:

► Your student, Juan, uses a wheelchair. His general education teacher has planned a field trip to a rural farm that is not wheelchair accessible. The teacher has told Juan he can't attend.
► You are teaching high school. One of your students has told you that last weekend he applied for a job at the local grocery store. In the interview the student told the manager he had a learning disability but that with specific directions he could do a good job stocking or bagging groceries. The manager told the student the job was not for a person with a learning disability.
► Your student, Sally, who is deaf, wants to participate in your school's volleyball team. The coach has told her she can't because he has no way to communicate with her.

Each of these scenarios describes a situation in which a student on your caseload is encountering discrimination based on his or her disability. Although you are not the person engaging in the discrimination, you are knowledgeable about it happening. Ethically, you have a responsibility to advocate or encourage your student and also the parent of the student to advocate for their rights under ADA (learn more about advocating in chapter 9).

Select Federal Laws Influencing Assessment of Students with Disabilities

Since the 1970s, educational laws have evolved to place more and more emphasis on the education of students with disabilities and accountability for that education. Table 4.2 provides an overview of some of the major federal laws that have influenced assessment of students with disabilities.

Table 4.2 Select Federal Laws Affecting Students with Disabilities

Law	Implications for Assessment
Section 504 of the Rehabilitation Act of 1973	Students have a right to testing accommodations such as extended time, bathroom breaks, and other assessment supports.
Education for All Handicapped Children Act of 1975	Nondiscriminatory assessment involves using multiple, validated, culturally, and linguistically appropriate measures to assess students with disabilities.
Individuals with Disabilities Education Act of 1990	There is now more emphasis on instruction and assessment practices occurring in the least restrictive environment.
Individuals with Disabilities Education Act of 1997	Students with disabilities are included in state and district assessments. Assessment for early intervention is further expanded due to child-find provisions.
No Child Left Behind Act of 2001	All students participate in state assessments and receive options for assessments with accommodations as well as alternate assessments for students who have the most significant disabilities.
Individuals with Disabilities Education Act of 2004	Schools and districts now pay much closer attention to the education of students with disabilities because their scores count toward adequate yearly progress (AYP) measures. IEP goals must be tied to the general education curriculum.

CONFIDENTIALITY

The primary focus of the Family Educational Rights and Privacy Act (FERPA) is protecting the privacy of student records.[9] FERPA is important because it protects the rights of students and parents. The law provides parents with the right to access and amend their child's educational records as well as some control over disclosure. The law defines *educational records* as those that contain information that directly relate to the student and are maintained by the educational institution or a party acting for the institution. Schools must have written permission from the parent or student (if a legal adult) in order to release any information from a student's educational record unless it falls under special circumstances.

- ▶ School officials with legitimate educational interest
- ▶ Other schools to which a student is transferring
- ▶ Specified officials for audit or evaluation purposes
- ▶ Appropriate parties in connection with determining financial aid for a student
- ▶ Organizations conducting certain studies for or on behalf of the school
- ▶ Accrediting organizations
- ▶ To comply with a judicial order or lawfully issued subpoena
- ▶ Appropriate officials in cases of health and safety emergencies
- ▶ State and local authorities within a juvenile justice system, pursuant to specific state law
- ▶ Directory information

Practice Your Knowledge of FERPA

Think about each of these scenarios. What would you do? Are the teachers violating FERPA?

1. Rob is meeting his general education colleague, Mrs. Smith, to discuss a student on his caseload, Jimmy. Rob instructs Jimmy in a resource setting for reading but for the remainder of the day Jimmy resides in Mrs. Smith's class. Rob is planning to discuss the most recent evaluation data with Mrs. Smith.

2. Suzie just completed grading her high school science tests. She knows her students are anxious to know their grades. She is considering leaving their graded tests outside her classroom for the students to pick up.

3. Maria just received a call from a probation officer for one of the students on her caseload. The officer would like some information regarding the student's behavior.

4. A parent of one of Rachel's students would like her to e-mail her son's recent grades.

5. Sam is meeting with one of his student's parents. He wants to show her that an intervention that worked with another student might apply to her son. He takes out the other student's IEP and classroom work to show the parent.

ANSWERS

1. Rob is not violating FERPA. It is okay to discuss student data with other colleagues who participate in instruction.

2. Suzie is violating FERPA. If she leaves the graded tests outside her classroom, any person walking by can see the grades for any student in her class.

3. Maria is not violating FERPA. She can share information about a student with a law enforcement officer.

4. Rachel is violating FERPA unless she has prior written permission from the parent to send grades electronically.

5. Sam is violating FERPA. He can't share information that specifically identifies another student.

Additionally, schools are required to notify parents and students annually of their rights under FERPA. Examples of items protected by FERPA include the following:

▶ Videotapes
▶ IEPs
▶ Photographs
▶ Evaluation data

Examples of items not protected by FERPA include the following:

▶ Records kept in your sole possession for your use only
▶ Security videotapes
▶ An overheard threatening remark made by a student

If you are ever unsure whether you are violating FERPA, it is best to err on the side of caution and not disclose information. Your principal and the record keeper at your school will also be well versed in FERPA and where and when it applies. Ask when you need help.

The Case of NCLB

Stacey Rice, University of Florida

It's no secret that special education teachers have plenty of things to think about on a daily basis. Planning instruction, grading papers, IEP meetings, and parent concerns are just a few of the things that may be on your mind today. With NCLB enacted in 2001, all teachers had to change their teaching and planning practices. Other terms that you have likely heard include *accountability, AYP, standard curriculum,* and *highly qualified.* Consider the case of Sandra, a veteran special education teacher:

> Sandra has long been using evidence-based interventions to help increase her students' knowledge and skills. However, with the implementation of NCLB, she has her general education colleagues making strides in their use of evidence-based practices as well as interventions to affect struggling students. Additionally, although data has always been an important part of monitoring IEP progress, Sandra has begun rigorously collecting data on her students to align with the NCLB requirements on accountability. This data helps provide more than an anecdotal picture of her students' improvement and helps her identify the areas in which each student needs additional instruction. The data she collects also helps her during parent–teacher conferences. Now she is able to communicate with parents using supporting data exactly how their child is doing in the classroom. Sandra has also noticed more attention from her principal since the implementation of NCLB regulations at her school. Previously, the majority of Sandra's students were excluded in the districtwide testing. Now, all of her students except one are included. In an effort to make sure her students are improving and perform well on the district annual assessment, Sandra meets biweekly with grade-level teams to discuss how their instruction is aligning with the state standards.

As you can see from the case of Sandra, NCLB has changed not only many of Sandra's practices, but also the practices of her general education colleagues. The regulation has made it more important for all the educators, administrators included, to be invested in the success of special education students.

DEALING WITH LEGAL CHALLENGES

Although the intention of regulations is for parents and schools to work together, parents and schools may disagree on what is appropriate for the student with a disability. In these cases, administrative agencies and courts are called on to make the final determination in a specific case. Courts can help to clarify a regulation and provide a legal standard. Appendix B highlights important court cases related to special education and describes how the determinations in these cases affect daily IEP decisions.

It is your responsibility as a special education teacher to implement legal requirements. If you know of a situation that does not follow the correct professional practice, it is your job to assist in complying with the law.

Consider the following situation:

> Sally is on your caseload and has been identified as having a specific learning disability. She comes to your resource room for reading but attends the general education classroom for all other instruction. Sally has an accommodation on her IEP for extended time on all exams. However, Sally's mom has told you the general education teacher will not give her extra time.

Tips for Resolving Difficulties

If you find yourself in a difficult situation there are several strategies you can try to ameliorate the problem.

Schedule a Time to Talk

In Sally's situation, you could set up a time to discuss the IEP with the general education teacher. Perhaps the teacher is unaware of the accommodations or has forgotten. Consider the communication tips outlined in chapter 3.

Offer to Assist

One way to help in difficult situations is to offer assistance. For Sally, you could suggest that she can take the tests with extra time in your classroom.

Seek Help

If you have been unable to resolve the problem, find someone to help. If Sally's general education teacher still won't provide extra time after you met with her, and she declined your assistance, find help. Your department chair or principal will be prepared to assist you with difficult situations.

There are some situations that are beyond your control such as when the parent is in disagreement with placement or practices that the IEP team decides. Your IEP team should make every effort to come to consensus with a parent. However, when this does not happen procedures are in place to help resolve the dispute.

Teachers as Expert Witnesses—Preparing for Due Process Hearings

Rachel Thomas, University of Florida

DUE PROCESS

There are three types of special education disputes that may lead to a due process hearing or a courtroom case:

► When parents of children with special needs want specific services for their child (examples include hearing aids and teacher assistants in the classroom)

► When parents want to dispute the classroom placement of their child

► When there are alleged violations of IDEA

Due process hearings occur before a case reaches a federal or state courtroom. IDEA allows states to have some flexibility in terms of due process hearings:

► They must decide on an impartial administrative hearing officer.

► Attorneys or special education teachers may be appointed to conduct the hearing.

Parents and the school system in question have the right to present their full positions at a hearing but the manner in which this happens is typically decided by the hearing officer.

SERVING AS AN EXPERT WITNESS[10]

An expert witness is different from an ordinary witness in that an expert is an individual who has had education, training, or experience that leads to specialized knowledge of a topic or field. Expert witnesses are allowed to give their opinion, whereas ordinary witnesses are allowed only to relay facts. If called on, you will have to testify. Remember that your role is important because you provide vital information to a judge who may be unfamiliar with children with disabilities. Important decisions may be made based on your testimony; therefore, your responsibilities for accurate portrayal should not be taken lightly.

TIPS FOR SERVING AS AN EXPERT WITNESS

► Give only factual information and your own interpretation of the facts available.

► Be prepared to share observations and evaluative information about the particular child.

► Keep the jargon and technical terminology to a minimum so the information you are giving is accessible to everyone.

► Make occasional eye contact and turn toward the judge when speaking.

► Testify in clear and certain terms. Avoid phrases like "kind of," "I guess," and "like."

► Only answer the questions asked.

► Avoid giving irrelevant information.

► Don't be surprised by personal attacks. Remain calm and respond with clear facts, not with anger or hostility.

► Avoid conversations with the opposing side.

► Provide information to prove your qualifications as an expert witness.

► Visit the environment where the hearing or trial will take place prior to the court date. This may help you feel more comfortable when testifying.

► Maintain communication with the attorney for your side.

► Remember, your professional judgments and opinions should always come before any type of loyalty to your employer.

Resolving Disagreements

Mediation is a process in which a qualified and impartial mediator aims to find resolution to a disagreement prior to formal litigation. A due process hearing can also be used to resolve a disagreement. In this case you can do the following:

- ▶ A complaint is filed with the state department of education but presided over by an impartial hearing officer.
- ▶ Cases only go to state or federal court on appeal.
- ▶ In rare cases, you may be asked to serve in a due process hearing or a court case as an expert witness.

TO SUM UP

- ▶ IDEA outlines provisions for the identification, education, and services for students with disabilities.
- ▶ Other laws also have implications for students with disabilities including civil rights legislation Section 504 and ADA.
- ▶ Confidentiality of student records is guided by FERPA regulations.
- ▶ Understanding the provisions of key laws can help you meet the needs of students with disabilities as legally required.
- ▶ When you are in a challenging situation related to the law or have questions, always seek assistance from a supervisor.

WHAT'S NEXT?

Now that you have a good understanding of the laws that apply to your everyday work, let's move on to some specifics about students. In the next chapter you will learn more about a key IDEA requirement, the development of IEPs for students with disabilities.

ADDITIONAL RESOURCES

- ▶ IDEA: http://idea.ed.gov/explore/home
- ▶ Wrightslaw: www.wrightslaw.com
- ▶ Special Education Law Blog: http://specialedlaw.blogs.com
- ▶ Special Education Advisor: www.specialeducationadvisor.com
- ▶ Edlaw: http://edlaw.org/wordpress
- ▶ Reality 101: http://cecblog.typepad.com
- ▶ Technical Assistance and Dissemination (TD&A) Network: www.tadnet.org
- ▶ Comparison of ADA, IDEA, and Section 504 (Disability Rights Education and Defense Fund): www.dredf.org/advocacy/comparison.html
- ▶ Early Intervention, Part C (National Early Childhood Technical Assistance Center): www.nectac.org/partc/partc.asp

CHAPTER FIVE

Developing Quality IEPs

In this chapter you will learn about:

- How to have a great start with IEPs
- Required IEP components
- How to plan for and conduct IEP meetings
- Who should attend and how to involve parents
- Transition planning and how to get students involved in their IEPs
- How to organize and lead an effective IEP meeting

Jamie noticed that four of her students' IEPs needed to be revised within the first month of school. She found an IEP form but had questions about what to put in some sections. She wondered about procedures for scheduling the meeting and who should attend. Although she had written mock IEPs in her preparation program she had never led a meeting. She also had questions about how to balance providing students with access to the general curriculum as well as meet their individual needs. Jamie took a deep breath and hoped that her mentor could walk her through one or two before she had to tackle these on her own.

It isn't surprising that one of the most challenging tasks for new special education teachers is facilitating the development of each student's IEP. The IEP committee must draw on its knowledge about the student's specific needs, research-based practices, and the varied supports and services necessary for the student to achieve important educational outcomes. In addition, specific forms and procedures for IEP development often vary across states and districts, leaving teachers to try to figure out processes in their settings. It also takes knowledge, skill, time, and commitment to work with others to make the IEP development process a meaningful one rather than just a compliance task.

THE IEP DOCUMENT

IEPs are written documents that are legally required for each child identified with a disability. IEPs might be understood as a map that outlines student goals and the necessary services and supports to help each child meet his or her goals:

▶ Must be based on meaningful data about student needs.

▶ Ensures that the student's education is individualized and standards based.

▶ Includes measurable academic goals and necessary supports.

▶ Describes the student's level of participation in the general education curriculum.

▶ Requires that peer-reviewed research (PRR) is incorporated in the design of special education services for the student. This PRR requirement extends to special education, related services, and supplementary aids and services to the extent practicable. This means that the IEP team should select and use academic and behavioral interventions that are supported by research because they are the most likely to be effective for the child. Other terms such as *evidence-based practices* are also used to describe those teaching practices supported by research.

▶ Provides a description of the student's participation in extracurricular activities and nonacademic activities, including lunch, clubs, and after-school programs.

▶ Ensures continuity of services as the child moves to another school.

The language in the IEP should be clear enough that a teacher in a different school or district will be able to understand and implement it. At the end of this chapter we list websites that include numerous examples of completed IEP documents for students with varied needs in elementary, middle, and high school.

THE IEP PROCESS

The IEP is developed through a process designed to encourage parents and school personnel to plan and communicate together to cultivate a program specific to the child's needs. The IEP meeting accomplishes the following:

▶ Helps the IEP team be thoughtful and proactive about supporting the student's needs

▶ Provides an opportunity for the IEP team to understand how the child currently performs in academic and nonacademic areas

▶ Allows the IEP team to collaboratively develop annual goals and determine needed services, accommodations, and supports

▶ Encourages the team to identify strengths and needs, problem-solve, and discuss concerns

TIPS FOR A GREAT START WITH IEPs

You will no doubt have questions about the IEP procedures in your district. It is important to ask for help and remember that writing IEPs becomes easier with experience. IEP forms and processes may also differ from those you used in college courses. It is important to note that some states have additional requirements for IEP documents beyond those included in federal law. This means that you need to take time to learn about IEP forms and expectations that are specific to your district. Here are some suggestions to help you tackle IEPs:

► Attend orientations and other special meetings about the IEPs in your district.
► Review district websites and manuals that explain district IEP procedures and forms.
► Observe your mentor or another special education teacher lead an IEP meeting.
► Ask your mentor to give you feedback when you participate in or lead your first meetings.
► Jot down IEP questions that you can ask your mentor during scheduled meetings.
► Ask your mentor for examples of model IEPs.

TIPS FOR DEVELOPING IEP COMPONENTS

Today the vast majority of students with disabilities are expected to learn the academic standards required of all students. Therefore, committees need to make sure that IEPs are aligned with the general education curriculum and also address individual needs. In this section, components of the IEP are described with examples of each. It is essential that IEP components be carefully linked to each other. For example, present levels of performance are used to determine annual goals, and special education services are designed and informed by PRR to maximize opportunities for student learning. Once the IEP is written, the IEP team monitors the student to assess his or her progress toward IEP goals and adjusts services as necessary. Figure 5.1 shows the relationships among key components of the IEP.

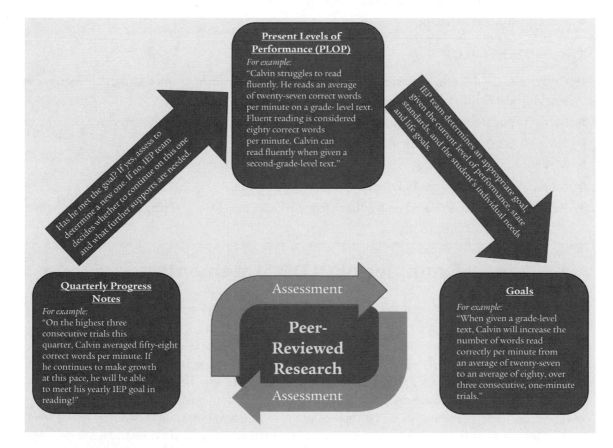

Figure 5.1 Interrelationships of IEP Components
Source: Elizabeth Bettini, University of Florida

Now that you have the big picture of how key components are related, we describe specific IEP components and provide tips and examples for writing each component.

Present Levels of Performance (PLOP)

The child's present levels of performance (PLOP) include information about academic achievement and functional performance, including how the child's disability affects his or her involvement and progress in the general curriculum.

▶ When writing PLOPs, focus on the child's strengths (i.e., what the child can do) and what is needed to help him or her achieve goals rather than using deficit language. For example, instead of writing that the student cannot read, describe developing reading behaviors (e.g., phonemic awareness, vocabulary development, listening comprehension).

TYPICAL SOURCES OF DATA FOR PLOP

▶ Data from mandated tests
▶ RTI or progress-monitoring data
▶ Psychological and academic tests
▶ Parent and staff observations
▶ Standardized achievement tests
▶ Curriculum-based measures
▶ Academic work samples
▶ Data gathered from related services personnel
▶ Data on student behavior

TIPS FOR WRITING PLOP

▶ Create a data folder for each student: include assessments, work samples, and other materials for showing the child's present level of performance.
▶ Solicit input from parents and service providers about PLOP prior to the meeting.
▶ Note areas in which additional data are needed.
▶ Makes notes about strengths and needs in key areas (e.g., reading, behavior).
▶ Summarize a draft of the PLOP data prior to the meeting.
▶ Revise the PLOP data based on feedback from others during the meeting.

Examples of PLOP Statements

ACADEMIC PLOP

Results of the Woodcock-Johnson Revised indicate that Jamal's basic reading level is at a beginning second-grade level. He was able to decode all of the first-grade sight words on the district's reading placement test and 25 percent of the second-grade list. He can consistently decode short vowel words (with some difficulty with the short *u*) but is inconsistent when decoding long vowel words. Jamal relies heavily on context clues in reading and scored at the fourth-grade level on the QRI, a measure of listening comprehension. Jamal loves to read and visit the library. He often chooses to reread books multiple times.

Elise is "non-verbal and uses many communication methods, including gestures, facial expression, eye gaze, vocalizations, word approximations, head nods for yes, head shakes for no, and use of a Dynavox 3100 augmentative communication device that she accesses with a head switch."[1]

Maya is on task for an average of 85 percent of the time when she works in a small-group setting and completes 80 percent of work when she is in a small-group setting, whereas, during whole-class instruction, Maya is on task for an average of 50 percent of class time and completes 60 percent of the assignments.

Annual Goals

It is easy to make similar goals and objectives and provide a "lunch menu" of accommodations, modifications, and adaptations, but it should be individualized!

Special education teacher

PLOPs should be directly related to annual goals: the IEP team uses present levels of performance data to determine the child's annual goals. These include measurable academic and functional goals designed to do the following:

▶ Meet the child's needs that result from his or her disability

▶ Allow the student to make progress in the general education curriculum

TIPS FOR WRITING ANNUAL GOALS

▶ Consider a range of student needs. Goals need to be aligned with the general education standards and also address individualized areas of need such as behavior, self-advocacy, social skills, and personal needs.

▶ Select goals that are most important and will make the biggest difference for the student. For example, if a student has significant behavioral needs that prevent her from making progress in the curriculum, it is essential that behavioral goals are included in the IEP.

▶ Focus goals on what the child will learn, not on activities or services. Whenever possible, write the goals in positive terms, indicating the desired behaviors (e.g., increase on-task behavior) instead of undesirable ones (e.g., decrease off-task behavior).

▶ Write measurable goals that include three components:
  • The goal
  • The conditions under which the goal will be met
  • The criteria for meeting the goal

Example of Annual Goals and Objectives in Academic and Nonacademic Areas

▶ Lilly will type an average of forty-five words per minute (goal) given an assigned passage on a fifteen-minute test (condition) with 98 percent accuracy (criterion).

▶ Jamal will read second-grade material (goal) aloud for five minutes at 115 to 130 words per minute (condition) with 98 percent accuracy (criterion).

▶ Dima will demonstrate mastery of the algebra 1 curriculum (goal) by completing the district algebra exam (condition) with 80 percent accuracy (criterion).

▶ Meg will demonstrate on-task behavior during thirty minutes of seatwork (goal) in math class (condition) for 90 percent of the time in three time-sampling observations (criterion).

▶ Juan will write a one-page essay in American history (goal) on an assigned topic in thirty minutes (conditions) that includes an introduction, relevant and factual details from the taught unit, and a conclusion and that includes no more than five mechanical errors (criterion).

Some goals indicate where the student is currently functioning as well as the annual goal. For example, "When given a prompt and three minutes to write, Kevin will increase the number of correct word sequences (sets of two sequential words or grammatical elements that are mechanically correct) from thirteen (present level) to thirty (annual goal)."

Short-Term or Benchmark Objectives

Short-term or benchmark objectives are the logical steps a child will take to reach a specific annual goal. IDEA 2004 only requires short-term objectives for students who take alternate assessments that are aligned to alternate achievement standards.[2] However, it is important to know that some states mandate short-term objectives for all students with disabilities. Be sure to know the requirements of your local school district. The following is an example of one student's annual goal and corresponding short-term objectives.

IEP Example

"The IEP team developed David's reading goal and objectives by examining the information in his PLOP. Then, they determined the skills that David needs to learn in order for him to be able to read at a fifth-grade level.

Annual goal: David will achieve a reading score at the fifth-grade level or above, as measured by the qualitative reading inventory.

Examples: Short-Term Objectives

▶ By October, when given a list of twenty unfamiliar words that contain short-vowel sounds, David will decode them with 90 percent accuracy on each of five trials.

▶ By November, when given twenty unfamiliar words that contain long-vowel sounds, David will decode them with 90 percent accuracy on each of five trials.

▶ By December, David will correctly pronounce twenty words with 90 percent accuracy on each of five trials to demonstrate understanding of the rule that when one vowel follows another, the first vowel is pronounced with a long sound and the second vowel is silent (e.g., ord*ea*l, c*oa*st).

▶ By December, David will correctly separate twenty words by syllables with 90 percent accuracy on each of five trials to demonstrate understanding of the rule that each syllable in a word must contain a vowel (e.g., lesson)."[3]

Special Education Services

IEP team members must outline the special education services to be provided to the child. The definition of special education services is complex. Fortunately, "the twenty opening words of special education's definition—specially designed instruction, at no cost to the parents, to meet the unique needs of a child with a disability—contain the core of the term's meaning."[4] The IEP committee team must use their knowledge of PRR to determine what special education services will best help the student meet his or her annual goals. In the following more information is provided about determining if special education is needed and what constitutes the IEP.

The IEP must determine what specially designed instruction is necessary to meet the needs of the child. Special education services may look very different for students given that the IEP must be individualized for each child. For example, special education for any student can consist of the following:

- An individualized curriculum that is different from that of same-age, nondisabled peers (e.g., teaching a blind student to read and write using Braille)
- The same (general) curriculum as that for nondisabled peers, with adaptations or modifications made for the student (e.g., teaching third-grade math but including the use of counting tools and assistive technology for the student)
- A combination of these elements

The education, services, and supports outlined in a child's IEP do not necessarily cover a child's entire education but rather those educational needs resulting from the child's disability. If the services and supports are needed for all activities throughout the school day, the IEP will cover all of these needs.

ADAPTATIONS AND MODIFICATIONS

The IEP will also include modifications and adaptations. A *modification* means a change in the level of what is being taught to or expected from the student.

- *Example:* Making an assignment easier so the student is not doing the same level of work as other students

An *accommodation* helps a student overcome or work around the disability without modifying expectations and standards.

- *Example:* Allowing a student who has trouble writing to provide answers orally. This student is still expected to know the same material and answer the same questions as fully as the other students but he doesn't have to write his answers to demonstrate content knowledge.

The following are examples of common modifications or accommodations:

- *Scheduling:* Giving the student extra time to complete assignments or allowing several days for testing
- *Setting:* Working in a small group or working one-on-one with the teacher

(Continued)

- ▶ *Materials:* Providing audiotaped lectures or books giving copies of teacher's lecture notes using large print books, Braille, or books on CD (digital text)
- ▶ *Instruction:* Reducing the difficulty of assignments, adjusting the reading level, or using a student or peer tutor
- ▶ *Student response:* Allowing answers to be given orally or dictated using a word processor for written work or using sign language, a communication device, Braille, or native language for a student whose native language is not English

Modifications and accommodations are meant to help a child to learn. For example, Jack is an eighth-grade student who has specific learning disabilities in reading and writing. He is in a regular eighth-grade class that is co-taught by a general education teacher and a special education teacher. Modifications and accommodations provided for Jack's daily school routine (and when he takes state or districtwide tests) include the following:

- ▶ Shorter reading and writing assignments
- ▶ Textbooks based on the eighth-grade curriculum but at Jack's independent (fourth-grade) reading level
- ▶ Test questions read and explained when he asks[5]

Adapted from NCHCY

Participation in General and Special Education

Students with disabilities should be placed in the least restrictive environment, participating in general education settings for academic and nonacademic activities to the greatest extent possible (see chapter 4). IEP teams make this decision by determining how much of the school day the child will be educated separately from nondisabled children or will not participate in extracurricular or other nonacademic activities. The amount or percentage of time that the student spends in general and special education is recorded in the IEP. If the student is to be placed outside of the general education classroom, an explanation must be provided in the IEP.

Example: Participation in General and Special Education

"Does this student attend the school he or she would attend if nondisabled?
X Yes ___No
If no, justify: *N/A*
Does this student receive all special education services with nondisabled peers?
___Yes X No
If no, justify (justification may not be solely because of needed modifications in the general curriculum): *Kimi requires instruction in cognitive strategies that enable her to better retain auditory material. She works with the speech-language pathologist to learn new strategies required to complete academic assignments. Special education and general education teachers collaborate to monitor progress.*
Ninety-nine percent to 80 percent of day inside the gen ed environment"[6]

Related Services

For some children with disabilities, related services are necessary to benefit from special education. For example, Alicia requires occupational therapy to improve her fine motor coordination, which is necessary for numerous school activities (e.g., writing, putting together puzzles). Philip requires counseling to learn anger management because his frequent outbursts interfere with his learning in the classroom. These related services are part of a free, appropriate public education and are provided at no cost to the parent.

IDEA requires a comprehensive evaluation to identify all special education and related services a child needs. Evaluations from therapists and counselors are often part of the present level of performance data. These evaluations may suggest the need for related services, such as the following:

► Occupational, music, and physical therapy
► Speech-language services
► Assistive technology
► Counseling or psychological services
► School nurse services
► Interpreting, orientation, and mobility services
► Parent counseling and education
► Transportation
► Medical services, if for diagnostic purposes or evaluation

Related services personnel should attend the IEP meeting when they have evaluated the child. The IEP team determines when related services will begin, how often they will be provided, for how long, and where they will be provided on the IEP.

Example: Schedule of Related Services

► Faisal will receive speech language therapy for two thirty-minute sessions weekly provided by the speech-language pathologist (related to annual goal four).

► Maddy will receive thirty minutes of occupational therapy each week by a licensed occupational therapist in her second-grade classroom (related to annual goal one), from the week of October 15 through the week of June 1.

► Evan will receive counseling twice monthly by a licensed psychologist in the library study room (related to annual goal two). Services will begin in October and the committee will reconvene in January to assess progress and determine whether continued services are needed.

Supplementary Aids and Services

The IEP team must consider supplementary aids and services to help students meet their goals. For instance, if Mary exhibits behavioral challenges that interfere with her ability to make progress on her academic goals, the IEP team creates a plan to address Mary's behavior. The following form is often included with the IEP to document that the committee considered needed supports.

Address All Areas Marked "Yes" in the IEP	Yes	No
Does the student's behavior impede his or her learning or that of others?		
Is the student an English language learner (ELL)?		
Does the student have special communication needs?		
If visually impaired, does the student need instruction in Braille or the use of Braille?		
Does the student need assistive technology devices and services?		
Is the student working toward alternate achievement standards, requiring alternate assessments?		
Does the student require specially designed physical education?		
Does the student require extended year services (i.e., service beyond the academic year)?		
Does the student require transition services according to state requirements or will he or she be sixteen or older during the implementation of the IEP?		

Accommodations in Assessment

IDEA also requires that students with disabilities take part in state and districtwide assessments, with test accommodation and modifications as needed. It is the responsibility of the team to determine needed accommodations in these assessments or determine if another type of assessment is needed (see chapter 10).

THE IEP MEETING

The IEP is your student's lifeline to success. It is imperative that you do your best in the development of this very important document!

Special education teacher

Required IEP Participants

A team of individuals, including school personnel and parents, are responsible for developing the IEP. The following individuals are required participants on the IEP team:

▶ The child's parents or legal guardian (if parents do not attend, attempts to involve them must be documented).

▶ The general education teachers and preferably all but at least one of the child's special education teachers or special education providers.

IEPs and Assistive Technology

Under IDEA 2004, IEP teams must consider whether assistive technology (AT) devices and services are needed to help students with disabilities meet their goals. Although the law requires that team members consider AT, specific guidance is not provided. However, states and districts may provide guidance. A popular guide is the *Wisconsin Assistive Technology Initiative (WATI) Assistive Technology Consideration Guide*, an excellent resource available for download at no cost.[7]

The following are examples of problems that would suggest a need to consider AT:

▶ Print size is too small.

▶ A student is unable to hear all that is being said.

▶ [The student has] difficulty aligning math equations.

▶ The student often needs text read to him in order to complete an assignment.

▶ Handwriting is so illegible that the meaning is impossible to decipher.

▶ The effort of writing is so slow or so exhausting that it is counterproductive.

▶ The student has difficulty finding key points on web pages.

▶ Current modifications are not working.

▶ The effort required to decode reading assignments is so difficult that the student loses track of the meaning.

▶ Student cannot organize assignments in a way that brings them to completion.[8]

Perspective on IEPs and Assistive Technology[9]

Penny Reed, Assistive Technology Specialist

I think that a good IEP team meeting is one in which all the members of the team, including the parents and the student, when the student is able to participate, have a voice in making decisions about all aspects of that student's IEP. First, they look at the present level of educational achievement and functional performance, and that level is well written so that you know exactly what the child is able to do or not do and where the challenges are. The IEP team then determines the goals for the coming year, talks them through, and all are in agreement about those, and then asks, "Okay, what do we need to provide so that this student can meet those goals? Where are the challenges? What things are we most concerned about?" And for those tasks and activities they look at assistive technology as well as other strategies that might help them. You've got to stop and think about the student and exactly what he's able to do and not able to do. And in the environment, what's there for him to use and what isn't? How much support does he have and how noisy is it, and things like that. What are the specific tasks, because you can't make an AT decision without knowing what the task is.

AT is not available for a specific disability. It's available to address specific tasks. One child with cerebral palsy will need a completely different set of assistive technology tools than another child with cerebral palsy. And one child with autism will require a completely different set of resources than another child with autism. We can't prescribe AT based on disability identification.

(Continued)

We have to look at the task that the student is struggling with. So that they're very task focused, they know exactly what the student can do and not do, now that it's based on what the task the student needs to do and where we're concerned about barriers that he's going to not be able to overcome without the assistive technology. You can't really do a good job of considering the need for assistive technology unless you're task focused, and you can't be task focused until you know what the goals are. For me, that's always been a significant piece. Many IEP forms ask you somewhere else in the IEP about AT as if it's a completely separate thing. So in some states it might come on the second or third page, and you haven't even developed the goals until two pages later. That's a problem for a lot of IEP teams because they're trying to think about it in isolation and, of course, then they don't have an answer. We're all driven by the order of the IEP that was developed by somebody who just thought it fit there nicely. And I used to put a sticky note on that page and come back to it because whether it's an electronic sticky note or it's a paper one, whatever form you're working in, you can't be driven by that. You've got to follow a thought process that makes sense for the participants.

> A representative of the school system, such as an administrator or special education teacher, who can fulfill the following:
>   - Is qualified to provide or supervise special education services
>   - Knows about the general curriculum
>   - Knows about the resources the school system has available
> An individual who can interpret the evaluation. Depending on the type of evaluation data (e.g., psychological testing or classroom-based evaluation data), this may be a school psychologist or a special educator.
> The student, when appropriate (see the section on transition plans on involving the student in the IEP meeting).
> Representatives from any other agencies that may be responsible for paying for or providing transition services (if the child is sixteen years or, if appropriate, younger).
> Other individuals invited by the parent or the school who have knowledge or special expertise about the child. This might include a relative, child-care provider, paraeducator, or a professional who provides related services.

IEP Notification

IDEA requires that parents receive notification early enough so that one or both have an opportunity to attend the meeting. It is important that the meeting is scheduled at a mutually agreed-on time and place. Most districts have form letters that are used to notify the parent about the meeting. This letter should include the purpose of the meeting, time, location, and who will be present. Some districts provide parents with a list of questions ahead of time that they might think about prior to the IEP meeting. These questions may include the following:

> How do you see your child's strengths and needs?
> Is there anything that you hope your child learns this year?
> What would you like for us to consider as we plan your child's program for this year?

Parent Participation

"Parents feel empowered because they believe their voices are heard and their values are reflected in the IEP."[10]

Teachers are very busy people and it is easy to focus on getting the IEP completed and signed instead of thinking about what parents and others have to contribute. This quote emphasizes the importance of making sure that the IEP team takes time to give parents a voice in the process and to work toward meaningful versus perfunctory participation (see chapter 3).

Parents can make important contributions to the meetings because they know their child well. For example, they may do the following:

▶ Provide information about their child's strengths, needs, and interests

▶ Identify what they would like for their child to learn

▶ Share concerns and suggestions based on their knowledge of their child over time

▶ Help establish long-term goals based on their vision for their child's future

To ensure meaningful participation, it is important to schedule interpreters for parents who are deaf or hard of hearing and for those who speak a language different from others at the meeting. Parents also have the option of participating in IEPs through conference calls or Skype.

It is important to exercise caution when bringing a written IEP to the meeting. When parents are asked to sign an IEP that was written before the meeting, they may view the process and their involvement as less important or pro forma. If you choose to bring a written IEP, clearly write the word *draft* on the IEP and explain to parents that you have recorded some ideas and your own thinking, and that it is not complete. During the meeting, record the input of others as decisions are finalized.

Teachers, principals, and district personnel may be responsible for facilitating IEP meetings. As you begin in the school, be sure to find out if you will have this responsibility. The guidelines in exhibit 5.1 should help you facilitate IEPs or be a more effective team member.

Exhibit 5.1 Facilitating an Effective IEP Meeting[11]

Preplanning for an IEP Meeting

Prior to holding an IEP meeting, several tasks need to be completed to ensure that the required team members are in attendance and that the information presented is organized. Begin planning for IEP meetings three to four weeks prior to the anticipated meeting time. This will give all team members ample time to prepare and ensure availability for them to attend the meeting.

- ▶ Plan the date and location of the meeting.
- ▶ Verify the time and date with parents or guardians first. Inform parents of who will be attending the meeting as well as the purpose of the meeting. You may also want to provide parents with information about how they can contribute to the meeting.
- ▶ Once the date has been verified with the parent or guardian, coordinate the time and location with the required team members. Federal law requires the following team members to be present at all meetings: parent or guardian, school district representative, special education teacher, and general education teacher representative. Do not invite too many persons whose participation may not be needed. Large numbers at IEP meetings guarantee a long meeting and can lead to parents feeling overwhelmed.
- ▶ All students should be encouraged to attend their IEP meeting. Students in ninth grade or age fourteen or older should be invited to the meeting. If the student does not attend, he or she should be consulted about interests and preferences regarding his or her educational program.
- ▶ Send a notice of the meeting to parents and enclose the parents' rights with the meeting notice. Be sure to keep records of all attempts to contact parents, parents' responses, and any other communication between the parents and the school.
- ▶ Begin to compile data for developing the present level of performance.
- ▶ Prepare statements on the strengths of the student as well as concerns that need to be addressed.

BEFORE THE IEP MEETING

The physical set-up of the room can contribute to a positive and effective IEP meeting. Note the following:

- ▶ Choose a room free from outside distractions with ample room for all team members to sit and have space to take notes.
- ▶ Consider providing water or beverages if the meeting will be longer than one hour.
- ▶ Alert office personnel to expect parents and make them feel welcome or have a team member meet the parents in the office and escort them to the meeting room.
- ▶ Consider waiting until the parent arrives before all team members enter the meeting room. It can be very intimidating to enter a meeting when all others have arrived and are already seated.
- ▶ Hold phone calls.
- ▶ Have pencils, paper, and copies of reports available for team members.
- ▶ Provide name tags with each participant's name and title.

BEGINNING THE IEP MEETING

When conducting an IEP meeting, it's important to set the tone and purpose of the meeting. With that in mind, the facilitator should consider the following:

- ► Welcome
- ► Introductions
- ► Explanation of the meeting's purpose and the expected outcome(s)
- ► The time parameters set aside for the meeting (include the time frame on the meeting invitation, for example, 2:00 to 3:00 PM)
- ► A reminder that if all agenda items are not addressed, another meeting will be held. This helps members to stay focused and to allow members to return to their schedules as planned.
- ► Explanation of the ground rules for the meeting (see following).
- ► Explanation of the standard for decision making and reaching consensus. This does not mean voting. Consensus means that the IEP team works together to develop an IEP that all can agree on or at least live with.
- ► Explanation of the procedural safeguards (see chapter 4). Be sure to also provide parents with a copy of this document.

CONDUCTING THE MEETING: GROUND RULES

When conducting the meeting, note the following ground rules:

- ► Remain child focused and child centered.
- ► Remain in the moment: turn off or mute all devices.
- ► Be an active listener and participant.
- ► Follow the agenda; however, record any non-IEP concerns as they come up and return to the agenda. Determine at the end of the meeting to whom the concerns need to be directed.
- ► Acknowledge all team members as valuable participants.
- ► Demonstrate mutual respect toward team members and their views.

MEETING ETIQUETTE FOR ALL MEMBERS

The following are suggestions for meeting facilitators and participants.

MEETING FACILITATOR

- ► Be open and encouraging.
- ► Serve as a catalyst by posing questions.
- ► Maintain harmony; remind participants of shared goals and appropriate meeting behaviors.
- ► Don't ramble.
- ► Don't control or dominate the discussion.
- ► Ask follow-up questions.
- ► If consensus can't be reached on an issue, discuss follow-up options.

MEETING PARTICIPANT

- ► Decide to make the meeting worthwhile.
- ► Exercise appropriate meeting behavior.

(Continued)

- Stay on topic; don't ramble.
- Study the agenda and assemble your information to share. Don't wing it.
- Practice listening skills; avoid engaging in sidebar discussions.
- Suggest closure for items that aren't resolved within allotted time.

DEALING WITH DIFFICULT SITUATIONS

If a meeting becomes difficult, facilitators should use the following tips to maintain a productive meeting:

- Remember: everyone wants to be heard.
- Stay calm. Don't be defensive.
- Be aware of body language and tone of voice. Sandwich problematic issues with positive statements. Remember that disgruntled parents walk away upset because of poor communication.
- Do not take complaints personally.
- Stay focused.
- Adjourn the meeting if it becomes nonproductive, discuss issues with your administrator, and reconvene at a later date.
- Maintain and bring clear, relevant data to any meetings; this will assist you in meeting due process timelines and monitoring progress on goals and objectives. It's easier to defend the student's program when there is data to support the school district's position.

FACTORS THAT CAN SLOW DOWN A MEETING

During a meeting, avoiding problems can lead to a more productive and shorter meeting. Whether you're a facilitator or participant, avoid the following:

- Arriving and starting the meeting late.
- Interrupting other participants.
- Having sidebar conversations.
- Making sarcastic comments.
- Letting unanticipated issues distract you from the agenda. If this occurs, record these as issues to resolve later and return to the agenda.
- Dominating the conversation.

ENDING THE MEETING

When ending the meeting, bring proper closure to the decisions made so that every team member understands personal responsibilities regarding the student's educational program.

- Consider all the parent requests; however, make recommendations based on data and professional expertise.
- Summarize the services being offered and any changes that are being recommended.
- Encourage the parent to review the IEP on receiving it and call with any questions.
- Complete, explain, and provide the prior written notice to parents.
- Thank the parents and team members for coming in and taking the time to meet.

With minor adaptations, from Henrico County Public Schools, Exceptional Education and Support Services. *Facilitating an effective IEP meeting*. Reprinted with permission.

TRANSITION PLANNING

Providing effective transition services is critical to helping students with disabilities prepare for adulthood and to help them gain the necessary education to pursue their postsecondary goals. Unfortunately, many students with disabilities drop out of high school; consequently, many are underemployed or unemployed and continue to live with their parents after high school. Students with disabilities also attend college at far lower rates than their nondisabled peers. To improve the opportunities that students with disabilities have to achieve success in adult life, transition services are designed to provide a coordinated set of activities based on the student's assessed needs, interests, aptitudes, and their postsecondary goals.

When Transition Plans Must Be Included

A transition plan is required to be in effect as part of the IEP when the student reaches sixteen years of age. This means that the IEP team should develop the transition plan while the student is age fifteen so it is in effect when the student turns sixteen. It is important to note that many students will benefit from even earlier transition planning, allowing more time for students to prepare for adulthood. Some states require that transition planning begin at age fourteen.

Requirements for Transition Plans

Transition plans address the following elements:

- ▶ The needs of the student, including strengths, skills, and interests, are used to make informed decisions about transition goals and activities.
  - Needs may be based on formal and informal assessments, interviews, and observations.
- ▶ Measurable postsecondary education goals in education, training and employment and independent living skills, if needed. For example:
  - After high school, Darla will enroll full-time in the hotel and restaurant program at Williard College.
  - After graduating from Williard College, Darla will work full-time managing a restaurant.
  - After high school, Raman will live in a group home and learn meal preparation, dressing, and personal care skills.
- ▶ A plan necessary to help students prepare to achieve postsecondary goals.
  - Academic preparation and training (e.g., specific courses or a course of study providing preparation in academics, career and technical education, vocational training, community college courses)
  - Employment (e.g., learning specific skills in employment settings such as part-time employment, supported job placement, internships, and shadowing to develop specific knowledge and skill such as résumé writing, interviewing, customer service, child care, technology)
  - Independent living (e.g., developing skills in using transportation, managing time and money, personal care skills)
  - Functional performance (e.g., self-advocacy, self -determination, goal setting, problem solving, social and interpersonal skills)

Some states include a specific transition planning form in the IEP. Forms include a place to identify a postsecondary vision and goals, disability-related needs, and an action plan needed to achieve the postsecondary goals (see the resources at the end of this chapter for examples).

Participants in Transition Planning

There are several important things to know about who needs to be invited to the IEP meeting if transition planning is part of the IEP.

▶ Student participation

In addition to the typical IEP committee, students of age must be invited to participate in their IEPs if it includes a transition plan. It is critical that students practice self-advocacy skills. Students need to know why they need it, what they need, and learn to ask for it as adults. If the student is unable or unwilling to attend, school personnel must take steps to ensure that the student's preferences and interests are considered (e.g., ask students about their preferences prior to the meeting).

▶ Representatives from participating agencies

Others who are responsible for providing (or paying) for transition services also must be invited to attend the IEP meeting. For example, the following individuals may be involved in transition services for certain students:

- Vocational rehabilitation counselor (required if paying for adult services)
- Assistive technology specialist
- Representative from the community if it relates to the plan
- Guidance counselor
- School nurse
- Social service agencies
- Juvenile officer
- Disability support services personnel from colleges or universities
- Advocates

Tips for Involving Students in Transition Planning

The transition planning process will be more meaningful if students and families receive guidance about transition planning prior to the meeting. Students and families need information about (1) the purposes of the transition meeting and (2) specific suggestions for preparing for the meeting.

Student-led IEP and transition meetings can help students meet critical self-determination goals, such as developing self-awareness, making decisions, setting goals, solving problems, and learning to self-advocate (see chapter 17 for a discussion of person-centered planning). Teachers can help prepare and coach students to eventually lead their own meetings. For example, students may become familiar with IEP forms and discuss their IEP individually with their teacher. As students become ready to lead, they may work with their teachers to prepare a PowerPoint presentation that includes material such as

Table 5.1 Interview Questions for Parents and Students[12]

Questions for Parents	Questions for Student
What are your hopes and dreams for your child?	What do you want to do when you become an adult?
In the next few years, what do you envision for your child in the domains of academics, social, independent living, vocational, community, and leisure?	In the next few years, what kinds of things do you want to learn and do? In school? At home? In the community?
What are your child's interests? What does he or she dislike?	What activities do you like to do? What activities do you not like to do?
What are some of your child's strengths? What are some of his or her weaknesses?	What are you really good at? What do you want to be good at?
What are your concerns for your child in the future?	Is there anything you are scared about in the future?

Adapted from Meaden, Sheldon, Appel, & DeGrazia (2010).

(1) how to open a meeting (e.g., welcome, introductions, purposes of meeting); (2) their strengths and needs overall and by course; (3) their interests and goals; (4) needed supports; and (5) questions that invite participation from others. Numerous resources about preparing students for leading their own meetings are provided at the end of the chapter.

Table 5.1 provides examples of the kinds of questions that families and students may wish to consider before the transition meeting so they are well prepared for what will be discussed.

IEP SUMMARY FORMS

IEPs are often long documents, sometimes ten pages or more. Exhibit 5.2 provides a summary form that teachers may use to keep key IEP information readily available. For example, summary documents can be used to share essential IEP information with general education teachers or paraprofessionals and as a reference for your own daily instructional planning. Be sure to check to see if the use of this form is consistent with your school guidelines for confidentiality.

TIPS FOR ORGANIZING THE IEP PROCESS

Set up an IEP file drawer or box with the following folders:

▶ Copies of blank letter forms inviting parents to the IEP meeting (most districts provide these) in multiple languages if needed

▶ Envelopes for letter to parents

▶ Blank IEP forms in multiple languages if needed

▶ Parent documentation sheet

▶ Copies of IEP meeting agenda

▶ An IEP folder for each student

Exhibit 5.2   IEP at a Glance (Elementary Level)

Name: _____   Grade and teacher(s): _____
_____
_____

Strengths: _____   Schedule: _____
_____   _____
_____   _____

Medical or health information: _____
Communication needs: _____
Crisis plan __Yes __No (If yes, attach)

IEP goals	Modifications or adaptations
Academic:	
Nonacademic:	
Behavioral, social, and personal:	
Other:	

Add names of all students to the calendar:

- ► Add the name of each student's IEP due date (e.g., Torrey Rex—IEP due).
- ► Three weeks before the IEP is due, record the date to begin (e.g., Torrey Rex—begin IEP planning).
- ► When new students are added, be sure to add their due dates as well.

PRACTICAL SUGGESTIONS FROM SPECIAL EDUCATORS

WHAT RESOURCES HAVE YOU FOUND TO BE BENEFICIAL WHEN DEVELOPING IEPS?

- ► District policies and procedures for writing IEPs
- ► District or state forms and examples of completed IEPs
- ► Forms available in Spanish and English (or other languages)
- ► Comprehensive student assessment data, including strengths and needs
- ► Skill hierarchies (commercial or teacher devised) for writing benchmark objectives
- ► Other teachers and mentors who have experience with the IEP process

WHAT APPROACH WOULD YOU SUGGEST FOR DEVELOPING IEPS?

- ► Actively involve the team to make it a meaningful document.
- ► Focus on collaborative IEP development rather than just going through the document.
- ► Emphasize individualization, noting student strengths and needs as well as skill levels.

WHAT ADVICE DO YOU HAVE FOR NEW TEACHERS?

- ► Realize that others may not know the rights of the students and parents or procedures governing IEPs for students with disabilities. It's your job to help educate others.
- ► Do not be afraid to advocate for students.
- ► Try to make the IEP something general education teachers, parents, and the student can understand clearly.

TO SUM UP

- ► IEPs are legal documents required for all students; teachers need to understand what goes in each component.
- ► The IEP team determines appropriate measurable goals based on the present levels of performance, state standards, and the student's interests, needs, and life goals.
- ► The IEP team must consider PRR in the design of special education services for students to help them increase their opportunities to meet their goals.
- ► The IEP meeting is important and all team members, including parents, need to be encouraged to have meaningful input into the planning for their child.
- ► Assistive technology is a required consideration in IEP planning; understanding how assistive technology can help is critical to decision making.
- ► Students can be active participants in the IEP meeting, and this is especially important for transition planning.

WHAT'S NEXT?

Now that you have the big picture and the details of writing IEPs, we will move on to ways to organize and manage your many responsibilities.

ADDITIONAL RESOURCES

IEP RESOURCES

▶ Examples of IEPs and transition plans: www.sagepub.com/gargiulo3estudy/pdf/Gargiulo_IEP.pdf and http://sped.sbcsc.k12.in.us/iStart%207/samples.html

▶ *A student's guide to the IEP:* http://nichcy.org/publications#lets

▶ IRIS Center. *Star legacy module: Assistive technology: An overview,* http://iris.peabody.vanderbilt.edu/at/chalcycle.htm

▶ Hammer, M. R. (2004). Using the self-advocacy strategy to increase student participation in IEP conferences. *Intervention in School and Clinic, 39,* 295–300.

▶ Konrad, M., & Test, D. W. (2004). Teaching middle-school students with disabilities to use an IEP template. *Career Development for Exceptional Individuals, 27,* 101–124.

▶ North Carolina Department of Public Instruction. Actual forms, in English and Spanish, including invitation letters, IEP forms, and examples and descriptions of how to write these forms: http://ec.ncpublicschools.gov/policies/forms/statewide-forms

▶ Wisconsin Department of Public Instruction: *A guide for writing IEPs,* http://dpi.wi.gov/sped/pdf/iepguide.pdf

TRANSITION SERVICES WEBSITES AND RESOURCES

▶ National Secondary Transition Technical Assistance Center: www.nsttac.org/content/about-nsttac

- See the *Team Planning Tool for Improving Transition Education and Services.* www.nsttac.org/sites/default/files/assets/pdf/pdf/complete_taxonomy_planning_tool.pdf

▶ NICHCY. (2009, September). *Transition "starters" for everyone.* Retrieved from http://nichcy.org/schoolage/transitionadult/starters

▶ PACER Center. *Transition planning and employment:* www.pacer.org/tatra/resources/transitionemp.asp

▶ Beach Center on Disability: www.beachcenter.org

▶ NICHCY. (2009, November). *Students get involved.* Retrieved from http://nichcy.org/schoolage/transitionadult/students

PART TWO

BECOMING AN ACCOMPLISHED EDUCATOR

CHAPTER SIX

Organizing and Managing Your Work

✓ **In this chapter you will learn about:**

- How to determine your roles and responsibilities
- How to set goals and plan for accomplishing tasks
- How to manage your time, tasks, and materials
- Tips for organization in a variety of teaching positions
- How to get ready for your first day of school

Beth's Wednesday: IEP meeting, bus duty, third-grade reading resource class, first-grade math resource, fifth-grade reading co-teach, co-planning with Mr. Sanders, lunch, third-grade team meeting, car pick-up duty, stop by Ms. Lowri's class to discuss Billy and Ms. Fallis's class to discuss Laura, planning, and paperwork.

Learning how to organize and manage your work is critical to your job because special education teachers have many responsibilities and roles. Well-organized special education teachers are able to manage assigned tasks and are well informed about their responsibilities. Effective special education teachers need to be master organizers; they know what, how, when, and where things need to be done.

Many new special education teachers feel understandably overwhelmed.[1] For example, new special education teachers often share concerns about materials, paperwork, role confusion, and managing time and caseloads. As Brad, a special education teacher, stated, "I've been inundated by paperwork, parent phone calls, and delivery-of-service questions with respect to my caseload of students and their schedules for next year. These are the times when I wonder how it's possible to teach a student the breadth and depth of curriculum I've imagined for them."

Taking time to understand your responsibilities and organize your work will set the foundation for a successful first year.

YOUR MANY ROLES AND RESPONSIBILITIES

Special education teachers serve in many different types of positions, including the following:

- ▶ Resource teacher
- ▶ Self-contained teacher
- ▶ Co-teacher
- ▶ Consultation teacher
- ▶ Itinerant teacher
- ▶ Case manager

Each of these positions is unique and involves a distinct collection of responsibilities that vary by context. You may be responsible for the following:

- ▶ Providing academic instruction
- ▶ Developing behavior and transition plans
- ▶ Co-teaching
- ▶ Assisting with personal care (toileting or feeding)
- ▶ Writing and monitoring compliance with IEPs
- ▶ Evaluating students as well as interpreting and communicating assessment results
- ▶ Maintaining data on student progress
- ▶ Consulting and collaborating with general education teachers, administrators, service providers, and parents
- ▶ Providing accommodations and modifications to the general curriculum
- ▶ Supporting a paraprofessional
- ▶ Creating schedules
- ▶ Advocating for students with special needs

Table 6.1 provides an example of one common role for a case manager position as outlined by Chicago Public Schools.[2]

Once you have accepted a teaching position, your first task (after sharing the good news with everyone you know!) will be to understand your roles and responsibilities. Your actual teaching contract may stipulate a broad role; however, your principal will be the key to unpacking your daily responsibilities. To help with this process, follow these steps:

- ▶ *Meet with your principal to review your roles and responsibilities.* Consider starting the conversation by expressing your enthusiasm for your work. You might say, "Dr. Smith, I am excited to get started at my new position. Would you review with me all my assigned responsibilities? I don't want to miss anything."
- ▶ *Write down each role and responsibility and ask questions for clarification.* For example, if your principal explains that one of your roles is to create a schedule for pulling students out of the general education classroom for resource services, you might ask, "Should I make a schedule only for the students on my caseload?" or "Will I need to coordinate with the general education teachers' schedules?"
- ▶ *Double-check your responsibilities with your mentor, team leader, or other special education teachers.* Your principal may not be aware of all the minor tasks typically required by your teaching role.

Table 6.1 Job Description for a Case Manager

Duties	Chicago Public Schools Case Manager Responsibilities
General tasks	• Coordinating all referrals for a full and individual evaluation to ensure that all required components are addressed and that the process is completed within sixty school days • Ensuring that all parental notices and consents for full and individual evaluations and placements are processed and that they are placed in student temporary files • Convening and chairing IEP conferences (including initial, special, and reevaluation eligibility determination meetings and annual reviews) and acting as the district representative • Arranging special education and related services for students within the school in accordance with the IEP and contacting administration to arrange placement in another school if necessary to implement the IEP • Consulting with the administrator regarding students who require low-incidence services or regarding problems that develop in the implementation of procedures • Finalizing the IEP documents in a timely manner • Ensuring that all relevant student data are entered into the online system in a timely manner
Prior to an IEP meeting	• Monitoring to ensure that all preconference activities are successfully completed within required timelines • Determining the date, time, and location of the IEP meeting with active participation of parents and other necessary team members • Preparing written notice to the IEP team (including parents) at least ten school days prior to the meeting • Determining which IEP team member will review previous evaluation reports and report as the evaluation representative at the annual review meeting • Preparing an agenda for the IEP meeting • Arranging accommodations for parents as necessary (e.g., interpreter or translator)
At the IEP meeting	• Acting as the district's representative to authorize services unless the principal or assistant principal is present • Starting the meeting with introductions of all IEP team members and ensuring that all required participants are present • Conducting the meeting by following an agenda and process appropriate for the purpose of the conference • Facilitating the completion of the IEP document at the meeting • Distributing copies of the completed IEP to parents, teachers, and related service providers at the end of the IEP meeting
Following the IEP meeting	• Informing all staff involved in the implementation of the IEP of their responsibilities to implement the IEP as written • Monitoring to ensure that all services delineated in the IEP are delivered • Ensuring that all teachers and related service staff who have a responsibility for the education of the student have access to the IEP or a paper copy of the IEP • Updating data entry in the student information system including the annual review dates, extended school year indicators, service provider, and related service codes • Coordinating all meetings related to IEP reviews and amendments when necessary

When you have a clear understanding of your responsibilities and roles, it is time to organize. This will set the foundation for the remainder of your organizational strategies, help you to establish a routine, and ensure that you are not overlooking any of your assigned duties. One way to accomplish this is to create a table containing each role, the assigned responsibilities, and any associated timelines. Once you have the table created, you can refer to it on a daily or weekly basis to double-check your accomplishments or fill in due dates in your calendar or planner. Exhibit 6.1 shows you an example of a roles and responsibilities organizational table.

GOALS AND PLANS EQUAL ORGANIZATIONAL SUCCESS!

Now that you are familiar with your roles and responsibilities, it is time to set goals and make plans to organize your tasks. It will take dedicated time to set goals and get organized but your year will run smoothly as a result. You will spend less time worrying about missed tasks, arranging information, and preparing materials, and spend more time doing what you love: teaching.

> I am a brand new teacher in a K–4 life skills classroom with nine children and two aides. I am trying to get ahead of the game now and figure out my classroom set-up, as well as that first day of school! I have no idea what that looks like or how to begin![3]

This blogger's plea for help describes how many beginning special education teachers feel the summer before school begins. Start with creating goals. You may be comfortable setting goals for student achievement but setting goals for accomplishing your own responsibilities is also important. Goal setting is helpful in maintaining focus, providing motivation, and gaining a sense of accomplishment. Not every task on your list needs a goal. Instead, choose tasks that feel particularly daunting, overwhelming, or time consuming. Use the following guide to create goals:

▶ Choose one task and review the timeline for completion.
▶ Break down the task into smaller steps.
▶ Assign every step a realistic due date.
▶ Post your goal somewhere visible.
▶ Check your progress.
▶ Celebrate your success.

Consider Emily's example:

> I was really worried about having my lessons plans uploaded in the online system for my principal to review by Friday afternoon. The first few weeks I stayed in my classroom until 9 PM. The online submission needed to include objectives, alignment with state standards and IEP goals, and the main lesson points. I started by breaking these into daily tasks and then I set my goal for completion of each. By doing this, I was able to leave reviewing my completed lesson plans for Friday. I stopped feeling stressed and knew I could get it completed.

Exhibit 6.1 Roles and Responsibilities Organizational Table

Role	Responsibilities	Timeline	Jan 7	Jan 14	Jan 21	Jan 28	Monthly
Instructor	Weekly lesson plans	Due to principal on Fridays	X	X			
	Gather materials	Weekly and daily	X	X			
	Grade and collect data	Daily and weekly	X				
	Report cards	Quarterly					
	Communicate with parents	Weekly notebook home	X	X			
Case manager	IEPs for all students on caseload	Every nine weeks enter data					
	Create schedules	Before school starts					
	Communicate progress to parents	Every nine weeks or per IEP					
	Ensure students receive accommodations	Monthly meeting with general education teachers					X
	Conduct manifestation determination—FBA	As needed					
Managing paraprofessionals	Plan weekly activities		X				
	Meet with paraprofessional about plans	Briefly daily, longer Friday afternoons	X				
Co-teach fourth-grade reading	Meet with Ms. Smith weekly to plan, review data	Meet on early release day		X			
Mentor teacher	Meet regularly	Meet every Thursday	X				
	Observe other teachers	November and January					
	Portfolio	Add data weekly	X				
Other	Morning duty	7:15–7:30 bus duty					
	Team breakfast	Once a month for team meeting					

Table 6.2 Emily's Goals

Task	Goal Due Date
Review student data	Monday
Align standards to state and IEP	Tuesday
Choose objective	Wednesday
Create lesson points	Thursday
Lesson plan revisions and submission	Friday

Emily organized her lesson plans by breaking down an overwhelming task into pieces. She tackled one piece per day and was able to accomplish her lesson plans and submit them to her principal on time every week. Table 6.2 shows Emily's written goals that she kept on her desk where she could see what she needed to accomplish every day.

Now think about the details of organizing your teaching life. Just as you need to have a good plan in place for student learning, you need a plan for your own organization. Following are ten keys to good organization. Each of the ten keys is discussed briefly and examples of implementation are provided.

Keep a Workable Working To-Do List

Refer to your responsibility table and goals to create a workable to-do list. Figure out what style is best for you but don't let your to-do list get too long. One way to make your list more manageable is to split your tasks into a daily list and a weekly list. Make sure to move tasks you were unable to complete from today's list to tomorrow's list. Also, consider using a smartphone application or online list to help reduce paper and keep your lists at hand. Many task management programs allow you to sync your to-do list so you can have access on your smartphone, iPad, or computer at any time. These task management programs include organizational features, such as delineating task lists, prioritizing tasks, and checking off completed tasks. Examples of free programs include Remember the Milk,[4] HiTask,[5] Toodledo,[6] Simplenote,[7] and Google Tasks.[8]

Use a Calendar

Even with a to-do list, it is still important to keep a calendar of important dates. Some tasks may have flexible due dates and others must be completed by specified times. You may want to keep a large desk calendar or track your dates electronically. You will also have meetings, trainings, or even field trips to include on your calendar. Having everything in one place will help you to plan for completing your daily, weekly, and monthly tasks on time. Most electronic calendars are also able to automatically sync with your e-mail, phone, and to-do list.

Jot Down Notes

Undoubtedly, you will be asked to assist with tasks that are not part of your direct responsibilities, such as these examples:

- The general education teacher may need your help modifying an exam.
- You may need to call a parent about a student's classroom behavior.
- A student may get suspended for the tenth day and you must send a notice for a manifestation determination.

You may not always have your smartphone with you or a computer handy so keep a notecard in your pocket to jot down important notes. Each time you need to complete a new duty, quickly write yourself a reminder on your notecard. When you get back to your classroom, you can add these to your to-do list. This strategy will ensure new tasks are not missed or forgotten.

Everything Has a Place; Put It There!

This timeless advice is true. Spend ten minutes at the end of each day returning everything to its rightful place. This may include filing papers in the correct folder, placing books on the bookshelf, and returning supplies to the closet. Taking this small amount of time every day will help keep your room uncluttered and reduce time wasted searching for items at a later date.

Send It Home or Throw It Away

Whenever possible, do not collect student work or unnecessary papers. You can keep student work in a folder for the week and send it home on Friday. When you are completing your daily filing, throw away papers that are not necessary. These might be flyers for trainings or notes about upcoming meetings. Once you have recorded dates in your calendar, dispose of the unneeded paper. This practice will help you manage your paperwork and save time sorting through papers later.

Use Color

When creating a place for materials, folders, or student work, use color to help you label. Using a variety of colors for different items will help you to remember where things go. For example, label all your bins for craft supplies orange and your reading materials blue. You might label folders that contain student data red. Color will also help when other teachers or students are assisting in putting things away.

Create a Routine

Keeping your teaching life organized is mostly about developing routines that work for you. Once you have your daily schedule set, find regular times to complete organizational tasks. For example, during your planning time, take five minutes to file the papers on your desk and update your calendar and to-do list. At the end of the day, take twenty minutes to grade papers. Once you develop routines for daily tasks, you will easily complete items on your to-do list.

Set Timers

If you find you are wasting time or avoiding a particularly aversive task, set a timer. For example, allow yourself thirty minutes to complete a draft of an IEP. During that time, avoid all other distractions. Devote yourself to only one task during the set time; do not answer e-mails, texts, or check your mailbox.

This strategy will help motivate you to complete the task in a certain time limit and reduce your likelihood of diversions.

Just Say No

As a first-year teacher, you may feel strange about saying no; however, you must learn how. You will have so many things on your plate. You do not want to add to your responsibilities by volunteering for things that are not important. For example, your principal may be looking for people to help with the technology plan. Even though you may be interested in technology, you can decline the opportunity if you are unsure that you will have time in your schedule for this responsibility. Once you are able to manage all your regular duties, you can volunteer for additional opportunities but protect your time as much as possible.

Delegate When Possible

You alone must handle many of your responsibilities; however, some tasks can be delegated. As much as possible, pass these tasks off to others. Have a paraprofessional handle the preparation of materials for the day or the reorganization at the end of the day. Have a parent prepare the folders of student work to go home on Fridays. A librarian might find books for you on a certain topic. Check your to-do list regularly and ask yourself if someone else can help with a task. The more you delegate, the better.

MANAGE YOUR TIME, MANAGE YOUR TASKS

As a special education teacher with many responsibilities, your time is valuable. There is no better way to save time than by managing and organizing your tasks. Sometimes it can be the littlest details that can make the biggest impact. It will take you about a month to settle in to your normal daily, weekly, and monthly tasks. As you start to develop routines, use these basic tips for maximizing your time:

- *Save difficult tasks for when you are fresh and alert.* If you try to take on your most challenging tasks at the end of a long and exhausting day, it will take longer and the quality may not reflect your best work. Try not to work on these demanding tasks when you are tired.
- *Complete small tasks while waiting.* Keep easily completed or minor tasks in a folder to take with you to meetings. If you are waiting for a meeting to begin, accomplish one of these tasks. Manage every minute of your time and you will manage all your responsibilities.
- *Limit the frequency of checking e-mail and office mail.* Set a time to manage your e-mail and stopping by the office. You might decide to check your e-mail once or twice per day. It is reasonable for you to stop by the office to check your box before and after school. Setting aside a specific time for checking mail helps to focus your time and reduces the likelihood you will be distracted.
- *Outline discussion points before attending meetings and making phone calls.* Take time to prepare a bulleted list of the important points you want to communicate for each meeting you attend. Not only will you have a reference of discussion topics, but you will also be able to stay focused in the meeting, keep your comments to the point, and decrease the likelihood of your time being wasted. For more information on conducting meetings, see chapter 3.
- *Check yourself.* If you find you are not getting enough of your tasks completed, log your time for a week. Write down everything you do all day long. This will help you to identify potential

problems. Perhaps you are chatting too much on your office visits or spending hours searching the Internet for lesson ideas. Knowing how your time is spent will help you to plan your time more wisely.

SETTING UP YOUR CLASS FOR SUCCESS

Your classroom is your home away from home. Good teachers strategically organize their classrooms because they know the classroom's set-up affects student interaction, learning, and behavior.

> *I love to set up my classroom before school starts. It is like being on an episode of HGTV. I create a room, surprise my students on the first day of school, and we live and learn there all year long.*
>
> Sally, special education teacher

The first step in setting up your classroom is design. Before you get out your paper to draw a diagram of your classroom, ask yourself the following questions:

▶ *Where will students keep personal materials? A desk? A cubby? Binders?* You may need a bank of cubbies or a place for students to store binders. If each student has a personal desk, it may be possible for materials to remain there.

▶ *How will students typically work? Independently? In groups?* If students will work in centers, it is likely you will have several tables with chairs. If you are providing direct instruction to a small group, you may need a group of desks in one area of the room. If you are working with kindergarteners, you may need dedicated floor space.

▶ *Do any students need special arrangements?* Review student IEPs prior to planning the organization of your classroom. Some students may have specific needs, such as working with a peer, sitting close to the teacher, or having independent work space.

▶ *What do students need to see? Vocabulary words? Math facts? Student work?* Your wall space is important. Most important, students should see your basic rules and procedures. Beyond this, make the most of your wall space. Determine how many areas of wall space you have and plan practically. Set up your wall space so it can be either easily changed (displaying student work) or will last for a month. For example, if you are focusing this month on summarizing skills, use one bulletin board dedicated to related information.

▶ *Where will you be? Moving around? At a small table? In front?* This answer is particularly important for influencing behavior management. If you will be working in a small group, you want to ensure you can still see the rest of the classroom. As you see in figure 6.1, if the teacher is at a designated teacher table, she can still see the students at their desks.

Once you have answered all the questions, sketch a diagram in pencil of your classroom before you start arranging items. Make sure your design takes into account all the important factors listed in the five questions just discussed. Once you are satisfied with your design, you can get to work. Do not be discouraged if you need to adjust your classroom plan during the first few weeks of school. As you learn more about your student needs and revise your lessons, it is likely you will adjust the structure of your classroom. You may need to move student materials to another area because you notice there is too much movement during small-group instruction. Be flexible and willing to make modifications.

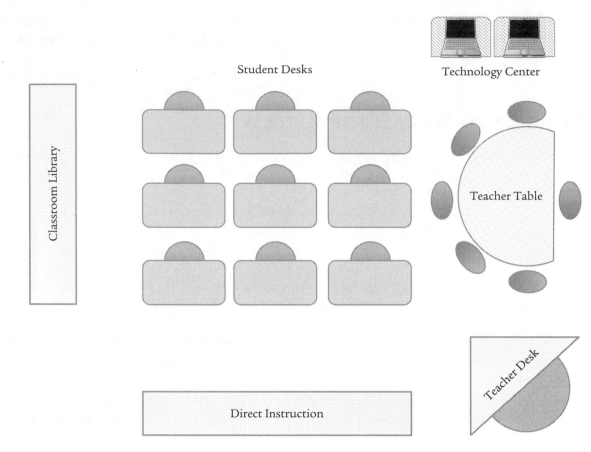

Figure 6.1 Scholastic Example Room Arrangement

CONSIDERATIONS FOR MIDDLE AND HIGH SCHOOL CLASSROOMS

If you are teaching in a middle or high school, your classroom design and organizational strategy will be different. Students will likely come in and out of your room all day long. Consider the following in your classroom design.

Student Seating and Routine

Keep seating charts for each class. If you have five classes and one hundred students, it will take a long time to learn where everyone is supposed to sit. Use your seating charts to take attendance and help you learn students' names and seats. Also, you may need to alter seating depending on your specific classes. For example, one class may need traditional rows of desks for more direct instruction and another class needs clusters of four desks to facilitate group work. During the first week of class, teach students routines for desk and table rearrangements. When you engage student help, this task can be completed before the bell rings allowing students to focus their attention on the day's academic objectives.

Wall Space

If you are teaching five classes on the same subject, you may be able to organize your wall space according to your academic units. However, often middle and high school special education teachers have many different subjects and levels. In this case, it may not be possible to devote bulletin boards to match your current instructional topic. Do not leave the walls blank and uninviting. Instead, you can post student work, hang motivational pictures and sayings, or allow students to design areas as a reward.

Class and Student Materials

It will be important for you to have an organizational system for class materials. You may consider color coding for easy access by you and the students. Also, think specifically about where you will keep materials and folders for students to easily find. Students need to be able to retrieve and return their books, pencils, folders, and other materials quickly at the beginning and end of class. Strategically placing these materials can help to maximize your teaching time.

Middle and high school teachers generally have a larger number of students. Because of this, managing student work and grading often becomes overwhelming. You may have ten students absent in one day who need make-up work or one hundred papers to grade. Consider the following to help you maintain organization.

Create a Designated Location for Turning in Work and Missed Work

Choose a location for turning in work close to the door. Students can drop finished assignments on their way out of the classroom to minimize distractions of getting up during class. Additionally, when you have a large number of students, you will have absences every day. You do not want to eat up your precious instructional time providing missed work to students. Instead, have a missed work folder for each class. You can even delegate this task to a responsible student: every day the student collects papers for students who are absent and places them in the missed folder. In this way, the student learns responsibility and you do not have to take your time to complete the task.

Keep a No-Name Folder

Undoubtedly, students will turn in work without writing their name on it. If you have a folder with no-name papers, students can access the pile and find their work independently. Attach an oversized or eye-catching pen to the assignment box to remind students to write their names on their papers if they forgot.

Use Technology

When possible, use technology to help you stay organized. Many middle and high school teachers have class websites updated with daily assignments and due dates. Some students may be able to keep a record and enter their own grades in a digital file. Not only does this minimize the work for you, but it also helps students learn to be accountable, set goals, and increase motivation to succeed. In the case of grading, you can double-check their entries. These are only a few examples of how technology can make your organizational work more manageable.

Keeping Your Student Data Organized and Accessible

Theresa Forte, Elementary School Teacher of the Year

ORGANIZE YOUR STUDENT DATA

Data is the most important tool for driving your instruction. One barrier you will face is an overwhelming amount of student data. If you do not have a system in place to keep data organized, you will become lost in piles of papers and assessment reports. This data is then not useful for informing instruction. Follow these simple directions to organize your student data.

CREATE A SINGLE ASSESSMENT MATRIX (BEST FOR CHAPTER TESTS AND UNIT TESTS)

► Place student names in alphabetical order.

► Across the top of the matrix, place a number to represent the assessment question.

► Use X marks in the box to represent the questions students missed.

► Last column for each student is the final score.

► Color code final grade to show if student reached mastery.

► Within the document, place the class average.

Example of Single Assessment Matrix											
	Q1	**Q2**	**Q3**	**Q4**	**Q5**	**Q6**	**Q7**	**Q8**	**Q9**	**Q10**	**Total Score**
Student A	X	X					X				70%
Student B		X									90%
Student C	X	X	X	X				X			50%
											Class Avg.: 80%

Setting up a single assessment matrix using this format allows you to see which skills you may need to reteach to specific groups of students, individuals, or the whole class. Looking at this particular matrix, it is obvious that the skill associated with question 2 needs to be retaught because all students missed this question.

In the beginning of the year, you likely know the schedule of required assessments your students will take in each subject area. Setting up a matrix to illustrate all assessments is important to show student progress during the school year.

CREATE A GROUP ASSESSMENT MATRIX FOR A SPECIFIC CONTENT AREA

► Place student names in alphabetical order.

► Across the top of the matrix, place the title of assessments.

► Place students' final scores in cells.

► Color code final scores to indicate mastery.

► Create a row for class averages.

► Create a column for beginning- and end-of-year benchmark assessments.

► Create a column for student growth.

Example of Group Assessment Matrix			
	Benchmark A, September	Benchmark B, January	Student Growth
Student A	53%	74%	+ 21 %
Student B	97%	84%	−13%
Class avg.	75%	79%	+ 8%

Setting up a group assessment matrix for single assessments of the same content area allows you to see overall trends easily. These matrixes are very useful for conferences with your general education colleagues, principal, and parents.

MAKE YOUR DATA ACCESSIBLE

Teachers are always scrambling for extra hours to complete tasks: your students are not the only ones with homework! On the days you are working at home, you will often need your data. With easy-to-use technology, your data can be accessible to you at any time: it is no longer necessary to purchase a rolling suitcase to lug home with binders full of handwritten paper and files. Several programs allow you to create accessible documents and tables that you can access, create, and edit anywhere you have an Internet connection.

Although there are many available programs that can provide assistance with electronic data, the following two are widely used and available for free.

GOOGLE DOCS FEATURES

▶ Password protection.
▶ Accessibility from any computer or mobile device. You could start your lesson at school and open it again at home or the coffee shop.
▶ Word processing documents, spreadsheets, and presentations that are compatible with Microsoft Office products.
▶ Collaborative format. You can invite people to participate in your documents. This can be helpful if you are co-planning with another teacher. You can both work on a lesson plan from home and can collaborate in real time using Google's chat feature as well.

DROPBOX FEATURES

▶ Password protection.
▶ Accessibility from your computer, laptop, or mobile device at any time. Materials are accessible anytime online by logging into the Dropbox site or offline through a computer application.
▶ File sharing. You can invite others to specific Dropbox folders to share files.

As with any data, it is always a good idea to keep backup files. If you save all your students' reading data in a file on Google Docs, save a copy on your flash drive, or print a copy to keep in your classroom. This ensures you never lose any necessary information.

THE TEACHER'S DESK

The teacher's desk is a potential location for clutter. It is easy to start piling up student work, correspondence from parents, meeting notes, or IEPs. A stack of papers can easily become overwhelming, increasing your stress. Keeping your desk organized is a simple way to eliminate undue pressure. In figure 6.2, see how Deanna Powers set up her desk for organizational success using a filing system and personal items.

Setting up your desk is not complicated. Follow these simple steps:

► Choose a desktop file holder such as a hanging file or stackable tray.
► Label the folders:
  ● To complete ASAP (you need to attend to immediately)
  ● To complete (work that must be done)
  ● To review (papers to read)
  ● To file (papers to be stored)
  ● To grade (student assignments or assessments)
► Always place papers in the designated area.
► Add something personal.

It might be overwhelming to sit down at your desk knowing you have a stack of work. Add something to your desk that will make you smile. This might be a family picture, a scene from the beach, or an important quote to make your desk more inviting.

When you sit at your desk before school, during planning, or after school, you can maximize your time because your paperwork will be accessible and your desk will be inviting.

Figure 6.2 Deanna's Desk[9]

Tips for Sharing Your Space with Others

Kristin Zimmerman, Special Education Mentor

Depending on your specific role and the resources at the school, you may not have your own classroom. You may work as a co-teacher and share a room with a general education teacher or you may split a classroom with a speech-language pathologist. Regardless of the reasoning, you will want your space to be accessible, organized, and welcoming.

GENERAL TIPS

Build a relationship with a coworker in your shared space with the following conversation starters:

- ► Introduce yourself.
- ► Ask about his or her teaching job.
- ► What does he or she like most about teaching? Dislike?
- ► Get to know him or her on a personal level.

Use technology effectively:

- ► Determine what technology is available.
- ► If only one piece of equipment is available in a shared room, create a schedule for usage.
- ► Maximize technology available by thinking of ways to decrease the things you need to carry from room to room.

TIPS WHEN USING ANOTHER TEACHER'S CLASSROOM FOR INSTRUCTION

PORTABLE ITEMS

- ► Put things you need to post in a classroom, such as rules and routines, in a binder to carry with you.
- ► Have access to easy hanging materials: magnet clips, Velcro, tape, pocket charts.
- ► Hang the items from the binder up in the room before class and remove at the end of class.
- ► Use available technology to increase portability (e.g., SMART Board, Google Docs, Dropbox).

STUDENT FOLDERS

- ► Have a folder for each student in the class for easy access to class materials.
- ► Use the folder to keep class materials. The folder may contain the class syllabus, notes, copies of PowerPoint slides from lessons, quizzes, and tests.
- ► You could also use the student folder for the class rules and routines.

(Continued)

Small Storage Space in Room

▶ Check with the teacher about providing a small space for your storage.

▶ Store materials you will use throughout the year or materials needed for a short-term project in your storage space.

▶ Plan an outline for each week that includes needed materials. Then collect and organize the materials for the week and place them in your storage space in the classroom.

TIPS WHEN SHARING A ROOM WITH ANOTHER TEACHER

Plan timing together:

▶ Set a time to discuss timing with the other teacher.

▶ Coordinate breaks to reduce distractions.

Organize furniture:

▶ Arrange furniture to maximize student focus and decrease distractions.

▶ Create two distinct spaces for each teacher's group of students.

▶ Use file cabinets, bookshelves, and standing bulletin boards as partitions to divide your space.

Consolidate materials:

▶ Use the same art project materials; for example, glue, scissors, crayons, markers.

▶ Keep one set of teaching materials if using the same program with different groups of students.

Create routines and processes for maintenance of classroom material:

▶ Keep space uncluttered and clean.

▶ Be respectful of the other person in the room.

▶ Clean up after yourself and your students.

▶ Keep desk area organized.

▶ Put shared materials away after use; don't make your colleague track down shared materials.

GET READY FOR YOUR FIRST DAY OF SCHOOL

Your first day as a teacher will be a special day you will always remember. Many new teachers are understandably excited and nervous. The following will help you to create a memorable first day for you and your students.

Create a First-Day Checklist

One way to assist you in completing all your preparation for the first day is to create a first-day checklist. Having all your tasks listed will relieve any anxiety about missed work and allow you to feel confident when the students arrive. Your checklist will need to be tailored to your specific role and responsibilities. Exhibit 6.2 provides an example to get you started.

PLAN FOR FUN AND KNOWLEDGE

The first day of school sets the stage for the remainder of your year. You want to create an impression on your students. Think about what you want them to feel about you and your classroom when they go home after the first day. Excited? Motivated? Comfortable? Interested? Strategically planning your first day can assist in creating the atmosphere you want.

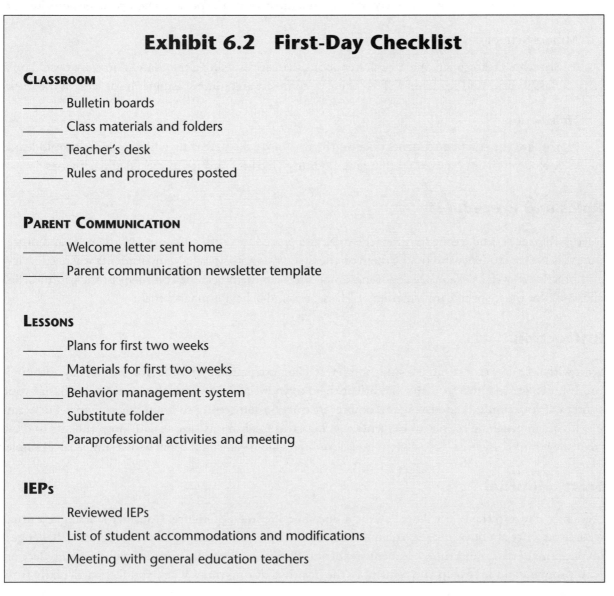

Exhibit 6.2 First-Day Checklist

CLASSROOM

_____ Bulletin boards

_____ Class materials and folders

_____ Teacher's desk

_____ Rules and procedures posted

PARENT COMMUNICATION

_____ Welcome letter sent home

_____ Parent communication newsletter template

LESSONS

_____ Plans for first two weeks

_____ Materials for first two weeks

_____ Behavior management system

_____ Substitute folder

_____ Paraprofessional activities and meeting

IEPs

_____ Reviewed IEPs

_____ List of student accommodations and modifications

_____ Meeting with general education teachers

Getting-to-Know-You Activities

On the first day, part of your time should be spent getting to know each other. Students will want to know about you and you will want to learn about your students. There are endless ways to accomplish this but remember some students will be extroverted and others will be shy. Planning activities that are fun and allow you to get to know one another is beneficial. Moreover, your grade level and subject should be considered. Here are some ideas to get your creative juices flowing.

Early Elementary

▶ All-about-me posters: students design posters with information about themselves.

Upper Elementary

▶ Snowball fight: students write three things about themselves on paper. Everyone crumples the paper and the class takes a minute to throw the papers in a snowball fight. When the timer goes off, each student picks up a piece of paper and must locate the person who wrote the note. Repeat.

Middle School

▶ Students create a personal newsletter about themselves using a template. These are posted on a class website and students will use these to complete an online scavenger hunt later in the week.

High School

▶ You are the teacher: students take on the role of teacher, creating what students should learn, including their preferred teaching methods (e.g., lectures, groups, projects) and activities.

Rules and Procedures

Successful teachers take time to review the rules and procedures with students. Having rules and procedures visible for students and telling them on the first day is not enough. Many students will need review and practice as well as examples and nonexamples to help them become confident in the routines. See chapter 7 for more specific information on classroom and behavior management.

Instruction

Start with activities that stimulate student interest. Plan instructional activities for the first day. Although you want to get to know students and orient them to your classroom, you also want to emphasize your content. If your time is limited, you can combine instruction and getting-to-know-you activities. For example, if you are teaching science in elementary grades, this might be as simple as asking students to draw what they think a scientist looks like; in middle or high school you could begin with a simple lab example.

Start a Journal

Your first day and the year that follows is a once-in-a-lifetime experience. Consider starting a journal where you write about your days. You may want to write daily or keep sections for successes, challenges, inspirational events, and funny student incidents. This journal will be useful to you as you reflect on your progress and may help you remember the positives during times when you feel particularly frustrated and overwhelmed.

Managing Your Job as an Itinerant Teacher

Stephanie Gardiner-Walsh, Itinerant Teacher, Deaf Education

Itinerant teaching was probably not covered in your preservice preparation program. It is a specialized field that requires a great deal of interpersonal skills, adaptation to a dynamic environment, knowledge of multiple grade levels, and management of many administrative styles and demands. On top of those basics, itinerant teaching also requires skills that other teaching positions do not require, including tire changing, for example. The following provides a glimpse into my six-year experience as an itinerant teacher.

LEARN TO CHECK AND MAINTAIN YOUR VEHICLE

Car maintenance is now part of your world. You will experience more frequent fueling, oil changes, and tire changes and drive more miles than your friends who stay at one school all day. Your vehicle is your office and you must be prepared to care for it during roadside emergencies. Here are some basics to master:

▶ *Check your oil.* This is simple and can be done once a week in less than two minutes. It can save your engine. Also, know what kind of oil your car uses.

▶ *Check your tire pressure and tire wear.* Correct tire pressure increases gas mileage and can save your life.

▶ *Understand your gauges.* Have your check engine lights inspected and make sure your temperatures and pressures are normal.

▶ *Learn how to change a flat.* Help may not always be readily available. Also, check your spare tire once every few months.

▶ *Don't skimp on maintenance!* Follow the recommended guidelines for belts, fluid changes, and other periodic maintenance. If you are unsure where to find guidelines, ask your dealer or local mechanic. Routine maintenance is required more frequently when you are racking up miles on back roads.

If this feels overwhelming or you have no idea how to start learning these skills, check out your local drivers' license center or refer to www.dmv.org/how-to-guides/vehicle-maintenance.php.

INVEST IN GPS, MOBILE MAPS, AND A CELL PHONE

Even after years of driving around a school system, you can guarantee that you will get stuck in some type of traffic jam and need to get around it quickly. Mobile maps or GPS are the best tools for doing so quickly. For the main routes you use daily, ask local people—they know all the best shortcuts! Preprogram your cell phone with all the schools you serve, parents you work with, medical facilities you collaborate with, and friends who are good at directing you. Your cell phone will enable you to contact schools to get help or to change your arrival time and can give you a quick chance to conference (using hands-free technology). *Please* follow cell phone safety rules.

(Continued)

DEVELOP A WAY TO REMEMBER NAMES, FACES, AND SCHOOLS

At every school you need to be able to identify the following:

- ▶ Secretaries (above everyone else!)
- ▶ Principal and assistant principals
- ▶ Guidance counselors
- ▶ Lead exceptional children teacher
- ▶ Psychologist
- ▶ Classroom teachers (with whom you work)
- ▶ Grade-level chairs

Keep a notebook or an electronic memo on your cell phone with locations and descriptions for each of these people. Here are two examples:

Happy Grove Elementary School.

Secretaries:

Mrs. Smith (brown hair, small, square glasses, always in bad mood, loves chocolate, desk on left)
Mrs. Jones (gray hair, adores her grandchildren, looks like my neighbor Janie)

DO NOT BE AFRAID TO APPROACH GRADE-LEVEL CHAIRS

As an itinerant, you are responsible for a range of grades. Having materials for every subject and every grade is impossible and expensive. Grade-level chairs can often access materials such as pacing guides, vocabulary lists, reference materials, classroom texts, manipulatives, old lesson plans, and worksheets to use with your students. Many itinerants spend their first few years reinventing the wheel before discovering that many school personnel are willing to give you materials to use if you just ask. The great thing about being itinerant is that you can ask multiple schools for materials; sometimes your best resources will develop from borrowing these materials across schools. The major problem with this system, however, is remembering where to return things at the end of the year. To avoid confusion, label materials that need to be returned with sticky notes and blank address labels.

PREPARE AN EMERGENCY EQUIPMENT KIT FOR YOUR SPECIALTY

Always keep emergency supplies in a small plastic box in your vehicle. Each specialty within itinerant teaching requires different tools that are frequently used and should be on hand at all times. Plastic shoe box–sized storage containers are ideal. Emergency kits may contain the following:

- ▶ Batteries: for any assistive devices or personal devices you use in the schools
- ▶ Repair kits: screwdrivers, electrical tape, and super glue
- ▶ Personal products: think hygiene for you and your students

- ► Office supplies: paper clips, stapler, and scissors
- ► Special items for your field: tubes, gels, stethoscopes, and medical supplies

INVEST IN MULTIPLE TEACHER BAGS

Your teacher bags will help you stay organized. Using teacher bags to organize school- and student-specific materials aids in a quick transition between schools. Many itinerant teachers have a bag specifically for their always-used items (e.g., agenda, planners, lesson plan book, laptops, writing utensils). Your second bag to carry into a school should contain student-specific materials. For example, at Happy Grove Elementary, you see two students and have a red bag with teaching materials for both of those students. After leaving Happy Grove, you go to Middle Brook High School where you serve three students. You need a separate bag to organize those materials. Multiple bags allow you to carry fewer materials at any given point in the day, will help you to keep important papers with the student they belong to, and will aid in organizing for substitutes. If you don't like carrying multiple bags, find another system that allows you to organize daily, weekly, and monthly materials into easy-to-carry, easy-to-grab groups.

EXPLORE THE AREA FOR GAS STATIONS, REST AREAS, FAST-FOOD LOCATIONS, AND WI-FI HOT SPOTS

As an itinerant teacher, fuel stops are often part of your day. Although I recommend fueling before your day begins, that is not always possible and fueling on the go is required. Make sure you can find a gas station in the peripheries of your service area as well as in the center. Knowing the distance you can travel after your fuel light turns on is critical to not having a breakdown. Not only do you need to fuel your car, you need to be able to find fuel for yourself. Classroom teachers will have access to the cafeteria if they forget their lunch. As an itinerant teacher, you will have fast-food restaurants and convenience stores to choose from. Finally, know where Wi-Fi hot spots can be located. As an itinerant, you often will not know in advance if one of your students is not in school. Take advantage of the unexpected planning time by using Wi-Fi to check e-mail, contact other teachers, plan lessons, and complete electronic monitoring. Contact parents and teachers as frequently as you can. If your laptop battery does not hold a charge for any length of time, invest in a power inverter so you can plug your machine into your vehicle.

ORGANIZE YOUR ATTENDANCE RECORDS, SERVICE RECORDS, FIELD NOTES, AND PROGRESS-MONITORING DATA

Similar to the teacher bag system, you need to have a way to track your service provision times and your student records. Ideally, everything should be kept in a filing cabinet with current IEP data. However, the reality is that you won't have the time daily to update files in every cabinet in every school. In your essential bag, set up a binder with a divider for each student you serve. Keep critical records including goals, progress monitoring, parent contact information, and student samples in each section. Keep these with you at all times so you can quickly open and check off your work during the day. This is also a great place to keep mileage tracking so that you do not short yourself at the end of the month.

(Continued)

INVENT AN ORGANIZATIONAL SYSTEM FOR YOUR CAR

Your trunk is no longer a place for groceries. You need your trunk to store materials and keep them organized, free from damage, and easily accessible:

▶ Small plastic milk crates for books, binders, planning materials, and teacher bags
▶ Soft crates for a change of clothes, spare snacks, and an umbrella
▶ Plastic grocery bag for trash in the footwell of your passenger seat
▶ Napkins because you will eventually spill something while having lunch in your car
▶ Sticky notes for quick phone messages you take in parking lots
▶ Small pencil boxes to use as prize boxes

In addition to keeping your car from being a mess, storage systems allow you to quickly access your teaching materials and turn your vehicle back into a car instead of a mobile office. Spending a few minutes and dollars at the start of your school year to organize yourself will save hours of searching to find the materials you need.

BEFRIEND OFFICE STAFF, ESPECIALLY THE HEAD SECRETARY

Anyone who works in a school knows the real boss is the secretary. The office staff people are your best friends. You may find it difficult to remember the location of teachers and staff people but the front office staff can guide you. It never hurts to bring small treats to introduce yourself and start off your relationship on a positive note. Establishing who you are, what you do, and explaining why you are constantly in and out of the building can save you and them headaches later in the year. Not only will befriending the secretary make coming and going from schools faster, it may also enable you to get access to copier codes, printers, and direct phone transfers faster than if you are unknown. Be courteous. Be sweet. Be complimentary. You will have a wonderful support if you are friends with the office staff.

TO SUM UP

▶ Special education teachers have many varied roles and responsibilities.
▶ Setting goals and plans for organization allows you to manage your time and tasks to avoid becoming overwhelmed.
▶ Organizational strategies can assist you in preparing your classroom purposefully to maximize instruction and your time.
▶ Strategically designing your first day will ensure fond memories and create a foundation for a successful first year.

WHAT'S NEXT?

You now have organizational strategies to manage your time and your work. Next, we will delve more specifically into strategies for classroom and behavior management.

ADDITIONAL RESOURCES

GENERAL ORGANIZATION TIPS FROM TEACHERS

▶ Mrs. McDavid: www.ourclassweb.com/sites_for_teachers_getting_organized.htm

▶ Mrs. Turhune: http://mrsterhune.blogspot.com/search/label/Organization

ORGANIZATION FOR SPECIAL EDUCATION TEACHERS

▶ National Association of Special Education Teachers. *Step by step guide to setting up your classroom*: www.naset.org/2366.0.html

▶ The Organized Special Education Teacher: http://organizedteaching.com/the_organized_sp_ed_teacher/index.html

▶ Wagaman, J. (2008, December 13). *Organization for the special education teacher*. Retrieved from http://suite101.com/article/organization-for-the-special-educator-a83908

▶ Bullard, C. (2003). *The itinerant teacher's handbook*. Hillsboro, OR: Butte Publications.

MORE FIRST-DAY ACTIVITIES WEBSITES

▶ www.teachhub.com/first-day-school-activities-students-love

▶ www.middleschool.net/back-to-school-activities.htm

▶ www.educationworld.com/a_lesson/lesson/lesson131.shtml

▶ www.superteacherworksheets.com/beginning-of-year.html

CHAPTER SEVEN

Classroom and Behavior Management

Elizabeth Bettini

University of Florida

In this chapter you will learn about:

- Promoting appropriate and preventing inappropriate behaviors by:
  - Setting up the physical environment of a classroom effectively
  - Establishing and reinforcing rules, expectations, and procedures
  - Creating a positive and caring classroom community
  - Providing engaging classroom instruction
- Teaching and reinforcing new skills for students with persistent and severe behaviors by doing the following:
  - Providing additional support to students with mild, persistent behavioral needs
  - Conducting functional behavior assessments and interventions

---

Javier and Cole are fourth-grade students who are included in a regular education classroom. Today, whenever Javier walks past Cole, Cole says, "Leave me alone, Javier!" This happened in math, during snack time, at lunch, and now during reading. Javier has ignored Cole's comments all day but finally he is tired of ignoring them so he slams his fist on Cole's desk, yelling, "What? You want me to do something to you?" Cole bursts out crying, turns to the teacher, and says, "Ms. Levin!! Javier threatened me!"

New teachers often struggle with managing their classrooms, and problematic student behavior is a major source of stress during the early years. Special education professionals are responsible for supporting students with a broad range of academic and behavioral needs. Although some students will need little more than clearly delineated expectations, others, like Cole, may need more intensive support. A key point to remember, though, is that all behaviors have a function or purpose. Cole doesn't act inappropriately because he is a bad kid but because his inappropriate behavior has worked for him in the past, allowing him to achieve something that he wants. In this case, Cole has learned that the best way to get attention from peers and staff is to provoke others. When peers threaten or make fun of him, he is at least getting attention. Because he doesn't know any equally effective, appropriate strategies for getting attention, he resorts to demanding it. Your job is to set up an environment that promotes appropriate behavior, prevents inappropriate behavior, and, for students like Cole, teaches and reinforces new behavioral skills.

It is sometimes tempting to blame students, parents, or other teachers when behavior problems occur. Yet blame does not solve anything—no matter where the problem behavior originated. It is more productive to keep in mind that your responsibility is to help the student develop new skills to be successful. If one of your students does not have sufficient skills in reading, for example, you would never blame or punish that student; you would teach him or her how to read. The same principle applies to behavior. When a student comes to you with insufficient behavioral skills, it is your responsibility to teach and reinforce new skills.

TIERED APPROACH TO PROVIDING POSITIVE BEHAVIORAL SUPPORT

Experts in the field of behavior and classroom management recommend using a three-tiered model of support for behavior, similar to the RTI model used for academics (see chapters 5 and 10).[1] As a special education professional, you may have responsibilities for each of the following three tiers depending on the setting in which you work (e.g., consulting, co-teaching, teaching in a full-time special education classroom):

Tier one: All students are provided effective, evidence-based classroom management. With effective classroom management, 80 to 85 percent of students will meet behavioral expectations.

Tier two: More intensive behavioral supports are provided for students who continue to struggle. In spite of tier one supports, about 10 to 15 percent of students will need additional support and instruction in order to behave appropriately.

Tier three: Interventions are intensive and individualized to help students learn and maintain appropriate behaviors in school. Only 1 to 5 percent of students will present extreme behavioral challenges, requiring tier three interventions.

In the following sections we provide specific guidance for each of the three tiers.

Tier One: Classroom Management

Many novice educators spend much of their time reacting to behavior: they yell, beg, punish, and cajole students who behave inappropriately and they leave at the end of the day feeling worn out and frustrated. What they don't realize is that the best classroom managers focus most of their energy on *preventing* inappropriate behavior rather than responding to it.[2] Most behavioral problems can be prevented through effective classroom management by doing the following:

- ▶ Set up the classroom environment effectively
- ▶ Develop clear rules, expectations, and procedures
- ▶ Create a positive and caring classroom community
- ▶ Provide engaging instruction

Set Up the Classroom Environment Effectively

As a special educator, you may be responsible for managing your own, separate classroom for students with special needs or you may support general education teachers as a consultant or as a co-teacher. No matter what your role, you will need to consider how to use classroom space effectively. Ideally, you will do this before students enter your classroom. Depending on your specific assignment you will need to arrange different areas:

- ▶ A desk area
- ▶ An area for direct instruction
- ▶ Areas for independent and group work
- ▶ Specialized areas such as a reading corner or an art table
- ▶ Bins for turning in homework

Take time to map out where you would like to place these areas, or if you co-teach, discuss arrangements with the general educator. As you create this map, think about how different spaces will be used, then arrange furniture accordingly. For example, spaces used for small-group work should allow students to sit together and see one another. Also think about traffic patterns: Where will students be walking? Will they have to walk in front of the whole class to sharpen their pencil? If so, that could be very distracting when you are conducting instruction.

When you organize your classroom, these basic principles will help you to minimize distractions and maximize academic instructional time:

- ▶ If there are materials that students will need to access during instruction, such as scratch paper or spare pencils, place them in a discreet location so that students aren't distracted when their peers get these materials.
- ▶ During direct instruction, seat students so that they do not view the door or other distractions such as the class pet or playground.
- ▶ Minimize transition time and save time by organizing class materials. You can enlist students' help with organization by requiring them to put things back where they came from and by offering incentives to help reorganize when necessary.
- ▶ Create ample room for students to work. Students have more appropriate social interactions when they have enough personal space to move and interact appropriately.[3]
- ▶ Make sure that you can see the whole room from any given point and you can move safely and quickly around the room. Strong classroom managers actively supervise their students by walking around the room and scanning their students' activities frequently. This will allow you to notice and address problem situations before they escalate.

Develop Clear Rules, Expectations, and Procedures

Mr. Kelly always begins his fourth-grade class by separating the class into five groups and gives each group one of the five classroom rules. Each group is responsible for creating a poster showing what the rule means. Each group presents its poster to the class, explaining why the rule is important and demonstrating how to follow it correctly. Mr. Kelly places the posters at the front of the room to remind students of the rules throughout the year. In addition, Mr. Kelly spends time teaching them what each rule means in different contexts. For example, he shows that, in the hallway, "Be respectful" means walking quietly, whereas at lunch, "Be respectful" means using kind language. After every vacation, Mr. Kelly spends time reviewing and reteaching these rules to help students remember what appropriate behavior looks like.

Now that you have your classroom set up, you need to do what Mr. Kelly has done: teach your students how to make the most of the space and the instruction that you have provided by following the rules, expectations, and procedures for your classroom. Some novice teachers spend only ten minutes reviewing these on the first day of school; that is a big mistake! Rules, expectations, and procedures must be taught and practiced if you expect students to follow them throughout the year. The time that you spend teaching them will pay off.

Rules, expectations, and procedures may, at first glance, appear to be synonymous, but they are actually different:

- ▶ Rules are explicit instructions about how to behave in the classroom.
- ▶ Expectations are implicit assumptions about what your students will do.
- ▶ Procedures are the coordinated ways that your class will accomplish tasks.

For example, if you have a *rule* that students should be active learners, you might *expect* that they will complete all of their work to the best of their ability, and you might have *procedures* for how they turn in that work.

Rules   Some novice teachers make the mistake of posting long lists of rules, barring all behaviors that the teacher finds inappropriate: "No gum, no cell phones, no talking, no texting," and so on. This is an incredibly ineffective approach to creating rules; you can't ban all possible inappropriate behaviors and it is difficult for students to recall. Instead, focus on developing three to five rules that are general, age-appropriate, and that tell students what *to* do instead of what *not* to do.[4] Exhibit 7.1 shows some examples of appropriate rules.

Exhibit 7.1   Sample Rules

1. Be Respectful	1. Safe Bodies	1. I am kind and caring.
2. Be Responsible	2. Attentive Minds	2. I work hard.
3. Be a Learner	3. Respectful Words and Actions	3. I am responsible for myself and my belongings.
4. Be Safe		

However, simply creating rules is not enough. You must also post, teach, and reinforce the rules, and when students engage in inappropriate behavior, you must respond appropriately.

Post the Rules   Mr. Kelly posted his rules well: at the front of the room. Rules should be displayed in a visible location, using engaging, age-appropriate language and materials.

Teach Students What These Rules Mean You should begin teaching the rules on the first day. You will do many different activities with students, so you should teach your students what these rules mean in the context of each different kind of activity. "Safe Bodies," for example, means something different inside the classroom than on the playground. During the first week of school, provide students with examples and nonexamples, and give them opportunities to interact with the rules by creating posters, acting out skits, or writing stories about the rules. Reteach this information after long vacations to help students return to a classroom mind-set.

Reinforce the Rules Although posting and teaching the rules is important, it is not enough. You also have to reinforce them by rewarding positive behaviors. You should have a continuum of rewards, ranging from small to large, so that you can address a continuum of behaviors. For example, Mr. Kelly has the following list posted in his room so that students will understand what rewards are available. Different rewards might be chosen depending on the behavior.

Continuum of Rewards

▶ Praise
▶ Reward raffle ticket
▶ Positive call home
▶ Lunch guest
▶ Five minutes extra recess (whole class)

Whole-class incentives, when used well, create positive peer pressure in which students encourage one another to behave appropriately:

▶ Place a jar on your desk and add one marble to the jar every time the whole class does a behavior (e.g., stays on task) that you have decided to target. When the jar is full, the class earns a pizza party or some other prearranged reward.

▶ Use tally marks on the board to track when the whole class does something good and provide a reward (e.g., an extra minute of recess) for every five tally marks.

It is important to use whole-class incentives in ways that foster community and that don't embarrass students who struggle. Incentives are intended to recognize appropriate behavior, not to punish students; you should never, for example, single out a student who has prevented the class from earning a reward.

Use Surface-Responding Techniques. When students do not follow rules, you may use a range of nonpunitive options, which are often called surface-responding techniques (see table 7.1).[5]

Use Punitive Consequences as Seldom as Possible. Sometimes, surface-responding techniques may be ineffective and you will have to provide punitive consequences when students break the rules persistently or when they engage in more severe behaviors. You should rely on punitive consequences only when all other options have failed because punitive interactions can have unintended negative consequences; they may provoke anxiety and fear in students and they reduce the quality of relationships between students and teachers.[6] The best consequences fit with the behavior. If a student cuts in line, the best consequence might be to require him or her to be at the back of the line the next time the class

Table 7.1 Surface-Responding Techniques

Technique	Explanation	Best for	Example
Precorrection	Reminding students of the expectations before an activity begins can prevent inappropriate behaviors for many students.	Before beginning an activity	*Before entering the hallway, Mr. Jamison reminds his class, "What does 'be respectful' mean in the hallway? That's right; it means we walk quietly so that we don't disrupt other classes."*
Proximity control	Simply walking next to a student or a group engaged in inappropriate behavior is a highly effective strategy for changing behavior.	When students are engaged in mild, problem behaviors	*Ms. Ting notices that one of the groups in her science lab is playing with the lab equipment. She walks near the group and stands next to them while continuing her instructions to the whole class.*
Praise appropriate behavior	Praising students who behave appropriately reminds others of the expectations and shows that appropriate behavior is appreciated.	Almost any time!	*When Mr. Little's class enters after lunch, some students begin doing their work and others continue talking. Mr. Little says, "Thank you for getting started on your bellwork" to on-task students.*
Nonverbal redirection	Nonverbal cues (e.g., eye contact, miming the appropriate behavior) communicate your expectations without disrupting instruction.	When students already know the rules	*While providing direct instruction, Ms. Olsen notices that Lisa is doodling instead of taking notes. While still instructing the class, Ms. Olsen makes eye contact with Lisa and mimes note-taking.*

Private Verbal Redirection

Technique	Explanation	Best for	Example
Restate rules	Restating your rules can remind students of what those rules mean in the present context.	When students forget the rules	*Kevin is leaving class without putting his materials away. Mr. Malone walks over to Kevin and quietly says, "Remember, Kevin, to 'be responsible' we put our materials away before we leave."*
Express interest	Expressing an interest in students' work communicates that their work is important to you.	When students are off task	*Ms. Roy notices that Jaime is checking e-mail instead of researching his project. She quietly says, "Jaime, tell me about your topic. What have you learned?"*
Two positive choices	Offering students two positive choices allows them to control their own choices and ensures that those choices will be positive.	When precorrecting or when students are making a poor choice	*Ms. Bair notices that Nicki has not been making progress on her essay. To precorrect at the beginning of class, she quietly says, "Nicki, would you like to work on the intro or the outline today?"*
Provide a rationale	Explaining why a rule is in place helps students understand that rules are important parts of being in a community, not arbitrary restrictions.	When less intrusive techniques have failed	*Mr. Vohs has used precorrection and proximity control but Mara continues to use lab equipment incorrectly. Mr. Vohs quietly says, "Mara, we need to follow the rules for the Bunsen burner because you can get hurt if you are not careful."*

goes out. If a student pushes another student at recess, then staying back from recess might be more appropriate. Consequences should always be delivered privately, in a calm and respectful tone, as soon after the inappropriate behavior as possible. Common consequences include the following:

▶ A phone call home
▶ Writing a note of apology
▶ Completing a reflection exercise
▶ Losing class privileges

Many teachers also use time-out as a consequence. However, you should be very careful about how you use time-out; it is only effective if a student is timed-out from an activity he or she enjoys.[7] If Tim hates math, then giving him a time-out during math class is a reward.

Expectations   Your expectations of your students matter. When teachers expect all students to learn, regardless of disability, they act differently, and their students are more successful as a result.[8] For example, a teacher with low expectations for a student might dismiss his or her inappropriate behavior, believing that it can't be fixed, whereas a teacher with high expectations will address the behavior respectfully and try to prevent it in the future. The student is more likely to make progress with the second teacher than the first.

You communicate your expectations to students in a number of subtle ways. For example, when you repeatedly call on the highest-performing students, you communicate that you do not expect lower-performing students to think about the answers. When you call on all students equally, you communicate that you expect them all to be thinking hard about the topic.

Praise

Praise is more than a simple reward for appropriate behavior; it also communicates your expectations and beliefs about a child. However, not all praise is equal. Some types of praise are more effective than others and some can actually be harmful. Effective praise is contingent, specific, and focuses on the student's choices, not stable characteristics.

▶ *Contingent praise:* Effective praise depends on the performance of a behavior or skill. If you praise students for poor performance, you communicate low expectations; if you praise them for working hard, you communicate that you expect and value effort.

▶ *Specific praise:* Effective praise also specifies exactly what the child did well. If Billy has been working on math problems while talking with Cheyenne, and you tell him, "Good job, Billy!" how will he know whether you are praising his math work or his conversation? If, however, you say, "Billy, you did a nice job of showing your work on those math problems," Billy knows exactly what he did well and he has a better understanding of your expectations for math class.

▶ *Focus on choices:* Effective praise focuses on choices that the child has control over, not stable personality attributes. Therefore, even if Gina has natural talents in writing, it is better to tell her, "I can tell that you really thought carefully about your word choice!" instead of "You are such a good writer!" The first comment communicates that her effortful behavior is responsible for her success, whereas the second comment communicates that she doesn't need to work hard to produce quality work.

Procedures   Routine tasks such as handing in homework, transitioning from one activity to another, getting materials for an activity, and collecting lunch money can take up tremendous amounts of class time if you do not have procedures for these activities. Procedures save time by routinizing these activities so that you and your students can devote your energy to academics rather than worrying about where the homework is or when students should give you their lunch money. Classes that spend less time on these types of activities are likely to have higher student achievement.[9] Similar to rules, procedures must be taught and repeatedly practiced at the beginning of the year. In well-run classrooms, students carry out these procedures with minimal direction.

Create a Positive and Caring Classroom Community

Positive behavior is more likely to thrive when relationships at all levels are trusting and supportive.
Epstein, Atkins, Cullinan, Kutash, and Weaver[10]

Rules, expectations, and procedures will gain little traction unless they occur within the context of caring relationships. Children who perceive their classrooms as caring, supportive environments are more likely to express an interest in academics.[11] You can create a positive, caring community by the following:

▶ Establishing strong relationships with your students
▶ Being consistent
▶ Using culturally relevant classroom management
▶ Emphasizing shared purpose rather than competition
▶ Actively teaching cooperation and communication skills

Relationships   By establishing strong relationships with students, you will decrease the frequency of discipline problems. You can establish strong relationships with your students by taking a personal interest in your students as people, not merely as students. Show empathy for challenges they face, even if those challenges seem trivial to you, and avoid sarcasm. When students come from different cultural backgrounds, make an effort to understand and show respect for their culture.[12]

Consistency   Consistency forms the basis for caring relationships. When students don't know what to expect, they must focus energy on figuring out your intentions, and they may feel anxious as a result. Consistency takes many forms. You can be consistent in your daily expectations, you can follow through when you say that you will do something, and you can have a consistent schedule and routine.

Teachers often believe that consistency requires them to treat all students the same but this is a mistake; in fact, research shows that effective teachers interact with different students according to their individual needs.[13] Consistency, therefore, means treating all students with the same *respect*, which will require you to individualize your interactions according to their needs. If your class is running a race, and Joey has a broken leg, you would never expect him to run the race the same way the other students do. Just as you might individualize Joey's participation in the race in order to treat him with respect, you should also individualize academic and disciplinary measures to meet students' individual needs. Consistency requires you to be fair to every individual, not to treat all individuals the same.

Culturally Responsive Classroom Management Cultural misunderstandings can interfere with caring relationships, and they can cause or exacerbate behavioral problems. For instance, research has shown than an African American or Latino student is more likely to be suspended or expelled than a Caucasian student who engages in the exact same behavior. African American and Latino students are also more likely to be labeled with emotional disabilities and placed in restrictive educational settings than Caucasian students. There are numerous possible causes for these discrepancies but one cause that has been identified is the gap between the cultural backgrounds of students and the cultural backgrounds of teachers: most teachers are middle and upper-middle class Caucasian women, whereas students come from an increasingly diverse array of backgrounds.[14]

No matter what your background may be or where you choose to teach you will work with students who come from different cultural backgrounds and who therefore have different understandings of what constitutes acceptable behavior. In order to develop positive and caring relationships with these students, you will need to cultivate an understanding of their culture and its expectations, which will require you to do the following:

▶ Make an effort to know students' families.
▶ Become familiar with the community in which students live.
▶ Understand, don't judge.
▶ Evaluate your practice.

The first step to understanding a student's culture is becoming familiar with his or her home life. Don't assume that just because a student looks like you that he or she comes from the same culture; culture is specific to families and communities and it varies widely within and among ethnic groups. Ask about how your students' families interact with one another, how they handle discipline, what goals they have for their children, and what makes them proud. Knowing these things will give you another perspective on behaviors that may seem problematic otherwise. For instance, if Isaiah's family tends to all talk at once, then you can understand why Isaiah doesn't wait his turn to speak in class; to him and his family, speaking over others is not misbehavior, it is normal. Instead of punishing him for this behavior, you can teach him to recognize situations when it is okay to interrupt and when he should wait his turn. Home visits, informal contacts with parents, and meetings can all help you to understand the specific family cultures within which your students have been raised.

Your students also exist within a community that rewards certain behaviors and punishes others. Unless you understand these community expectations, you may make inappropriate assumptions about your students' behaviors. For instance, Caucasian educators often assume that African American boys who walk with a certain gait are troubled, even though these patterns of movement are respected and valued in some communities.[15] Be aware that your expectations will frequently differ from those of your students' community. Seek to understand the history and importance of these expectations as well as how they specifically affect your students.

In order to understand your students' cultures, you must first recognize and release any judgment you may have toward cultures that are unfamiliar to you; the minute you judge, you have placed a barrier between yourself and your students. Instead, look for strengths in your students' cultures. There is something about every culture that you can learn from. You don't need to agree with everything about every culture but you do need to make an effort to understand and respect your students' heritage.

Ms. Halpin comes from a middle-class, suburban town in New England. She just began teaching in a low-income, rural community in New Mexico. She assumes that because she and most of her students are all Caucasian, they share the same cultural background and, as a result, she doesn't make any effort to develop an understanding of their culture. One day, her student Abby shares that her family owns several guns, that her home is "off the grid," and that her family stockpiles supplies in case of an apocalypse. Several students share that their families have made similar provisions. Ms. Halpin has never heard of living off the grid, and she assumes that these students' parents are radicals. In the staff room, she refers to them as *crazies*.

Another teacher, Mr. Bender, hears Ms. Halpin make this comment and decides to speak with her about it privately. He tells her that Abby was in his class the previous year and that her family has some real strengths. For instance, they have extensive knowledge of nature. Abby's mother is able to identify most birds by sound and she knows a lot about all of the plants in their ecosystem. As a result, Abby has been raised with a deep appreciation for nature and science. Mr. Bender also shares that Abby's family has had some negative experiences in the past, which have led them to make the choice to live off the grid. He says that he does not agree with all of Abby's parents' beliefs but he understands why they hold those beliefs and he feels genuine respect for them. He encourages Ms. Halpin to get to know Abby's parents before judging them.

Finally, you should evaluate your own practice. Examine your own expectations; do they align with the expectations of your students' cultures? If not, you may need to either rethink some of those expectations or explicitly teach students how to meet your expectations. You should also take time to examine your academic and behavioral data, such as referrals, report cards, and attendance records. If you notice that students from a specific cultural background tend to receive more referrals, fail more exams, or miss school more frequently, then you should spend some time figuring out why this is occurring; cultural influences that you are completely unaware of could be affecting students' performance in your class. In these cases, you can seek advice from colleagues, administrators, and, when appropriate, students' parents. Ask them to look at the data or to come observe you. They may notice something about your practice that is culturally problematic for your students and they may be able to provide suggestions for how you can provide more culturally responsive classroom management.

Cooperation, Not Competition Cooperative relationships among students are also critical for supportive and caring classrooms. Students in competitive environments are less likely to interact in cooperative ways and they are less likely to follow the rules.[16] Instead of fostering competition, you can foster a sense of shared purpose by encouraging students to support one another and by celebrating the diverse talents of different students. One way of focusing on a shared purpose is to emphasize mastery learning as opposed to grades or class rank. For example, if you say, "Wow, Ben, you did better than most other students!" you have just taught Ben that he is in competition with his peers. However, if you say, "Wow, Ben, I can see that you really have developed a strong understanding of this concept! Do you think you could explain how you did this to your group?" you have just taught Ben that mastering the content is important and that he can play a role in helping others master that content. When the focus is on extrinsic indicators of learning, such as grades, then students have an incentive to inhibit one another's learning in order to advance their own position; when the focus is on collective learning goals, then students have an incentive to support one another.

Teach Communication and Cooperation Skills Students cooperate and support one another better when they are explicitly taught how to communicate and work together effectively. You can foster more productive cooperative activities by teaching students to actively listen to one another, to criticize constructively, and to resolve conflicts. In group activities, assigning roles within the group (e.g., recorder, materials manager, etc.) can also help minimize conflict.

Provide Engaging Instruction

Providing effective and engaging instruction is one of the most powerful ways to promote positive behavior and prevent inappropriate behavior. When students are engaged in academics, they are unlikely to be simultaneously engaged in inappropriate behaviors.[17] Engaging instruction includes the following:

- ▶ Creates frequent opportunities for success
- ▶ Moves quickly
- ▶ Uses interesting and varied materials

Creating Frequent Opportunities for Success   Success is intrinsically rewarding so lessons that provide many opportunities to succeed are reinforcing for students and may lead to higher engagement and better behavior.[18] Creating many opportunities for success does not require you to lower your expectations but it does require you to teach concepts at the students' instructional level and provide frequent opportunities for students to demonstrate mastery as you teach. For example, when teaching a concept that has multiple steps, you can provide multiple opportunities for students to demonstrate mastery of each individual step before moving to the next step and before requiring students to demonstrate mastery of the concept as a whole.

Moving Quickly   Fast-paced instruction can increase on-task behavior and student responses. When teachers increase the instructional pace, they tend to provide more frequent opportunities for students to engage with content and more frequent opportunities for students to succeed.[19] A brisk pace communicates to students that time for learning is important and should not be wasted.[20] Teachers often believe that they should slow down when students lack understanding but this is a mistake; although you may choose to spend more time on a concept that students struggle with, the pace at which you engage students with that concept should be brisk.[21] Whole-class and mixed-responding techniques can be used to provide fast-paced, successful opportunities for students to be engaged.

Whole-Class and Mixed-Responding Techniques

Many novice teachers use only one type of responding technique to engage their students: they call on individual students. This is one of the most ineffective ways to engage students because only one student at a time can participate. Whole-class and mixed-responding techniques engage multiple students simultaneously and are thus more effective at providing frequent opportunities for students to experience success.

Whole-class responding techniques allow you to quickly scan the room and determine who understands the concept and who needs more instruction. You can then adjust instruction according to students' needs by spending more time on the concept if many students are still struggling or by moving to a new concept if most students have mastered it. When you monitor and adjust instruction according to students' needs, you are more likely to offer instruction at an appropriate level for all students and more students will be engaged as a result. Table 7.2 shows some whole-class responding techniques.

Table 7.2 Whole-Class Responding Techniques

Technique	Definition	Best for	Example
Choral responding	The whole class answers a question out loud at the same time.	• Repetitive memorization activities • Questions that have simple answers	*Mr. Lin wants students to memorize their times tables. He rapidly asks them a series of multiplication questions and requires all students to answer simultaneously.*
Thumbs up, thumbs down	Students respond to a question with thumbs up or a thumbs down.	• Yes or no questions • Agree or disagree • True or false	*When reviewing for a social studies test, Mr. Hanson makes a series of statements. Students use thumbs up or thumbs down to signal whether the statement is true or false. Students then explain to their partners why the answer was true or false.*
Signaling	Students respond to a question by holding up a certain number of fingers.	• Multiple-choice questions	*Ms. Nelson puts the following key on the board: 1. noun; 2. verb; 3. adjective. Ms. Nelson points to words in a sentence and students hold up the appropriate number of fingers in response. When all students have answered, Ms. Nelson asks one member of each group to share the correct answer with the group.*
Response cards	Students use dry-erase markers to write their answers to questions on small whiteboards or on laminated paper. Students then hold up their answer.	• Short answers • Math problems • Visual answers	*In algebra, students solve for x on scratch paper, then write their answers on response cards. They all hold up their response cards at the same time. Mr. Garcia scans the room, asks one randomly selected student to explain the correct answer to the class, and moves on to the next question. He does this until the majority of students are consistently answering correctly.*

However, whole-class responding techniques may not always be appropriate. For instance, the answer to a reading comprehension question is unlikely to fit onto a small whiteboard. In these cases, a mixture of group and individual responding techniques may be more effective at promoting appropriate behavior than individuals responding alone.[22] Table 7.3 show a few examples of the many different mixed-responding techniques.

(Continued)

Table 7.3 Mixed-Responding Techniques

Technique	Definition	Best for	Example
Think-pair-share	Students think about a complex question and discuss their answers with a partner. Call on random students to share their answers.	Answers that will differ from one student to another, such as the following: • Justifying an opinion • Making a plan • Developing an idea	*After reading an editorial, Ms. Munoz asks her students to think about one part of the author's argument they agree with and why they agree. She gives students a think sheet and one minute to process their thoughts. She instructs students to discuss their thoughts with their partners. She then calls on randomly selected students to share.*
Signal and share	Students first signal their answers simultaneously, then share individually.	• Explaining an answer that can be signaled	*Mr. Oblanksy asks students to signal true or false using a thumbs up or thumbs down. When all students have signaled, he calls on two randomly selected students to share why they chose their answers.*

Using Interesting and Varied Materials   No matter what responding technique you use, your instruction should use high-interest materials. Teachers can make content more interesting by relating it to topics that students care about and by demonstrating how it will benefit students. Activities may be more interesting when they are varied so that students are not required to do any one type of activity (e.g., independent seat work, group work) for long periods of time.

Tier Two: Small-Group Academic and Behavioral Interventions

In spite of strong efforts to prevent behavioral challenges, some students (15 to 20 percent) will still struggle to meet the behavioral expectations that you have set for your class and will need more intensive behavioral support.[23] Students who persistently engage in inappropriate behaviors that are not dangerous to themselves or others may benefit from tier two behavioral interventions. Common tier two behavioral interventions include the following:

▶ Reteaching rules and expectations
▶ Social skills instruction
▶ Check-in/check-out systems

Reteaching Rules and Expectations

If some students consistently struggle with a behavioral skill, you may need to reteach this skill in a small-group setting. The students may have forgotten what the behavioral expectations are in a particular context or they may not have mastered the skill in the first place. For instance, if three students in your class consistently break the uniform policy, you might consider doing a small-group activity in which they classify various clothing items as acceptable and unacceptable. If some students consistently run in the hallway, you can provide additional instruction in appropriate hallway behavior with opportunities to practice and additional supervision.

Social Skills Instruction

Some students may have persistent problems with social interactions. In these cases, targeted instruction in social skills may be required. For example, a particular social group may be especially prone to conflict and might benefit from small-group instruction in conflict management. Several students may struggle to make friends because of social skills deficits and may benefit from a safe, supportive place to engage in guided social interactions during lunch. Tier two social skills instruction should be targeted to the needs of students with mild social skills deficits.

Check-in/Check-out Systems

Another option for students who persistently struggle with mild, inappropriate behaviors is check-in/check-out systems, in which a staff member with whom the student has a strong relationship holds students accountable for their behavior on a daily or weekly basis. This intervention may be most effective for students whose inappropriate behavior helps them to obtain attention.[24] Check-in/check-out systems usually involve a behavior rating system in which the student's teachers record information about the student's behavior on a paper that the student hands in to the intervention coordinator and to parents. The intervention coordinator or the parents then provide rewards or consequences based on the student's behavior. These rewards and consequences should be determined in advance through a behavior contract. For instance, if Maria struggles with talking in class, her behavior contract might be as shown in exhibit 7.2. The behavior rating system associated with this contract might appear as shown in exhibit 7.3.

Exhibit 7.2   Behavior Contract

I, _____, will strive to attend to lessons in class. I will strive to raise my hand when I want to talk in class, and talk out of turn one time or less per class period. If I am able to achieve my goal for four out of five classes on a given day, I may select one of the rewards listed below. If I achieve my goal in fewer than two out of five classes on a given day, I will spend five minutes of my lunchtime working on an assignment that I didn't attend to.

Exhibit 7.3   Check-in, Check-out

Class	Number of Times Hand Raised	Number of Times Talking	Teacher Initials and Comments
Math			
Reading			
Science			
Social Studies			
Writing			
	I achieved my goal in ___ out of five classes on _____ (date). Student signature: _____ Parent signature: _____		

Principles of Effective Rewards

Reward systems, such as those used for students in check-in/check-out interventions, are more likely to be effective if the rewards meet the criteria for effective rewards.

▶ Rewards are intended to recognize appropriate behavior, not punish inappropriate behavior. Therefore, rewards should always be stated positively, as something that is earned, not something that is taken away. For instance, remind Beatriz that she can "earn five minutes of computer time" by finishing her assignment but do not tell her that she will "lose computer time" if she doesn't finish.

▶ Several reward choices should be available because, if only one reward is possible, then the student may tire of this reward or the student may have days when this reward is not motivating; if the only reward available is food, what happens when Kyle is not hungry? Options increase the likelihood that one of the rewards will be motivating.

▶ The rewards should be selected by the student to ensure that they are motivating to him or her. Giving Billy basketball time is unlikely to be effective if he doesn't like sports.

▶ Rewards should be as small and infrequent as necessary to motivate the student. If, for instance, ten minutes on an iPod at the end of the day is enough to motivate Joseph to change his off-task behavior, then ten minutes at the end of every class is unnecessary.

▶ Rewards should always be delivered as soon after the desired behavior as possible. If Isaiah meets his goals today and you don't reward him until a week later, he is unlikely to associate the reward with the behavior.

▶ Rewards should be faded as soon as they are no longer necessary to maintain the appropriate behavior. You can help facilitate this process by focusing students on intrinsic rewards for good behavior. For example, Anthony may receive computer time in exchange for work completion but you can focus on intrinsic rewards by asking him, "Anthony, how does it feel when you finish your work on time?"

No matter which tier two intervention strategy you select, you must monitor the effectiveness of the intervention. To do this, you will need to collect data on the behavior. If the student's behavior does not change in a reasonable time frame, you should check to ensure that the intervention is being implemented accurately. If not, then you need to assess and remedy any barriers to implementation; if it is being implemented accurately and is still not working, then you will need to try either another tier two intervention or you will need to progress to a third tier intervention. These decisions should be made as a team with parental involvement.

Tier Three: Individualized Interventions

When students do not respond to tier two interventions or when their behaviors are severe enough to cause safety concerns, a tier three intervention is warranted. In spite of excellent preventive efforts, some students (1 to 5 percent) may present extreme challenges to order and safety in the school; they may destroy classroom environments, hurt other children, become violent, or try to hurt themselves. Alternatively, they may withdraw, hide, and avoid social interactions in spite of their teachers' best efforts to engage them. Frequently, these students have emotional or behavioral disabilities, including psychiatric diagnoses such as bipolar disorder, depression, or oppositional defiant disorder. These students require the support of caring teachers who believe that they can be successful and who have expertise in conducting functional behavioral assessments (FBAs). In this section, we provide a brief overview of the following:

- ▶ The FBA process
- ▶ Principles for developing function-based interventions
- ▶ Common, evidence-based interventions

The FBA Process

FBA is an evidence-based procedure for assessing severe problem behaviors. Federal law states that all students with special needs who exhibit persistent problem behaviors must have an FBA and a behavior plan that is based on that FBA.[25] The FBA process can seem daunting at first, but it is actually based on the very simple premise that all behaviors have a purpose or function; all humans do certain things because those things have helped them in some way in the past. You may say *please* when you ask for something because this behavior has generally been more effective at getting you what you want than demanding; you may smile when greeting a friend because this behavior has generally led to more positive interactions than if you scowl; you may go to the kitchen when you are hungry because this behavior has generally led you to food that satisfied your hunger. An FBA is a systematic way of thinking about how a student's extreme behaviors may help the student achieve something that he or she wants. An FBA has two major steps:

- ▶ Defining the problem behavior
- ▶ Determining the function or purpose of that behavior

Defining the Problem Behavior   The first step in doing an FBA is to determine what the target behavior is: What does the student do that is problematic in school? Note that if you are changing a behavior it should be something that is a problem, not something that is merely abnormal; students may engage in many unusual behaviors that are not problematic. If Blake works best while standing at the back of the room, and this behavior does not cause problems for his academic performance or for other students' access to instruction, then it is not necessary to complete an FBA for this behavior. However, if Blake goes through other students' belongings while working at the back of the room, then this behavior is a problem.

If a behavior is a problem, then it should be identified clearly, using an objective and observable language.[26] If MaryEllen throws books and curses, say, "MaryEllen throws books and curses," not "MaryEllen has a fit." When behavioral problems are stated clearly, they can be observed and measured more easily; different observers might disagree about what constitutes a fit but they are unlikely to disagree about whether MaryEllen has thrown a book or cursed. Agreement about a behavior allows the team of people working with a student to communicate clearly with one another and with the student.

Determining the Function or Purpose of That Behavior   Once a problem behavior has been defined, you need to determine what function it serves. What does the student get from the behavior? Consider the following example:

> Sam is a ninth-grade student who gets good grades in math and science but generally gets Ds and Fs in language arts. In his English class, Mr. Lingstrom tells the class to get

their books out. Sam gets his out. The teacher then tells Sam to read a passage aloud. Sam punches his desk, throws his book, and says, "F*** you, I'm not doing shit!" Mr. Lingstrom sends Sam to the principal's office, and Sam is sent to in-school suspension for the remainder of the day.

What purpose did Sam's behavior serve? Is he just a jerky kid? Or did he achieve something that he wanted? To determine the function of a behavior, you need to observe the antecedents (what came before) and the consequences (what comes after) of the behavior. An ABC (antecedent, behavior, consequence) chart, as shown in table 7.4, can help you organize your observations.[27]

Note that Sam followed directions when he was told to open his book. He only behaved inappropriately when he was told to read aloud. Sam's behavior was triggered by the direction to read in public, and it helped him escape from this activity. In this case, Sam avoided potential embarrassment by cursing at Mr. Lingstrom. He does poorly in reading and doesn't want to reveal this fact to the rest of the class. Sam has learned that acting inappropriately—by cursing, punching, and throwing things—allows him to escape a task that is highly unpleasant for him. In technical terms, the function of his behavior is to escape from an aversive activity, reading aloud. Over the course of his school years, Sam may have missed a lot of class time because this strategy has worked so well. This missed class time only exacerbates his struggles in reading as he falls further and further behind his peers.

In Sam's case, an observation was helpful to understanding the function of his behavior but observation is only one possible method of data collection. Other methods include the following:

▶ Interviews with teachers, parents, the student, and sometimes peers can help you to better understand what function the behavior serves. Interviewees can provide information about what behaviors are of concern, when the problem behaviors do and do not occur, and why they believe the behaviors occur.

▶ A review of the student's records can also help to isolate when the problem began and when it is most likely to occur.[28] Sam's disciplinary record, for example, likely shows a pattern of high rates of discipline referrals during reading class and low rates in math.

When students engage in high-intensity, low-frequency behaviors, it may be impossible to observe the behavior as it happens, and these other methods of data collection may be your primary source of information about the behavior.[29] If, for instance, Zack bites other students one to two times per month, then his behavior does not occur frequently enough for you to observe it within a reasonable observation time frame but you can gather information from others who happened to be present during an incident. These other observers can complete an ABC chart after the fact, and you can interview them to obtain greater depth of information about the antecedents and consequences of this behavior.

Table 7.4 ABC Chart

Antecedent	Behavior	Consequence
Sam's teacher told him to open his book.	Sam opened his book.	Class continued.
Sam's teacher asked him to read aloud.	Sam punched his desk, threw his book, and cursed at his teacher.	Sam was sent out of the room and did not have to read aloud. He spent the day in suspension.

Exhibit 7.4   Common Behavioral Functions

The functions of most behaviors fall within six categories, encompassed by the function matrix: they may help students to avoid attention, objects, activities, or sensory experiences, or they may help students to access attention, objects, activities, or sensory experiences. After completing an ABC chart, the function matrix, as shown here, can help you determine the purpose of the behavior you've observed. This matrix represents these six possible functions, and can help you think about which one is relevant for your student.

Function Matrix[30]

	Access	Avoid
Attention		
Tangibles and activities		Sam avoids reading aloud.
Sensory		

Sometimes the relationship between behaviors and their functions may be more complex:

- ► Behaviors may have multiple functions: talking in class may help Amanda to access peer attention *and* avoid class work.
- ► Some behaviors may have different functions in different contexts: kicking students on the playground may help Jacob to avoid peer interactions, whereas kicking students in class may help him to access adult attention.
- ► A variety of behaviors may all have the same function: Carla may scream, hit, sleep, and talk in order to avoid schoolwork.

To address these complex situations, you should collect data about the student's behavior in all of the settings in which it occurs.

Principles for Developing Function-Based Interventions

When the function of a behavior is known, you are able to address it much more effectively. Researchers have repeatedly found that when interventions are based on the function of a behavior, they are more effective than interventions that are designed without considering behavioral functions.[31] Function-based interventions (FBIs) are organized plans for teaching students how to replace their inappropriate behavior with a behavior that is more acceptable, but that also achieves the same function. Developing an FBI requires two steps:

- ► Choose an appropriate replacement behavior
- ► Select an intervention strategy

Choosing an Appropriate Replacement Behavior   The first step of an FBI is selecting an acceptable replacement behavior. The replacement behavior must achieve the same function as the problem behavior and it should be acceptable to all members of the students' team. Consider the following example.

Liam is a very active third-grader, who seems to move constantly; he runs around the perimeter of the room, he jumps up when he raises his hand, he taps his pen, he kicks the desk in front of him, and he rocks his chair on the rare occasions that he sits in it. He is very smart but never seems to finish any assignments. The special education teacher, Mr. Giani, conducts an FBA and determines that the function of Liam's behavior is to allow him to move (accessing sensory). In the intervention plan, Mr. Giani states that the replacement behavior is "Liam will stay quietly in his seat." He offers Liam incentives for every period that he stays in his seat. The plan has been in place for two weeks now but Liam has not earned a single reward.

What did Mr. Giani do wrong? His major error was that he chose a replacement behavior that did not achieve the same function as the problem behavior. Liam's behavior allows him to move, whereas staying quietly in his seat does not allow him to move at all.

Mr. Giani consults the district behavior specialist, Ms. Hendricks, who writes a new replacement behavior: "Liam will move in class using sensory tools and appropriate spaces." She gives Liam a box of quiet sensory tools, such as theraputty, and teaches him that when the teacher is talking he may play with any of these tools while he attends to the lesson. She ties a theraband around the legs of his chair and teaches him to kick this band when he wants to move his feet. She gives him a clipboard, puts a line of tape on the floor at the back of the room, and teaches him that he may complete independent work on the clipboard while walking on the line of tape. She also works with the classroom teacher to assign Liam classroom tasks that involve movement, such as collecting books at the end of a lesson and erasing the board.

Liam clearly needs to move frequently, and Ms. Hendricks has created ways for him to move that are appropriate in the classroom. Rather than kicking another student's desk, he kicks a theraband; rather than tapping his pencil, he plays with theraputty; rather than running around the perimeter of the classroom, he walks his line of tape while working.

> Recall the case of Sam, who threw books, cursed, and punched his desk to escape from having to read aloud. What replacement behavior would you select for Sam? Remember that the replacement behavior must achieve the same function as his problem behavior: in his case, it must allow him to escape from the embarrassment of reading aloud in front of peers.
>
> A good behavior for Sam might be speaking with his teachers at the beginning of the school year to tell them how he feels about reading aloud. If a situation arises in which reading aloud is an essential part of a lesson, the teacher can alert Sam in advance, so that he has an opportunity to practice the relevant passage with his special education teacher before he is required to read in front of peers. Sam's special education team may also decide to provide Sam with remediation in reading. Sam is thus able to use appropriate behaviors to avoid the embarrassment of reading poorly in front of his peers.

Selecting an Intervention Strategy Once you have selected an appropriate replacement behavior, the next step is to determine how to get the student to do this replacement behavior. As you think about how to proceed, two questions may help you direct your efforts:

▶ Can the student perform the replacement behavior?
  No: Your intervention must teach the student how to do the behavior and reinforce the student for doing the behavior more accurately than in the past.
  Yes: Proceed to question two.

► Is the setting in which the behavior occurs run effectively?

No: Your intervention must involve working with staff to improve the setting. See tier one classroom management strategies for ideas.

Yes: If the answer to both questions is yes, then your intervention must change the antecedents and consequences that maintain the behavior.[32]

Example: Selecting an Intervention Strategy

William is a first-grade student who is very popular in his class. At lunchtime, Ms. Minos has witnessed William eating food off of the floor, pinching girls, and throwing paper airplanes. Other students watch and laugh when he does this. More seriously, he has been in two fights. Many other students gathered to watch the fights because William told them that Will Smith was coming. Ms. Minos decides that the function of William's behavior is to access peer attention and that the replacement behavior should be getting attention in more appropriate ways.

Ms. Minos now needs to select an intervention strategy that will get William to seek attention appropriately. She asks herself if he knows how to do the replacement behavior and she observes that William often does get peer attention appropriately. Therefore, she decides that he does know how to do the replacement behavior. Ms. Minos next asks herself if the environment is structured effectively and she decides that it is; William's teachers are using evidence-based practices and there is adequate supervision.

Therefore, because William knows how to do the replacement behavior and the setting is run effectively, Ms. Minos decides to adjust the contingencies associated with William's behavior so that he gets more peer attention for appropriate behaviors and less for inappropriate behaviors. She decides to actively create opportunities for William to get a lot of peer attention. She sets up a reward menu for William, which states that if William behaves appropriately during recess, he is allowed to put on a small show in the cafeteria during lunch. Ms. Minos also assigns him leadership roles in class, such as collecting lunch money and passing out materials. William clearly has strong leadership and social skills; rather than punishing William, Ms. Minos channels these skills into more appropriate directions.

Common Evidence-Based Interventions

Interventions should be tailored to the function of a student's behavior; no one intervention will be effective for every single student. However, some interventions have a strong evidence base. These interventions entail the following:

► Teach the student to do the replacement behavior

► Alter the antecedent conditions or the consequences of the behavior

All interventions are most effective when they are implemented within an effectively run environment; therefore, you should also consider whether the environment needs to change to support the intervention.

Teach the Student to Do the Replacement Behavior For students to do the replacement behavior, they must first know how to do it. If they don't know how to do it, you need to teach them. Depending on the behavior and the student's skills and needs, you may teach the replacement behavior using direct instruction, a cognitive behavioral intervention, or social skills instruction.

Cognitive behavioral interventions (CBIs) have been effective with students with emotional and behavioral disabilities.[33] CBIs teach students to regulate their own behavior by changing their thought processes. For instance, if Xavier becomes violent in order to relieve frustration, a CBI might teach him to identify the triggers that cause him frustration and to consciously change the way he thinks about these triggers. CBIs focus on changing students' inner dialogue, or self-talk.

To implement a CBI, you will need to provide direct instruction in the strategy you want the student to use. Direct instruction involves (1) modeling self-talk associated with the strategy, (2) providing cues to remind the student of the steps in the strategy, and (3) conducting role-plays to help the student practice using the strategy. Additionally, you need to provide feedback when you see the student using the strategy and provide opportunities for students to reflect on how he or she used the strategy and whether or not it was effective.[34]

Sample CBI Strategy

If Rebecca curses when she is confused by her schoolwork, you can teach her to change the way she thinks about confusing assignments by ABC-ING:

▶ *A B*ig breath!
▶ *C*onfusion is okay and normal.
▶ *I* can learn this!
▶ *N*ow try.
▶ *G*ood job! or ask for help.

Some students' behavioral challenges may stem from deficient social skills. For example, if Jose struggles to understand other students' body language, he may feel threatened when other students are near him and respond violently. If Kyle does not know how to join group conversations, he may feel excluded from group activities and be mean to other students as a result. In these situations, students must be explicitly taught appropriate social skills.

You can instruct students in appropriate social skills using direct instruction by teaching them the appropriate social behavior, modeling it, allowing them to role-play the behavior, and then reinforcing them for performing it correctly. For example, if Tyler hides because he doesn't understand other students' emotions and therefore finds social situations confusing, you can teach him to recognize the meanings of different facial expressions and you can teach him some appropriate ways to respond. You might show him pictures of emotional expressions such as happy, sad, confused, or angry, and have him repeatedly identify these emotions using flashcards or pictures from a magazine. You can help him practice responding to these emotions in appropriate ways using role-plays, and you can support him in structured interactions with "safe" peers before expecting him to interact in more complex situations, such as the playground.

In some cases, it may be appropriate to use CBIs to help students self-regulate their social behaviors. Tyler, for example, might benefit from a step-by-step strategy that helps him to assess his peers' emotional expressions and select an appropriate response. You could teach him to STTAR:

1. *St*op: What is the other person feeling?
2. *T*hink: How can I respond respectfully?

3. *Try it!*
4. *Assess: How did it go?*
5. *Repeat!*

Alter the Antecedent Conditions or the Consequences of the Behavior   If a student already knows how to do the replacement behavior, and the environment is effective, then you need to adjust the contingencies that maintain the behavior by changing the antecedents or the consequences. When you adjust the contingencies, keep the function of the behavior in mind. If Jamie's behavior helps him escape from math class, then ignoring the behavior is unlikely to be effective. If, however, Jamie's behavior functions to get the teacher's attention, then ignoring the inappropriate behavior may be effective. There are two different ways that you can adjust the contingencies:

▶ You can adjust the antecedents.
▶ You can adjust the consequences.

Antecedent-Focused Interventions   Antecedent-focused interventions prevent the behavior from occurring by changing the conditions that led to the behavior. For instance, if Henry bangs his head against the wall in noisy environments in order to escape from them, then an antecedent-focused intervention would focus on making the environment a quiet place to learn. If Fabian runs from school in order to escape a student whom he fears, then an antecedent-focused intervention would either eliminate all possibilities for him to encounter that student or help him create a more positive, trusting relationship with that student.

When students' behaviors function to help them escape from academic tasks, academic interventions are an effective antecedent-focused intervention. Recall the case of Sam, who cursed, threw things, and punched his desk in order to escape from having to read aloud. Providing Sam remediated reading instruction would eliminate the need for him to escape from reading aloud. Similarly, if Lisa sleeps in math class in order to avoid math instruction, then an effective intervention would include, among other components, remediation in math and additional support during math instruction.

Consequence-Focused Interventions   Interventions that are focused on consequences should do two things:

▶ They should eliminate reinforcement for the inappropriate behavior.
▶ They should provide extra reinforcement for the replacement behavior.

When the plan is first implemented, it is critical to provide a lot of extra reinforcement for the replacement behavior. This reinforcement can then be slowly reduced as the student becomes increasingly adept at the replacement behavior.

Planned ignoring is an effective and common strategy for students whose behavior helps them access attention. When doing planned ignoring, teachers simply follow these guidelines:

▶ Ignore the inappropriate behavior (eliminating reinforcement for inappropriate behaviors).
▶ Provide extra attention for appropriate behaviors (reinforcing the replacement behaviors).

The first couple of times that you do planned ignoring, the student's behavior may get worse rather than better as the student tries harder to access the reinforcement that he or she is used to. If you give in and provide attention during this process, you will make the situation worse because this teaches the student that escalation is effective at getting your attention. However, providing extra attention for appropriate behaviors should help ameliorate this problem.

Eliminating reinforcement is especially difficult when a student's behavior functions to get peer attention. Recall the case of William, who told students that Will Smith would be videotaping his fights at recess. In his case, William's teachers created special opportunities for him to secure positive peer attention instead of behaving inappropriately. In other situations, you may choose to actively recruit peer support for the behavior plan (permission from the student's parent should be obtained prior to doing this). For example, if Allison throws spit wads, crawls on the floor, and barks in order to get peer attention, you might consider recruiting peers to pay attention to her when she is behaving appropriately and to ignore her when she engages in these behaviors. You may need to provide peers with some kind of reinforcement for assisting with the behavior plan because ignoring those types of behaviors may be challenging.

Other behaviors may have different functions and require different adjustments of the contingencies:

▶ If Calvin has learned that people give him a stuffed animal when he screams, withhold the stuffed animal when he screams and give it to him when he asks for it politely.

▶ If Victoria has learned that hitting other students leads to in-school suspension (ISS) with a teacher she likes, let her go to ISS as a reward when she has demonstrated an appropriate behavior.

▶ If Luke has learned that ripping up his paper allows him to escape from math class, laminate his math work, provide an escape card that allows him to take a short break once every ten minutes during math class, and provide more supportive math instruction.

In some cases, it is impossible to deny reinforcement for the problem behavior. For instance, if Greg runs into walls in order to access sensory stimulation, then his behavior is maintained by a reinforcer (the feeling of running into a wall) that you cannot control. In this case, you must put extra energy into providing reinforcement before the inappropriate behavior occurs. So, if Greg usually runs into walls after lunchtime, take him out of lunch a few minutes early and provide him with an appropriate sensory experience that mimics the one he is seeking. An occupational therapist can help design this activity to meet Greg's individual sensory needs.

For high-frequency behaviors, it may be appropriate to use a structured reinforcement system in which a student's behaviors are tracked throughout the school day and reinforcement is provided at regularly specified intervals. These systems provide structure and predictability for students, they help teachers remember when and how to reinforce students, and they can also be used to track behavioral changes over time. These systems can be structured in a number of different ways, depending on the student's needs and ability level:

▶ Some systems use points to reinforce students. These points are then exchanged for rewards at a later time. Rewards should meet the criteria listed in the "Principles of Effective Rewards" section.

▶ Others use objects, such as fake money, instead of points, to meet the needs of students who process concretely. These objects are then traded for rewards at a later time.

▶ For students who are unable to delay gratification for a later time, these systems may provide immediate rewards rather than using points or objects in an exchange system.

▶ A self-monitoring component, in which students monitor their own behaviors, should be included when possible.

Such systems should be tailored to the individual needs of the student. The point sheet shown in exhibit 7.5 can be used with any student who understands numbers.

Exhibit 7.5   Sample Point Sheet

Safe hands: +1 point
Kind words: +1 point
Work completed: +2 points
Organized materials: +2 points
Cross out numbers to demonstrate how many points a student has earned.

1 2 3 4 5 6 7 8 9 10 11 12 13 14 15 16 17 18 19

20 21 22 23 24 25 26 27 28 29 30 31 32 33 34 35

35 points = choice of:

Five minutes computer time	Time with Ms. Debbie
Positive phone call home	Reward from treasure chest
Play basketball outside	Play with class pet

Older students with more skills may be able to handle more complex reinforcement systems. For example, the point sheet in exhibit 7.6 requires the student to self-monitor four different behaviors and score his own behavior on a scale from 0 to 2. It also requires the student to calculate the percentage of points earned and correlate those with information located elsewhere. Therefore, this system would only be appropriate for a student with more advanced skills.

Exhibit 7.6   Sample Point Sheet

	I sought attention appropriately	I was on task during class	I used kind language	I used a strategy from my list if I felt frustrated
Math:	S: 0 1 2	S: 0 1 2	S: 0 1 2	S: 0 1 2
	T: 0 1 2	T: 0 1 2	T: 0 1 2	T: 0 1 2
Reading:	S: 0 1 2	S: 0 1 2	S: 0 1 2	S: 0 1 2
	T: 0 1 2	T: 0 1 2	T: 0 1 2	T: 0 1 2

S = Student ratings of his or her own behavior

T = Teacher ratings of the student's behavior

0 = The student did this behavior for less than half of the class period.

1 = The student did this behavior for at least half of the class period.

2 = The student did this behavior for the whole class period.

95% of points = privileges from gold sheet

85% of points = privileges from green sheet

75% of points = privileges from yellow sheet

< 75% of points = no privileges today

Point systems can be completed daily and sent home to parents so that the student's entire team knows how the student is making progress toward his or her behavior goals. The points earned can also be graphed so that long-term trends in behavior, such as consistent improvements or declines, are more easily observed and analyzed.

Incorporating self-monitoring into FBIs increases their efficacy.[35] Depending on the behavior of concern, students may keep a tally of appropriate and inappropriate behaviors, they may rate their behavior on a scale, or they may track the duration of a behavior. This helps students to become more aware of their behaviors. Here are some examples:

▶ If Leah struggles to stay on task, provide her with a timer that vibrates every five minutes. When it vibrates, Leah records on a form whether she was on task.

▶ If Silas struggles to manage frustration, he can use self-monitoring to rate how frustrated he felt during a class and to list what strategies he used.

Self-monitoring can be challenging for students and must be explicitly taught, reinforced, and monitored.

Restraints

In some cases, the problem behavior is physically dangerous to the student, peers, or teachers. When this is the case, you may have to intervene physically in order to protect yourself and your students. However, you should never intervene physically unless you have been trained to do so because physical restraints can be dangerous to students and staff; students have died during improperly conducted restraints. Restraints are a very serious form of intervention and they should only be used to ensure safety. Restraints are *not* intended to enforce compliance, to punish students, or even to protect school property.[36]

If you find that restraints are becoming common in a setting, you should consider evaluating that setting to determine why they are occurring. It is possible that they are being misused or that they can be prevented through more effective classroom management and better relationships between students and staff. Safety should always be a paramount consideration but you should never rely heavily on restraints to ensure safety.

EVALUATING THE INTERVENTION

Once you have an intervention in place, you must assess its effectiveness by collecting data on a student's behavioral progress. The problem behavior and the replacement behavior should be systematically measured. If behaviors improve within a reasonable time, then the intervention has been effective and your next challenge is to ensure that the team continues to implement the intervention for as long as the student requires it. If behaviors do not improve within a reasonable time, then the intervention has not been effective and you must evaluate why it failed. You should first consider whether the intervention was implemented accurately; if it was not, the team should evaluate and address any barriers to implementation. If the intervention was implemented accurately but was ineffective, you should ask yourself the following questions:

▶ Was the function accurate?
▶ Did the replacement behavior achieve the same function as the problem behavior?

► Does the student know how to do the replacement behavior yet?

► Does the classroom provide adequate reinforcement for the replacement behavior?

► Is the classroom environment effective?

The answers to these questions will determine how the team decides to move forward.

TO SUM UP

► Effective classroom managers focus on preventing behavior challenges.

► You can prevent most students (80 to 85 percent) from engaging in inappropriate behavior by doing the following:

- Setting up the classroom environment effectively
- Establishing clear and reasonable rules, expectations, and procedures
- Creating a caring classroom community
- Providing engaging instruction

► Some students (10 to 15 percent) will need more intensive support, including opportunities to relearn the rules, social skills instruction, and check-in/check-out systems.

► For students with more severe behavioral needs (1 to 5 percent), you will need to assess the function of their behavior and provide intensive function-based interventions.

WHAT'S NEXT?

Now that you have the essentials of classroom management, it's time to think in more depth about how you can provide supportive instruction for all of your students.

ADDITIONAL RESOURCES

TIER ONE

► A series of video demonstrations of tier one classroom management strategies: https://louisville .edu/education/srp/abri/primarylevel/focus/behavior

► A series of video demonstrations of the application of tier one strategies with students with autism: https://louisville.edu/education/srp/abri/primarylevel/student/asd_msd

► A series of video demonstrations of engaging instructional strategies: https://louisville.edu /education/srp/abri/primarylevel/classroom/group

► Video demonstrations of tier one classroom management strategies: www.teachingchannel.org /videos?landing_page=Classroom1Culture1Behavior1Landing1Page&gclid=CPjhpsHzm7ACF QFeTAodcwtyWg

► Database of awards and certificates that can be used in a reward system: www.teachervision.fen .com/awards/resource/6076.html?detoured=1

► A series of webinars and tutorials on classroom management: http://iris.peabody.vanderbilt.edu /tutorials.html

TIER TWO

▶ Database of resources for conflict resolution: www.teachervision.fen.com/safety/teaching-methods/55815.html?detoured=1

▶ Database of forms that can be adapted when implementing tier two and tier three interventions: www.teachervision.fen.com/classroom-discipline/resource/6283.html?detoured=1

▶ Database of resources for implementing check-in/check-out programs: http://miblsi.cenmi .org/MiBLSiModel/Implementation/ElementarySchools/TierIISupports/Behavior/Target BehaviorInterventions/CheckInCheckOut.aspx

▶ Guidance and resources for conducting effective social skills instruction: www.pbisworld.com /tier-1/teach-social-skills

TIER THREE

▶ A tutorial on understanding behavior: http://serc.gws.uky.edu/pbis

▶ A series of resources on conducting FBAs and FBIs: http://cecp.air.org/fba/default.asp

▶ Resources on conducting effective FBAs and FBIs: http://cte.jhu.edu/courses/pbis/ses5_act3 _pag1.shtml

▶ Resources on conducting effective FBAs and FBIs, including case studies, forms, and tutorials: www.specialconnections.ku.edu/~kucrl/cgi-bin/drupal/?q=behavior_plans

CHAPTER EIGHT

Collaboration and Co-Teaching

In this chapter you will learn about:

- Fundamentals of collaboration
- How collaboration works in various service delivery models
- How to work in inclusive settings
- How to effectively communicate, plan, and keep records in collaboration
- How to help others adapt and modify curriculum and teach effective behaviors
- Different models of co-teaching
- Strategies to aid in successful co-teaching

Sarah, a second-year special education teacher, is co-teaching a fifth-grade social studies class. She is nervous and excited about her new role. Her principal organized common planning time for the two teachers but Sarah is worried about feeling like an outsider in the general education classroom. She knows that Mrs. Stokes, the general education teacher, has been teaching for twenty years, and Sarah wonders if her ideas will be valued. She thinks about her first meeting with Mrs. Stokes and how she will approach the conversation.

Sarah's concerns about her co-teaching role are similar to those of many special educators. Historically, teaching was a more autonomous profession: teachers were the captains of their individual classrooms and had limited working relationships with their colleagues. This is no longer true in many schools. Collaboration is a necessity and not just a preference if the needs of students with disabilities are to be met in general education settings.[1] As a special education teacher, one of your roles is to work with general education colleagues, paraprofessionals, and other service providers.

> *Collaboration with general educators is half of my job. My students are in my classroom only for an hour and spend the rest of the day with their other teachers. It is critical I work with the general education*

teachers to ensure the students receive the services and instruction they need to make growth. By meeting regularly with the general educators, we can pool our knowledge and create strategies together for student success.

Maggie, experienced special education teacher

As more special education students receive services in general education, collaboration is imperative for student success. Although the amount of time required of you will differ depending on your specific job assignment, every effective beginning special education teacher will engage in some collaboration.

FUNDAMENTALS OF COLLABORATION

Anyone who has worked on a group project knows that collaboration isn't always easy. Some people want to complete work early and others delay. Some group members dedicate more time and others do only the minimum required. There is not a special ingredient in education to solve these challenges. During your career you will engage in collaborative relationships with varying levels of ease and difficulty. Marilyn Friend and Lynne Cook outline defining characteristics for collaboration.[2] These apply to all types of collaboration and co-teaching relationships. Understanding these fundamentals is critical to your success as a special education teacher.

DEFINING CHARACTERISTICS FOR COLLABORATION

▶ *Parity:* Parity means *equal.* Each person who participates in collaboration must be an equal partner whose decisions and contributions are equally valued.

▶ *Mutual goals:* All people in collaboration must have at least one mutual goal. This is typically for the student's needs to be met and improve student outcomes. Professionals need not agree on all the strategies to reach the goal but a shared goal helps to focus collaboration and find common ground.

▶ *Voluntary:* People can't be forced into collaboration. Sometimes this happens in school settings because an IEP often necessitates collaboration between special and general educators. If you encounter someone who is completely against collaborating, seek assistance from your administrator.

▶ *Shared responsibility, resources, and accountability:* Share. This seems simple enough but sharing is critical for successful collaboration. Educators actively engage in decision making together, share materials and resources, and share responsibility of student outcomes.

UNDERSTANDING COLLABORATION IN VARIED SERVICE-DELIVERY MODELS

Ideally, the nature and frequency of collaboration will be determined through assessing the services your students need. In different service delivery models, more or less collaboration is necessary. Consider the varied collaboration activities among special educators working in four types of classrooms.

Self-Contained Classroom

Ed's students are in his classroom nearly all day. Five of the eight students receive all academic instruction from Ed. During special activities and lunch, all of the students participate with their grade-level peers. Three students receive some of their instruction from grade-level general education teachers.

To address these varied arrangements, Ed meets weekly with the general education teacher. Ed provides assistance with each student's behavior plan and works with the general education teacher to discuss and problem-solve difficult situations. He also meets daily with the paraprofessional who works in his classroom and periodically with the speech-language pathologist and school counselor, who also provide services to some of his students.

Resource Services

Suzie provides services to students with disabilities in a resource classroom. All of her students have a general education teacher and they attend her classroom for a specified amount of time, typically thirty to ninety minutes. Suzie meets with the four general education teachers weekly to discuss how students are progressing, to identify knowledge and skills areas she can reinforce in the resource classroom, and to identify needed accommodations.

Co-Teaching

Terry is a full-time co-teacher in middle school. He co-teaches with two different general education teachers, Dave and Judith. Dave and Terry co-teach two classes of math and Judith and Terry co-teach three classes of science. Terry shares a common planning time with Judith and the two meet daily to discuss plans and assessments. Terry meets with Dave once a week to co-plan for the following week.

Consultation

Anyana provides consultation for forty-five high school students receiving all of their instruction in general education. She typically meets with all twenty-six general education teachers on a varied basis depending on the needs of the students. She has three students on her caseload who require more frequent collaboration with their respective teachers, so she meets with these teachers biweekly. During the meetings, Anyana discusses student progress, provides assistance with accommodations, and suggests ideas or other services to address students' needs.

Although all four teachers work in different service delivery models, each is responsible for collaborating with at least one general education colleague and often other service providers. Once you receive your job assignment, your first step in collaboration is determining with whom you will need to meet and how often, and the type of information you discuss or exchange.

Response-to-intervention (RTI) is another area in which collaboration is necessary for successful implementation. RTI may exist in different delivery models and many of the guidelines for collaborating in RTI apply to collaborating more generally.

Collaboration in RTI

Ideally, RTI is neither a general education nor a special education initiative but rather a total school initiative with the goal of optimizing instruction for all students, including those who are struggling with language and literacy. Within this framework for identifying and supporting students who experience difficulties, collaboration among educational professionals and with students and their families is imperative for RTI to be successful.[3]

TIPS FOR SPECIAL EDUCATION TEACHERS IN COLLABORATING FOR RTI

Actively participate:

▶ You are only one member of the RTI team but you play an important role.
▶ Be deliberate, intentional, and ongoing in your efforts to make time for collaboration.
▶ Have a dedicated meeting time as well as structure to optimize collaboration.

Encourage a shared vision and common goals:

▶ Use your student data to help form shared vision and goals for collaborative decision making.
▶ Share your resources and expertise to help meet student assessment and instruction goals.
▶ Listen to others. Their knowledge from various backgrounds and training can help the RTI team affect a diverse group of students.

Agree on common language:

▶ Because the language of RTI is complex, be sure to have an open discussion during a collaborative meeting to create a shared language. For example, what do tiers one, two, and three mean to you and your team?
▶ Remember to be sensitive and clear when discussing an issue. Make sure you understand your team members' ideas as well.

Attend training together:

▶ Use multiple forms of trainings to help you strengthen your and your team's collaborative skills and professional knowledge.
▶ Be open to learning strategies from your colleagues or working with your team to adjust strategies based on new information.

Focus on research-based interventions:

▶ Share research-based strategies with colleagues.
▶ Try new strategies offered by other collaborators.

COLLABORATION IN INCLUSIVE SETTINGS

The IEP team determines the extent to which each student participates in the general education settings; however, ongoing collaboration among the team members serving students with disabilities is needed. Good communication and planning take work, and chapter 3 provides specific suggestions for communicating well with the varied individuals you need to work with to ensure strong relationships. Traditional teaching structures must be altered and modified throughout the year in general education settings to facilitate student success. Inclusive settings require collaboration between general and special educators to facilitate student success but it is important to acknowledge that collaboration is not always easy. The following guidelines are important to create strong teacher collaboration and inclusive services for students with disabilities.

Strategically Match Students and Teachers

As much as possible, try to place students in classrooms that most effectively meet their needs. Most scheduling happens prior to the beginning of the school year. Take some time to review student IEPs and records, and have discussions with teachers and paraprofessionals about student needs and possible placements. Other special education teachers, paraprofessionals, counselors, and administrators may provide valuable input and suggestions about creating placements and schedules that work for specific students. As an example, consider Stephen, a fourth-grade student with a disability. Stephen's IEP team met at the end of third grade and determined he would be moved from his self-contained classroom to the general education classroom for all instruction except for a small portion of reading instruction, which he would receive in a resource setting. His previous special education teacher maintained an extremely structured environment with lots of opportunity for positive reinforcement. Stephen began this year with Mrs. Smith. Although Mrs. Smith was positive and excited to have Stephen in her class, she kept a loose instructional schedule, often changing her class's activity schedule during the day to allow more or less time for activities as required. She liked to try new things so students rarely had the same routine. Stephen struggled in this atmosphere, unsure of what to expect, and was often confused. He did not complete his work and often caused behavior disruptions. The IEP team met after nine weeks, and instead of moving Stephen back to a self-contained room, they moved him to Mr. Bankston's room. Mr. Bankston had clearer routines and an instructional schedule that rarely varied. Stephen quickly blossomed in his classroom and had a successful remainder of his fourth-grade year.

Clarify Expectations

When a student moves into an inclusive setting, one of the most important goals is to make certain everyone knows the expectations of everyone involved. All participating parties should be able to identify the expectations for the following:

- ▶ The general education teacher
- ▶ The special education teacher
- ▶ Students
- ▶ The parents
- ▶ General education peers

Clear expectations eliminate confusion and create a positive starting point for collaborative work.

Meet Student Needs in General Education

As a special educator your primary goal is always to meet student needs. The IEP team will determine each student's specific needs and how the needs can be met in general education. You are the center of the process facilitating communication, guiding implementation, and assisting others in providing services. It is critical that student learning goals are clear, including academic, behavioral, social, and any other goals.

Monitor Student Progress

How will you know you are meeting student needs? How will you know that the student is making adequate progress on his or her designated goals? Even if you are following the IEP plan and everyone knows expectations and is providing services, student progress is not ensured. As special educators, we know plans and services often need altering. Monitoring each student's progress will provide information you need to ascertain if students with special needs are in fact demonstrating growth in academic, behavior, and other areas in an inclusive setting. Student data will also assist you in collaborating with other service providers in adjusting instructional or behavioral practices. Ultimately, student progress is essential.

Check Your Bs

Successful inclusive settings necessitate collaboration. As you collaborate with others, certain actions help and others hinder the process. Take some time to think about your own actions and how they reflect on the collaborative process. Use the four Bs to help you.

Believe in the Process

It is critical that you believe the current inclusive setting can be a successful environment for meeting student needs. Remember that collaboration is powerful and has the potential to improve student outcomes.[4] This belief is particularly important to express when serving as the caseload manager and facilitator of collaboration.

Be Understanding

Each service provider brings a different perspective to the table. Perspectives are typically based on a person's preparation, previous experiences, and beliefs.[5] Diversity of viewpoints allows a team to creatively solve challenging situations. However, differing positions can also create struggles in reaching agreements and can disrupt communication. Reflecting on others' perspectives can assist you in keeping communication flowing and successfully facilitating collaboration (for detailed information on communication, see chapter 3).

Be Flexible

Flexibility can aid in working with others. Each person enters the collaborative process with a different set of skills and knowledge. No one person is always correct. You may not always agree that an idea is the best one but compromising and willing to try new strategies will assist you in the overall process.

Be Respectful

As the special education teacher, you are the case manager of the student and most often the leader of a collaborative effort. In this role, it is essential to maintain respect for others you are partnering with and remember you are all equal partners in meeting the needs of students.

Sometimes it is challenging to be flexible and supportive when working with your colleagues. There are times when your general education colleagues do not want to work with your students or are resistant to using practices that support students with disabilities, even though they are required to do this according to the students' IEP. In these instances, you will need to know how to deal with resistance.

Dealing with Resistance When Working in Inclusive Settings

Dimple Malik Flesner, University of Florida

As a beginning special education teacher, you often have the opportunity to bring diverse materials into the classroom and try out a variety of progressive teaching techniques. However, other teachers may not welcome these ideas or be willing to share their own. You will need strategies to handle and overcome resistance to collaboration. It can be frustrating, and you will sometimes feel the need to stake your claim and insist on certain ideas and instructional methods. Instead, focus on building and modeling a sense of community: you can assert yourself in ways that do not intimidate others or ignore their concerns. If identified and managed correctly, resistance can actually enhance professional growth and provide rich opportunities for reflection and renewal. You should always do the following:

▶ Be aware of resistance.

▶ Identify sources of resistance.

▶ Develop proactive strategies for dealing with resistance.

You will be aware of the school climate and the teachers who resist collaboration within the first few weeks of the school year, if not sooner. Drawn from Bondy's and Brownell's "Overcoming Barriers to Collaboration among Partners-in-Teaching,"[6] proactive strategies to overcome resistance and collaborate with your general education partners include the following:

▶ Foster time and create relationships with other teachers.
  - Teachers are always limited on time, yet we have to find ways to increase communication and spend time together. Then, we become comfortable with each other, begin to understand different perspectives, and even find common ground. Take the initiative to establish communication with other classroom teachers.
  - Eat lunch or share your planning period with other teachers. Invite teachers to come into your classroom to plan projects or special events. Seek help in creating behavior management plans. Attend grade-level and team meetings with ideas and questions. Join the school's social committee and attend fundraisers and community events with other teachers. Often, these meetings and conversations will give you powerful insights into the motives behind individual teaching styles and practices and also help you to think about your personal trajectory in the field of education.

▶ Cultivate collaboration and communication skills.
  - Collaborative skills and open communication are instrumental in overcoming resistance from colleagues. Ask yourself, Am I a good listener? Do I encourage others to share their ideas and perspectives? Do I use clear language and state personal opinions and areas of disagreement tactfully? Do I acknowledge others' skills, experiences, creativity, and contributions without passing judgment or being critical? Can I navigate through challenges and negotiate to achieve a mutually beneficial outcome and problem solve? Can I admit when my idea is not the best and come

(Continued)

to a mutually beneficial decision? A key part of collaborating and communicating is showing sensitivity. Each individual must genuinely believe that he or she is an equal and valued partner. We all need respect and support as we struggle to define and redefine our roles and responsibilities. This includes a sense of parity in which the special educator and general educator recognize each partner's contribution, even though proficiency may be different.

► Set a common goal and share responsibility.

- Of course, our goal and responsibility as teachers is to focus on our students. However, the demands and realities of classroom teaching are mentally and physically exhausting. Often, teachers are using every ounce of energy to get through the day in one piece! Nevertheless, we must always come back to what is best for our students and our commitment to their growth. To meet the challenge of inclusion as well as fulfill legislative requirements, special and general education must come together, and such collaboration allows teachers to share knowledge and embrace responsibility. Thus, particular teaching interests and expertise can be used to address specific student needs; over time, this shared knowledge becomes more collective. If we maintain student learning and progress as the focus and goal of collaborative efforts, we will be successful. This step is critically important because if discomforts or differences come up, teachers will be able to return to the shared agenda, refocus their intent and efforts, and work as partners united in a common goal.

Remember, changing thinking and work styles is a process. Building a collaborative relationship is not a remote event but a series of events that requires time. It will take time for other teachers to change their ideas of and beliefs about teaching. Missteps and setbacks are common. Resistance is a natural product of trying something different and moving forward.

SMALL STRATEGIES TO MAKE A BIG IMPACT ON COLLABORATION

Sometimes small actions can make a big difference in the collaborative process. You will play the lead in the majority, if not all, of your collaborative relationships focused on students with special needs. Being proactive can assist in laying the groundwork for successful collaboration. Take the following steps when working with others.

Set a Regularly Scheduled Time for Communication

Teachers are busy people. Your first step in collaborating is to set a time to regularly communicate. Look at schedules, find common times, and put it on the calendar. Respect this dedicated time and do not let other meetings or appointments interfere. By doing this, you increase respect and show value for your co-collaborator's time.

Provide Immediate Assistance

There will be times that problems arise and your general education colleague needs immediate assistance. As much as possible, find a way to provide help quickly. General education teachers want to feel supported. Although it is not expected, this gesture of support will go a long way in strengthening your collaborative relationship.

Give Positive Feedback

Everyone enjoys positive feedback, a pat on the back, or recognition for hard work. Take a little time to notice the hard work of your general education peer. At the beginning of your next regularly scheduled meeting or even in the lunch line, make a comment. This could be as simple as one of the following:

> I noticed a change in Billy's attitude. I think it is because of the shift in your reward system. He told me all about it and I can tell he is loving your class.

> I just wanted to mention the difference I see in Chelsea's fluency already. You only began the new strategy a few weeks ago, and it has already made a difference. I can't wait to see her timing results this week.

HELPING GENERAL EDUCATORS

One of the roles in collaboration may be to assist your general education colleagues. By providing assistance to general education teachers, you will help the teachers and the students with disabilities in their classrooms.

Provide Accommodations, Adapt Curriculum, and Modify Behavior

> *This year, I am expected to meet with each teacher while he or she plans lessons and assist in the process while providing accommodations and modifications for the students who have IEPs.*
>
> Theresa, second-year special education teacher[7]

The IEP team gets together to determine a course of action to meet a student's needs. Now, the general education teacher goes back to the classroom and provides the accommodations, adapts the curriculum, and modifies behavior. Some accommodations are simple, such as moving a student to the front of the class. Others are more complicated, such as changing the way instructional material is presented. Many general education teachers may feel uncomfortable providing accommodations because they simply do not know how. It is your responsibility to help ameliorate this problem and to ensure students with disabilities receive the accommodation and modifications they need to access the general education curriculum.

Communicating the IEP

General education teachers need to know their responsibilities related to implementing the IEP. An elementary teacher may have only two or three students with disabilities whereas secondary teachers could have twenty students. Regardless of the number, the first task is making sure everyone is informed.

Create Cheat Sheets

Help yourself and the general education teachers. Create a cheat sheet with a list of each teacher's students and their accommodations. Use initials instead of student names and be sure to still keep the information confidential.

MRS. SMITH

J.B.

Student should face teacher at all times.

Provide directions twice.

Provide timing warning.

M.R.

Preview assignments.

Chunk long assignments.

Provide answers verbally.

Highlight text.

Keep all your cheat sheets in a folder organized by teacher name. The general education teachers or other service providers can keep theirs in an easy-to-access location.

Meet with Professionals Involved

Preferably before school or immediately following an IEP meeting, set a time to meet with all personnel involved in the implementation of the IEP (i.e., general education teachers, paraeducators, therapists). At this meeting, review the IEP and specific responsibilities for accommodations and modifications. This is also a good time to hand out your cheat sheet and offer assistance (more information about this in the next section).

Monitor Implementation

Set a regular time to meet with service providers. Go through each accommodation or modification and check to see how they are being implemented. Use conversation starters to monitor implementations so you will not been seen as a compliance micromanager. Try these questions to help you find out information:

> "How is J.B. doing with his seating arrangements? What did you come up with for your center time?"

> "What strategy are you using to allow M.R. to preview assignments? Is it working for M.R. to give her answers verbally?"

Make Yourself Available

You want your general education colleagues to be able to access your assistance. Do not wait for them to ask specifically for your help. As a first-year teacher, many of your peers may feel uncomfortable knocking on your door or they may feel they are burdening you. You can remedy this situation by doing the following.

Offer to Meet Make yourself available to general education teachers even when it is not your regularly scheduled collaborative time. You might even ask questions to help start conversations about students. Here are some ways to offer your time:

▶ At the end of your regularly scheduled meeting: "I just wanted to mention that I am always in my room during planning time. I am always happy to help with figuring out accommodations."

▶ "I can stop by your room to check on Billy's modification of the behavior system. I have some time before school. I can help you get his area ready."

▶ "If you need any assistance with adapting the reading lesson for Sam, just send me an e-mail. I can find some time tomorrow or Wednesday and we can work on it together."

Provide Suggestions General education teachers will look to you for expertise. Don't assume just because a teacher has eight years of experience that he or she knows how to implement all accommodations or modifications. As you work with different general education teachers you will learn what level of support each teacher needs. One way to help is providing suggestions, either verbally or written.

CO-TEACHING

This year, I am so lucky to be co-teaching with a wonderful colleague (and she is probably reading this right now, too!). Having a general education teacher who is willing to accept you into her classroom is really one of the most important things when it comes to successful co-teaching.

Theresa, second-year special education teacher[8]

Co-teaching is a typical collaborative role in many inclusive schools. The assumption of co-teaching is that two teachers with different skill sets can come together to benefit all the students.[9] Co-teaching is not as simple as assigning two teachers to teach together. If you have been assigned to co-teach, there are many possible models for structuring instruction. Table 8.1 provides four examples of co-teaching models.

Each model has pros and cons. Figuring out what is best for you, your co-teacher, and your students is one of your first tasks. You may decide to switch between models. What you want to avoid is becoming a highly paid classroom aide. Table 8.2 provides guidance on what co-teaching is and what it is not.

Table 8.1 Co-Teaching Models[10]

Co-Teaching Model	Description
Parallel	• Divide the class. • Both teachers teach same content.
Centers	• Divide content and students. • Teach mini-lessons. • Switch groups and repeat. • Typically includes independent work center
Alternate	• Divide by one large group and one small group. • Smaller group is higher-needs students; teachers alternate who teaches this group.
Teaming	• No division. • Alternate providing instruction and supporting students.

Table 8.2 What Co-Teaching Is and What It Is Not[11]

Co-teaching is . . .	Co-teaching is not . . .
Two or more professionals working together, including certified or professional staff	A teacher and an assistant, paraeducator, teacher's aide, or parent volunteer
Conducted in the same classroom	When a few students are pulled out of the classroom on a regular basis
Conducted with heterogeneous groups	Consistently pulling a group of students with special needs to the back of the general education class
When both teachers plan for instruction together	
When each teacher has different expertise that is valued by the other	When one teacher plans all lessons and the other walks in to the room and asks, "What are we doing today and what should I do?"
When both teachers provide substantive instruction together, have planned together, and share or trade off tasks, such as homework, teaching content, facilitating activities	When one teacher consistently observes or walks around the room as the other teaches the lesson
When both teachers agree how to assess and evaluate progress for all students	When each teacher grades "his" kids or when the general education teacher grades all students and the special education teacher surreptitiously changes the grades and calls it "modifying after the fact"
When IEP goals are kept in mind along with the curricular goals and standards for that grade level	
When teachers maximize the benefits of having two teachers in the room by ensuring that both teachers actively engage with students	When teachers take turns being in charge of the class so that the other teacher can get caught up in grading, photocopying, making phone calls, or creating IEPs, or when students remain in the large-group setting in lecture format as teachers rotate talking at them
When teachers use different co-teaching models, including team teaching, station teaching, parallel teaching, alternative teaching, and one teach–one observe, one teach–one drift	
When teachers reflect on the progress and process, offering one another feedback and planning for needed changes in teaching styles, content, activities, and other items pertinent to improving the teaching situation	When teachers get frustrated with one another and talk about it with others in the teachers' lounge or when one teacher simply tells the other teacher what to do and how to do it

THE CO-TEACHER RELATIONSHIP

When you first meet with your co-teacher, establish a good relationship and work together to make decisions. Follow these steps to help guide you.

Before School Begins

Working together to plan your co-teaching classroom before school begins will help prepare you for your co-teaching assignment. Before you meet with your co-teacher, learn as much as you can about the students in your classroom and what their needs are. Are there special accommodations or modifications to the curriculum that need to be made? Information about student needs will help your co-teaching team choose a model of co-teaching that matches your content, student needs, and your comfort level.

Building Relationships

You will spend a lot of time with your co-teacher. One of the most important elements is making sure you have a good working relationship. During your first meeting take some time to share a little bit about yourself and your excitement and commitment to the co-teaching process.

Review the Student and Content Goals

Next, review student needs and content goals for the year. Having a clear picture of requirements, mandated by the state and the IEP, is necessary before making decisions.

Make Important Decisions

Discuss the following questions with your co-teacher. Answers will help to clarify the model, roles, and parameters of co-teaching.

- ▶ What model of co-teaching best suits our students and content?
- ▶ When will we plan?
- ▶ What is our behavior management system?
- ▶ Who will handle problem situations?
- ▶ How will we arrange the room?
- ▶ What routines will be set up?
- ▶ Who will give directions?
- ▶ How will we share resources?
- ▶ How will we grade students?
- ▶ How will we show students and parents that we are equal partners?

It is also a good idea to ask about preferences or things that tend to cause friction. Knowing this up front can help you in choosing responsibilities and avoiding conflict.

- ▶ What tasks do you love?
- ▶ What bothers you?

When beginning a co-teaching relationship, there are many things to discuss. Use exhibit 8.1 to help guide your conversations and eliminate misunderstandings.

Exhibit 8.1   Checklist for Co-Teaching[12]

Successful co-teaching relies on effective communication. It's surprising how simple matters, if not clarified, can lead to misunderstandings that interfere with co-teaching success. Some of the fundamental issues to address are described here. You may have others to add. Before and during the co-teaching process, be sure to discuss the following:

_____ Instructional content and outcomes, including the topics being taught and your priorities for what students should learn.

_____ Planning, including when it will occur and who is going to take responsibility for each part of planning. If planning is not shared, one person may feel overburdened.

_____ Instructional format, including how the lesson will be delivered and by whom.

_____ Parity signals, that is, how you will make clear to yourselves and students that each of you shares the same status. This includes how to do introductions to students, parents, and others, as well as classroom allocation of adult space (e.g., desks, chairs, names on board).

_____ Instructional space, that is, how to arrange students in a way that is instructionally relevant but not distracting to other learners, nor stigmatizing to any one group.

_____ Noise or how the sound level in the room will be monitored and adapted. Noise could include teacher voices, instructional activities, student voices, and environmental sounds.

_____ Classroom routine, including each teacher's expectations for how the class will operate. This includes everything from headings on written assignments to permission for the bathroom.

_____ Discipline and determining acceptable limits for student behavior and the system of rewards and consequences for behavior.

_____ Grading, including the basis for grades as well as who will assign them. The effect of instructional modification on grades is also an important topic.

_____ Teaching chores, including who scores assignments on tests, duplicates materials, reserves films, contacts speakers, arranges field trips, and so on.

_____ Feedback, including when you will meet to assess the co-teaching arrangement and how you will discuss successes and challenges.

_____ Pet peeves or other aspects of classroom life critical to you, including everything from the organization of materials, the way students address teachers or seek assistance, or the fact that it really bothers you when someone opens your desk drawer without asking.

_____ Other topics important to the partnership.

A Survival Guide for New Special Educators, by Billingsley, Brownell, Israel, and Kamman. Copyright © 2013 by John Wiley & Sons, Inc.

One General Education Teacher's Perspective on Co-Teaching

Carol M. Bland, University of North Carolina at Greensboro

I learned about co-teaching in a master's-level course about collaboration. When I read about co-teaching for the first time, I knew my resource teacher for special education, Ms. G, and I could be successful in co-teaching our inclusive first-grade classroom. Ms. G and I already had an established relationship. We trusted each other, had common goals, and shared a teaching philosophy based on a conviction that all students belong to the classroom learning community. With this relationship firmly in place, we had already overcome one of the biggest challenges in co-teaching: finding the right co-teacher.

With support from our building principal, we began to explore co-teaching formats for our language arts block each morning. Planning time was a challenge for us. Our personal schedules and determination to effectively deliver instruction in a co-taught format drove us to weekly planning meetings on Sunday afternoons in a coffee shop. We arrived with the teacher's guide for our school's language arts program and supplemental materials to guide our planning for guided reading, word study, and writing activities. Spread out across a large table, we thoughtfully assigned students to three groups. Next, we carefully decided which activities each group would complete during a station-teaching approach. I led guided-reading groups, Ms. G directed writing activities, and a paraeducator or student intern conducted word-study activities from a scripted word-study program with the third group.

We introduced this station-teaching approach to our students by using an explicit, direct instruction method to ensure that our students understood the stations, what they would do at each station, and how they would move from one station to the next. With role-playing and practice sessions at each station, we conquered the logistics of station teaching before trying to introduce any content. This made our station-teaching experience run very smoothly from the beginning.

After we gained confidence in our station teaching and attended a co-teaching conference, Ms. G and I branched out into other approaches to co-teaching. We followed Marilyn Friend's guidelines for using parallel teaching, alternative teaching, teaming, and one teach–one assist to vary the delivery of our instruction, based on the curriculum content and the needs of our students. Through co-teaching, we were able to accomplish much more than we could have achieved on our own. Our weekly meetings gave us a chance to continually monitor student progress and adjust student groups and our teaching activities accordingly. It is important to note that we did not always group our students by ability. In order to build community in our classroom and allow students to learn from each other, students were grouped in many different ways throughout the school year. Through co-teaching, all our students gained access to the general curriculum and received appropriate differentiated instruction to meet their needs.

Finding the right co-teacher and making a commitment to a designated planning time are important to successful co-teaching but a sense of parity between the co-teachers is most important. In this essay, I refer to *our* classroom and *our* students. It is critical that both teachers have ownership of all the activities and instruction taking place in the classroom and share responsibility for all student learning. When Ms. G and I used teaming, we made sure we each did an equivalent amount of talking. When we used the one teach–one assist approach, we varied

(Continued)

who taught and who assisted. At curriculum nights, we presented the language arts curriculum together, making sure that parents understood that both teachers would teach their children. We evaluated assignments together and assigned grades together. We solved problems together and celebrated our students' successes together. We were a team in every way.

Can co-teaching be challenging? Yes. Is co-teaching time consuming? Absolutely. Do obstacles get in the way of effective co-teaching? Of course. However, when co-teaching is understood to be an effective method for teaching all students in inclusive classrooms, the barriers can be overcome. Co-teachers who trust and respect each other, set common goals, hold similar teaching philosophies, and are willing to share resources, responsibilities, and accountability can enjoy many professionally rewarding experiences and enhance the educational opportunities for all their students.

CHARACTERISTICS AIDING IN SUCCESSFUL CO-TEACHING

Co-teaching is not an exact science. There are many variables, including student needs, content, instructional strategies, administrative support, teacher personalities, and knowledge. However, co-teaching relationships may be enhanced by strategies that enhance collaboration more generally:[13]

▶ *Valuing each other:* Value the expertise of your co-teacher. Take time to appreciate your co-teacher's unique skills and learn from them.

▶ *Displaying a willingness to collaborate:* Show a positive attitude and optimistic outlook about your working partnership.

▶ *Focusing on students:* Focus co-teaching on student needs in order to facilitate maximum professional growth.

▶ *Negotiating:* Respect each other's opinions, listen, share personal concerns, and settle differences together.

▶ *Developing parity:* Evenly represent the daily responsibilities of the general and special educator.

▶ *Using unique skills:* Use unique strengths to make a significant contribution to help students achieve more.

BARRIERS AND HOW TO OVERCOME THEM

Even with the best intentions and armed with collaboration skills, you may encounter some of these common barriers to co-teaching. Use the following guide to help you identify possible barriers and potential strategies to overcome them.

Barrier: Time

If the co-teachers do not have enough time to plan and make decisions, co-teaching can go awry.

Strategy: Set dedicated time and seek help.

First, try to find a common regularly scheduled time to meet that both parties agree to make a priority. If you cannot find a common time, ask your administrator for help. Your principal may be able to relieve you from other duties (before or after school) to help give you time.

Barrier: Differences in commitment

One teacher may be taking on the majority of the workload, whereas the other is not prepared.

Strategy: Change models and focus on positives.

When you are having trouble with your co-teacher's commitment to the process, change models to provide more equal allocation of responsibilities. Also, find ways to show your co-teacher the difference his or her contribution makes to the outcomes of students, which will increase his or her commitment.

Barrier: Differences in styles

Teachers who are accustomed to working independently may have a different instructional or management style that they are comfortable with and do not want to change methods.

Strategy: Negotiate.

Attempt to negotiate some minor adaptations to the existing management or instructional plan to meet your students' needs and your own.

KEEPING COLLABORATIVE RECORDS

No matter what type of collaboration you engage in, documenting the process is important. You will have more than one collaborative relationship and you cannot expect to remember all your conversations. Keeping collaborative logs is essential and serves several purposes.

Assists Collaborative Team in Noting Successes and Challenges

Collaborative logs can help team members identify patterns in students' behaviors. Over the course of six months you may not notice that each time the general education teacher begins a new unit, Jerry engages in problematic behavior. By reflecting on the collaborative log, you can easily see this behavioral pattern and work with the general education teacher to better prepare Jerry for learning new information.

Provides Information for the IEP Team

Not all members of the IEP team are present for the implementation of services. The collaborative log can help in IEP meetings to make important decisions about future services. For example, if the special and general education teachers meet weekly to implement a specific accommodation and the student is still struggling, the IEP team can use this information to change accommodations.

Serves as a Record of Your Responsibilities

There will be times that you may need to prove you have met your responsibilities. What if a parent does not think you are working together to meet his child's needs? What if a general education teacher does not provide an accommodation and tells the principal you did not inform her? Your collaboration log will show documentation of the meetings and your role in collaboration. You may also need this information at your evaluation meetings with your administrator.

Your school or district may already have a log template. If not, creating a collaborative log does not need to be complicated. Create a log of either the student or the teacher you work with and include a simple chart with the date, people in attendance, topic discussed, decisions made, and action steps taken. Exhibits 8.2 and 8.3 are examples of teacher and student logs.

Exhibit 8.2   Teacher Collaboration Log

Teacher: Mrs. Smith, general education
Teacher: Ms. Lotty, special education

Date	Student Discussed	Topic	Decisions Made	Actions and Responsible Parties
Sept. 4	John	Problem in science	Implement reminders before lab	Mrs. Smith
	Billy	Reading test score	n/a	n/a
	Joe	How to adapt the social studies lesson	Meet to work together	Set date for 9/7 to adapt together

Exhibit 8.3   Student Collaboration Log

Student: Joe Brown

Date	People in Attendance	Topic	Decisions Made	Actions and Responsible Parties
Sept. 4	Mrs. Smith and Ms. Lotty	How to adapt the social studies lesson	Work together	Set date for 9/7 to adapt together
Sept. 5	Ms. Lotty and Suzie (para)	Transitions	Keep Joe at end of line	Suzie

TO SUM UP

► Collaboration is a necessary role for special educators.

► Collaboration is student focused and based on principles, including parity, shared goals, shared responsibility, and respect.

► Co-teaching is a common delivery model that allows general and special education teachers to share instructional responsibilities to meet the needs of students.

► Special and general education teachers working together on a common goal can increase the likelihood of improving student outcomes.

► Service delivery models and individual student needs will dictate the amount of collaboration necessary.

► Pay attention to your own dispositions and use proactive strategies to strengthen collaborative relationships.

► Have a plan for helping general education teachers provide accommodations, adapt curriculum, and modify behavior.

► Keeping records of collaborative relationships helps to maintain your focus and provides documentation of your progress.

WHAT'S NEXT?

Now that you have strategies to effectively collaborate to meet student needs, the next chapter focuses on supporting your students.

ADDITIONAL RESOURCES

COLLABORATION

▶ Center for Effective Collaboration and Practice: http://cecp.air.org/schools_special.asp

▶ IRIS module: *Collaboration:* http://iris.peabody.vanderbilt.edu/resources.html

ACCOMMODATIONS, ADAPTATIONS, AND MODIFICATIONS

▶ National Dissemination Center for Children with Disabilities, *Supports, modifications and accommodations for students with disabilities:* http://nichcy.org/schoolage/accommodations

▶ Teacher Vision: *Adaptions and modification for students with special needs:* www.teachervision.fen.com/special-education/resource/5347.html

▶ IRIS Module: *Accommodations:* http://iris.peabody.vanderbilt.edu/resources.html

CO-TEACHING

▶ National Dissemination Center for Children with Disabilities: *Co-teaching: General and special educators working together:* http://nichcy.org/schoolage/effective-practices/coteaching

▶ Co-teaching Connection: www.marilynfriend.com

▶ Access Center: www.k8accesscenter.org/index.php/category/co-teaching

CHAPTER NINE

Supporting Your Students

In this chapter you will learn about:

- How to establish strong student–teacher relationships
- How to motivate your students
- How to advocate for students and assist students in self-advocation
- Culturally responsive teaching
- How to help your students gain organizational skills and responsibility

Jordan is a sixth-grade student who receives instruction in English, math, science, and social studies from Mrs. Johnson, a special education teacher. Jordan attends PE and art for his elective. At the end of the year during scheduling Jordan came to Mrs. Johnson about a concern: "I really want to take band next year but Mr. Fudge (the counselor) says that I can't." When Mrs. Johnson followed up by asking Mr. Fudge about the problem, he responded, "We never put special education students in band. The band director wouldn't allow it. Jordan can choose PE, art, or computers."

Being a special education teacher is so much more than instruction and improving student gains; you will also have other responsibilities and commitments concerning your students. Jordan is not allowed to sign up for band because of an ongoing exclusionary practice used by the counselor and the band director. Mrs. Johnson has to decide if she is going to let this practice continue or advocate for Jordan and his rights. As a special education teacher, one of your roles will be to serve as an advocate for your students, and as they grow older assist them in self-advocating. In order to do this, you will need to have a strong relationship with your students. If Jordan didn't feel comfortable with Mrs. Johnson, he never would have told her about his problem.

Special educators have other important responsibilities as well. For example, many students struggle and have been unable to find success at school. As such, students may resist instruction and teachers must find ways to motivate them. Some of the other important skills you need to teach your students aren't included in their reading or math books but may be just as important as the academic skills. For instance, valuing individual cultural diversity and building on multicultural backgrounds will assist students in respecting themselves and connecting with others who are different. Other skills such as helping students with organization and gaining responsibility will not only aid them academically but also throughout their lifetime in relationships and work.

THE STUDENT–TEACHER RELATIONSHIP

I always loved Mr. Harralson; everyone did. He just took the extra time to get to know us, and we all worked extra hard for him.

Maggie

Nearly everyone can recall an extraordinary teacher from childhood. Maybe the teacher was funny, told interesting stories, or really showed a particular interest in learning. Whatever the reason, it was essentially about the connection formed between the student and teacher. Promoting student–teacher relationships is not about being liked or remembered favorably. Positive relationships are powerful, supporting students' academic performance,[1] behavior,[2] and adjustment[3] in school.

Student–teacher relationships develop over the course of the school year through a complex intersection of student and teacher beliefs, attitudes, behaviors, and interactions with one another.[4]

TIPS FOR FOSTERING POSITIVE STUDENT–TEACHER RELATIONSHIPS

Positive student–teacher interactions are critical for establishing a sound relationship foundation. This foundation is important during times when students struggle and to help understand student needs.

Get to Know Your Students—Talk to Them!

Students know you care about them when you listen and show an interest in their lives. Here are some simple topics and examples of questions to ask your students:

Ask about other classes: "How are you doing in math class?"

Ask about their home life: "What did you do this weekend?"

Ask about after-school activities: "How is it going on the baseball team?"

Once you have initial responses try to remember important information and ask follow-up questions such as, "I know you were having issues with Mr. Frank last week. Have you been able to resolve the problems?" or "Did you win your big game on Friday?"

Caution: One problem you may encounter is students wanting to share information during inappropriate times. One way you can still show your interest and not sacrifice instructional momentum is to say, "I really want to hear more about that. Let's talk about it while we are walking to lunch."

Share Appropriate Personal Information

Relationships can't be just one sided, with one person sharing all the information and the other person being a closed book. Students want to know you are a real person, with a real family and outside interests. Sharing appropriate personal information is important in supporting your student–teacher relationship. Use table 9.1 to help you distinguish appropriate from inappropriate personal information to share.

Be Available to Help

The student–teacher relationship will be strengthened when students know you are available to help when they are struggling. Whether this is during class, before school, or after school, students want to know they can access an adult for assistance. If you can't help with a particular problem, you can assist by locating someone who can help (counselor, another teacher).

Communicate High Expectations

You can have a classroom where everyone gets along but high expectations are a necessity for a strong student–teacher relationship. Telling students you believe they can achieve goals and then helping them do it shows students you care about them and what they can learn. Ultimately, you are communicating that you believe in the student.

Find the Good and Build on It

How you deal with behavior will undoubtedly affect your relationships with students. The key here is to find and focus on the good things students are doing, recognize them, and build from there. Positive feedback communicates that you notice what students are doing right and you care enough to comment on it.

Have a Short-Term Memory for Negatives

There will be days when you or your students struggle. Try to start every day fresh. If you are always rehashing the negative moments from yesterday or last week, it will be difficult to build on your positive relationship. Holding a grudge will not help you or the student. Let go of the challenging situations and focus again on the good. This attitude communicates to students that you will move forward when things are tough.

Table 9.1 Guidelines for Sharing Personal Information with Students

Appropriate	Inappropriate
My dog was so naughty last night, he ate my favorite shoe!	I am so stressed out because I have too many loans to pay and my washing machine just broke.
My husband is on a work trip in California.	My husband and I had a romantic weekend away. We walked on the beach holding hands and snuggled in bed all morning.
I stayed up too late last night watching the big game! I just couldn't go to sleep not knowing if the Gators were going to win.	My youngest cousin who is still in high school just got arrested for fighting and doing drugs.

MOTIVATING YOUR STUDENTS

Suzie is excited about the unit she has planned for teaching summarization. Her class walks in on Monday morning and Suzie's excitement quickly begins to diminish. She watches DeShawn put his head on the desk, Sean groans as she announces the topic, and Chelsea appears to be writing a note and not paying attention at all.

Clearly, student motivation is a necessary foundation for learning. Without student motivation, even the most well-planned lessons will fail. When students arrive in your classroom unmotivated it is normal to feel frustrated. Your students will have varying backgrounds and experiences that contribute to their motivation. You may not be able to change the past but you can make a difference today, in your class.

There is not one right way or special recipe for motivating students. First, you will need to pay attention to the age, level, and interests of your students. This basic information will help you foster motivation. Use the following tips to help you cultivate student motivation.

Show Your Enthusiasm

Motivation 101: Enthusiasm is contagious.

Don't: "I hate math, too; let's just get it over with."

Do: "Fractions are up today, and I love them because you get to break things apart!"

Make It Relevant

Find some way to make the content relevant and connect it to the students' lives. Ask yourself the following:

▶ Why is it important for students to know this information?

▶ What value does this information have for students?

At the very beginning, make the topic interesting for students and they will be motivated to learn more.

Find the Sparkle in Their Eyes

As you teach your students it will become more apparent what really excites them. As much as possible, build on interests. If your students love technology, try to incorporate projects that allow them to use their skills. If your students hate reading but love skateboarding, find a way to weave the interest into lessons.

Pinpoint Currency

Try different ways to extrinsically motivate students. Your school may have systems, such as points for reading books or coupons for good grades. For difficult-to-motivate students, work with parents and other teachers to figure out appropriate motivating factors. For an elementary student this could be as simple as lunch with the teacher; for a high school student it might be a homework pass. Be open to trying different things.

Pump It Up with Peers

Peers can be extremely motivating. Having students work together in groups, creating goals, competing, and encouraging one another can aid in motivation, particularly with adolescents.

Let Students Take the Reins

Student self-assessment is a great tool to help improve student motivation. When students set goals and are in charge of monitoring their own progress, it helps to make their learning meaningful.

Set Them Up for Success

Students may not be motivated because of past failure in school. In these cases, creating lessons and assignments in which students are likely to be successful can help with motivation. Once students taste success, they will be more interested in learning.

Praise, Praise, Praise

Who doesn't like to receive praise? If you are doing well on a task you will naturally be more motivated to do it again. However, if you are constantly struggling, you will be more likely to give up and quit. If you want to keep your students motivated, find ways to celebrate even the smallest successes. Students crave positive feedback. They will work harder to gain more of your positive praise.

Motivating Adolescents

Angela Jones, Behavior Resource Teacher

Adolescents are at a particularly difficult age to motivate. Why? Well, they have a lot to figure out. Everything is changing for these little monsters (just kidding). They experience changes in their bodies, relationships with their parents and friends, and responsibilities. Adolescents with disabilities are likely to have lower self-esteem than their peers because they haven't met success as often in school and this may lead to difficulty with their parents and teachers. No wonder they are not the cheerleaders of your class. Now that you understand why they may be acting this way, here are some tips to get them motivated!

BE CARING AND CONSIDERATE

Adolescents are not that hard to figure out. If they think you don't care about them, then they will not care about your instruction. Yes, they are teenagers and perhaps the drama is a bit too much but their problems are very real to them. Sometimes all it takes is one question from you to show your care and concern: "What can I do to help?" When students genuinely know you care, they will do anything for you.

GET THEIR ATTENTION

It is not surprising when a student who doesn't read well is less than ecstatic about reading instruction. Your first step in this uphill battle is to get the student's attention. For adolescents, one strategy is implementing the wow factor. Think of nontraditional ways to start your lesson:

▶ Find a funny YouTube video relevant to your topic.
▶ Use cool technology, such as Google Earth, to introduce a location.

- ► Use music, like the *Mission Impossible* theme, to start your lesson.
- ► Have a comic on the board when they walk into class.

LAUGH AND HAVE FUN

Humor can help students cope with many of their personal issues and reduce anxiety and stress. Laughing and having fun can assist adolescents in connecting with one another and you. One way to get the ball rolling is to laugh at yourself. Sometimes adolescents take everything too seriously. When they see you lighten the mood, they will follow suit.

Caution: Adolescents may engage in humor at the expense of other students. Teachers need to model and monitor for appropriate positive humor in the classroom.

FIGURE OUT WHAT MAKES THEM TICK

Get to know your students, not just their test scores and reading level. Try to learn at least one interesting fact about each student. This may seem like a daunting task when you have fifty to one hundred students throughout a day. Make yourself little notes to help in your seating chart or attendance. Try to incorporate their interests or stories in your lessons. Also, allowing their personal creativity to show helps their ownership and motivation.

CELEBRATE THE SMALL SUCCESSES

Find ways to celebrate successes. Adolescents have notoriously rocky self-esteem and yet are amazingly self-centered. They crave attention. When the class has finished a challenging week, celebrate with a "we made it to Friday" activity. Give a "way to go" postcard to a student who improved on a test. Write words of encouragement and *congratulations* on the top of their homework. Talk positively about your students around campus and to other teachers.

USE TECHNOLOGY

How you present your lesson and how the students interact with the content is one arena offering opportunities to engage adolescents. Your students may be more technologically savvy than you are. Using technology to convey the content and allowing students to use technology to show their knowledge will help to motivate students even when the content is not naturally motivating or difficult. A perfect example was an algebra teacher who used the popular Angry Birds game to motivate her students.[5]

Examples of technology for student use in content interaction:

- ► Webquests
- ► SMART Board
- ► iPads
- ► Cameras
- ► Wikis and blogs
- ► Gaming

ADVOCATING FOR AND WITH YOUR STUDENTS

Advocating for your students is a vital role you will play as a special education teacher but often without specific responsibilities and timelines. A concrete responsibility is the number of IEPs you have to manage. For advocacy, your role is a bit more complicated. Instead of a particular time, advocating is more situation and student sensitive, that is, specific circumstances will necessitate your advocacy for students. Additionally, as an advocate you must consider each student's unique needs. Consider these scenarios:

> Ms. Hall receives a call from Antonio's mom. She is concerned that Antonio is not receiving extra time for his tests, as indicated on his IEP, in the general education classroom. When Ms. Hall meets with Antonio he confirms that his fifth-grade teacher tells him that he has to finish his tests with the rest of the class.

> Mr. Santos is running an IEP meeting for Yadira, a student in his self-contained class who struggles with her behavior. Yadira spends nearly all her day, except lunch, in the special education environment. She has expressed interest in attending regular classes. Mr. Santos feels Yadira is ready to move to the general education environment for her specials. Yadira's mom and the counselor do not want to make any changes.

> Treyvus is a middle school student who attends all regular classes and one learning-strategies class for extra academic support. Treyvus, usually a happy and relaxed student, has recently been agitated and seems stressed. Mrs. Ball, his special education teacher, cannot get Treyvus to talk about the problem. Mrs. Ball asks some other students who tell her that Treyvus is getting teased by a group of kids because he is a slow reader.

In each of these scenarios, the student needs specific teacher support. The special education teacher must consider the situation, the student's needs, and determine how to best advocate. Your role as an advocate is to speak for your students when they are unable to do so for themselves and assist in making sure their needs are met. Although this may sound simple, advocacy is often one of the most difficult tasks for teachers. You are often advocating because of resistance or difficulties faced by the student. Although you may feel like storming into a colleague's classroom or slamming down the IEP law, hard-nosed strategies are not likely to benefit your students. Instead, think strategically about ways to advocate that will lead to positive outcomes.

Strategies for Advocating for Your Students

▶ *Ask questions and listen.* Start by asking questions. This strategy will help you better understand the whole situation and the issues involved.

▶ *Provide information.* Use what you can to help show why it is important to change or implement a practice. Knowledge and examples can help to convince others about how the student will benefit.

▶ *Be prepared for conflict.* Before engaging in conversation, think about the concerns the other person may raise. Prepare yourself by practicing appropriate responses that defuse conflict and focus on student needs.

▶ *Avoid blame.* Try to avoid blaming others for problems. Instead, focus on how you can help facilitate a solution.

▶ *Foster connections.* Much of the resistance students and teachers encounter is because of unfamiliarity or lack of preparation in handling student needs. Personal connections help to build trust, and ultimately your advocacy will be better received.

Teach Your Students to Advocate for Themselves

Advocating for your students is important but supporting your students in self-advocating is fundamental to their success throughout their lifetime. Self-advocacy skills are critical for students with disabilities as they transition out of school and into adult life.[6] When students leave high school, they are expected to take responsibility for learning and life needs. Students must be able to communicate their strengths and needs and even offer strategies for others to assist them. The age and ability of your students will determine how much advocacy you take on or how much you need to support them in self-advocating. Students need long-term practice in self-advocacy and you can assist with this by starting even with the youngest students.

Facilitating Self-Advocacy

Self-advocacy skills can be learned and practiced in any subject area. Use the following guide to assist you in incorporating self-advocacy skills[7] in your lessons.

Increase Student Awareness of Strengths and Needs

Students cannot self-advocate if they cannot communicate their strengths and needs:

▶ Teach about disability, specifically, facts about their disability, what it means, and providing positive examples of people with disabilities and accommodations that were necessary for success.
▶ Provide students with practice in expressing their successes and challenges.
▶ Describe progress on classwork and assessments so students understand where they are performing well and struggling.

Involve Students

Involve students in their education:

▶ Provide opportunities for choice.
▶ Involve or have students self-monitor progress.

In a lot of cases, the late elementary years are a perfect time to begin inviting students to attend and participate in IEP meetings. Here are some suggestions for including students in the process:

▶ Begin engaging in the IEP process by simply sharing how school is going. You can help students prepare for the meeting by listing successes or difficulties during the year and writing any specific strategies they feel are helpful. Role-playing an IEP meeting allows students to practice and can ease anxiety about speaking in a roomful of adults.

► Next, students can take on a larger role in the IEP by drafting goals they hope to accomplish and steps necessary to meet the goals. You can help students prepare by assisting in aligning their personal goals with appropriate standards.

► Finally, many students, with ongoing practice, can gradually take on responsibility to lead the IEP process, indicating their self-identified goals and supports they need to meet the goals. At this stage the remainder of the IEP team provides guidance and suggestions for the student.

Teach, Model, and Practice Self-Advocacy

There will be many opportunities to teach, model, and practice self-advocacy. You can help by incorporating self-advocacy skills in your lessons. For example, one element of self-advocacy deals with problem solving. Include opportunities for students to do the following:

► Identify problems
► Gain knowledge to help with the problem
► Brainstorm strategies to address the problem
► Voice opinions and solutions

Other skills to build on self-advocacy include the following:[8]

► Self-awareness
► Knowledge of rights
► Leadership skills
► Effective communication

Collaborate with Parents

Parents have the unique potential to advocate with and support students with disabilities across a lifetime. You can collaborate with parents to determine the best strategies for encouraging student self-advocacy skills. Talk with parents about how you are fostering self-advocacy and share successes in promoting student independence and responsibility. Actively working with parents will give you deeper insight into your students' backgrounds and what the family values and expects long term. (For more information about collaborating with parents, see chapter 3.)

CULTURALLY RESPONSIVE TEACHING

Students from different cultural, linguistic, and economic backgrounds can and do achieve academic success. You may have students in your class who will be learning English as a second language, who live in poverty, or come from different religious or cultural backgrounds. Each classroom context is unique but you need to be equally prepared to engage with all students. Students' backgrounds and experiences affect how they participate in education. Consider the following scenarios, cultural considerations, and how the teacher can be more culturally responsive:

Dominik is having difficulty getting along with his peers. The other children complain he is always touching them and talking to them too closely.

Cultural consideration: Dominik comes from a Polish family in which touching is how you show someone that you like them.

Culturally responsive practice: Discuss with the class about personal comfort of proximal space. Encourage students to communicate their personal comfort level by role-playing and practicing in pairs.

Mrs. McCray relies on cooperative learning groups in social studies. Jose often asks to work by himself and when forced to work in a group remains silent.

Cultural consideration: Jose's previous teacher in Nicaragua only lectured and emphasized students' role in the classroom as recipients of knowledge rather than constructors of it.

Culturally responsive practice: Start small by allowing Jose to work with one peer or provide choices for completing assignments in groups or independently.

Mr. Hill has assigned a girl in each group to debate against a boy. Chung Ae, a Korean student, stands up to do her debate, remain silent, and then runs from the room.

Cultural consideration: Chung Ae's Korean family believes strongly in traditional gender roles. Chung Ae has been taught that women do not argue with men.

Culturally responsive practice: Provide other opportunities for Chung Ae to give her opinion, with a group of girls or in written format.

In each of the scenarios, the students acted a specific way in accordance with their cultural practices and in each scenario the students' actions could easily be misunderstood. You can see why it is especially important to know about your students and avoid misinterpretations of behavior based on cultural differences. Knowing each student as an individual will help to avoid stereotyping students' behaviors or beliefs because of a specific cultural characteristic. Being a culturally responsive teacher is something you will likely have to continually work at because your student population will always be changing. However, there are similar characteristics of culturally responsive teachers that can help guide your actions. Specifically, culturally responsive teachers do the following:[9]

▶ Connect instruction to student backgrounds and interests
▶ Have high expectations for all students
▶ Learn about cultures and how students are different
▶ Believe all students can succeed
▶ Create a classroom community
▶ Show care for students
▶ Find ways to communicate and include all families

More than anything else, learning about students' cultural backgrounds and experiences involves being open, flexible, and caring. Students bring many gifts and talents to their education, and when teachers learn what these are, student learning is always enhanced.[10]

Tips for Supporting Students from Multicultural Backgrounds

Rachel Thomas, University of Florida

As our schools become more and more diverse, chances are your classroom will have students from a range of cultural backgrounds. Use the following tips in supporting culturally diverse students.

SELF-REFLECT

▶ Your own background and experiences influences who you are as a teacher. You need a clear idea of your own cultural identity and an understanding of any stereotypes or dispositions you may have regarding race and culture. It is important to self-reflect to raise your awareness. One way to do this is to keep a journal about your beliefs and practices.

BUILD RELATIONSHIPS

▶ Foster relationships with students and their families by learning as much as you can about students' cultures, languages, interests, home life, and any challenges they may be facing. This knowledge will help you understand student behavior in the classroom and in sharing information about student learning to parents.

▶ Cultivate diverse peer relationships. Students want to feel a part of the school environment. Having friends can go a long way to help a student feel connected and accepted in the classroom.

CELEBRATE DIVERSITY

▶ Respect individual differences. Although it will be important for you to highlight commonalities of students, it is equally important to value different backgrounds and experiences. Find opportunities to celebrate these differences together and learn from each other.

▶ Nurture individual voices. Some students are naturally outspoken and others are less so. Make a concerted effort to have every student's voice heard. This communicates to your students that each person, no matter his or her view, is an equal contributor to the class.

PROMOTE DIVERSITY IN ACADEMICS

▶ Communicate high expectations for the success of all students and explicitly teach the rules of the culture of the classroom and school.

▶ Use interactive and collaborative instruction to help include all students in the learning process. It is especially important to provide an equal opportunity for students to respond and interact in classroom activities.

▶ Make learning meaningful to all students. Find ways to connect the content to the students' experiences and backgrounds.

HELPING YOUR STUDENTS STAY ORGANIZED AND LEARN RESPONSIBILITY

I forgot my book.

Can I borrow a pencil?

I put the signed letter in my binder but my binder is missing.

Students with disabilities frequently struggle with organization and responsibility. For instance, some students may forget verbal assignments, lose homework papers, and arrive without appropriate materials. Why is it so important that students manage their materials and time? First, students who arrive at class prepared will have more time on task for learning. Second, good organizational skills are important life skills for outside of school. You can help your students manage their work and learn organizational strategies and responsibility. Start by pinpointing potential problem areas, such as student desks, notebooks, book bags, and lockers. Tackle each area, one at time. There are several ways to get students organized. The following are basic guidelines to assist you.

Keep Organization Compact

If possible, have students organize their work in one place. For example, instead of having five different binders, use one binder with five sections and a three-hole punch to keep papers in place. Each area of the binder is labeled and a zipper pouch holds pencils and pens. One binder keeps students from rifling through different binders, confusing papers from different classes and losing them altogether.

Color Code

Designating different areas with colors is another useful strategy. It is not always possible for students to keep one binder, particularly in secondary classrooms. Using colors can assist students in knowing where different papers go and in being prepared for each class.

Use a Calendar or Planner

Keeping a daily assignment calendar or planner is helpful for any student but can be an especially useful tool for students with disabilities. Teachers may give verbal directions but students might not remember them by the next class. By the time the well-intentioned student sits down at night to do the homework, recalling the assignment might be impossible. Students at different ages and abilities can use calendars in varied ways; you can help to facilitate the process:

▶ Print labels with your homework assignment for young students or students who have difficulty with writing. This saves time and ensures the assignment is written correctly.

▶ Do a quick planner check during the last minute of class or a peer check when each partner checks to make sure assignments are written in the planner.

▶ Provide incentives for correctly kept planners. Check them on a weekly, monthly, or semester-long basis. This encourages students to maintain their planner properly.

Exhibit 9.1 Student Daily Organization Checklist

Task	Monday	Tuesday	Wednesday	Thursday	Friday
Before School					
Homework, signed papers					
Pencils, pens, calculator					
Backpack					
During School					
Turn in homework					
Hand in completed classwork					
Put all papers in correct folder					
Write assignments on calendar					
Double-check assignment directions for understanding					
After School					
Complete homework					
Clean out folder and backpack					
Check supplies and restock (paper, pencils)					

Follow Routines

One of the most critical pieces of teaching organization is practice! By creating regular routines, students develop good habits in managing materials. Using a checklist (see exhibit 9.1) can assist students in controlling their work and gaining confidence in organizational skills and feeling responsible for their own work.

TO SUM UP

▶ Build appropriate student–teacher relationships by dedicating time and effort, communicating, and focusing on positive student actions.

▶ Motivate students by showing enthusiasm, linking content to student interests, providing praise, using peers, and fostering independence.

▶ Advocate for your students when they are unable to do so themselves. Teach self-advocacy skills to assist students throughout their lifetime.

▶ Be culturally responsive by intentionally and systematically designing lessons to enhance instruction and the learning environment for all students.

▶ Teach organizational skills to students and reinforce with routines to help them learn responsibility.

WHAT'S NEXT?

Now that you have added strategies to your toolbox to support your students, we move on to effective assessment practices, a crucial part of understanding your students and planning instruction.

ADDITIONAL RESOURCES

▶ Minority Student Achievement Network: *Resources for educators: Student–teacher relationships:* http://msan.wceruw.org/resources/educators_relationships.aspx

▶ National Dissemination Center for Children with Disabilities: *Students get involved:* http://nichcy.org/schoolage/transitionadult/students

▶ Wrightslaw: *Special education advocacy:* www.wrightslaw.com/info/advo.index.htm

▶ LD OnLine: *Transition and self-advocacy:* www.ldonline.org/article/7757

▶ National Education Association: *Online resources for culturally responsive teachers:* www.nea.org/home/16723.htm

▶ Teaching Organizational Skills: *ADD/ADHD:* http://suite101.com/article/teaching-the-adhd-child—part-11-a6115

CHAPTER TEN

Assessment and Knowing Your Students

> **In this chapter you will learn about:**
>
> - How legal requirements inform our assessment practices
> - How standards inform our assessment practices
> - To interpret standardized assessments
> - Two progress-monitoring methods that support instructional decision making
> - Decision-making strategies for testing accommodations and modifications
> - Ways to determine which students qualify to receive alternate assessments

Katie, a first-year special education teacher, wanted to get a head start on the school year, so she reviewed the IEPs for all the students on her caseload. She read through assessment reports from the school psychologist, progress charts from last year's performance, and the students' report cards. All these data! Sometimes the formal assessments from the school psychologist were not consistent with how the students did in their classes. She felt overwhelmed and wondered how to begin planning instruction for her students based on these assessment records. Finally, she decided to take these assessments into account but also conduct her own assessments once she got acquainted with her students.

As a teacher, you will constantly make instructional decisions based on assessment results. Accomplished teachers realize that evaluating student understanding and progress goes hand in hand with instruction. Essentially, *assessment* is the umbrella term we use to consider the broad topic of evaluating how students are and should be progressing. Assessment includes formal assessments (that provide a way for us to learn how students are performing compared to their peers) as well as informal assessments (that let us understand how students generally do within specific skills, content areas, or tasks).

Individuals often use the term *assessment* to argue for and against many school initiatives, laws, and policies. Assessment, therefore, has been implicated with negative reactions because of issues such as the achievement gap between students with and without disabilities. In fact, in searching for the terms *assessment* and *education* in major national newspapers, the following headlines emerged:

▶ Testing and Teaching Aren't at Odds (*Washington Post*)
▶ Flawed Policy on Testing Drives Schools to Cheat (CNN Online)
▶ If Students Fail History, Does It Matter? (CNN Online)

Despite the negative associations with assessment, it is a critically important aspect of instructing students with and without disabilities. Without the information that assessment provides, how would we know whether the instruction we are providing is making a difference?

YOUR STATE STANDARDS AND THE CCSS

Instruction in K–12 settings closely aligns with content-specific instructional standards developed by each state. Currently, each state has processes in place for developing and implementing content standards as well as for assessing students based on those standards. These standards intend to provide a roadmap to school districts to ensure that students receive the skills necessary to succeed in postsecondary education and work environments. Additionally, there is a movement toward adopting the CCSS,[1] which are intended to provide consistency among the states in expectations for student outcomes. To learn more about the CCSS, you can go to www.corestandards .org. The developers of these standards stated that the rigor of these academic content standards provide a historic opportunity for students with disabilities to gain meaningful access to effective instruction.

Whether discussing the state or national standards, there is great emphasis on aligning student IEPs with these standards. In other words, all students will be assessed against the standards, including students with disabilities and English language learners. Similar to other assessments, students can qualify to receive testing accommodations when taking the state assessment or they may qualify to be assessed against alternative assessment standards, which will be discussed in the following sections.

WHY TEST IN RELATIONSHIP TO THE STANDARDS?

It is important to see if students are making progress toward a predetermined set of standards to make sure that they are learning the skills necessary to succeed as they move through the grades and into postsecondary life. Using the standards to gauge student learning allows teachers to determine whether instruction is resulting in necessary student gains. If students are not making anticipated gains, schools and school districts can allocate resources to support student learning in weak areas.

EDUCATIONAL LAWS AND ASSESSMENT

Since the 1970s, educational laws have evolved to place more and more emphasis on the education of students with disabilities and accountability for that education. Chapter 4 provides information about the major federal laws that have influenced assessment of students with disabilities.

RELATIONSHIP BETWEEN THE LAWS AND YOUR ASSESSMENT PRACTICES

The legal requirements surrounding assessment can be quite complex and confusing. Students cannot receive special education services without an initial comprehensive, nondiscriminatory evaluation. The IEP team uses the results of the nondiscriminatory evaluation to determine if the student qualifies for special education services. In order to qualify for special education services, a student must have a diagnosis of one of thirteen disability categories (see appendix A).

Why Is Nondiscriminatory Evaluation So Important?

Generally, when making disability determination decisions, it is critical to accurately assess and avoid mislabeling a student with either having or not having a disability. The school has an obligation to safeguard against mislabeling students. For example, it is important to know whether a student is struggling because of issues such as (1) poor instruction, (2) limited English proficiency, or (3) other issues that may be influencing academic performance (such as a health condition).

One major issue with which we have had to historically contend involves disproportionate representation of students from culturally diverse backgrounds in special education. This occurs when students from one cultural or linguistic background is either over- or underrepresented in special education as compared with peers from other groups. Although there are many issues that contribute to disproportionate representation, the assessments certainly can play a role if the assessment is given in a manner not consistent with the unique needs of the student.

Multitiered Systems of Support or RTI and Intervention

Many schools have adopted a tiered instructional support process in which students who struggle with learning receive increasing intensity of instruction and supports that meet their individual academic and behavioral needs. This is done prior to any discussion of qualifications for special education services. The two most common terms for these systems include *multitiered systems of supports* or *RTI*. These programs provide multitiered instructional and behavioral supports to students who struggle so that they can receive more intensive and individualized instruction regardless of whether they have a disability. Multitiered supports in different school systems have varied features but common approaches include universal screening of all learners, multitiered instructional models, and consistent progress monitoring.[2]

Universal Screening

Universal screening is designed to identify students who may be struggling or are at risk for academic failure. Often all students participate in universal screening.[3] These assessments are typically brief and take little instructional time. School districts that implement an RTI model typically use state proficiency standards as benchmarks for the universal screenings. There is not one agreed-on universal screening that all schools use to identify struggling learners. Rather, there are many options that include state proficiency standards, performance on a norm-referenced test (such as the Woodcock-Johnson Test of Achievement reading or math assessment subscores), or performance on curriculum-based measures as benchmarks for the universal screenings. If your school uses a universal screening, you will be provided with a performance score or percentile under which students will be identified as potentially struggling in the assessed area. Schools use the information from universal screening in different ways. Some schools will automatically provide more intensive supports to students who perform poorly on the universal screening. For example, if students perform below the twenty-fifth percentile on an achievement assessment, they may be identified as needing more intensive supports and interventions. Other schools will use the information from the universal screening as a starting point for further, more targeted, and individualized assessment. As a new special educator in a school district implementing RTI, you will likely receive the local benchmarks for your grade level and content as well as the types of universal screenings that all the students will undergo.

Multitiered Instructional Supports

School districts will organize their tiered systems differently with varied numbers of tiers, varied systems of instruction and interventions, and with different instructional personnel providing supports throughout the tiers of intervention. The most common RTI system involves a three-tiered model in which students receive increasingly individualized and more intensive instruction as they progress up the three tiers of support. An example of such a model may have the following general structure:

▶ *Tier one:* The core instruction for all students involves use of evidence-based practices tied to the state standards. Teachers monitor student progress and assess whether students are progressing and making gains. Additionally, all students are assessed through universal screening.
▶ *Tier two:* If students struggle in tier one, as displayed through universal screening and progress monitoring data, students may receive supplementary small-group instruction in order to provide more intensified instructional supports. Progress monitoring also increases in frequency.
▶ *Tier three:* If students continue to struggle in tier two, the students receive more individualized and intensive instruction. This instruction may occur individually or in small groups. In many school systems, nondiscriminatory evaluation associated with special education services occurs at this point.

Providing appropriate academic supports to students with and without disabilities under an RTI model rests heavily on accurate assessment information. As a new special educator working within an RTI framework, consider the following recommendations:

▶ Students should be allowed to move fluidly and rapidly between tiers based on their instructional needs. If you conduct progress-monitoring checks often, you will know when students need additional supports.
▶ Students can simultaneously be in different tiers for different instructional areas. For example, a student can be in tier one instruction for learning fractions in math class, tier two instruction in writing, and tier three instruction in reading comprehension.
▶ Tiers of instruction do not equate to instructional placement. For example, tier three is not necessarily always special education.

PROGRESS MONITORING AND CURRICULUM-BASED MEASURES

Regardless of whether your school includes a robust RTI system, you will most likely conduct, interpret, and communicate about student performance regularly. One type of common classroom assessment involves evaluating how well students master a particular benchmark or objective. This type of assessment is called *mastery measurement*. Most classroom assessments fall into this category when teachers assess whether students understand various short-term, content-specific concepts and skills. Once students demonstrate mastery of these concepts, the teacher moves to different concepts and skills. These assessments provide information about how well students understand concepts but they do not provide adequate information about how students progress over time on critical skills necessary for long-term school success.[4] Progress monitoring allows teachers to determine whether the students are benefitting from the instruction or whether they need additional support on long-term curricular skills.

One well-established form of progress monitoring is called *curriculum-based measures (CBMs)*. In CBM, students are evaluated on specific instructional skills used as indicators of academic proficiency.[5] As students learn, their scores are graphed so that teachers and students can observe progress and adjust instruction based on the data. Because CBMs do not take a great deal to administer, they can be administered frequently and provide a great deal of information about student progress over time.

Pamela Stecker, Erica Lembke, and Anne Foegen provide a helpful five-step guide to implementing progress monitoring.[6] Within these five steps, we offer a few specific suggestions for conducting progress monitoring with your students:

▶ Select the appropriate measurement materials depending on the skills you would like to assess.
- If you are assessing overall reading comprehension, for example, consider reading comprehension questions tied to grade-level passages. If grading mathematical computational fluency in single-digit multiplication, consider measuring the number of correctly answered single-digit multiplication problems answered in one minute.

▶ Evaluate whether the measurement materials are reliable and valid.
- You can learn about the reliability and validity of commercial progress-monitoring tools on the National Center for Response for Intervention website (www.rti4success.org /progressMonitoringTools).
- If creating your own CBMs, consider whether they truly measure the same tasks or skills over time. Teachers may inadvertently slightly alter the tasks or skills being assessed by changing the difficulty level of the tasks (e.g., changing the readability level of a reading comprehension CBM) or changing the task (e.g., changing from single-digit multiplication to single-by-double-digit multiplication). In both cases, the validity and reliability of the CBM is compromised and it would be difficult to interpret changes in the students' performance.

▶ Administer and score the CBM. It is important to consistently administer CBMs and provide immediate feedback to students so that they can track their own progress and compare current to past scores.
- These should be provided at regular intervals. You should consider developing a schedule for data collection. For example, you can choose to assess your students weekly, every two weeks, or monthly.
- Once you score the CBMs, graph the results with your students so that they can see their progress.

▶ Use the data from the CBMs to set new instructional goals.
- If the student is making steady progress toward an instructional goal, you can likely assume that the instruction is effective. When the student meets the desired goal, you should develop new goals that increase the complexity or difficulty of the tasks.

▶ Use the data from the CBMs to judge the effectiveness of instruction.

- If progress-monitoring data reveal that the student is not making adequate progress toward the instructional goal, you should consider ways of altering your instructional practices to better meet the needs of your students.

Progress Monitoring Graph

Andy is a seventh-grader who is working on answering inference questions within grade-level text. His teacher, Mr. Rodrigues, has been working with Andy on increasing his reading comprehension with the goal of reading at grade level by introducing him to numerous reading comprehension strategies. With these strategies, Andy's reading level has dramatically improved. Mr. Rodrigues uses a system of progress monitoring along with curriculum-based measures so that he knows whether Andy is making progress or whether he needs to alter his instruction. In early March, Andy met his previous goal of answering inference questions on fourth-grade-level passages with 80 percent accuracy and has transitioned to fifth-grade-level text. Figure 10.1 shows the chart that Mr. Rodrigues and Andy have maintained to track his progress. From this chart, Andy and Mr. Rodrigues are fairly confident that they can move to a new skill next week but Mr. Rodrigues would like to have at least one more data point before doing so.

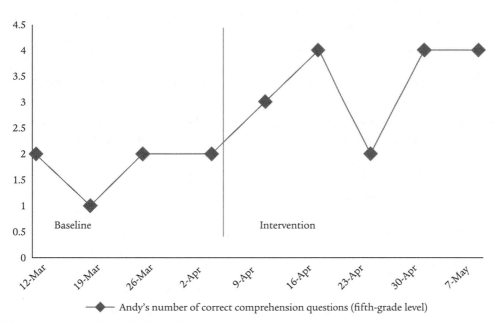

Andy's number of correct comprehension questions (fifth-grade level)

Figure 10.1 Progress Monitoring Graph

Generally, the key to progress monitoring and CBM includes the following:

▶ Consistency in assessing student progress

▶ Focusing on long-range goals

▶ Making instructional decisions based on CBM data

FORMAL OR STANDARDIZED TESTS

In addition to progress monitoring and classroom assessments, you will be required to know how to interpret formal or standardized tests. These assessments enable you and other instructional decision makers to compare students to one another to identify whether the students are progressing well as compared to their peers.

Norm-Referenced Assessments

These assessments measure students against similar peers in the population. When considering how students perform on norm-referenced tests, we essentially compare them to others of the same age and grade level to determine if they are performing at, below, or above the average range. There is a great deal of terminology associated with norm-referenced assessments. Appendix C clarifies some of the common jargon in order to help you interpret norm-referenced assessment results.

You will encounter a wide variety of assessments, and each school district typically relies on a set number of assessments in making eligibility decisions and tracking student progress. Although certainly not a comprehensive list, table 10.1 provides examples of common standardized assessments that you may encounter as a special education teacher.

Table 10.1 Examples of Common Standardized Assessments Used in Schools

Assessment Type	Example Assessments	Further Information
Intelligence tests	Wechsler Intelligence Scale for Children–IV	Intelligence test for ages six through seventeen
	Stanford-Binet Intelligence Scale (5th ed.)	Intelligence test for ages two through eighty-five
	Kaufman Assessment Battery for Children (2nd ed.)	Intelligence test for ages three through eighteen
Achievement tests	Woodcock-Johnson Test of Achievement–III	Achievement test for ages two to ninety plus in areas such as reading, writing, math, and vocabulary
	Kaufman Assessment Battery for Children	Achievement assessment for grades K–12 across multiple reading, writing, and mathematics areas
	Stanford Achievement Test	Assessment for grades K–12 across multiple content areas including writing, science, and social studies
	Wechsler Individual Achievement Test–III	Assessment for grades preK–12 in areas such as oral language, reading, writing, and mathematics
Content-specific assessments	Dynamic Indicators of Basic Early Literacy Skills (DIBELS)	Curriculum-based measure of early reading skills including decoding and phonemic awareness
	Brigance Comprehensive Inventory of Basic Skills–Revised (CIBS-II-R)	Criterion referenced assessment of preK–9 in areas such as reading and ELA (e.g., oral reading, comprehension, spelling, and writing) and math (e.g., algebra, geometry, data analysis, and measurement)
	KeyMath Diagnostic Assessment (3rd ed.)	Norm-referenced individualized assessment of broad mathematics skills
	STAR Math Enterprise	Computerized assessment of mathematics for grades 3–12 in areas such as numbers and operations, algebra, geometry, and data analysis

ASSESSMENT ACCOMMODATIONS AND ADAPTING CLASSROOM TESTS

Assessment accommodations create a leveled playing field in which students with disabilities can demonstrate their knowledge in a manner that is not hindered by their disability.

Eligibility for Assessment Accommodations

Teachers often wonder whether students should be provided with testing accommodations during classroom assessments as well as on high-stakes tests. Generally, if students have an IEP or a Section 504 plan, they may be eligible for testing accommodations. Those accommodations are determined by the IEP team or the Section 504 plan committee and are also dependent on whether the accommodations would compromise the validity of the assessment. Accommodations should be individualized and meet the specific testing needs of the students. A very helpful resource is the National Center on Educational Outcomes (www.cehd.umn.edu/nceo/default.html). This website provides a list of allowed accommodations by the different states as well as an accommodations manual helpful in selecting assessment accommodations.

Typical Assessment Accommodations

Assessment accommodations are any changes made to an assessment format or environment that help students demonstrate what they know on the assessment but do not change the constructs being tested. When done well, these accommodations should increase the validity of the assessments because they should offset issues that would prevent the students from demonstrating what they know.

It is important, however, to understand which accommodations are allowable on various assessments. For example, allowing someone to read sections of a reading assessment may compromise the validity of that assessment. Your school district's special education department should have accurate information about which assessment accommodations are allowable for the various district-mandated assessments. Generally, there are four areas to consider for assessment accommodations:

▶ *Presentation accommodations:* These provide changes in how the assessment is presented. Common presentation accommodations include the following:
- Changing the presentation materials, for example, large print, Braille, or a plain English version of the assessment
- If it does not compromise the validity of the assessment, teachers can do the following:
  - Read aloud and clarify the directions or the test items.
  - Provide a text-to-speech software or audio-recorded version of assessment questions and items.
- Allowing students to use assistive technologies usually used by the student

▶ *Response accommodations:* These involve changes in the way students show their knowledge on the assessments:
- Providing a larger version of the answer sheet if it is separate from the rest of the assessment
- Allowing the student to indicate answers in the following ways:

- Mark their answers in the test booklet. Later, a teacher or proctor can transfer the answers to the answer document.
  - Verbally provide answers to either a scribe or into an audio recorder.
  - Point toward correct answers.
- Allowing assistive technologies usually used by the student:
  - Calculator
  - Brailler to record Braille answers
  - Computer, AlphaSmart, or other word processor with functions such as spell and grammar check, word prediction software, and so on
  - Augmentative and alternative communication devices to communicate answers

▶ *Timing accommodations:* These involve changing the timing requirements of the assessments:
- Changing the time of day when the assessment is given
- Providing breaks during the assessments to allow students to rest, eat, use the restroom, and so on
- Providing multiple test sessions rather than requiring the student to complete the assessment in one session

▶ *Setting and environment accommodations:* These involve changing the setting in which the student completes the assessments:
- Determining the best place for the student to complete the assessment
- Allowing for individual or small-group settings with reduced distractions
- Allowing assistive technologies usually used by the student including seating and posturing furniture

Tips for Determining Students' Assessment Accommodations

▶ Once the team agrees on assessment accommodations, make sure that you document these on the student's IEP or Section 504 plan. If an accommodation is not documented on either the IEP or 504 plan, the student cannot receive those accommodations on either classroom assessments or the state assessments.

▶ Involve the student as much as possible in deciding and evaluating assessment accommodations.

▶ Collect data on how and when student performs while using the assessment accommodation(s). You may ask the following questions:
- Does the student consistently use the accommodation(s) that are provided or does the student use the accommodations only under certain circumstances?
- When the student uses the accommodation(s), does he or she perform better?
- Is the student resistant to using the accommodation(s)? If so, why?

▶ Many assessment accommodations require a certain degree of planning prior to implementation. Make sure that you give yourself advanced time for such planning.
- Make sure there is an available room for small-group or individual assessment administration.
- Arrange for large-print answer sheets prior to testing day.
- If the student dictates answers to a scribe, make sure to arrange for this person well in advance.

Common Mistakes in Providing Assessment Accommodations to Students with Disabilities

As a new special educator, determining and implementing assessment accommodations may appear intimidating. The following describe a few common mistakes that new teachers make when giving assessment accommodations to students with disabilities:

▶ Providing every single type of possible testing accommodation "just in case" the student might need them. This common mistake occurs because new teachers want to make sure that they have covered all bases when it comes to the types of supports a student may need in taking an assessment. Unfortunately, when students are offered accommodations that they may not necessarily need, they may rely on those supports regardless of need and become dependent on them.

- Remember that students are entitled only to those accommodations that are necessary to level the playing field for those students.

▶ Expecting too little from students with disabilities. Sometimes teachers assume that students with disabilities cannot perform certain tasks and skills. When assessment accommodations are considered with this lowered expectation, students are provided supports that they do not need. Sometimes, they are offered assessments that neglect higher-order thinking skills because of the expectation that they cannot perform more complex tasks and analyses.

- Always consider the grade-level standards and assume that the student can learn the skills necessary to perform on assessments. Make sure that your decisions are supported by data!

▶ Allowing students to use testing accommodations on state assessments or other high-stakes assessments that are not used during the student's regular instruction and assessment. Sometimes, students receive accommodations on state assessments that they have never used prior to that assessment.

- If students do not need a particular testing accommodation during regular instructional and assessment times, they cannot receive them on state assessments.

ALTERNATIVE ASSESSMENTS

In some cases, students with disabilities will have difficulty meaningfully accessing information necessary to perform on assessments, even with accommodations. In these cases, alternate assessments should be considered.

Determining Which Students Should Participate in Alternate Assessment

Eligibility to take the alternative assessments differs from state to state but several principles exist:

▶ You cannot simply use a student's diagnosis to determine if a student qualifies to take the alternative assessment. Simply stating that a student has a disability does not automatically result in an alternate assessment.

▶ Similar to assessment accommodations, the IEP team must make an individualized decision to determine if a student should be assessed using an alternative assessment method.

Different Types of Alternate Assessments

Alternate assessments should focus on core academic content and should measure student progress toward grade-level standards. The following are explanations of the three types of alternate assessments that students may qualify to take.

Alternate Assessment Based on Alternative Achievement Standards (AA-AAS)

These assessments are intended for students with the most significant cognitive disabilities.

- ▶ AA-AAS involve a different definition of how much students need to know in order to be proficient in grade-level content.
- ▶ Typically, the AA-AAS requires students to know grade-level content at a lower complexity and breadth.
- ▶ According to federal regulation, less than 1 percent of students should qualify to take the AA-AAS.

Examples of AA-AAS include assessments such as checklists, portfolios, and performance assessments that demonstrate students' proficiency on grade-level content standards.

Alternative Assessment Based on Modified Academic Achievement Standards (AA-MAS)

These assessments are intended for students with disabilities who work on grade level but they require additional time to master the content.

- ▶ Students who qualify for the AA-MAS can be from any disability category.
- ▶ Students who qualify for the AA-MAS learn the general education standards but are not expected to achieve grade-level proficiency.
- ▶ AA-MAS aligns to the grade level in which the student is enrolled but items on the assessment will be less difficult than items on the general assessment. According to the National Center on Educational Outcomes, other differences may include the following:
  - Fewer test items on the assessment
  - Use of pictures alongside text to enhance understanding
  - More white space on the pages
  - Reduced choices within multiple-choice items
  - Use of simpler language

Alternative Assessment Based on Grade Level Achievement Standards (AA-GLAS)

These assessments are intended for students with disabilities who work on grade level but need testing procedures that are not included in the general assessment or cannot be achieved through regular assessment accommodations.

- ▶ Few states have this assessment option, but according to the National Center on Educational Outcomes, it is anticipated that more and more states will institute this option in the future.
- ▶ Students who qualify for the AA-GLAS cannot demonstrate their level of proficiency on the assessments with the typical types of accommodations available on the assessments.

FEEDBACK AND GRADING

Grading student work, especially of students with disabilities, can seem confusing. You may wonder how to balance grading with providing meaningful feedback to help your students improve their performance. You must adapt when grading students with disabilities who receive individualized instruction. Grades based on adaptations of systematic processes provide meaningful information to students and their parents. If teachers provide inconsistent and informal observations, the grades that students receive can offer confusing information.[7] Check your school's grading policies because it will likely provide specifics relating to grading adaptations for students who receive special education services.

Lee Ann Jung and Thomas Guskey outline four common grading myths:[8]

Myth one: Students who have IEPs, 504 plans, or are ELLs cannot legally receive a failing grade. The authors explain that if students receive all the supports and accommodations outlined in their IEPs, they are eligible for the entire range of grades attained by their peers.

Myth two: Report cards cannot identify a student as receiving individualized instruction. The authors explain that although transcripts cannot include information about IEPs, 504 plans, or ELL status, these topics can be included on report cards. However, they also explain that this information should appear on report cards only if absolutely necessary to explain a student's progress.

Myth three: Transcripts cannot identify information about curriculum modifications. The authors explain that although transcripts cannot include information about IEPs, 504 plans, or ELL status, schools can legally indicate whether the curriculum was modified. They also indicate that this is perhaps the most common grading and reporting myth.

Myth four: Obtaining higher grades increases students' self-esteem. The authors note that this myth is perhaps the most dangerous of the grading myths. They indicate that increases in self-esteem arise only when increased grades are a direct result of increased performance that accurately reflects achievements associated with that increased performance.

To accurately assign grades to students with disabilities, Jung and Guskey suggest the following steps:

Step one: Ascertain whether the student can meet the grade-level standard(s).

Step two: If it is decided that the standard(s) cannot be met, decide what types of adaptations should be made to the standard(s).

Step three: If it is decided that the standard(s) should be modified, decide on the appropriate standard(s).

Step four: Base the grades and student feedback on the modified standard(s).

Step five: Provide accurate communication of student progress toward the modified standard(s).

These five steps provide a systematic way for IEP teams to decide how to evaluate students with disabilities. Generally, remember that providing feedback to students involves more than assigning grades several times each year. The majority of assessment feedback that teachers provide to students involves formative feedback. This feedback is ongoing and provides more immediate information to the students about their performance. See the section on curriculum-based measures for more information about formative assessment.

Grading Adaptations in Inclusive Classrooms

William D. Bursuck and Tammy L. Barron,
University of North Carolina at Greensboro

There are two ways that grades can be adapted so that they communicate information about students more effectively: classroomwide grading adaptations that benefit all students, including students with disabilities, and individualized grading adaptations that are carried out only for students with disabilities as specified on their IEPs. Both types of grading adaptations are summarized in table 10.2. However, before deciding to employ any grading adaptations, teachers should ask themselves the following questions:

1. *Are students working toward the same learning standards as the rest of the class?* Most students with disabilities are expected to meet the same general education curriculum standards as their classmates without disabilities. The exception is students with significant intellectual disabilities who follow an alternative curriculum and are graded solely on the basis of their IEPs. The needs of most students with disabilities can be met using classwide grading practices, though even students with mild disabilities can benefit from individualized adaptation as well.

2. *Is student progress being frequently monitored?* Report card grades come out only four times per year. Often struggling students and their parents require more frequent feedback than that. Students and parents may also require feedback on factors not often accounted for in traditional grading systems such as effort, progress, and the use of learning strategies.

3. *Are students receiving accommodations that result in reasonable access to the general education curriculum?* Instructional accommodations allow students with disabilities to access the general education curriculum by minimizing the impact of their disability on meeting classroom demands. It is important to be sure the appropriate instructional accommodations are in place prior to making a grading adaptation. Otherwise, students' grades will be a reflection of their disability and not their academic achievement.

4. *Have you identified your purposes for grades and articulated them clearly?* As already stated, grades can have various meanings and serve an array of purposes. Miscommunication of student progress can occur and the value of grades can be undermined if the purpose for grades are not discussed and agreed on by the teacher, parents, and the student.[9]

CLASSROOMWIDE GRADING ADAPTATIONS

Classroomwide grading adaptations can be used with all students and include making changes to letter grades and monitoring progress more frequently. Changes to letter grades clarify letter grades by supplementing them with other ways of evaluating and reporting student progress such as rubrics, written or verbal comments, logs of student activities, and portfolios. Examples of classroomwide grading adaptations are shown in table 10.2.

Remember that changes to letter grades do not have to be written on the report card itself. In fact, this may be impossible to do with commonly used automated grading computer programs that have limited preset comments available. Talking to parents or sending a separate letter for clarification may often be more appropriate. In addition, although adding information

Table 10.2 Grading Adaptations in Inclusive Classrooms

Whole-Class Grading Adaptations		Individualized Grading Adaptations	
Making Changes to Letter and Number Grades	**Example**	**Changing Grading Elements**	**Example**
Comments	Some students scored below benchmark levels during RTI assessments but earned As and Bs in reading on their report cards. The teacher writes comments to show that the reading level of material in the students' reading groups was below grade level.	Base all or part of the grade on progress on IEP objectives.	Jean's IEP indicates that she should score 95 percent or better on a set of twenty multiplication problems. The teacher determines she will earn an A if she meets this goal, a B if she scores between 85 and 94 percent, and so forth.
Activity logs	Teacher uses electronic activity logs showing students' performance solving word problems. Parents are given the results for review on a weekly basis.	Base all or part of the grade on performance on prioritized content and assignments.	The teacher determines that it is essential that Darren learn the phases of the water cycle based on the standard course of study for the current unit. Darren is given an assessment that tests only his knowledge of these core concepts.
Rubrics	All students are given a list of specific criteria to earn a passing grade in a tenth-grade civics project on supply and demand. Each element of the project is worth a set amount of points. Teachers use the rubric when grading the project and send a copy of the rubric home with the students.	Emphasize learning strategies and effort in a balanced grading system.	Amy is working on using a learning strategy to answer complex math problems correctly. She demonstrates appropriate use of the strategy on a think-aloud assessment.
		Change the value of grading elements.	Amy's effort learning the strategy and her correct use of the strategy are counted into her grade for the term.
Reporting progress more frequently	Students who are struggling with literary terms in ninth grade are assessed weekly using a brief three- to five-minute vocabulary test to determine their skill in using morphemes to understand words.	Grade on basis of improvement.	Michael earned 40 percent correct on the last spelling assessment. This week, he earned 60 percent. His teacher raised his grade to a C for showing 20 percent growth.
		Modify grading weights and scales.	April's IEP team decided to count homework completion as 30 percent of her grade, rather than the usual 10 percent, to motivate her to continue completing her homework.

(Continued)

is generally quite helpful, additional information should never state that the student is receiving special services; this would be a violation of student confidentiality.[10] Finally, reporting progress more frequently helps students and parents better understand their final report card grades and prevents the inevitable surprises that occur when progress is reported infrequently (e.g., "I thought Jean was doing so well and now you tell me she is not?").

INDIVIDUALIZED GRADING ADAPTATIONS

The second type of grading adaptations, also described in table 10.2, is individualized grading adaptations, which are carried out only for students with disabilities as specified on their IEPs. They are called for when a learner has a moderate to severe intellectual disability and modified curricular expectations, but can also be used when a learner has a mild disability and is already receiving a series of appropriate classroom accommodations. Merely having an IEP, trying hard, failing because of missed work, or receiving inappropriate accommodations by itself is not enough to qualify a student for an individualized grading adaptation. Individualized grading adaptations are done systematically in conjunction with a student's IEP, and as such are legally binding. Individualized grading adaptations include two types: changing the grading elements and changing the value of the grading elements.[11]

Changing the grading elements involves changing what specifically counts toward earning a grade, such as basing all or part of the grade on progress on IEP objectives, on performance on prioritized content and assignments, and emphasizing learning strategies and effort in a balanced grading system. Descriptions and examples of each of these are shown in table 10.2. Although all of these adaptations have the benefit of connecting students' IEPs to how they are evaluated in the general education classroom, care must always be taken to ensure that the standard of access to the general education curriculum is maintained.

Changing the value of the grading elements means that teachers may base part of the grade on improvement over past performance and modify grading weights and scales.[12] Descriptions and examples of each of these types of individualized grading adaptations are shown in table 10.2. Changing the value of grading elements has the potential advantage of motivating students with disabilities because they can earn a higher grade. However, caution is advised when using these adaptations. When grading on the basis of improvement, students may become dependent on special contingencies or may lack the skills needed to improve. The lack of increased performance standards when using modified grading weights and scales may undermine students' incentive to improve. Modifying grading weights and scales may also be perceived by classmates as unfair.

ASSESSMENT CONSIDERATIONS AT THE HIGH SCHOOL LEVEL

One of the most controversial assessment issues involves high-stakes graduation exit exams. These exams are considered high stakes because the consequences of not passing them have serious consequences for young adults. For students with disabilities, this is a very significant issue. Because of these exit exams and other graduation requirements, states have developed alternative options that allow students with disabilities to exit high school but with an alternative to a regular high school diploma.[13] In fact, recent statistics point to the fact that only approximately half of all students identified with a disability complete high school with a regular diploma.[14]

There are serious consequences to receiving an alternative high school diploma. In fact, many post-secondary institutions do not value alternative diplomas highly. One study found that many postsecondary admissions boards view students with these alternate diplomas similarly to those students who dropped out of high school.[15] It is, therefore, incredibly important to support most students with disabilities in attaining a regular high school diploma.

If you are working with secondary students with disabilities, you should investigate the following questions:

► What are the graduation options for students with disabilities?
► Does the state require exit exams for graduation? If so, what options are available to students with disabilities?
► What are the consequences of partaking in a nontraditional exit exam?

Ethical Considerations

As evident throughout this chapter, assessment practices present considerable ethical concerns because the administration, interpretation, and educational decisions based on assessment can alter a student's educational experiences. The Council for Exceptional Children has developed standards for professional practice that can guide how we consider the ethical use of assessment practices for students with disabilities:[16]

► Use assessment instruments and procedures that do not discriminate against persons with exceptionalities on the basis of race, color, creed, sex, national origin, age, political practices, family or social background, sexual orientation, or exceptionality.
► Base grading, promotion, graduation, and movement out of the program on the individual goals and objectives for students with exceptionalities.
► Provide accurate program data to administrators, colleagues, and parents based on efficient and objective record-keeping practices for the purpose of decision making.
► Maintain confidentiality of information except when information is released under specific conditions of written consent and statutory confidentiality requirements.

Generally, these standards are intended to remind us to use assessment practices to make instructional decisions in the best interest of students.

Providing Assessment Results to Parents

Parents and guardians play a vitally important role in the education of their children with disabilities. As part of the IEP team, they provide critical information that informs their child's education. We cannot assume, however, that they have the necessary knowledge of assessment practices to participate fully in conversations about assessment needs or results. When communicating assessment results to parents or guardians, therefore, you must remember that they may not understand many of the concepts you are attempting to communicate. For example, percentiles are often difficult for parents to understand because they confuse percentiles with percentages. You may say that the student's scores fell within the fiftieth percentile, and they will hear 50 percent (or failing). Also, remember that hearing about a student's assessment results can be emotionally challenging for parents, so be sensitive when providing feedback. Given the many pitfalls that may occur in communicating with parents about assessments, Salvia, Ysseldyke, and Bolt provide a list of helpful suggestions:[17]

▶ Have frequent communication with parents and guardians about their child's progress. The authors stated that parents and guardians may not know if their child struggles unless you communicate this information with them.

▶ Make sure that you communicate strengths as well as weaknesses. By highlighting both, you provide a more holistic picture of the child as a learner and avoid the pitfall of focusing only on the negative.

▶ If the parents and guardians speak a language other than English, provide a translator to communicate assessment information.

▶ Be mindful of the parents' and guardians' cultural background and how it might affect their understanding of assessment information.

▶ Try to schedule meetings at times that are convenient for parents and guardians to attend. Because parents may work during the day, for example, they may not be able to attend meetings during school hours.

▶ Explain the purposes, procedures, and results of assessments. The authors suggested that it may be helpful to schedule a premeeting to provide background information about the various assessments so that parents feel prepared to participate in the meeting about assessment results and educational planning based on those results.

▶ Do not use acronyms, unnecessary jargon, or technical language when communicating assessment results. The authors suggested erring on the side of using easier language to explain assessment information rather than language that is too technical.

▶ Focus on solutions and meeting the instructional needs of the students and avoid any discussions of blame about past educational decisions that may have not been successful.

TO SUM UP

▶ Familiarize yourself with the content standards that your students are required to meet and align assessments to these standards.

▶ Work with general education teachers to develop testing accommodations and modifications that are consistent between instructional assessments and district and state assessments.

▶ Make instructional decisions based on data from multiple assessments. No one assessment provides the full story!

▶ Know the legal requirements and district policies for assessing students for special education services.

▶ Communicate assessment results to parents and guardians in a clear fashion and avoid assessment jargon whenever possible.

WHAT'S NEXT?

You now understand more fully the assessment issues that inform educational decision making for students with disabilities. We will now shift gears toward focusing on effective instruction. Specifically, we will emphasize ways of proactively planning instruction that meets the needs of all learners through the lenses of universal design for learning, instructional technologies, and assistive technologies.

ADDITIONAL RESOURCES

► Intervention Central: www.interventioncentral.org

► National Alternative Assessment Center: www.naacpartners.org

► National Center on Educational Outcomes: www.cehd.umn.edu/nceo/default.html

► National Center on Student Progress Monitoring: www.studentprogress.org/default.asp

CHAPTER ELEVEN

Universal Design for Learning and Technology

In this chapter you will learn about:

- How to use the UDL framework to guide your instructional planning
- How to integrate instructional technologies into your instruction
- How to determine which ATs support the unique needs of students with disabilities
- Resources that support UDL, ATs, and instructional technologies

Julia, a new special educator in a suburban elementary school, saw the value of UDL early on: "My caseload is huge and I can't be in every classroom all the time. Because I work with the general education teachers on UDL, at least I know they are thinking about the kids with disabilities while they plan. The kids are learning, so the general ed teachers have bought into this."

As a special education teacher, you probably place a great deal of emphasis on making sure that your students can access learning. Historically, teachers, parents, and advocates for students with disabilities have had to work very hard to make sure that students with disabilities have this access. In recent times, though, we have shifted the conversation away from simple access to meaningful access.

This chapter addresses various ways of supporting meaningful engagement of students with disabilities through three related areas of instruction: universal design for learning (UDL), instructional technologies, and assistive technologies (ATs). All three areas support meaningful access but they do so differently. This chapter provides general strategies and additional resources for you to access to gain further information about each of these three areas.

Students with disabilities are not one large category of students who struggle in similar ways. In fact, when you observe your students, you will likely find that they are quite different from each other. You can meet the needs of the diversity of your students through proactively planning in a manner that addresses UDL, instructional technologies, and ATs.

UDL, Instructional Technologies, and ATs

▶ *UDL:* An instructional planning framework for proactively addressing barriers in the curriculum to support students with diverse learning needs and benefit a broad range of students. This is accomplished, in part, through considering how to represent information in multiple ways, providing multiple ways for students to demonstrate their understanding, and planning for multiple ways of engaging students in learning. If you are planning a lesson that is universally designed, you will look at the curriculum, materials, assessments, and resources as flexible so that students' strengths, interests, background knowledge, and individual needs can inform the instruction. For example, rather than an eighth-grade math teacher simply providing examples of math problems on the board and then assigning homework, the teacher could provide YouTube videos illustrating the big ideas, tie those ideas to real-world mathematics, and allow students to use various technologies to assist them in learning the concepts. There is no one way to "do UDL," but this chapter will provide you with some guidelines to help inform your planning so that it aligns with the principles of UDL.

▶ *Instructional technologies:* The diverse range of technologies used to support student learning and engagement. Some technologies are useful across various content areas and can include common computer software programs such as word processing. Other instructional technologies are more content specific. For example, geography, math, and science teachers can find different uses for Google Earth to expand understanding and illustrate content-specific concepts.

▶ *ATs:* Technologies that support the individual needs of students with disabilities. Unlike instructional technologies, which benefit a wide range of students, assistive technologies are much more individualized. These range from low-tech objects such as pencil grips to high-tech software for communication, physical mobility, and other instructional needs.

Similar to the new teachers described in the following passage, you may feel overwhelmed by concepts such as UDL, instructional technology, and AT. Although these teachers are aware that these may be powerful tools, they just do not know where to start.

Doug teaches in an inclusive eighth-grade science class. This is his first year teaching in a school with a heavy focus on UDL and technology integration. He has gone to some professional development activities and is beginning to align his instructional practices with UDL into his science instruction. He commented, "I see how to use instructional tech in science. I just don't know how to integrate UDL with science inquiry."

Claire teaches in a self-contained classroom for students with autism spectrum disorders. She hopes to encourage her team to support integrating her students into the general education setting more and more. Her students have various low- to high-tech ATs that support their learning. She hopes to work with the general education teachers to plan using the UDL framework so that her students can be successful in the general education classroom. She also hopes to meet with her district's AT coordinator to help her learn how to better use the technologies that her students are using to communicate.

Doug and Claire have two very different concerns. Doug is in an inclusive setting and is trying to integrate UDL into a set science curriculum. His school has made a commitment to using the UDL framework to support diverse learners. Claire is hoping to introduce UDL into some general education classes so that her students can be successful in those settings. She also realizes that she needs to become more proficient in AT because her students require a combination of UDL and AT to be successful. As you read this chapter, it may be helpful to consider your own instructional needs as well as Doug's and Claire's dilemmas.

PLAN ENGAGING AND ACCESSIBLE INSTRUCTION THROUGH UDL

Universal design in education has an interesting history. In fact, it originated from architectural planning of spaces that are accessible to people with physical disabilities! This section provides a short history of UDL and then offers specific suggestions for implementing UDL in your instruction.

A Brief History

UDL offers an instructional planning framework to help teachers consider how to provide engaging, challenging, and accessible instruction to diverse learners. The history of UDL has its roots in architectural design when architects began to consider how to design buildings that are accessible to people with physical disabilities and also that would benefit other people using the buildings.

This movement to build physically accessible buildings was brought to the forefront of architectural design because of the ADA, which stated that public buildings such as schools and courthouses had to comply with physical accessibility standards. Initially, buildings had to be retrofitted to make them accessible with supports such as ramps and widened doors after the buildings were constructed. These fixes were not elegant or aesthetically pleasing, looked like an afterthought, and were often awkward to navigate or use.

Because of issues resulting from after-the-fact retrofitting, architects then started planning for accessibility as they were designing new buildings. They found that if they proactively designed accessibility into their designs, the buildings could not only be more aesthetically pleasing, but also useful for a broader population beyond just people with disabilities. For example, automatic doors helped people with limited mobility as well as parents pushing strollers, shoppers with arms full of groceries, and even people busy texting.

In the 1980s, the Center for Applied Special Technologies (CAST) began to apply the architectural concepts of universally designed buildings to education as a framework that teachers can use to proactively design instruction to minimize barriers and address the needs of a broad group of academically diverse students.

THE BASICS OF UDL: REACH AND ENGAGE YOUR STUDENTS IN MULTIPLE WAYS

You should consider UDL to be a roadmap for planning instruction in a way that reduces the learning barriers faced by many students with disabilities and at the same time increasing their learning opportunities.[1] None of your students are alike. They have different motivations for learning, different areas of strength and weakness, and different goals. UDL allows you to plan with this diversity in mind.

When looking at planning and teaching from this perspective, UDL no longer seems like a "special education thing." In fact, although UDL greatly benefits students with disabilities, because it focuses on the overall diversity among our students, it also benefits ELLs, students at risk for academic failure, typical learners, and students receiving gifted education services.

THREE PRINCIPLES OF UDL: MULTIPLE MEANS OF REPRESENTATION, ACTION AND EXPRESSION, AND ENGAGEMENT

The main goal of planning in a manner that is consistent with UDL is to consider the level of flexibility that you build into your instruction as well as in the materials that are available to your students. This flexibility can be understood through the three guiding principles of UDL: multiple means of representation, action and expression, and engagement. Figure 11.1 describes these principles.

Multiple Means of Representation

Planning for multiple means of representation in your instruction means that you acknowledge that students have preferences in how they acquire new information. Some students may learn quite well by listening to the teacher and taking notes. For many students, however, this form of instruction is not efficient or engaging. Therefore, when you plan your instruction, consider building flexibility into the ways that you present information to your students. Examples of providing multiple means of representation are listed in table 11.1. These strategies are important for providing students with alternatives and options for accessing instructional content.

Multiple Means of Action and Expression

Allow and encourage students to demonstrate their knowledge in different ways. Strategies for doing so include offering choices in how students demonstrate their understanding. Although you may include more traditional assessment options such as tests and worksheets, consider offering options for the following ways of presenting knowledge as well:

▶ *Multimedia presentation:* Technology continues to evolve and offer more options for students to present their understanding (see table 11.2 for technology options).

▶ *Collaborative projects rather than individual assessment options:* Collaborative projects allow students to work in an unstructured group that demonstrates knowledge and choose from specific jobs in presenting that information. There is a lot of information out there about how to group students in collaborative groups. Consider the needs and interests of your students when you create collaborative groups so that you can assign group roles that the students will find interesting. Also consider how you can use online collaborative tools such as Google Docs (http://docs.google.com) or wikis such as Wikispaces (www.wikispaces.com) or PBworks (www.pbworks.com) to further facilitate collaboration.

Multiple Means of Engagement

Provide options that motivate, interest, and challenge students in learning. In order to plan instruction in this manner, it is important to consider how students can engage in content. This may be especially

I. Provide Multiple Means of **Representation**	II. Provide Multiple Means of **Action and Expression**	III. Provide Multiple Means of **Engagement**
1: Provide option for perception	4: Provide options for physical action	7: Provide options for recruiting interest
1.1 Offer ways of customizing the display of information	4.1 Vary the methods for response and navigation	7.1 Optimize individual choice and autonomy
1.2 Offer alternatives for auditory information	4.2 Optimize access to tools and assistive technologies	7.2 Optimize relevance, value, and authenticity
1.3 Offer alternatives for visual information		7.3 Minimize threats and distractions
2: Provide options for language, mathematical expressions, and symbols	5: Provide options for expression and communication	8: Provide options for sustaining effort and persistence
2.1 Clarify vocabulary and symbols	5.1 Use multiple media for communication	8.1 Heighten salience of goals and objectives
2.2 Clarify syntax and structure	5.2 Use multiple tools for construction and composition	8.2 Vary demands and resources to optimize challenge
2.3 Support decoding of text, mathematical notation, and symbols	5.3 Build fluencies with graduated levels of support for practice and performance	8.3 Foster collaboration and community
2.4 Promote understanding across languages		8.4 Increase mastery-oriented feedback
2.5 Illustrate through multiple media		
3: Provide options for comprehension	6: Provide options for executive functions	9: Provide options for self-regulation
3.1 Activate or supply background knowledge	6.1 Guide appropriate goal-setting	9.1 Promote expectations and beliefs that optimize motivation
3.2 Highlight patterns, critical features, big ideas, and relationships	6.2 Support planning and strategy development	9.2 Facilitate personal coping skills and strategies
3.3 Guide information processing, visualization, and manipulation	6.3 Facilitate managing information and resources	9.3 Develop self-assessment and reflection
3.4 Maximize transfer and generalization	6.4 Enhance capacity for monitoring progress	
Resourceful, knowledgeable learners	Strategic, goal-directed learners	Purposeful, motivated learners

© CAST

Figure 11.1 Universal Design for Learning Guidelines 2.0[2]

Table 11.1 Multiple Means of Representation

Suggestions for Multiple Means of Representation	Examples and Resources
Including technologies such as digital text to allow for features such as text-to-speech, digital tagging, and embedded dictionaries	You may have access to e-readers (such as iPads and Nook by Barnes and Noble). There are also free or inexpensive text-to-speech software for desktop computers. Students can then make choices in how they access information.
Using graphic organizers or interactive reading guides to accompany reading assignments	Provide explicit instruction in using the graphic organizers or reading guides to move students toward independent use when possible (see chapter 13 on reading for more details). Students can then have various ways of independently and collaboratively accessing the big ideas.
Integrating multimedia options for representing major concepts	Consider websites such as iTunes U, Khan Academy, and TeacherTube (web addresses provided at the end of the chapter). These options enable student choice and increased independence.
Providing text options at different readability levels	Your district resource center or library may have leveled books. Google's advance search option provides leveled-reading search results. Other search engines with readability levels are provided at the end of the chapter. Students can thus access content at their own reading and knowledge levels.
Embedding choices in how students access information	Provide options for print or digital materials (including multimedia). Offer students support in choosing content. Allow for collaborative work or peer coaching in accessing information.

tricky for older students with disabilities because they may associate school and learning with disengagement because of a history of failure in particular subjects. For example, if a student has experienced years of failure and frustration in areas such as mathematics, reading, science, or writing, engaging students in these activities necessitates teachers to plan instruction that provides alternatives to the type of instruction that has resulted in students' acceptance of failure and frustration. Suggestions for promoting meaningful instructional engagement across the subject areas include the following:

▶ Simulations and video games that promote instructional content. These learning experiences are often tied to content standards and are becoming more and more available. For example, Filament Games (www.filamentgames.com) has created learning video games across diverse content including science, social studies, mathematics, reading, and even career development. Similarly, companies such as PhET (http://phet.colorado.edu) and Gizmos (www.explorelearning.com) provide interactive simulations around instructional topics related to many instructional concepts taught in K–12 instruction. Many students find virtual play an engaging way of accessing instructional content and at the same time develop deeper understanding.

Table 11.2 Technology Options for Expressing Understanding

Technology	Presentation Type	Websites and Resources
PowerPoint	Slide presentation software from Microsoft that is not free but is available on most computers in schools as part of the Microsoft Office Suite	http://office.microsoft.com
Keynote	Slide presentation software from Apple that is not free but is available on many Apple computers	www.apple.com/keynote
Open Office	Free slide presentation that is similar to PowerPoint and Keynote	www.openoffice.org
Prezi	Free presentation software that helps you create digital posters that can be presented in nonlinear ways and that allow presenters to import media seamlessly	http://prezi.com
Inspiration and Kidspiration	Visual mapping software that allows for concept diagrams and maps; it is not free but many schools have it	www.inspiration.com
Audio and video podcasting	Audio or video recordings that teachers or students can upload online to either open or place on password-protected sites	Free podcasting sites such as iTunes U, http://podbean.com, http://podcastpickle.com
iPod Touch, flip cams, and other video-capturing technologies	Video-capturing devices that allow for podcasting and video presentations	Devices such as iPod Touch (http://apple.com/ipodtouch), Sony Bloggie cameras (http://store.sony.com)

▶ Virtual tours are another means by which students can learn about complex instructional materials, especially in learning science and social studies content. For example, Google Earth (http://earth.google.com) provides ways of seeing our Earth from multiple perspectives including under water, from satellite views, and even back in history.

UDL and Instructional Planning

Although the principles of UDL seem simple and logical, actually planning in a manner that is consistent with UDL takes a great deal of upfront thought. One helpful resource in considering UDL planning is an instructional process developed by the UDL–Implementation and Research Network (see exhibit 11.1). You can access this tool as well as others at http://udl-irn.org.

GENERAL HINTS FOR IMPLEMENTING UDL

When you first consider how to plan in a manner consistent with UDL, you will find that it takes time to do so in a way that meets the needs of diverse learners. Consider the suggestions on page 198.

Exhibit 11.1   UDL Instructional Process[3]

As a framework, UDL requires educators to think proactively about the needs of all learners. Educators implementing UDL should use a backward design instructional process that incorporates the following five steps.

STEP ONE: ESTABLISH CLEAR OUTCOMES

Establish a clear understanding of the goal(s) of the lesson (or unit) and specific learner outcomes related to the following:

► The desired outcomes and essential student understandings and performance for every learner (What does learning look like? What will students be able to do or demonstrate?)

► The desired big ideas learners should come to understand and their alignment to the established standards within the program of study

► The potential misunderstandings, misconceptions, and areas in which learners may meet barriers to learning

► How goals will be clearly communicated to the learners in ways that are understandable to all learners

STEP TWO: ANTICIPATE LEARNER NEEDS

Prior to planning the instructional experience, teachers should have a clear understanding of the learner needs within their environment:

► Learner strengths and weaknesses specific to lesson and unit goals

► Learner background knowledge for scaffolding new learning

► Learner preferences for representation, expression, and engagement

► Learner language preferences

► Cultural relevance and understanding

► Curriculum barriers (e.g., physical, social, cultural, or ability level) that could limit the accessibility to instruction and instructional materials

STEP THREE: MEASURABLE OUTCOMES AND ASSESSMENT PLAN

Prior to planning the instructional experience, establish how learning is going to be measured:

► Previously established lesson goals and learner needs

► Embedding checkpoints to ensure all learners are successfully meeting their desired outcomes

► Providing learners with multiple ways and options to authentically engage in the process, take action, and demonstrate understanding

► Supporting higher-order skills and encouraging a deeper connection with the content

STEP FOUR: INSTRUCTIONAL EXPERIENCE

Establish the instructional sequence of events:

► Develop intentional and proactive ways to address the established goals, learner needs, and the assessment plan.

(Continued)

- ► Establish a plan for how instructional materials and strategies will be used to overcome barriers and support learner understanding.
- ► Create a plan that ensures high expectations for all learners including the needs of the learners in the margins (i.e., struggling and advanced).
- ► Integrate an assessment plan to provide necessary data.

Considerations should be made for how to support multiple means of the following:

- ► *Representation:* Teacher purposefully uses a variety of strategies, instructional tools, and methods to present information and content to anticipate student needs and preferences.
- ► *Expression and action:* Student uses a variety of strategies, instructional tools, and methods to demonstrate new understandings.
- ► *Engagement:* A variety of methods are used to engage students (e.g., provide choice, address student interest) and promote their ability to monitor their own learning (e.g., goal setting, self-assessment, and reflection).

STEP FIVE: REFLECTION AND NEW UNDERSTANDINGS

Establish checkpoints for teacher reflection and new understandings:

- ► Did the learners obtain the big ideas and the desired outcomes? (What data support your inference?)
- ► What instructional strategies worked well? How can instructional strategies be improved?
- ► What tools worked well? How could the use of tools be improved?
- ► What strategies and tools provided for multiple means of representation, action and expression, and engagement?
- ► What additional tools would have been beneficial to have access to and why?
- ► Overall, how might you improve this lesson?

Collaborate with General Education Teachers

Because UDL is not intended to only support struggling learners and students with disabilities, it is important to work with the general education teachers in implementing UDL in the general education classrooms. General educators may not have a great deal of knowledge about UDL or even of the barriers in the curriculum that would result in many students struggling, so they will rely on you to help them integrate the principles of UDL into their practices.

Your Skills in Implementing UDL Will Improve Over Time

When considering implementation, think about degrees of implementation rather than a rigid yes-or-no approach in which teachers are either implementing UDL fully or not at all. In your own planning, you will find that planning for UDL is time consuming to develop and takes time to implement. Start with planning one lesson using the UDL framework, reflect on the lesson, and then move toward large goals such as planning an entire UDL unit. If you consider small steps toward UDL, you will be more likely to succeed. Also, in working with general education teachers, there is a danger that they will think that you want to change their entire teaching approach if you suggest too many changes at once. If you consider the continuum of UDL implementation, you can begin by making small changes that are consistent with UDL rather than attempting to change your entire teaching practice at once.

What Instructional Supports Are Available to You and the General Education Teachers with Whom You Work

These supports include technologies, staff, and curricular materials available to the teachers. Being realistic about what can be done is incredibly important but so is pushing past the status quo toward better instruction.

Using the UDL Framework to Support ELLs

Wenonoa Spivak, University of Cincinnati

UDL WITH ELLs: APPLICATIONS OF SELECTED PRINCIPLES

ELLs may have difficulties in acquiring and expressing knowledge. It is estimated that it takes up to seven years for ELLs to acquire literacy in academic English that is equivalent to their native speaking counterparts. UDL offers a framework through which content can be made accessible to ELLs. This case study will offer ideas and tips for working with ELLs with regard to selected UDL principles.

MULTIPLE MEANS OF REPRESENTATION

This first principle of UDL includes some critical components that can support the "what" of learning for ELLs by how information is presented. This principle includes such things as clarifying vocabulary, mathematical notation, and symbols and activating or supplying background knowledge.

IN PRACTICE

- ▶ Present a language objective to the students for every lesson.
- ▶ Define key terms in the students' first language (L1). You can do this in homogeneous L1 groups or individually and share in a whole-group setting.
- ▶ Deepen the ELLs' knowledge of key vocabulary. Begin with a paragraph containing key vocabulary words in context. Incorporate reading strategies by reading for a general idea of the passage as a whole. Continue on to the word level with specific definitions of words and a discussion of affixes that can help with cross-content understanding and metacognition.
- ▶ Students can be charged with finding content vocabulary words in texts that are interesting or new to them, highlighting their occurrences, defining them, and presenting the information to the class.
- ▶ Show videos or play songs that demonstrate the vocabulary terms in context.

(Continued)

▶ Allow the use of tools to assist: electronic translation tools and digital text applications that can read words, sentences, and passages can help ELLs pick up on prosody and inflection in their target language (L2) of English.

▶ Gradually decrease the use of these supports so that the ELLs take over the digital text reader's role as they adjust to the pronunciation, rate, and inflection of the reading.

▶ Additionally, some publishers offer books that are modified for challenged readers (often called *hi-lo books*) and these can be tools that teachers can incorporate initially or in conjunction with the course text as the ELL improves in English literacy.

Tools

Tool	Website	Description
Click, Speak	http://clickspeak.clcworld.net	This is a simple, free program for students to have web pages read to them to improve English literacy.
Applied Language Solutions	www.appliedlanguage.com /web_translation.shtml	This program enables students to translate pages and entire websites into another language.
Learning Suffixes	www.vocabulary.co.il/suffixes	This website offers different activities for students at different levels.
Vocab Ahead	www.vocabahead.com	Students and teachers can watch and create their own vocab videos.
Visuwords	www.visuwords.com	This program offers an online graphic dictionary and thesaurus that illustrates relationships between words.
Vocabulary self-collection	http://ohiorc.org/record/3804 .aspx	This site provides an explanation of the vocabulary self-collection strategy and how to incorporate it into your classroom.
Brain POP	www.brainpop.com	This site offers a great way to illustrate vocabulary in context and reinforce the meaning of words.
Graphic organizers	www.graphic.org/concept.html	This is a website that offers ideas to create graphic organizers for display and enactment of background knowledge.
Hi-lo books	www.resourceroom.net /comprehension/hilow.asp	This is a website with a list of books that are adapted to challenged or reluctant readers.

MULTIPLE MEANS OF ACTION AND EXPRESSION

The second principle of UDL includes important considerations of how to help ELLs express what they know within the content. ELLs have potentially differing proficiency levels in English so it is important that teachers remember that their conversational proficiency may be very different from their ability to express themselves in academic writing. This principle includes having access to tools and technologies, multiple media for communication, appropriate goal setting, planning and strategy development, and monitoring progress.

- ▶ As the ELLs become accustomed to the new vocabulary, determine a range of ways that they could demonstrate their knowledge of the vocabulary and main ideas.
- ▶ After the paragraph and definitions, students can express their understanding of the concepts through drawing a picture representing the big idea of the lesson and labeling the key vocabulary words.
- ▶ Next, try to incorporate a way in which the big ideas could be demonstrated through motion or a kinesthetic activity.
- ▶ Students can record themselves thinking aloud or as they read and decode a text passage to demonstrate how they approach these tasks.
- ▶ Students write their language objective and content objective at the top of their progress-monitoring sheet and complete the expected steps to reach their goals.
- ▶ Using a flow-chart process, students can create a visual representation of their goal-setting and progress-monitoring process.
- ▶ Teachers can present students with outlines at differing levels so that ELLs who are struggling with organization and progress can complete the required information.

Tools

Tool	Website	Description
Yodio	www.yodio.com	Students can record messages and commentary that explain photos or steps in a process.
SAM Animation	www.samanimation.com	Students can turn their content into stop-motion animated videos.
Flipcam, bloggie, or iPod Touch		Students can video content from class projects, homework, field trips, and so on to present to the class or teacher.
Camtasia	www.techsmith.com/camtasia-screencasting-1011.html?gclid=CJzF5dWB0qwCFWICQAodl0lm9Q	Students and teachers can try a thirty-day trial with no cost. This program captures everything occurring on the desktop and can include a video of the user as he or she narrates what is occurring on screen.
Goal-setting worksheets	www.abcteach.com/directory/middle-school-junior-high-goal-setting-3297–2–1	This site offers a collection of worksheets for goal setting.
Flow charts	http://arb.nzcer.org.nz/strategies/flowcharts.php	This site offers sample flow charts that students can complete as they document and monitor their progress.
Webspiration	www.mywebspiration.com	Classroom teachers can purchase subscriptions of this program that will help students create visual representations of brainstorming, organizing, planning, and executing their ideas and progress.

MULTIPLE MEANS OF ENGAGEMENT

The third principle of UDL addresses important concepts such as individual choice, relevance, value, and authenticity. The amount of choice that teachers need to provide to ELLs varies with

(Continued)

students, of course; therefore, these ideas and activities provide differing levels of support. The following resources offer options for ELLs to explore their interests and see how vocabulary and language interact in contexts that are engaging to them.

IN PRACTICE

▶ Offer students choices for topics that they can explore within the content area.

▶ Often teachers present ELLs with options that help them express their cultures; however, if your ELLs have been in the United States for a long period of time, they may be less interested in this option.

▶ Including books in the ELL's native language in the classroom as a supplement to the book in English can encourage relevancy and engagement with the text. If the student is literate in L1, this can provide a way for the ELL to access the text in English.

▶ ELLs who have difficulty taking notes on the content in the classroom can be provided with a copy or outline of the teacher's notes at the end of the class period to ensure that they do not lose crucial content.

▶ When in groups, each member can be assigned a different portion of the text to read for comprehension. This jigsaw text-reading approach can reduce the workload for ELLs and encourage group collaboration.

Tools

Tool	Website	Description
Flipboard app	http://itunes.apple.com/us/app/flipboard/id358801284?mt=8	You can add any RSS feed to this app to explore tons of different content areas. Students are bound to find something here that interests them.
Book Adventure	www.bookadventure.com/Home.aspx	Students can search books to find something that interests them, monitor their reading progress, and take quizzes.
Word Generation	http://wg.serpmedia.org	This program embeds academic vocabulary in text passages about issues under discussion in the country.
National Geographic	www.nationalgeographic.com	This site offers videos, stories, photographs, and text in an interactive way that helps make cross-content knowledge relevant and authentic to students.
ePals	www.epals.com	Students can connect with other students via the Internet to share information, ideas, and learn about content in new ways.

You can learn more about UDL by going to the following websites:

▶ Center for Applied Special Technology (CAST): www.cast.org
▶ Center for Universal Design, North Carolina State University: www.ncsu.edu/project/design-projects/udi
▶ National Center on Universal Design for Learning: www.udlcenter.org
▶ The Universal Design for Learning Implementation and Research Network (UDL-IRN): www.udl-irn.org
▶ The IRIS Center UDL module: http://iris.peabody.vanderbilt.edu/udl/chalcycle.htm

USING INSTRUCTIONAL TECHNOLOGIES TO SUPPORT STUDENTS WITH DISABILITIES

You have probably noticed that many strategies that support meaningful access and engagement make use of instructional technologies. Although we can argue about whether or not technology is absolutely necessary to implementing UDL fully, there is no arguing about the fact that instructional technologies can greatly enhance instruction by providing tools and materials that extend beyond static instructional materials. By providing technology tools that reduce barriers to learning, students can focus on learning and higher-order thinking skills.[4]

An example illustrating the power of technology is the spelling and grammar–checking application within word processing programs. Most people have used this feature (regardless of whether they have a disability). Spell and grammar check have changed the way we write! In the past, we spent time looking up words and unfamiliar sentence structures or used them inaccurately in our writing. Now, we write, are notified of incorrect words or sentence structures as they appear, and correct them during writing processes. Regardless of whether students have a disability, this technology can be helpful. You may still be asking yourself what does it mean to effectively integrate instructional technologies into our teaching practices and how does this apply when considering the needs of students with disabilities.

Where Do I Begin?

Technology is constantly changing and is used in education in increasingly more creative ways. When considering how to integrate the technologies available to you, think of ways of using it in your instructional delivery as well as by your students. This can be a daunting task, especially if you are not naturally drawn to using technology. Many teachers are overwhelmed by technology and simply do not attempt to integrate technology into their instruction. It is important to recognize that although it can be time consuming and difficult to learn how to use technology, technology can open the door to student learning and engagement in a very powerful way. You probably have two very important resources to help in learning new technologies: other teachers in your school and technology-savvy students. One way to begin exploring new instructional technologies is by exploring those technologies on your own and then seeing how to use these same technologies to support your students. Also, remember that learning any new technology takes time.

▶ *Gain basic skills in using the technology.* There is always a learning curve. Expect that it may take you time to learn how to use new technologies. Teachers who are effective technology users are not necessarily "techies." They are teachers who understand the power of using technology to support students with disabilities and then persevere through the learning curve! Using powerful instructional technologies is worth the time you will spend in learning how to use them.

▶ *Integrate the technologies into your own teaching.* Using instructional technologies requires more than simply knowing how to use them generally. In fact, one of the most frustrating things you will experience when you receive professional development in the various instructional technologies available in your school is that often this professional development will focus only on the general use of the technologies and not on ways that you can meaningfully integrate the technologies into your own instructional practices. Anticipate that this process can be as time consuming as learning how to use the technologies in the first place. With almost any effective instructional technology, you can find numerous resources on the Internet to support content-specific or skill-specific technology integration.

▶ *Teach the students how to use the technologies strategically.* Just as you need time to learn how to use new instructional technologies, your students do as well. Make sure that you build time into your instructional plans to introduce new technologies, explain the benefits of using the technologies to support learning and engagement, model using the technologies, and allow students practice with the technologies. For example, when introducing students to software that allows for text-to-speech so that the students can hear their written products as a proofreading strategy, you can begin with telling the students a story about when you were in school and you were required to turn in written assignments, you read through your work but missed a number of errors. You can explain that now there is software that allows students to hear what they write so that they can catch written errors more effectively. You then model using the software with writing that has errors. Next, students should have a chance to do the same. You would expect students to use the technology independently only after they have the tools to do so.

General Instructional Technologies and Student Learning

You will not find the same technologies in any school that you visit. There is such a wide range of technologies available in schools and even in classrooms within the same schools. Therefore, you cannot assume that when you start teaching, you will have a set group of technologies to support students. Generally, there are common technologies that support learning across the different subject areas and more specific technologies that address the specific instructional content of the content areas. In this section, we will explore general and content-specific technologies.

One of the first things you will probably do when you begin teaching in a new school is explore the resources, materials, and technologies available to you and other teachers to support student learning and engagement. Instructional technologies have sometimes been categorized as those used by teachers versus those used by students. This distinction is becoming less relevant as we have come to realize that teachers should not always be the ones delivering content for students to consume. Instead, teachers are more and more looked on as facilitators who allow students to have choice and autonomy over some aspects of their learning. So, when examining instructional technologies, try to avoid the trap of considering some technologies as teacher technologies and others as student technologies. Rather, consider how those technologies can be used to maximize student learning, allow for flexibility, and fit within a UDL framework.

In typical classrooms, you will usually find a few desktop computers, a projector, and a teacher computer. In classrooms with more technology, you may also find additional technologies.

Interactive Whiteboards

These systems involve an interactive display connected to a central computer and an overhead projector. You and your students can interact with the board with a stylus marker and even your hands. There are many classroom uses for an interactive whiteboard but unfortunately many times these are used as expensive overhead projectors because teachers do not have the professional development, time, or resources to use these technologies in a meaningful way. If you have access to an interactive whiteboard, you should consider how it can be used to support your students' learning and engagement. Tips for integrating interactive whiteboard into your instruction include the following:

▶ Consider the numerous ways of engaging students with the whiteboard: as an interactive center, having students come up to the board during discussions, problem solving, and illustrating concepts. For example, when teaching students metacognitive strategies such as finding patterns among items, you can have students brainstorm items on the interactive whiteboards, brainstorm categories, and then have the students physically move their items on the board to fit under the categories. In this way, the students are engaged and not just watching you interact with the technology.

▶ There are numerous resources you can access to learn how to use the interactive whiteboard and get tips for how they support student learning. These resources include the following:

- *Promethean Planet* (www.prometheanplanet.com/en): This website offers a range of supports for using interactive whiteboards. Although the resources specifically target teachers who use Promethean whiteboards, the teacher blogs and suggestions can be applied to other interactive whiteboards as well.

- *SMART Inclusion* (http://smartinclusion.wikispaces.com/Smart+Inclusion+Home): This wiki provides information on using a variety of technologies but focuses primarily on the use of SMART Boards to support students with disabilities.

▶ Observe other teachers who use interactive whiteboards to get ideas for how to integrate them into your own instruction. Often, you will get the best ideas and suggestions from other teachers in your building or school district.

Classroom Response Systems (Clickers)

This technology allows you to ask your students multiple-choice questions and get immediate feedback from all your students in real time. These are helpful for getting feedback about student understanding, attitudes, or any other information that you want to get without putting students on the spot. Because students can simply input their answers into their clickers, they often feel more able to express themselves than raising their hands in class. Additionally, the students' response data can immediately be graphed and displayed so that students can see their responses either with or without their names and IDs. Hints for using classroom clickers include the following:

▶ During classroom discussions or lectures, you can keep students actively engaged by having them use clickers to answer questions throughout the class.

▶ For struggling learners, you can use the clickers to reinforce learning, review previous information, and get information about students' comfort with the information learned.

▶ You can find many resources for using interactive clickers. Many of these resources are on teacher websites such as Clickteaching (http://clickteaching.com) and the Denver Public Schools' teacher technology resources information page about clickers (http://teachertechresources.wikispaces.dpsk12.org/Clicker+Resources).

▶ Similar to other new technologies, learning to use clickers to support educating students with disabilities takes time.

Mobile Learning Devices

With the advent of mobile devices such as iPads and the Samsung Galaxy, students can now access and interact with information with much more flexibility. When thinking of the UDL framework, it is easy to see how mobile learning devices can enhance learning within each of the three UDL principles:

▶ *Multiple means of representation:* Students can access digital text, videos, and simulations.
▶ *Multiple means of expression and action:* Students can take notes, capture video, or create digital presentations of their learning.

▶ *Multiple means of engagement:* Students can engage in educational video games or simulations as well as integrate probeware or other devices with these mobile learning devices.

Video Games

There is a growing body of literature that suggests that video games hold great power to support the learning of students with disabilities. Educational video games, sometimes called *serious* video games, have a dual purpose. The first purpose is to help students learn specific content areas. The second purpose is to engage students in learning through game play. Consider how to integrate video games into your instruction through these means:

▶ Find video games that are tied to educational standards or the skills that your students need to learn. More and more, video game developers include information about the academic standards addressed by their games. These are useful as you map the content you are responsible for teaching.

▶ Look for effective game features. You can learn a great deal about whether an educational video game is useful by playing the game yourself. Good video games will have features such as the following:

  • Progressively more difficult levels as students master skills
  • Features to help students when they are stuck within a level
  • Options for customizing the game to meet student needs
  • Data collection that you can access or download

▶ Think of creative ways of integrating video games into your instruction. You can consider options such as having a gaming center for small-group collaborative work, allowing students to play as part of homework if they have access to computers at home, or even including game play as part of whole-group instruction so that you can strategically stop and discuss gaming decisions tied to instructional content.

▶ Communicate the purpose of the video games to parents and other teachers in order to explain their purpose, how they will address instructional content, and how the game will be used during class time. In this way, you will avoid misconceptions and misinformation about the use of gaming in learning.

Instructional Technology and Content Area Instruction

Technologies can support content area instruction in numerous ways. In fact, assisting students to become proficient in the technologies specific to the various content areas helps acculturate students into those disciplines, so it is important to learn which technologies content teachers are using so that you can support students in their use. For example, students are expected to use graphing calculators in math classes, and without this knowledge, students struggle with the basic procedures required to succeed in these courses. In science courses, students may use probeware to measure temperature, barometric pressure, or a number of other data within scientific inquiry. For students with disabilities, these technologies can foster improved access and increase motivation to study. If the students are not proficient in using these technologies, they can present frustrating barriers.

Although instructional technology can be used to provide access, engagement, and support to students with disabilities, sometimes these technologies can limit student engagement if they are not developed in an accessible manner. For example, some digital content is formatted with proprietary software that is locked, making it incompatible with software such as text-to-speech and other assistive technology options. When choosing instructional technology, therefore, it is critical that you ask yourself two questions:

► Is this technology engaging and enriching?

► Does the technology have limitations that limit my students' access?

If you look at instructional technologies from a UDL perspective, you will find yourself making more informed decisions about which instructional technologies you will use. Remember, proactive planning is the key. Content-specific technologies will be discussed in further detail in chapter 16.

ATs TO SUPPORT STUDENTS WITH DISABILITIES

You've read that the purpose of UDL is to provide you with guidelines for planning instruction that meets the needs of your diverse learners. Even when you implement UDL to its fullest, some students will still need additional supports and technologies to help them meaningfully access the content. This is where ATs come in. You can plan your lessons with multiple means of representation, expression and action, and engagement in a manner that meets the needs of most of your students, but some of your students may still need individualized technologies such as a Braille reader to access Braille text, an augmentative communication device to communicate, or another specific form of technology to meet his or her individual needs. Even with the most proactive planning, UDL will never replace the need for individualized ATs because there will always be some students whose needs are specific and unique.

What Are Assistive Technologies?

The purpose of AT is to provide students with the means necessary to accomplish tasks that they could not otherwise do independently. In this way, they will be more successful in accessing the general education curriculum, communicating with peers and teachers, and being more independent. *AT* is a legal term that is defined as those technologies that support the needs of people with disabilities. There are several definitions of AT but the one that teachers should be most familiar with is the one from IDEA. IDEA defines AT as two related constructs: AT devices and AT services.

AT Devices

According to IDEA, an AT device is "any item, piece of equipment, or product system, whether acquired commercially off the shelf, modified, or customized, that is used to increase, maintain, or improve functional capabilities of a child with a disability."[5] The purpose of AT devices, hence, is to improve the abilities of students who have been diagnosed with one of the IDEA-defined disabilities (see appendix A for more information about disability categories under IDEA).

AT Services

IDEA stipulates that AT devices be accompanied with AT services to help students access their AT devices. IDEA states that an AT service is "any service that directly assists a child with a disability in the selection, acquisition, or use of an assistive technology device."[6] It is important to consider AT as devices and services because of the following:

► Students, teachers, and families may need support in how to best use an AT device to support students with disabilities.

► It is expected that as a child learns to use a new AT and whose needs change over time, additional tweaking and problem solving may be necessary to ensure that the student benefits from the AT device(s). Systematic data collection and reassessment are necessary to ensure the student's AT is appropriate in meeting his or her ongoing needs.

IEPs and Assistive Technologies

The latest reauthorization of IDEA states that students with disabilities have a right to AT devices and services. More specifically, AT must be considered as part of the IEP process for all students who receive special education. The determination of how AT would support students with disabilities must be made on an individual basis. For example, not all students with reading disabilities benefit from text-to-speech software. The goal of AT is to help students be more successful and independent so its use must be an individual decision based on the strengths and needs of the individual student.

Continuum from No-Tech and Low-Tech to High-Tech AT

There is a continuum of low-tech to high-tech AT devices. Unfortunately, AT has often been equated only with high-tech technologies that support students with the most significant disabilities. When people think of AT, they often think of alternative and augmentative communication that assist students who are nonverbal. Although these are certainly considered AT, they represent only one kind of AT device.

Low-tech AT

There are many devices that are considered low-tech AT. Sometimes, the best option for addressing specific barriers is through simple solutions that requires no or very little technology. Examples of low-tech AT that you will probably have access to include the following:

► Pencil and pen grips to support hand positioning while writing
► Highlighters to indicate main ideas in text
► Magnifying glass or screen magnifier to see small text
► Sticky notes for note-taking
► Adapted eating utensils to support hand positioning while eating
► Adapted paper with raised lines, larger spaces between lines, or other variations

High-tech AT

As technologies increase in sophistication, they become more high tech and typically more expensive. Examples of high-tech AT include the following:

► Software programs to assist with academics such as text-to-speech and voice-recognition software
► Hardware devices such as computers and mobile devices with various supports
► Classroom amplification systems
► Braille keyboards, printers, and translator software
► Voice-output devices for augmentative communication

Determining Appropriate AT for the Individualized Needs of Students with Disabilities

It will be important for you to consider the unique situations of your students in order to fully understand their needs for AT. There are several well-accepted methods of determining which AT devices and services best meet the needs of students with disabilities. One process that you may likely find helpful is the SETT process,[7] which was designed as a flexible method of making informed, collaborative decisions about AT considerations in a manner that can be incorporated into the IEP process. SETT is an acronym for *student*, *environment*, *tasks*, and *tools*. This process will help you and the rest of the instructional team consider your students' AT needs in a manner that focuses first on the student and then on devices and tools. This process also encourages AT decisions to be made collaboratively by the IEP team, with significant input from the student and parents.

Student: The first thing that the team must do is consider the needs of the student. The team should identify the student's areas of strength and need as well as areas that the student finds interesting and motivating.

Environment: Next, the team should consider the environment(s) in which the student may benefit from AT. This includes the typical settings we consider such as classrooms but also other settings such as the cafeteria, gym, playground, and other environments that the student experiences. When making environmental considerations, it is important to be as descriptive as possible so that you can begin to pinpoint the barriers within the environment clearly.

Tasks: Once the environment is fully explored, the team must consider the specific tasks that the student is expected to perform in various environments in order to meet his or her goals.

Tools: Once the team has fully considered the student, environment, and the tasks, the members are ready to deliberately match tools to the tasks that the student needs to perform in the environments where those tasks take place.

Although appearing sequential, the order of consideration is flexible. The only exception is that tools should always be considered last. Often, the natural inclination is to search for a tool or solution first without considering the other factors—student, environment, and tasks that the student needs to complete. Thinking about tools first forces the student to fit the tool when in fact we want the tool to fit the student.

The SETT process is designed to be cyclical. The process starts only when you and the team have fully explored how AT devices and services can support your students in meeting their goals. You then should continue with data collection on how the device is being used by the student. In doing so, consider the following questions:

▶ To what level of independence is the student using the AT? For example, does the student need further support in order to independently use the AT device?

▶ Are you noticing any resistance to the AT by either the student or others in his or her environment? For example, are you noticing that the student does not want to use the device?

▶ Is the student using the AT in one environment and not in other environments? For example, is the student using the AT device in English but not in social studies?

▶ Do the teachers and other school personnel promote the student's use of the AT device? If not, does there need to be additional support to the teachers to help them further support the student in using the AT device to meet his or her goals?

You can learn more about the SETT process of determining which AT devices and services best meet the needs of students with disabilities at www.joyzabala.com.

Depending on the complexity of the AT device, there may be professionals in your school or district who can support you in promoting AT use for students who require AT. For example, speech, occupational, and physical therapists may be extremely helpful in assisting in the process. You can also sometimes enlist the support of the student's peers to promote AT use.

You can find online supports for ATs at the following websites:

► Closing the Gap: http://closingthegap.com
► Assistive Technology Industry Association: http://atia.org/i4a/pages/index.cfm?pageid=1
► Quality Indicators for Assistive Technology Services: http://natri.uky.edu/assoc_projects/qiat/
► Wisconsin Assistive Technology Initiative: www.wati.org

TO SUM UP

► Your students will have a range of strengths, needs, and interests.
► Planning instruction based on the principles of UDL allows you to proactively meet the needs of students with diverse learning needs.
► Explore the range of technologies available through your school district from the perspective of how these technologies can help meet the needs of your students.
► Simply using technology does not mean that you are planning instruction that is universally designed. You need to learn what it is and how technology supports student learning.
► When students need further individualized technology supports, go through the SETT process to determine the AT that best supports their needs.

WHAT'S NEXT?

Now that you have a good understanding of how UDL, instructional technologies, and AT can support diverse learners, we will discuss lesson planning and effective instructional practices.

ADDITIONAL RESOURCES

INSTRUCTIONAL WEBSITES

► K–12 and university content available at iTunes U: www.apple.com/education/itunes-u
► Instructional content website that allows students to progress through gradually more complex learning, take content quizzes, and track their progress, with numerous resources for teachers, including content mapping to the CCSS and access to student data: http://khanacademy.org
► Online community of shared instructional videos similar to YouTube: http://teachertube.com

SAMPLE TEXT-TO-SPEECH SOFTWARE

► Free and paid versions of text-to-speech software that will read text from word processing, PDF, and web pages: www.naturalreader.com
► Free text-to-speech software that supports numerous foreign languages: http://espeak.source forge.net

▶ Apple Computers and Windows-based computer (Vista, 7, and newer) build accessibility features into their systems. You can do an Internet search about the accessibility features within both platforms to learn about text-to-speech and speech-to-text options.

SAMPLE SPEECH-TO-TEXT SOFTWARE

▶ *Dragon Naturally Speaking:* This is probably the most common voice recognition software on the market. This software is not free but many school districts hold site licenses for this software to support students with disabilities.

▶ *Dragon Dictation:* This software can be downloaded as a free app from the iTunes store if you have access to iPads or iPod Touch devices. However, you must have Internet connectivity to use this app.

CHILD-FRIENDLY SEARCH ENGINES WITH READABILITY LEVELS

▶ A search engine developed by librarians that includes educational content with readability levels and is organized by general search and common topics: www.kidsclick.org

▶ A search engine referred to as an Internet public library with information organized by general searches and common topics: www.ipl.org

PART THREE

MASTERING EFFECTIVE PRACTICES

CHAPTER TWELVE

Effective Instructional Practices and Lesson Planning

In this chapter you will learn about:

- How to plan instruction according to state content standards
- Strategies for planning courses, units, and individual lessons
- How to implement the components of the direct instruction model
- How to teach cognitive strategies
- How to make guided discovery instruction more explicit for students with disabilities

Don, a teacher educator, uses this anecdote to illustrate the importance of planning: "As I was observing a beginning special education teacher, I realized that he had not thought carefully about the words he wanted to use in his decoding lesson. He had included poultry *in his activity designed to help students work on spelling multisyllabic words. I had recommended that he use spelling to help students learn different regular syllable types, such as consonant vowel consonant. If you are trying to help students learn common syllable types, then* poultry *is not a great word to use. It is not phonetically regular. Like many beginning teachers, I just don't think this teacher understood how much he would have to plan each component of the lesson."*

It is critical to engage in thorough planning when you are first learning to teach. In this particular scenario, the teacher did not think carefully about each word that he selected for instruction. Some of the words were appropriate and others were not, therefore perhaps confusing students and limiting their opportunities to learn. Planning lessons carefully and using effective instructional principles are foundational to designing instruction that improves academic outcomes for students with disabilities.

PLANNING FOR EFFECTIVE INSTRUCTION

Careful planning enables beginning special education teachers (and all teachers) to avoid mistakes that can confuse students. Careful planning also helps teachers focus on instructional and behavioral goals that are most important for helping their students achieve. For most students with disabilities, instructional planning requires collaboration between the special and general education teachers; otherwise, students with disabilities will not receive the cohesive instruction they need to make progress, and there is danger that they will not have sufficient opportunities to access the general education curriculum and practice needed strategies and skills. Such scenarios will not allow students with disabilities to meet content expectations in the general education curriculum and will put them at risk for not obtaining a standard high school diploma.

How to Approach the Planning Process

To plan effectively, it is important for beginning special education teachers to work with their general education partners to identify the content area standards that they must address through whole-class and more intensive instruction. Most special and general education teachers use the CCSS (www.core standards.org). Teachers should also be able to find the CCSS or their state's content standards on their state's department of education website.

Once special and general education teachers are familiar with their state's standards, they can begin planning instruction. In planning for students with disabilities, special and general education teachers should identify those standards that will be difficult for students to achieve and should discuss specific problems students with disabilities will encounter in meeting the standards:

▶ Will their problems be related to their abilities to understand the instruction needed to reach the state standard or will their problems be related to difficulty accessing and representing information? For instance, will they have difficulty learning because they are not fluent readers or will they have difficulty demonstrating their knowledge because of severe spelling problems when writing or an inability to organize their ideas?

▶ Will students with disabilities have problems achieving the standard because they do not have prerequisite skills in place, such as a thorough understanding of how place value works when solving two- and three-digit multiplication problems? These sorts of learning problems should be identified and addressed through goals in the students' IEPs.

Using Assessment to Inform Planning

The answers to these questions depend on assessment information that general and special education teachers have collected. This information can include data collected from various measures:

▶ Curriculum-based measures
▶ Information from observations of a student's classroom performance
▶ Interviews with a student about completed work or tests
▶ Data from checklists of skills and strategies that a student demonstrates
▶ Work samples

For more detailed information about the assessments that can be used, see chapter 10.

As a special educator you play a primary role in collecting, analyzing, and interpreting, for each of your students, assessment data that can be used in the planning process. In addition, you should consider the extent to which your general education colleagues may need assistance in interpreting the data to determine the difficulties that students with disabilities will experience in achieving content area standards.

Three Frameworks for Planning Curriculum, Units, and Lessons

Planning the curriculum for a class can daunting. Deciding what to emphasize in a curriculum that must address multiple content standards is no small task, either. Fortunately for teachers, there are available frameworks that can be used to simplify the planning process. Several of these strategies come from the Content Enhancement Series developed by Donald Deshler and his colleagues at the University of Kansas, Center for Research on Learning, and include frameworks for course planning, unit planning, and lesson planning. Although it will take some time and practice to use these strategies, they can help you develop clear expectations about what students will learn.

Clear expectations also will help students with disabilities better organize the information you are teaching, and they will help you communicate better with parents. By providing students and parents with expectations, students can talk with their parents about what they will be learning and their requirements for participation in the classroom environment.

Course Planning

If students with disabilities receive most of their instruction in general education classrooms, course planning will be the general education teacher's primary responsibility because he or she provides access to the general education curriculum. As a special education teacher, you will collaborate with the general education teacher to help him or her plan accessible instruction. Even when you provide intervention instruction in a pull-out setting, you should plan collaboratively with your general education colleagues to ensure that students with disabilities are accommodated. Regardless of the arrangement, it is important to focus instruction on essential concepts and strategies or the big ideas of the curriculum because they allow you to provide more in-depth instruction related to key curricular ideas and teach in more focused ways to help students develop deeper conceptual understanding in a content area.

The SMARTER planning process,[1] one of the content-enhancement strategies developed by Donald Deshler and his colleagues at the University of Kansas, is a strategy to help you and your general education colleague determine these big ideas (according to the CCSS or a specific state's content standards) and organize the content they will address around them. Once you have decided on the big ideas and critical content, you can identify difficulties that your students will encounter, how you will address those difficulties, and how you will assess whether or not students learned the curriculum. Thus, the SMARTER planning process can be a very effective tool for helping you work collaboratively and deliberatively with your general education partner.

SMARTER is an acronym that teachers can use to guide instructional planning. It helps teachers pose critical questions about the content to be learned, organize the essential concepts in a visual map, analyze aspects of the content to determine what difficulties it might pose for certain students, determine ways to overcome the learning difficulties students might encounter, help students understand what they are expected to learn, and help students evaluate the degree to which they learned the key ideas.[2] The SMARTER acronym directs teachers to use the following steps when planning for students:

▶ *S*hape the critical questions
▶ *M*ap the critical content
▶ *A*nalyze for learning difficulties

► *Reach enhancement decisions*
► *Teach strategically*
► *Evaluate mastery*
► *Revisit outcomes*

Table 12.1 provides a description of each step and suggestions for implementation.

Although using an approach such as SMARTER for course planning is time consuming, it helps teachers organize instruction for students with disabilities. Additionally, this approach helps you and your general education colleague clarify your goals for instruction, develop a rationale for why those goals are important, and communicate more clearly with parents, colleagues, and administrators about your instruction and what you are trying to accomplish.

Unit Planning

After deciding how to organize the course content, take the next step with your general education colleague: planning individual units of instruction. Once again, you identify a method for determining the critical content for the unit and how students will learn the content because this will improve the organization of instruction and students' ability to learn. The unit organizer[3] can be used for this purpose. The unit organizer includes a graphic organizer that helps students identify relationships between big ideas of the unit, questions they should be able to answer on unit completion, strategies needed to answer questions, and assignments they must complete along with completion dates. In implementing the unit organizer, teachers work through three steps:

► Identify the unit's big ideas and consider the relationship among those ideas
► Identify the knowledge and skills you want students to have at the unit's completion
► Consider the evidence you want to collect to evaluate the extent to which students acquired these knowledge and skills

Represent the unit's big ideas and relationship among the ideas using a semantic map. By organizing the unit's big ideas and supporting details graphically, the curriculum's organization becomes conceptually transparent to the general and special education teachers. If the semantic map is shared with students, it then becomes a road map for the teachers and students: you and your students can continually refer back to the map to ensure ideas and relationships between them have been adequately addressed and that students have demonstrated each of these ideas through some sort of assignment, quiz, or test.

Critical questions and the type of strategic approach students require (e.g., compare and contrast) are included below the semantic map. Carefully consider the sorts of issues students might encounter when attempting to learn the concepts or strategies outlined in your unit. For instance, will students have difficulty reading the text that you selected? If so, is there any way that you can modify the text or select supplementary texts that are simpler but help students learn the concept? Can you find videos that support student learning or online resources that the student can watch or listen to?

The assignments that will be used to assess the students' knowledge and skill are listed to the side of the organizer. As you and your general education colleague design assignments and quizzes, consider whether these assessments align with your intended goals, whether students have the skills to participate in the assignments or quizzes, and whether students can demonstrate their knowledge in a different way. For instance, if you want students to demonstrate compare-and-contrast or cause-and-effect relationships, ask questions that are more advanced than recalling information. You might also allow students to develop a visual that demonstrates how one event causes another and then record a description of the cause and

Table 12.1 Steps and a Description of the SMARTER Strategy

Steps of the SMARTER Strategy	Description of What the Teacher Does
Shape the critical questions	Ask yourself what the big-idea questions are that can focus and organize your course instruction. For example, in a middle school US history class, you could include some of the following questions to focus your course: (1) What were the major events that shaped the formation of our democracy? (2) How is our current system of government a reflection of those major events? (3) What are the major periods of US history? (4) What were the main cultural and political forces at work during those major periods of history? (5) How have tensions over human rights influenced our history? The list should include about ten questions. A longer list suggests that you might want to rethink exactly what the big ideas are.
Map the critical content	Visually represent the critical content to be learned under each of the critical questions. Developing a graphic organizer of the content to be learned will help you communicate with students how the big ideas of the course will be organized. It will also help you and your general education colleague to think carefully about how ideas are organized and make any needed revisions to the content.
Analyze for learning difficulties	Consider how you want students to learn the content and demonstrate their learning. You and your general education colleague should analyze the type of learning difficulties students are likely to encounter (e.g., if you want students to read primary sources in history, you might want to consider how their reading problems can be addressed). Being clear about the learning difficulties you expect students to encounter allows you and your general education colleague to be proactive in designing instruction by using strategies that make the content more comprehensible and accessible (e.g., using text-to-speech software or having students work with a peer to read text and answer questions).
Reach enhancement decisions	At this point, select approaches and strategies for remediation that address the skills and strategies students with disabilities need in order to be successful with the content. You can use information contained in the different chapters of this book to make decisions about how to represent content for students with disabilities, the strategies students will need to learn the content, and how to assess the degree to which students have learned the content.
Teach strategically	The main point of this step is to help students become partners in the learning process. If you are working with a general education teacher, this is the point at which your special education expertise is especially helpful. You can help your general education colleague understand how to use graphic organizers (see chapter 16) to explain how information in the course is taught and learned, clarify strategies you will teach that enable students to better comprehend and generate text, and employ technology to support student learning. The remaining chapters in this book will help you and your general education colleague teach strategically.
Evaluate mastery	You can help your general education colleagues determine how to evaluate students' ability to learn content and determine how instruction might need to change as a result. At this point, consider the types of difficulties students may encounter when representing their knowledge. The information in the chapters on UDL and assessment should be helpful to you. Additionally, comparing the instructional techniques you used to those discussed in this book is also helpful.
Revisit outcomes	You and your general education colleague should consider how well you achieved your goals and revise curriculum content for the following year.

effect using speech-to-text software. Taking the time to consider the learning challenges in advance helps you plan instruction that is more accessible to all students. Exhibit 12.1 provides an example of a unit organizer for social studies and the Florida Sunshine State Content Standards that it addresses.

Lesson Planning

Once you have planned units of instruction, you are responsible for planning individual lessons. Whether planning a co-taught lesson or an intervention lesson, be clear about how your particular lesson will help students achieve a particular content standard or an IEP goal. Also, simultaneously think about what you want students to achieve at the end of the lesson and how they will demonstrate content mastery. Lesson

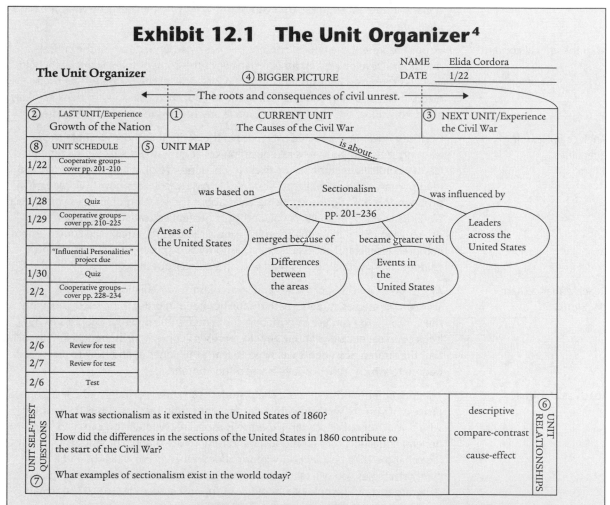

Exhibit 12.1   The Unit Organizer[4]

The Unit Organizer

NAME Elida Cordora
DATE 1/22

④ BIGGER PICTURE

← The roots and consequences of civil unrest. →

| ② LAST UNIT/Experience Growth of the Nation | ① CURRENT UNIT The Causes of the Civil War | ③ NEXT UNIT/Experience the Civil War |

⑧ UNIT SCHEDULE

1/22	Cooperative groups—cover pp. 201–210
1/28	Quiz
1/29	Cooperative groups—cover pp. 210–225
	"Influential Personalities" project due
1/30	Quiz
2/2	Cooperative groups—cover pp. 228–234
2/6	Review for test
2/7	Review for test
2/6	Test

⑤ UNIT MAP

is about...

Sectionalism
pp. 201–236

was based on → Areas of the United States

was influenced by → Leaders across the United States

emerged because of → Differences between the areas

became greater with → Events in the United States

⑦ UNIT SELF-TEST QUESTIONS

What was sectionalism as it existed in the United States of 1860?

How did the differences in the sections of the United States in 1860 contribute to the start of the Civil War?

What examples of sectionalism exist in the world today?

⑥ UNIT RELATIONSHIPS

descriptive

compare-contrast

cause-effect

Standard 1: Use research and inquiry skills to analyze US history using primary and secondary sources.

Standard 5: Examine the causes, course, and consequence of the Civil War and Reconstruction including its effects on American peoples.

Lenz, B. K., Bulgren, J. A., Schumaker, J. B., Deshler, D. D., & Boudah, D. A. (2006). *The unit organizer routine.* Lawrence, KS: Edge Enterprises, Inc.

Note: The instructor's manual for this routine is available in conjunction with professional development workshops. Go to www.edgeenterprisesinc.com for details as well as research results.

focus is essential to designing cohesive activities and ensuring that you are addressing the right content, strategies, and skills with your students. Lesson focus is a key identifier of effective instruction. In addition to developing focus, you will want to think carefully about how new information is introduced and old information is reviewed, how you intend to practice the content of the lesson, and how you will evaluate whether or not students learned the content. For instance, if the lesson focuses on developing student understanding of a concept, consider the method you use to introduce the content, what background knowledge you need to build, what examples you use to help students learn the concept, how you help students identify the main features of the concept, how you help students apply their understandings of the concept to a novel problem or situation, and how you assess whether or not students have learned the content. Although numerous lesson-planning frameworks exist, one that has been researched for general education teachers working with students with disabilities is the lesson organizer planning framework, a planning approach designed to complement course and unit organizers.[5]

The lesson organizer is structured in such a way that it allows teachers to focus their efforts and help students see the big picture of the lesson. The mnemonic CRADLE is used to guide teachers through the steps of planning a lesson (see table 12.2). Additionally, teachers produce a graphic organizer to help students see the organization of the lesson (see exhibit 12.2).

▶ *Consolidate goals:* Introduce the topic and describe why it is important. Frame the topic in words the students understand, identify relationships between content taught in the lesson, and name a strategy they might use to learn the content.

Table 12.2 Steps and a Description of the CRADLE Lesson-Planning Strategy

Strategy Step	Description of Step
Consolidate goals	Teachers help students understand the goals of the lesson by (1) naming the topic of the lesson plan (e.g., food groups), (2) paraphrasing the topic in words the students understand (choosing a balanced dietary intake), (3) identifying the important relationships that students need to look for within the lesson content, and (4) naming the strategy or strategies students will be using to achieve learning outcomes.
Review knowledge	Teachers help students build background knowledge needed for the lesson by reviewing topics from previous lessons and student background knowledge or experiences.
Assemble anchors	Teachers develop a visual anchor for connecting the new information to previously learned information. The purpose of an anchor is to graphically depict the previous information, connect to new information, and illustrate how new information fits within the unit or students' background knowledge.
Describe and map content	Teachers use a visual graphic organizer to further detail how the lesson's information is connected to previous learning and the unit. The graphic organizer is developed by drawing arrows between information (e.g., balanced diet to combination of foods) with more detailed, bulleted information below each subtopic.
Link content to anchors	Teachers link visual anchors to students' lives by using visual resources that further connect the students' experiences to the content.
Explore questions and tasks	Teachers offer students a series of questions that communicate outcomes of the lesson and indicate what the students should be able to answer at the end of the lesson. These questions are listed in section seven of the organizer, describing the expectations students must meet. In this way, students are aware of what they need to learn to be successful, and teachers are directed in their teaching to ensure that the questions are answered as a result of their instruction.

► *Review knowledge:* Build background knowledge. In this step, you identify the prior knowledge students need to understand the topic and consider how to develop it.

► *Assemble anchors:* Develop a graphic that illustrates how new information is connected to the broader unit of study.

► *Describe and map content:* Use the graphic you developed to show relationships between information to be learned in the unit. The graphic organizer should help students see the main topics to be covered and the key subtopics to be included under each main topic.

► *Link content to anchors:* Link elements of the graphic to students' lives through the use of stories or examples.

► *Explore questions and tasks:* Develop questions that focus on the lesson outcomes you desire. These questions help students understand what they need to learn in order to be successful, and they will help you ensure that your instruction is organized in such a way that students will be able to answer the questions.

Exhibit 12.2   A Graphic of the Lesson Organizer Routine[6]

The Lesson Organizer

Lesson Organizer | ④ UNIT or BACKGROUND: Nutrition | DATE: _____ NAME: _____

② **Relationships**	① **LESSON TOPIC**	③ **Task-Related Strategies**
Describe	Food Groups	

⑤ *Lesson Map*

is about

US RDA — by understanding — **choosing a balanced dietary intake** — by following — **Serving sizes and amounts**

by following — **Food pyramid**

by understanding — **Combination foods**

Which includes
· Variety
· Maintain healthy weight
· Types of fats
· Focus diet on fruit, vegetables, and grains

Food pyramid
· Bread, Cereal
· Fruits
· Vegetables
· Meat, Poultry
· Milk, Cheese
· Fats, Sweets

Combination foods
Such as
· Protein, complete and incomplete
· Classifying combination foods
· Identifying hazards

Serving sizes and amounts
Including
· In relation to labels
· Look at serving size
· Identify serving sizes

⑥ *Challenge Question*

⑦ *Self-test Questions*	⑧ *Tasks*
1. What are the six food groups? 2. What are the US RDA recommendations? 3. How do we classify combination foods using the US RDA?	1. Food recall activity 2. Read lessons 1 and 2 and answer review questions

Lenz, B. K., Marrs, R. W., Schumaker, J. B., & Deshler, D. D. (1993). *The lesson organizer routine.* Lawrence, KS: Edge Enterprises, Inc.

Note: The instructor's manual for this routine is available in conjunction with professional development workshops. Go to www.edgeenterprisesinc.com for details as well as research results.

Though the planning strategies recommended in this chapter require time, our work with teachers suggests that careful planning pays off. Teachers are more likely to provide focused, engaging instruction when they consider how the content they are teaching relates to broader objectives, consider how the different examples they have selected are related to the concepts they want to teach, think carefully about how they will access background knowledge, consider the questions they will use to assess student learning, and consider the language they will use to introduce ideas.

USING EFFECTIVE INSTRUCTION

Once you have designed your lesson, consider the instructional approach best suited for teaching the content of your lesson. If your lesson focuses on developing a skill, such as decoding syllables with vowel diagraphs (e.g., *oa, ea*), then you will want to use a direct instruction approach. Direct instruction approaches, when combined with the use of manipulatives or visuals, can be useful for helping students build conceptual knowledge in mathematics. For teaching students strategies, such as summarization or an approach for solving word problems, you will want to use cognitive strategy instruction. Explicit approaches can be used to teach students with disabilities to engage in inquiry and analysis in the different content areas. These approaches guide students through a structured process whether learning about a phenomenon in science or analyzing literature and historical texts. Finally, peer-learning structures can be used to develop conceptual understanding, skills, and strategies for students with disabilities.

Direct Instruction

Direct instruction is an approach that makes explicit for students what they need to do to complete a task or apply a concept. Direct instruction is a well-researched and useful approach when teaching students who struggle to learn a skill, such as decoding; helping students learn how to apply mathematical concepts to procedures, such as using manipulatives with regrouping in addition; and helping them develop fluency with certain skills, such as developing the ability to decode common word patterns (e.g., *oat* as in *bloat* and *goat*). The components of direct instruction and examples of how it can be applied are illustrated in table 12.3.

Cognitive Strategy Instruction

To become more proficient learners, students with disabilities need to learn effective strategies for understanding text, decoding novel words, writing organized papers, solving mathematical word problems, and studying for exams. Such strategies help students determine how to approach challenging tasks and perform them more effectively and efficiently. Cognitive strategy instruction is an approach to instruction that involves direct instruction methods and a more cognitive approach to modeling and guided practice, that is, teachers work with students to help them see how accomplished learners think while completing a task. Cognitive strategy instruction is designed to teach students how to think strategically when completing a task by helping students learn the processes that an accomplished learner uses (e.g., looking for repeating ideas when developing a summary statement or separating main ideas from details when creating summary statements). Research on reading comprehension, writing instruction, and mathematical word problem solving has demonstrated that teaching strategies to students with disabilities, particularly those with learning disabilities and emotional and behavioral disorders, can be helpful in improving their academic achievement.

Table 12.3 Direct Instruction Model

Component of the Model	Purpose	Example Using Addition with Regrouping
Introduce the topic for the lesson.	Make students aware of the lesson purpose.	"Today we are going to be using our base ten blocks to learn regrouping with addition. The base ten blocks will help us understand how to change ones to tens in addition problems."
Review needed information for the lesson.	Help students connect new information to previous learning.	"We have been working on regrouping with base ten blocks for a couple days. Can anyone show me how you can use your base ten blocks to show fifteen ones? Now, can you show me how that would be regrouped using the tens and ones blocks?" Reviewing several examples will be important to ensure that all students remember the concept you have taught.
Model the new skill using precise language and several examples.	Help students understand the steps involved in solving a problem or completing a task.	"Today, I am going to show you how to use regrouping with base ten blocks when solving an addition problem. I will do each step of the problem and ask you to follow along using your base ten blocks. Let's look at this problem. What number is on top? (answer: fifteen) How can you represent fifteen using tens and ones blocks? Now, what number is on the bottom? (answer: seven) How can you represent seven using your tens and ones blocks? Now, what two numbers do we need to add together? (answer: fifteen plus seven) With addition problems, we always begin adding the numbers on the right. So what two numbers will we add together? (answer: five and seven) Yes, you will add five ones to seven ones. Can you do that with your base ten blocks? Okay, you have twelve ones blocks, so you need to regroup. How can you regroup twelve using tens and ones blocks? (Students show the answer.) Yes, you would have one ten block to represent the one set of tens and two ones blocks. In your problem, you are going to write a one on top of the one on the left to show that you are adding it to the one ten that is already there. Now how many tens do you have? (Students answer.) Yes, you have two tens, so bring down the two in the tens place. How many sets of ten do you now have? (Students answer.) Yes, you have two. So, you have two tens and how many ones? (answer: two) Yes, so what is your answer? (answer: twenty-two) Yes, twenty-two."
Provide guided practice with corrective feedback.	Help students learn how to apply what they are learning while receiving considerable support.	Have students solve problems step by step while observing their progress. "First add the numbers in the ones column using their base ten blocks and show me your answer." Watch students do this and provide corrective feedback. For instance, if a student said that seven plus six equals twelve, you might say, "Let's recount the seven and six blocks together. What is the answer?" However, if the student answered correctly, the teacher acknowledges the correct response.

Component of the Model	Purpose	Example Using Addition with Regrouping
Provide independent practice and monitor student progress.	Help students move toward using procedures and processes on their own while solving problems and completing a task. Students should demonstrate they have some facility with the knowledge or skill before moving on to this step. Independent practice can be used over time to build fluency.	If the students are able to solve five problems with only minimal assistance at each step, give them five more to solve by themselves. Of course, observe them as they solve problems to provide corrective feedback. If some students are not ready to work independently, have them work with a peer to solve the problems.
Provide application or generalization.	Help students apply their newly acquired knowledge or skill to novel problems.	Use two-digit addition with two digits on the top and two digits on the bottom. Of course, if students cannot apply their knowledge easily, intervene by asking questions to help them apply their knowledge. For instance, you might say, "Where do you start in the problem? How did we show tens when we were regrouping before?"

In the chapters on reading, writing, and mathematics, we present other strategies that you and your general education colleagues can teach to students with disabilities and other struggling learners. You can help students learn cognitive strategies when they use a modified version of direct instruction that helps students understand how they can think while completing a task. Table 12.4 shows the steps of effective cognitive strategy instruction and how those steps can be applied when teaching students with disabilities to understand text.

You should also help students examine how the strategy influences their performance and encourage them to make positive attributions. Unfortunately, many students with disabilities have problems that affect them academically and therefore develop a maladaptive attribution style.[7] That is, because of repeated struggles in school or with peers, they begin to see failure in academics and social situations to be the result of inferior intelligence, their personality, or other circumstances beyond their control. For example, when they receive a poor grade on an exam, students with disabilities might conclude that they are not smart enough or because their teacher's tests are too confusing. These maladaptive styles are problematic because they often lead students with disabilities to give up easily when completing a task, refuse to try a task that they perceive is too difficult, or depend too much on others for help with the task.[8] These maladaptive attribution styles then compound problems created by students' disabilities.

Learning cognitive strategies or any skill depends, however, on developing a positive attribution style or the view that by learning effective skills and strategies and employing effort you can achieve more. You can help change students' attributions by showing them how their level of effort and strategy is related to their performance of a task.[9] For example, if students use a summarization strategy and answer more questions correctly on an assignment, then you can tell them that their improved performance was related to their use of more effective strategies. You can also point out when poor performance is related to weak effort or forgetting to use certain skills. For instance, you can show a student that he missed a number of mathematics problems because he made simple calculation errors or forgot

Table 12.4 The Cognitive Strategy Instruction Model

Step of the Cognitive Strategy Instruction Process	Purpose of the Step	Example
Introduce the strategy and build a rationale	Helps students understand what the strategy is and what it will help them to do; fosters commitment to learning.	"When you summarize text, you learn to state the main points of the text briefly in your own words. Learning how to summarize information helps to understand the main ideas better and remember what you read or heard. Can anyone tell me why it might be important to summarize in school? How about when describing a movie you just watched to your friend?"
Explain and model the steps of the strategy	Helps students learn the steps of the strategy and how to think when using the strategy.	"Today, I am going to show you how to use a summarization strategy. While I demonstrate the strategy, I will talk aloud so you can see how I think while using the strategy. First, I am going to read the passage. Okay, now that I am done reading, I have to ask myself if the first sentence of the passage helps me to summarize the passage. Well, the first sentence talks about Carolina wrens and how they are a common bird in the Southeast, so I guess the passage is likely about Carolina wrens. So let me see if that is correct. Well, the passage goes on to talk about what the wrens eat, how they build their nests, and how they take care of their young. Those are all things that the wrens do to survive, so I think I can summarize the passage in a short sentence. This passage is about Carolina wrens and how they survive in the Southeast."
Guided practice	Helps students learn to use the strategy with various types of texts.	Summarization is a difficult strategy to learn so you may want to start modeling summarization with expository text. Many times the first sentence of an expository passage contains the main idea and then the important details supporting the main idea are described in the paragraphs that follow. This structure makes expository text easier to summarize than narrative text.
Independent practice	Helps students practice the steps of the strategy to mastery.	Students practice using the summarization strategy with different types of expository text.
Generalization	Helps students use the strategy with different sorts of materials in different settings. Work with your general education colleagues to prompt students to use the strategy in their classes.	At this point, you might show students how they can use summarization with different types of texts or in situations when they have to paraphrase what others are saying. Be sure to reinforce students when they use the summarization strategy in other classes and situations.

steps when he refused to write down all the steps of the problem. If students exhibit anxiety or frustration when performing a task, you can teach them to make positive self-statements while using the strategy (e.g., "I know essays are hard for me, but if I calm down and use the strategy I learned for planning a persuasive essay, I can secure a passing grade.") Finally, make sure that students understand that being smart is not the most important factor in success. Instead, teach them what it means to work hard by employing effective strategies, being conscientious in their work, not giving up, and setting reasonable goals or standards for themselves.

Explicit Approaches to Acquiring Inquiry and Analytical Skills

Inquiry approaches, directed largely by student interests or questions, are considered best practice by scholars in science and social studies; however, such open-ended approaches do not work well for students with disabilities. These students do not always have the knowledge or skills to engage in such an approach, and sometimes their nondisabled peers do not incorporate their comments and efforts into the group project. However, students with disabilities, just like other students, benefit from well-structured opportunities that deepen their conceptual knowledge, allow them to engage in inquiry about a topic, and help them think more analytically. To ensure that students with disabilities have these opportunities, researchers in special education have developed explicit approaches for engaging students with disabilities in inquiry and analysis in content areas.

Similar to all effective instruction, these approaches depend heavily on teachers' abilities to focus on the most important concepts and understandings they want students to develop. Thus, the planning strategies described previously will be essential to establishing this focus.

Knowing exactly what you want to teach will allow you to better accommodate the needs of students with disabilities so that they can learn science or social studies content, for example. Thomas Scruggs, Margo Mastropieri, and Cynthia Okolo described why clarifying what you want to teach before structuring the science or social studies learning experience is important.[10] They highlighted the case of a fourth-grade science class in which the teacher suggested that a blind student not participate in a unit that required the use of a microscope. The parents insisted, however, that the child be taught alongside her peers. Their insistence caused the fourth-grade team to rethink their approach—realizing that the student did not have to learn the content by using a microscope but could learn it with physical models and accompanying explanations. This case is a great example of why planning is so important: once you know where you are headed, you can figure out different approaches for getting there.

Once you have decided what to teach, many of the following approaches will help you to achieve your objectives. These approaches will involve planning and creating materials but their impact on the engagement of students with disabilities during instruction and subsequent achievement will be worthwhile.

Coached elaborations involve explicit questioning techniques that help students to understand phenomena.[11] When using coached elaborations, teachers help students to develop more inductive reasoning by using open-ended but structured questions to guide student thinking. For instance, when talking about how animals develop certain characteristics to survive in their ecosystem, the teacher may ask the following questions about Carolina wrens:

Teacher: Today, we are going to be talking about the characteristics animals have to survive in their ecosystems. This animal is a Carolina wren. It lives in dense bushes and undergrowth close to the ground. Let's look at some of its characteristics. What do you notice about the color of the bird?

Student: It is brownish with a lighter belly.

Teacher:	Now, we know that the bird lives in dense bushes close to the ground. Why do you think it is brown on top?
Student:	Because that way it blends in with the tree trunks and sticks near the ground.
Teacher:	Yes, there would be a lot of tree trunks and stems of bushes near the ground, and they would be more likely to be brown. Could we say that the color of the wren is one of its characteristics that it has developed to protect itself from predators in an ecosystem?

The teacher would then proceed to discuss other characteristics of the Carolina wren, drawing student attention to how those characteristics help the animal survive. Then, the teacher might move to another animal and ask students to discuss the features of that animal that allow it to survive. Next, the teacher would ask students to describe the features of animals that enable them to survive in an ecosystem and discuss how those features might differ depending on different types of ecosystems. For instance, students could be asked to predict how a bird in the desert might differ in characteristics from the Carolina wren. To wrap up the lesson, the teacher would help students draw conclusions about the ways in which animal characteristics evolve to ensure their survival in an ecosystem. To effectively coach students, carefully plan key questions in advance to ensure that students focus on the most essential features of concepts. Additionally, anticipate challenges students may experience when responding to questions, such as focusing on the information that is most important, so that you can prompt students in ways that will improve their understanding. For instance, if the student was not able to describe why the Carolina wren's feathers might be brown, then you might prompt him to look at the underbrush and describe its color, asking the student to consider why the colors of the underbrush and Carolina wren might be similar.

Coached elaborations can also be combined with experiments in which students with disabilities work with their peers to develop knowledge of a concept. Lucinda Spaulding and Jenny Sue Flanagan wrote about providing effective science instruction to students with disabilities and showed how chemical changes could affect matter.[12] Specifically, they described an experiment in which students are asked to examine what happens when hydrogen peroxide is mixed with yeast. Students participate in the experience and then record what they observed with their peers. They are then provided with other substances to mix and asked to record their predictions about what might happen and then observe what actually happens. They are also provided with a chart to record their observations that helps them focus on whether or not the change was physical or chemical. For instance, they are asked to record if they see a gas produced, a change in temperature, or a change in color. At the end, they are provided with a graphic organizer that helps them develop the definition of chemical change by discussing its characteristics and examples and nonexamples.

Such guided inquiry approaches can be very helpful to students with disabilities because they are not dependent on the ability to consume information from text or access extensive background knowledge. These approaches are time consuming, however, so you and your general education colleagues will need to take specific care to focus your efforts on the most important concepts to be learned in the content area standards.

Project-based learning that employs explicit structures and strategies can also be used to promote students' skills of analysis and development of historical concepts. In project-based learning, students explore real-world problems and challenges in order to develop a deeper understanding of the subjects they are studying. Students are directed to work together to generate questions they would like to answer. To support student learning, teachers can use organizers, such as compare-and-contrast charts, for students to record the information they are learning, and use strategies to help students develop persuasive arguments and summarize information.

As an example, Cynthia Okolo, Ralph Ferretti, and Charles MacArthur have conducted research examining how students could learn about historical periods and concepts by engaging in projects that involved reading first- and second-hand accounts of history (also known as primary and secondary sources).[13] These researchers developed units for upper elementary and middle school students with disabilities that would help them learn about immigration and its causes. The researchers' intent was to help students understand the ways of life that led to migration. As part of the inquiry process, the students worked in small groups to use a migration and conflict schema to organize the information they were collecting. This schema was designed to help students identify the reasons that people migrated and how their migration brought them into conflict with other groups of people. While completing the framework, they were encouraged to consider immigrant versus nativist views of immigration and how clashes in those views often resulted in conflicts. Students also read mostly primary sources of information that historians would read to develop a historical account. To support learning, students were also provided with compare-and-contrast organizers to help them examine similarities and differences between the different groups of people they were investigating (e.g., two students who emigrated from Guatemala to Los Angeles and the immigration of eastern European Jews and Chinese). Additionally, students were taught a persuasion strategy to help them develop a reasoned approach to persuading others of their opinion.

In using a project-based approach, you and your general education colleague will need to consider accommodations and instructional supports students need. For instance, students may have difficulty reading primary sources so you may need to use speech-to-text software, develop summaries to accompany the source, or find sources that are written in simpler language. Additionally, if you use graphic organizers to help students organize and display information they are collecting, you need to ensure that they know how to use the organizer. The same is true with any strategies you use to help students complete the project. Finally, breaking down projects into manageable parts to be completed will help all students but such an approach will be particularly helpful to students with disabilities.

Cooperative Learning Approaches

Cooperative learning strategies help to address the diverse needs of students with disabilities, particularly in general education classrooms. In this section, we first describe the elements of effective cooperative learning activities. Then, we outline strategies that have received support from the research literature in general and special education.

Elements of Effective Cooperative Learning

Four different elements must be present in cooperative learning situations: interdependence, individual accountability, collaborative goals, and group processing.[14] Interdependence requires students to understand the need for all group members to help the group attain certain learning goals. To foster interdependence, teachers can ensure that all students have an important role to play in the group and that they have the skills necessary to perform the role. It would be best if teachers assigned students to roles to ensure that this happens. Students should be encouraged to reflect on how well they worked as a group. Teachers should be clear with students about the goals that they want them to accomplish as a group (e.g., developing a summary of the chapter and identifying everyone's contribution to that summary). To improve group processing, teachers need to provide feedback about how well students operated as a group and provide reinforcement for effective group performance. Effective group work will also require students to have collaborative skills, including how to provide positive support to peers, ask questions in respectful ways, and listen to other viewpoints. Teachers must model these collaborative skills and provide plenty of opportunities to practice and receive feedback. Finally, finding ways to create individual accountability is important. For example, students might receive an individual grade for their contributions to a group project. Additionally, students can be taught to monitor their own progress in the group; for example, students can be asked to reflect on how they contributed to their group that day.

Classwide Peer Tutoring (CWPT)

Charles Greenwood and his colleagues developed CWPT to help students with disabilities and other at-risk learners in inclusive classrooms.[15] CWPT is a well-researched strategy in which students work with a peer to practice reading and spelling skills, such as oral reading, spelling phonetically regular words, and learning sight words. CWPT is appropriate for learning skills and practicing them to a high degree of fluency. To implement CWPT, teachers use the following steps:

▶ Rank the students according to their achievement in a particular area, such as their oral reading fluency.

▶ Divide the class in half, with students in the top half of the distribution in one group and students in the lowest half in the other.

▶ Pair the students using the following strategy. The highest-scoring student in the class is paired with the highest-scoring student in the lowest half of the class. The second-highest-scoring student is paired with the second-highest-scoring student in the lowest half of the class. Continue pairing students in this way until you have paired all students. The purpose of pairing students in this way is to eliminate frustration that may be caused when a highly competent student is paired with a student who is experiencing extreme difficulty in an area. Also, when pairing students, you should consider personality issues or other issues that might contribute to students' ability to work together successfully.

▶ Discuss guidelines for working together. After students are paired, you will talk with them about how to work with peers. You will discuss not only the procedures for working together, but also how to work together. As an example, one of the authors of this book worked with a second teacher who taught students collaborative skills by talking with them about what it means to be on a team and how to define the positive and negative behaviors of teammates. She then helped students practice the procedures associated with distributing materials and moving to work with peers before starting the CWPT process.

▶ Teach students how to respond to peers' correct responses and mistakes. Students are directed to reinforce their partner for correct responses. Students are also directed to provide students with the correct answer if they cannot respond in three to five seconds. If the student performs the task incorrectly, then the other student says, "No, that is not correct," and provides the correct answer. This part of the CWPT process should be taught when students learn collaborative skills and procedures for working together.

▶ Start the CWPT process by having the higher-achieving student do the task first. For instance, this student might read for three minutes or spell ten words.

▶ Have students switch roles while the second student does the task.

Peer-Assisted Learning Strategies (PALS)

PALS are similar to CWPT in format. In fact, students are paired and taught the skills of working together in the same way. Doug and Lynn Fuchs, along with several colleagues, have conducted extensive research using PALS in reading and mathematics. Like CWPT, most of the research has been conducted in elementary school but the strategies have also been researched with middle school and high school students. The PALS for reading incorporates oral reading fluency, summarization, and prediction.[16] Students use PALS in the following way:

▶ The stronger reader reads aloud for five minutes, followed by the weaker reader reading the same text aloud for five minutes.

▶ If one of the readers misses a word, the peer tutor stops him or her and says, "Stop, that word was not correct. Can you figure it out?" If the reader cannot read the word correctly in four minutes, the tutor says, "That word is _____. What word?" The reader repeats the word and then is asked by the tutor to read the sentence again.

▶ The stronger reader then proceeds to read for another five minutes stopping after each paragraph to "shrink the paragraph" or summarize. When summarizing, readers are taught to "name the who or what," "tell the most important thing about the who or what," and "say the main idea in ten words or less."

▶ After the stronger reader summarizes, the weaker reader then proceeds to read new material, stopping to summarize after each paragraph.

▶ Once each reader has read for five minutes, the stronger reader engages in "prediction relay" before reading for five minutes again. In prediction relay, the stronger reader makes a prediction about what will happen next, proceeds to read about a half a page, and then stops to see how accurate his or her prediction was. At that point, the stronger reader summarizes what he or she read and then makes another prediction. Then the stronger reader repeats the process one time.

▶ After the stronger reader has read one page, the weaker reader reads for five minutes, employing prediction relay and paragraph shrinking just as the stronger reader did.

PALS can also be adapted for nonreaders. In this instance, the nonreader can read one sentence after the stronger reader has read it or the weaker reader can choral read with the stronger reader.

PALS has been applied to learning mathematics concepts and basic computations with elementary and high school students.[17] In one study, researchers used PALS to help first-grade students learn about number quantities.[18] Tutoring pairs were given number lines, individual beans, ten beans on a popsicle stick, a number array from one to a hundred, and a spinner with greater-than and less-than symbols and before-and-after terms. Tutoring pairs used these manipulatives to practice concepts that were introduced in class: (1) recognizing numerals and representing them with fingers; (2) recognizing numerals and representing them with objects; (3) ordering numerals on a number line and comparing them using more, equal, or less; (4) learning addition, subtraction, and equal symbols; (5) representing addition and subtraction equations using beans; (6) using beans and popsicle sticks to understand ones, tens, and the concept of regrouping; and (7) using beans and popsicle sticks to add and subtract with regrouping.

Collaborative Strategic Reading

Collaborative strategic reading is a cooperative learning approach developed by Janette Klingner and her colleagues to help students learn strategies for comprehending expository text.[19] In this strategy, students are taught to use four strategies in heterogeneous cooperative learning groups:

▶ *Preview:* Before reading a passage, the students discuss what they know about the topic and predict what they think the passage will be about.

▶ *Click and clunk:* While reading the text, students are directed to highlight difficult words, concepts, and ideas in the passage that they need to better understand. They are also encouraged to use specific fix-up strategies to make sense of these difficult ideas, including rereading the sentence, rereading the sentences before and after the unknown or confusing words or ideas, breaking the word into understandable chunks and trying to decode it, and looking for a prefix or suffix that students know.

▶ *Get the gist:* Students are directed to restate the most important idea in a paragraph or section in ten words or less by focusing on the who or what and the most important thing about that who or what.

▶ *Wrap up:* After reading, students create a summary of the ideas learned and generate questions that could be asked on a test.

Jigsaw

In this cooperative learning approach, students are assigned to heterogeneous groups, and each student in the group becomes an expert on a particular topic.[20] For instance, students might be studying mammals and are asked to pursue a topic related to mammals (e.g., the foods they eat, how they reproduce, their main characteristics). The expert groups then meet with other experts in the room about their respective topic to review the information they have gathered. Once the expert groups have compiled their information in an organized form, they return to their heterogeneous group and share the information they have acquired while their group members ask questions. After all the individual experts have presented and the group has studied the information, individual quizzes are provided. The jigsaw approach is perfect for content area instruction, particularly in science and social studies, and can be used to gather information that students will later use to write reports.

Numbered Heads Together

Students are assigned to heterogeneous groups of four or five students and count off by number. The teacher then poses a question to the group and asks students to put their heads together to develop an answer. After allowing students time to develop their group responses, the teacher calls out a number. All students with that number raise their hand and the teacher selects one to state the answer. Students can also hold up their answer on whiteboards. Larry Maheady and his colleagues used this strategy to help students improve their performance on science tests but it could also be used for all content area subjects.[21]

TO SUM UP

▶ Become familiar with your state's content area standards. These can be found on your state's department of education website.

▶ Use diagnostic assessments and progress-monitoring assessments to determine the specific difficulties your students will have when learning content area standards.

▶ Use content standards and information about your students' needs when planning with your general education colleagues.

▶ Work with your general education colleagues to ensure that parents and students know how students with disabilities will be accommodated in general education classrooms and how intervention instruction will be used to help students in the general education curriculum.

▶ Be clear about how instructional approaches will be used to meet course, unit, and lesson goals.

WHAT'S NEXT?

In the chapters that follow, you will learn more specific information about how to teach reading, writing, mathematics, and content area instruction. Careful planning and effective instructional strategies will be essential for implementing this content.

ADDITIONAL RESOURCES

▶ Teacher Vision is a website that contains information that can be used for lesson planning, collaborating with general education teachers, developing accommodations, and much more. Many tips are available for free but for a reasonable fee you can obtain many other materials: www.teachervision.fen.com

▶ The ERIC Clearinghouse on Disabilities and Gifted Education also contains a section with links to websites focused on lesson planning: www.hoagiesgifted.org/eric/faq/lesnplan.html

▶ The Center for Research on Learning offers information about the unit organizer and content area instruction on their website: http://clc.kucrl.org/video/classroom-instruction-in-the-academic-disciplines

▶ *Kagan Cooperative Learning* book provides extensive information about how to structure cooperative learning activities and different cooperative learning structures: www.kaganonline.com/google/cooperative_learning/?gclid=CLDT46u6uakCFQsE5Qod_DYi8g

▶ Access Center provides information about meeting standards, instruction, and other special education issues: www.k8accesscenter.org/index.php/category/standards-assessments

CHAPTER THIRTEEN

Teaching Reading

In this chapter you will learn about:

- A framework for providing reading instruction and evidence-based instructional strategies to support skill development in reading
- How to provide instruction within an RTI framework
- How to integrate technology into instruction

Jada, a first-year special education teacher, was surprised to discover how much there is to know about teaching reading. She had always been a strong reader and had no idea what was involved in helping children with reading disabilities. "I didn't have any training to be a special education teacher, so I lacked a lot of the knowledge I needed. I had no idea what a cvc *word was or what a* cvce *word was. Now, I realize you have to know a lot to teach reading."*

Most students with disabilities experience difficulties learning to read and write. As a beginning teacher, you are likely going to spend a sizable portion of your assignment developing the literacy abilities of your student. Knowing the fundamentals of instruction in this area and evidence-based practices you can use to support your students will be critical. Since the advent of the No Child Left Behind Act, reading instruction in schools has received considerable emphasis. Many districts have hired reading coaches to help teachers use evidence-based practices in their instruction. Reading coaches are one source of assistance you can rely on for improving your instruction. Unfortunately, writing has not always received the same emphasis, even though developing skill in this area is essential for success in secondary and postsecondary environments. Given that students with disabilities are likely to exhibit substantial problems in both these areas, you will need to acquire knowledge and skill to support them.

A FRAMEWORK FOR TEACHING READING

The National Reading Panel,[1] composed of leading reading researchers, outlined five key areas of instruction that should be emphasized in any reading curriculum. These key areas provide a framework for assessing and instructing students with disabilities.

- ▶ *Phonological awareness:* The ability to hear and manipulate individual speech sounds in words (e.g., a child can hear that *chair* is composed of two phonemes, even though it has five letters).
- ▶ *Phonics:* The ability to attach individual speech sounds to letter patterns in order to decode the words (e.g., a child knows that *ch* makes one sound and *air* makes another and can blend these two patterns together to say */chair/*).
- ▶ *Vocabulary:* Involves knowledge of words, including the various meanings of individual words and the role they play in a sentence (e.g., *jam* can refer to something you eat [a noun] or something can be *jammed* in the door [a verb]).
- ▶ *Fluency:* The ability to rapidly recognize word patterns and individual words, and read connected text with ease. Fluency is important to reading text smoothly and is a skill that predicts students' ability to comprehend text.
- ▶ *Comprehension:* The ability to understand text presented orally or when it is read aloud.

In each of these areas, teachers can draw on evidence-based strategies to support student growth.

PHONOLOGICAL AWARENESS AND PHONICS (BASIC DECODING)

Phonological awareness and phonics are areas of considerable difficulty for many students with disabilities, particularly those with reading disabilities.[2] To improve students' skill in these areas, you can teach students to work with rhyming words, blend and segment the individual sound and letter patterns in words using strategies that help students actively process each sound and associated letter(s), and manipulate individual sounds in words. For very young students (those in kindergarten) who lack any letter sound knowledge, teachers should focus on isolated phonological awareness instruction. Isolated phonological awareness instruction does not involve letters and teaches students to recognize rhyming words, segment words into syllables, blend individual sounds in words, and segment individual sounds in words. As soon as students learn some letter sound associations involve consonants and short vowels (e.g., /a/ in *cat*), then teachers should link sound instruction and letter (grapheme) instruction, making phonological awareness instruction a cornerstone of phonics instruction. Strategies for teaching phonological awareness and phonics are listed in table 13.1. These strategies are important for helping students actively process each phoneme and its associated graphemes and will ultimately enable students to consolidate their alphabetic knowledge, a skill necessary for fluent decoding.

When teaching the strategies in table 13.1, you will need to use direct instruction routines. As pointed out in chapter 12, direct instruction involves review, modeling, guided practice, and independent practice. For instance, when teaching segment to spell, the teacher would review the vowel and consonant sounds she will be using in the routine. Then, she would model how to use the strategy.[3]

> I am going to give you a word: *hat*. I want you to listen to the word, say it slowly to yourself, and tell me the first sound. In *hat* (she says it slowly), the first sound is /h/. I know that *h* is the

Table 13.1 Strategies for Teaching Phonological Awareness and Early Phonics Skills[4]

Name of Strategy	Explanation of Strategies
Rhyming words	Students are given a key word (e.g., *ball*) and then asked to select the word they hear that rhymes with *ball* (e.g., *fall, stall, small*). Students can also play matching games with pictures that represent rhyming words. This strategy is appropriate only for students who cannot blend and segment individual sounds.
Blending sounds and syllables	First students are taught to blend syllables or onsets and rimes. For instance, teachers might say two syllables (*mag* and *pie*) and then ask students to blend them together. Having students hold their hand under their chin and counting how many times their chin drops when saying a multisyllabic word will help them segment these words into their individual syllables. Additionally, they might say /p/ and /ink/ and ask students to blend them together. Once students can blend syllables and onsets and rimes, then they learn to blend individual sounds into words. For instance, the teacher might say, "Let's say these sounds together: /c/, /a/, /t/," emphasizing each sound as she goes. Then, she asks the students to say the word, requiring them to blend the sounds together to say /cat/.
Sound manipulation	In this strategy, teachers ask students to eliminate or replace syllables or sounds in words. For instance, a teacher might ask a student to say *tulip* without the *tu-*. Or, say *blink* without the *b-*.
Stretched blending	Once students learn a handful of consonants (*m, n, l, t, p*) and one short vowel sound (*a*), they can start blending sounds and their associated letters. In stretched blending, the teacher points to each letter and asks students to hold its sound until she moves to the next letter. The key here is holding out the sounds and pointing to the letters. Such a strategy combined with stretched segmenting helps students acquire the alphabetic principle.
Segmenting	In the beginning students learn to segment multisyllabic words into syllables, starting with two-syllable words. Thus, if a teacher says *baseball,* the student is expected to say *base* and *ball*. After students master segmenting syllables, then teachers might ask them to state how many sounds are in *tell* or *gate*. Once students can identify how many sounds they hear in a word, they will be asked to say each sound.
Segment to spell	Once students have acquired some sound letter knowledge, then they can use spelling to reinforce their alphabetic knowledge. In the segment-to-spell routine, students are given a word (e.g., *fat*) and then taught to say each sound of *fat* and select the letter associated with that sound. For instance, the student hears the word *fat*. The teacher then asks the student, "What is the first sound in *fat*? What letter makes the /f/ sound?" The teacher may then ask the student to write the word *fit*. This routine helps students to understand how manipulating sounds can change the way the word is pronounced and spelled. Additionally, to create variety, this routine can be used with letter tiles, paper and pencil, magnetic letters, and so on.

letter for the /h/ sound, so I am going to write the letter *h*. What is the second sound in *hat*? (asks students) Yes, it is /a/. What letter makes the /a/ sound? (asks students) Yes, it is *a*. Now say the word (asks students). Yes, it is *hat*.

After modeling two or three words, the teacher would then ask the students to work with words, providing assistance until students can use the strategy with little help.

Once students learn words that have one-to-one letter sound correspondences or the closed syllable, short vowel words (consonant-vowel-consonant [cvc] words or consonant-consonant-vowel-consonant [ccvc] words, such as *plan*), they begin to work with words that have increasingly complex spellings. A basic scope and sequence for decoding is provided in table 13.2.

Table 13.2 A Scope and Sequence for Learning Decodable Words: Kindergarten through Third Grade

Type of Word	Examples	Rule to Teach
cvc or vc words	*cat, bat, tip, mop, up, cup, bet*	Help students understand that when the word ends in a consonant, it closes the door on the vowel and makes it say its short name. Students with reading disabilities often have considerable trouble distinguishing between short vowel sounds so you may need to spend a lot of time with these sounds.
ccvc, cvcc, cccvc, or cvccc words	*plan, flat, rest, mist, street, strap, chap, lash, catch*	*Blends:* Teach students that some consonants come together but you hear each sound. These are called *blends* because you blend each sound together. *Digraphs:* Once students learn blends, you can help them understand that when consonants come together, they sometimes make one sound. These are called *digraphs.*
cvce (or magic *e* words) and ccvce words	*cave, stove, kite, mute, Pete, crave, blame, shame*	Help students understand that the *e* on the end of words is magic; you don't hear it but it makes the vowel before it says its name. First work with cvce words that do not contain blends or digraphs, then add these words.
r-controlled words	*fur, star, for, stir, her,*	Show students how vowels change their sounds when you add *r.* For instance, show them what happens when you change *stat* to *star.*
cvvc, ccvvc, or cccvvc words	*boat, bloat, cream, stream, loom, groom*	Just as with consonants, you will teach students that sometimes two vowels come together to make one sound; usually this sound is long and usually it is the first sound that says its name. Vowel digraphs are difficult for all children, especially students with reading disabilities. Be prepared to create multiple opportunities to practice these sounds.
Words with inflected endings (-*s,- es, -ies, -d, -ed, -ing*)	*cats, fishes, flies, caked, hopped, fished, flying, making, hopping*	Students need to be taught rules for adding these endings. For instance, when you have two *ss* or a consonant digraph at the end of a word, you can add *-es.* Or, when you have *y* at the end of the word, you change it to *i* before adding *-es.*
cvccvc words	*rabbit, mitten, rattan*	Help students learn that when two cvc words come together, both syllables have short sounds, and you divide the syllable between the consonants (the *rab/bit* rule).
cvcvc words	*tiger, camel, maple*	Help students understand that when there is only one consonant between two vowels, the first vowel is usually long (the *ti/ger* rule). Sometimes, however, the vowel is short (the *cam/el* rule), so they should sound out the words both ways to see what makes sense. If you teach the tiger and camel rules, you can help students remember to say the long vowel first because the tiger usually eats the camel.

(Continued)

Table 13.2 Continued

Type of Word	Examples	Rule to Teach
cvccvc words with blends and diagraphs	*panther, freshness, wishful, restful*	Help students understand that consonant blends and digraphs usually stay together when you are dividing words into two or more syllables (the *pan/ther* rule).
Words derived from root words	*grew* and *growth, orthodontia* and *orthography, physique* and *physiology*	Help students understand that English is also a morphological language, that is, words are spelled somewhat consistently based on their smaller meaning units or morphemes. For instance, *grew* and *growth* maintain similar spellings and meanings, even though their pronunciation and spelling changes somewhat.

In teaching students increasingly complex words, you should highlight the orthography or spelling of those words using strategies such as segment to spell (described earlier) and decoding by analogy.[5] In the latter strategy, teachers select key words that help students learn novel words. Key words should include the common rimes; for example, *-oat, -air, -eet, -ill*. When introducing the decoding by analogy strategy, you can use these steps:

▶ Present the rationale for the strategy. Tell students you are going to help them become good word solvers by teaching them to recognize word parts they know in new words. You might also ask them at this point why being a good word solver would be helpful.

▶ Introduce a key word that contains a commonly used rime (e.g., *boat*). Talk with students about how *oat* is almost always pronounced with a long *o* and a /t/ sound.

▶ Provide a list of words with *-oat*. Ask the students to use what they have learned to solve the word. For example, "What letters are in *boat*? What parts of the word do you recognize?" (Students should say *-oat*.) Point to *b* and ask, "Okay, so we know what *-oat* says. What sound does *b* make? Let's blend them together stretching out the sounds. What is the word? That's right, *boat*."

▶ When finished blending words, have students use segment to spell to emphasize the words' orthography again.

As you teach single syllable words, such as *cat* and *boat*, you can teach students the associated syllable type. Doing so will make it easier to introduce multisyllabic words. The six syllable types are as follows:[6]

▶ Closed syllables follow the vc, cvc, ccvc, cccvc, cvcc, or cvccc pattern.

▶ Open syllables always end in a vowel, such as *be-, re-, she-*.

▶ Vowel team syllables include vowel digraphs (e.g., *steam*).

▶ Magic *e* syllables include cvce words, such as *stake*.

▶ *F*-controlled syllables include *r*-controlled patterns, such as *-er*.

▶ Stable final consonants include *-tion, -le, -ing, -al, -ble*.

DECODING MULTISYLLABIC WORDS AND PROMOTING MORPHOLOGICAL AWARENESS

In about third grade, students begin to decode multisyllabic words. If students with disabilities have been taught syllable types, they can use this knowledge for dividing syllables.[7] The easiest syllable division rule to teach is *rab/bit*. When teaching the rabbit rule, you show students first how to put a dot over the vowels. Second, you would ask students if they saw a syllable type in *rabbit* by pointing out the *rab* and the *bit*. Finally, you would let students know that when you have two cvc syllables coming together, then you divide the word between the consonants. After mastering the *rab/bit* rule, you can teach students three other rules for dividing syllables (e.g., *ti/ger*, which shows students how to divide syllables after the open syllable; *cam/el*, which shows students how to divide after the consonant if the tiger rule does not work; and *pan/ther*, which helps students learn to keep consonant digraphs and consonant blends together when dividing words).

While students are learning about syllables, they should begin to learn about morphemes. Morphemes are small meaning units in words, and when students can work easily with morphemes, they are said to be morphologically aware. The first foray into developing morphological awareness involves teaching students to use inflected endings when decoding or to note the singular or plural form of nouns or verb tense when writing. For typically developing students, this occurs in about second grade.[8] When introducing inflected endings, you help students understand that words can be changed in ways that alter their role in a sentence or communicate plurality. Showing students how base words change spelling when you add endings (e.g., *fly* to *flies*) helps them learn about the role that morphemes play in the English language—the spelling remains intact or similar but the meaning never changes.

In about third grade, students start learning about affixes (or prefixes and suffixes) and base words. Base words are root words that retain their meaning and, for the most part, their spelling when affixes are added (e.g., *forgive* in *unforgiving*). When learning about affixes, students should learn the most common ones first (e.g., *re-*, *un-*, *dis-*, *-tion*, *-able*). Students can play with words to see how adding affixes changes the meaning of words, the way they are used, and the way they are pronounced. Doing so helps to improve a students' morphological awareness or their ability to decode and understand the smaller meaning units in words. To promote knowledge of affixes, it helps to teach students prefix and suffix families (e.g., *dis-*, *mis-*, *un-* all mean *not*). Teachers can also use activities that involve manipulating prefixes and suffixes to change the meanings of words.

Once students understand base words and affixes (toward the end of third grade), they can be taught more complex roots that are based in Greek and Latin (e.g., *aud-* in *audible* and *trans-* in *transport*). Learning about Greek and Latin roots also helps students become morphologically aware.[9] Table 13.3 provides examples of strategies and activities that can be used for teaching morphological awareness. Using these strategies and others helps students become more word conscious, an ability that should enable them to learn more novel words on their own.

Students can also learn cognitive strategies for decoding multisyllabic words once they have some knowledge of syllable types and prefixes and suffixes. One such strategy that has been taught successfully to third-grade students is BEST.[10] The BEST strategy provides students with a process for decoding words:

Break apart the word into parts you recognize (prompt students to use what they have learned thus far about syllables, rimes, affixes, and base words).

Examine the stem (or word parts they recognize).

Say the parts.

Try the whole thing (to see if it makes sense).

Table 13.3 Strategies and Activities for Improving Students' Morphological Awareness[11]

Strategy or Activity for Teaching Morphological Awareness	Explanation of Strategy or Activity
Introducing inflected endings using direct instruction and word sorts	Begin the lesson by helping students understand that you can add word endings that will make words plural or mean more than one or change the tense of the word in a sentence. Students need to know that tense relates only to verbs or action words and it indicates when something is done. Show the student the base word and then add the ending. For example, show students that they will add -s to most words when they make them plural (e.g., *hen* to *hens*); however, for some words they will add -es. Then you teach them the rule for adding -es (e.g., when words end in a diagraph or double ss, you add -es). Practice doing this with a few words. Once students can state the rules, then you can use word sort, in which students categorize words on cards according to whether they are spelled with -s or -es.
Sentences that help students understand how inflected endings are used	Teachers can present sentences that contain correct and incorrect use of inflected endings or morphemes and ask students which word makes more sense. For example, you might ask students to read the following two sentences, remembering their syllable division rules. "The rabbit went hopping down the trail." Or "The rabbit went hoping down the trail." Ask the students which word makes more sense. Then, ask them to tell the difference between *hopping* and *hoping*. Once they identify the difference, then you can remind them of the rule.
Prefixes and suffixes dice game	Students have two die, one with prefixes on it and another with base words. First, make sure students understand the meaning of the base words. Second, let students roll the dice to make new words. Third, ask students the meaning of the new word and help them understand the difference between real words and nonsense words (e.g., you would not use *mis* with *satisfied*).
Morpheme webs	Webs can be used to help students see relationships among prefixes, suffixes, base words, and Greek and Latin roots. A base or root word can be placed in the center circle and other morphemes that can be joined with the root or base are put in separate circles. Then you discuss with the students how new words can be formed using the web.
Morpheme triangles and rectangles	When teachers want to explore three- and four-syllable words, they can use morpheme triangles and rectangles. For example, you might want to explore the word *inspector*. You would ask the students to tell you how many syllables are in the word and what those syllables are (encourage students to use the rules they learned for dividing syllables). Once the word is divided into syllables, point out the root *spect* and ask if they know of other words that contain the word *spect*. Encourage students to talk about words such as *spectacles, spectator,* and *inspection*. Ask what these words seem to have in common; you are trying to help them understand that *spect* refers to looking at something or examining it. Then get them to focus on the other syllables *in-* and *-tor* and what they mean. Finally, ask the students to put all the word parts together and discuss what they believe the word *inspector* means.

Strategy or Activity for Teaching Morphological Awareness	Explanation of Strategy or Activity
Continue to use spelling to emphasize morphological patterns	You will want to have students spell words listening for the morphemes and applying the spelling rules. When practicing any of the multisyllabic words, have students first say each syllable they hear, then work on spelling those syllables with corrective feedback from you. For example, when teaching students how to discriminate between words spelled with an -s versus -es, you might ask students to spell *fish* and then *fishes, hen* and then *hens.* Always use error correction when they miss words that emphasizes the rule.

Students are taught the BEST strategy using the process for teaching cognitive strategies outlined in chapter 12.

VOCABULARY INSTRUCTION

Many students whom you work with require explicit instruction in vocabulary in order to more effectively comprehend text. In the previous section, we discussed strategies for improving morphological awareness as a tool for improving vocabulary knowledge. In this section we focus on strategies for developing word-level knowledge. To enrich students' vocabulary knowledge, you want to help them understand that words often have varied meanings and play different grammatical roles in sentences. Students who have a rich understanding of words are more likely to use their knowledge to better comprehend text. There are many strategies available for teaching vocabulary; these strategies involve rich discussion about words, helping students connect new words to their background knowledge, and developing linkages between words that are connected conceptually.

Strategies that do not work, however, include looking up words in the dictionary and writing definitions, memorizing synonyms and antonyms, and taking weekly tests on ten or more vocabulary words.[12] When students learn dictionary definitions, they often end up using these words to write odd sentences. For example, two definitions of *usurp* in the online version of *Merriam-Webster Dictionary* are "to take or make use of without right" and "to take the place of by or as if by force" (www.merriam-webster.com /dictionary/usurp?show=0&t=1310306180). When a student was asked by his teacher to look up this word and then write a sentence using the word, he wrote, "The thief tried to usurp the money from the safe." Most would agree that this is an odd use of the word *usurp.* So, what can you use instead to help students with disabilities improve their vocabulary?

▶ *Select words that are appropriate for students to learn,* words that will enrich their daily oral vocabulary, their writing, and their ability to comprehend text. Appropriate words, referred to as tier two words by prominent vocabulary researchers Isabel Beck, Margaret McKeown, and Linda Kucan are richer words that are synonyms for more common words that students already have in their vocabulary (or tier one words).[13] For instance, *splendid* is a richer word than *great* and *delightful* is a richer word than *nice.*

▶ *Use student-friendly definitions.* Student-friendly definitions help students understand words in ways that they can be used appropriately in context. You can find student-friendly dictionaries, such as *Cobuild: New Student's Dictionary,* or access such dictionaries online. The *Longman Dictionary of Contemporary English* (www.ldoceonline.com) is one such example. In this dictionary, *usurp* was defined as "to take someone else's power, position, job, etc. when you do not have the right to." Merriam-Webster also has a student-friendly version of their dictionary, called *Word Central*, that provides students with definitions and vocabulary games they can play.

▶ *Use strategies that promote conversations about words.* Strategies, such as Text Talk, help students learn the meaning of tier two words. In Text Talk, teachers read and discuss the story with the students. They then introduce the target words one at a time, asking students to repeat the word after the teacher. You can then use either the student-friendly definition of the word or read the word in context and ask students what they think the word might mean. If you choose the later, you might want to use a sentence that helps to reveal the meaning of the word. Discuss the meaning of the word and how you might use it in different sentences. Students can help to generate some of these sentences in the discussion. Ask the students to repeat the word while focusing on decoding the different letter sound patterns in the word. Finally, create activities in which students have to interact more with the words. For instance, when working with words, you can ask them to tell you if they have ever seen a person usurp something in a movie or story. Students can also complete sentences to deepen their understanding of word meanings (e.g., "I could tell I was getting drowsy because . . .").

▶ *Teach students how to use context to understand words.* Teaching students how to use context clues to decipher a word's meaning can help them learn as many as a thousand words in one year. Table 13.4 includes context clues you can teach to students to use to understand words. You can teach these clues by modeling for students how to use these clues to decipher the meaning of words. Of course, you should limit the number of context clues you teach students in any one lesson.

▶ *Promote generalization of new words.* Finding ways to encourage students to use words they are learning in different settings is important. For example, you can engage students in word sightings, where they are reinforced for noticing when words they are learning are used in another context.

Table 13.4 Context Clues Students Can Use While Reading[14]

Type of Clue	Explanation of the Clue and an Example
Definition clue	Usually the word is defined or explained in the same sentence or in a nearby one: The *atmosphere* is the earth's outer covering of air. It was *serendipity* when she found her ring at the bottom of her closet. After months of looking, she never expected to find her ring again.
Description clue	The unknown word is described with other words: Mary is a *diligent* student who studies constantly.
Example clue	Several words or ideas are presented that are examples of the unknown word: The lantern *illuminated* the cave walls so well that we could see spiders crawling all over them. The Christmas lights *illuminated* the snow and made the neighborhood look like a sparkling wonderland.
Comparison clue	The unknown word is depicted using similarities among persons, ideas, and objects: The *stealth* thief was as quiet as a mouse when he broke into the house and moved through the rooms picking up what he could take easily.
Contrast clue	Words or ideas are used to depict the difference between the unknown word and other concepts: Bill is somewhat *cantankerous* but his girlfriend is so enthusiastic and pleasant.

PROMOTING FLUENCY AT THE RIME, WORD, AND CONNECTED-TEXT LEVELS

When students automatically decode word parts, such as *fl-*, *str-*, *-oat*, and *-an*, they can tackle multisyllabic words more effortlessly. In fact, when competent decoders encounter a novel word, they divide it into recognizable parts and quickly put those parts together to decode these words successfully.[15] Similarly, fluent readers, or those who read text effortlessly, can easily and quickly recognize individual words in terms of decoding them and deciphering their meaning.[16] Such effortless processing of individual words and text allows students to focus on comprehending text. To promote fluent reading, teachers need to focus on four key areas: (1) automatic decoding of word parts, (2) rapid recognition of common decodable words and other common phonetically irregular sight words, (3) building fluency with oral and silent reading, and (4) rapidly retrieving a word's meaning. The last component of fluent reading was discussed in the previous section. Strategies for developing fluent reading in the other areas are discussed in the following.

Rapid Word-Part Recognition

Segmenting words with letters is one way of helping students build the type of alphabetic knowledge that will allow them to rapidly recognize word patterns. Incorporating reviews in phonics lessons that focus on spelling word parts will also assist students in developing automaticity because spelling is a form of segmenting. Finally, rapid practice with word parts will help students develop the automaticity they need.[17] Some methods that can be used to build automaticity at the word part level include constant time delay, chorally reading flash cards with word parts and then chanting their spellings, concentration, and rapid practice with word parts (e.g., students say a word part as quickly as possible after viewing it).[18]

Constant time delay involves seeing the word part, waiting for a second, and then rapidly saying the word part when you cue the student to do so. You can also show students the word part, ask them to repeat it after you (using choral response), and then ask them to spell each letter aloud on cue. Students can also play a game of concentration with the word parts, and when they turn over matching cards, they have to say the word part aloud. Rapid practice with word parts also works. Once teachers know that students recognize the word parts, they can encourage them to say them rapidly when presented with the word parts on flash cards.

Rapid Word Recognition

To help students quickly decode individual words, teachers must work toward automaticity with common decodable words or regular words and sight words that are irregular, such as *said*. The strategies mentioned for developing rapid recognition of word parts can also be used to facilitate rapid word recognition. Lists of common regular and irregular sight words can be found on line. Ray Reutzel and Robert Cooter Jr., however, caution that once students learn to rapidly recognize the 107 most commonly occurring words, there is little benefit to be gained from engaging in sight word practice to commit the remaining 823 common words to memory.[19] These researchers recommend that teachers focus on Susan Zeno and colleagues' word list shown in table 13.5.

Fluent Reading of Connected Text

Fluent reading involves reading text accurately and with appropriate phrasing at a quick but comfortable pace. To develop fluent reading, students with disabilities need practice in decodable and

Table 13.5 107 Most Common High-Frequency Words[20]

the	as	but	about	your	how	also	back
of	are	by	up	which	than	down	where
and	they	were	said	do	two	make	know
to	with	one	out	then	may	now	little
a	be	all	if	many	only	way	such
in	his	she	some	these	most	each	even
is	at	when	would	no	its	called	much
that	or	an	so	time	made	did	our
it	from	their	people	been	over	just	must
was	had	there	them	who	see	after	
for	I	her	other	like	first	water	
you	not	can	more	could	new	through	
he	have	we	will	has	very	get	
on	this	what	into	him	my	because	

From Zeno, S. M., Ivens, S. H., Millard, R. T., & Duvvuri, R. (1995). *The educator's word frequency guide.* Reprinted by permission of Touchstone Applied Science Associates, Inc.

connected text.[21] Decodable text contains many phonetically regular words. Teachers typically choose decodable text that supports a particular decoding pattern as a way to help students generalize their knowledge of decoding patterns to reading real words in text. Although decodable text is helpful for fostering automaticity, it is insufficient. Real word text is not always decodable; therefore, students need practice reading connected text at their reading level. To facilitate fluent reading, you can choose to use a research-based fluency-building program, such as Great Leaps!, QuickReads, or Read Naturally. You can also use several research-based strategies with decodable and connected text. Most of these strategies are based on the concept of repeated reading. When students with reading disabilities repeatedly read text, they are likely to become more fluent. Repeated reading strategies include the following:[22]

▶ *Echo reading* involves the teacher modeling how to read a sentence or a passage and then the students read the same sentence or passage after the teacher.

▶ *Choral reading* involves the teacher and the students reading text aloud together. Often students will engage in choral reading after the teacher has read the passage or story to them.

▶ *Partner reading* involves students reading to each other. The strategy can be used in either general or special education classrooms. If used in a general education classroom, either you or your general education partner should divide the class in half and assign the top reader in the class to the top reader in the lower half of the student distribution. You then assign the remaining students in a similar fashion until the lowest student in the top half of the distribution is assigned to the lowest student in the class. Once students are assigned partners, you need to demonstrate how they will work together successfully. This involves teaching students behaviors associated with being a good partner, including providing one's partner with encouragement, providing appropriate wait time to recognize a word or self-correct, and pointing out in a neutral tone mistakes that were made and asking your partner to reread the sentence using the correct word.

After learning appropriate partner behaviors, then partner A (the stronger reader) first reads the passage. While partner A is reading, partner B marks words missed and keeps track of how many words are read. Once partner A is finished, partner B provides appropriate feedback. Then, the pairs switch and the procedure is repeated. *Classwide peer tutoring* and the *peer-assisted learning strategies* are routines that incorporate partner reading intended to develop fluency (see chapter 12).

Another important strategy for promoting fluency is to help students set fluency goals and then chart their progress. Such a strategy promotes responsibility for learning. Help students set reasonable goals. For instance, if a student is reading fifty correct words per minute (cwpm), it will not be appropriate to set a weekly goal of one hundred cwpm. Once students set their goals, they chart how many words they read correctly during a one-minute timing. When students reach their goals, it is important to acknowledge their progress before setting new goals.

PROMOTING READING COMPREHENSION

Many students with reading disabilities lack effective strategies for comprehending text or do not have sufficient knowledge of text structure to use in the comprehension process.[23] To help students with disabilities become more effective readers requires instruction in effective comprehension strategies and text structure. Research has shown that students can improve their comprehension when they are taught to make predictions, summarize text, make inferences from text, and self-monitor text when reading.[24] Table 13.6 contains examples of strategies that can be taught to students to improve their comprehension. Effective instruction in these strategies requires the use of instruction routines for teaching cognitive strategies (see chapter 12).

Table 13.6 Effective Comprehension Strategies

Name of Strategy	How to Teach the Strategy
Making predictions	Students are taught to look at the title of the text and pictures to make an educated guess about what the book is about. Or students are taught to use their knowledge of what has happened in the text to make predictions about what might happen next. In order for this strategy to be effective, students must work with the teacher and their peers to look for evidence in the text that either confirms or disconfirms their predictions.
Summarization	Students can be taught several processes for summarizing text. One strategy that has been used effectively for students with learning disabilities is *Paraphrasing Strategy* by Jean Schumaker, Pegi Denton, and Donald Deshler.[25] In this strategy students are taught to read the passage, ask themselves about the main idea and details, and put the passage in their own words. Summarization is difficult to teach; however, when students learn to summarize, not only will their comprehension increase, but so will their ability to write effectively.
Self-questioning while reading	Students need to be able to monitor how well they are understanding text while reading. To help them with this process, students can be taught to ask themselves the following questions: Can I restate the main points I just read? Did I understand what I just read or do I need to go back and reread? Do I understand how main ideas or events are related in the paragraph or passage?

Exhibit 13.1   Story Map Organizer

Setting: Where and when did the story occur?	*Characters:* Who were the major characters?
	Who were the minor characters?

Problem: What was the main problem in the story that needed to be resolved?

Name three major events in the story:

1.

2.

3.

Solution: How was the problem resolved?

A Survival Guide for New Special Educators, by Billingsley, Brownell, Israel, and Kamman. Copyright © 2013 by John Wiley & Sons, Inc.

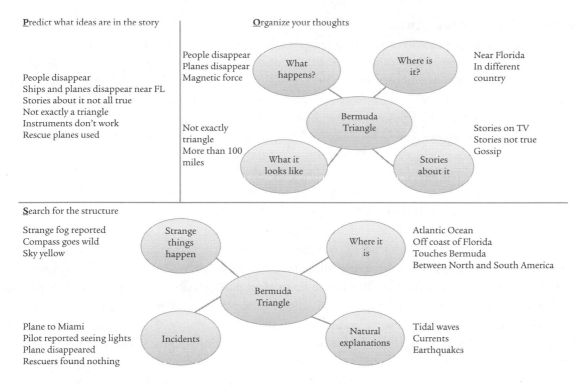

Predict what ideas are in the story

People disappear
Ships and planes disappear near FL
Stories about it not all true
Not exactly a triangle
Instruments don't work
Rescue planes used

Organize your thoughts

People disappear
Planes disappear
Magnetic force — **What happens?**

Where is it? — Near Florida
In different country

Bermuda Triangle

Not exactly triangle
More than 100 miles — **What it looks like**

Stories about it — Stories on TV
Stories not true
Gossip

Search for the structure

Strange fog reported
Compass goes wild
Sky yellow — **Strange things happen**

Where it is — Atlantic Ocean
Off coast of Florida
Touches Bermuda
Between North and South America

Bermuda Triangle

Plane to Miami
Pilot reported seeing lights
Plane disappeared
Rescuers found nothing — **Incidents**

Natural explanations — Tidal waves
Currents
Earthquakes

Summarize. Summarize the main idea in your own words. Ask a "teacher" questions about main idea. Evaluate. Compare. Clarify. Predict.

Figure 13.1 The POSSE Strategy[28]
Englert, C. S., & Mariage, T. V. (1991). Making students partners in the comprehension process: Organizing the reading "POSSE." *Learning Disability Quarterly*, 14, 123–138.

Narrative and expository texts have different structures. Understanding text structure can improve students' comprehension and ability to write effectively.[26] For improving comprehension of narrative texts, students can be taught to identify the major elements of stories, such as the plot or problem of the story, main and minor characters, sequence of main events in stories, and setting. In exhibit 13.1, we provide an example of a story map that teachers can help students learn to complete using the cognitive strategy instruction approach described in chapter 12.

Researchers have also developed graphic organizers for helping students understand expository text. One such strategy is POSSE.[27] In this strategy, students are taught to use five strategies and a graphic organizer to comprehend the main ideas and key details in expository text. First students are taught two prereading strategies, predicting and organizing background knowledge. With the teachers' guidance, students make predictions about an expository text and organize their predictions according to the major categories their ideas represent. Second, during reading, students are taught to work in groups to search for the author's text structure or how the author organized ideas. After discussing the text structures, students move to the summarization step. At this point, students work through short sections of the text to identify the main idea for a section. Once the main idea is identified, the student leader for the group poses a question about the main idea and elicits responses from peers that help elicit relevant details about the main idea. Finally, students evaluate what they have learned by first comparing their summaries of the text with their original predictions. Once they compare their predictions and final summaries, they ask clarifying questions about various ideas presented in the text. Finally, students predict what they think the next section of the text will be about. In figure 13.1, we provide an example of the POSSE strategy.

Response-to-Intervention

Special and general education teachers working in an RTI framework can use the strategies presented in this chapter to provide tiered instruction. Creating a cohesive instructional approach for students with reading disabilities, however, will require ongoing collaboration between the general and special education teacher. Decisions will have to be made about what strategies will be taught to all students in tier one instruction and what strategies will be taught selectively, based on student need, to students in tier two and tier three instruction. Likely, as the special education teacher, you will be providing tiers two or three instruction in those areas where students are struggling most.

The instructional focus of tiers two and three should be determined through ongoing individual assessments conducted mainly by the special education teacher and analyzed collaboratively with general education colleagues. Curriculum-based measurement in reading is a type of assessment that can provide special and general education teachers with a quick assessment of how students with disabilities and other struggling readers are responding to instruction.[29] As discussed in chapter 6, curriculum-based measures are particularly useful for making quick judgments about students' overall progress in reading. Curriculum-based measurement can include oral reading fluency probes or cloze passages obtained from a basal curriculum, intervention curriculum, or measurement system such as the DIBELS. In addition to curriculum-based measures, special education teachers will want to administer diagnostic assessments to secure a deeper understanding of students' strengths and needs in the specific areas of reading. There are many diagnostic reading assessments available such as the Core Phonics Survey and the Diagnostic Reading Assessment. The Core Phonics Survey is available free online (www.scholastic.com/dodea/Module_2/resources/dodea_m2_tr_core.pdf) and provides in-depth information about students' letter sound knowledge and decoding skills. The Diagnostic Reading Assessment is available commercially and provides information about students' strengths and needs in phonemic awareness, decoding, vocabulary, fluency, and comprehension.

To be useful, curriculum-based measures and diagnostic assessments must be collected over time to determine if students with disabilities are profiting from the research-based reading instruction being provided or if instructional interventions should be changed or delivered with more intensity to meet student needs. Additionally, progress on these assessments can be used to determine if students should move into a different instructional tier.

SPECIAL CONSIDERATIONS FOR ELLs WITH LEARNING DISABILITIES

Students learning a different language, or ELLs, have specific difficulties that can be compounded by a reading disability. These challenges include (1) hearing and pronouncing specific English sounds (e.g., Korean-speaking students struggle to distinguish between /p/ and /f/), (2) recognizing words and retrieving their meanings because of insufficient vocabulary and decoding knowledge, (3) comprehending English grammar structures (syntax), and (4) understanding figurative language. Although students with reading disabilities also can exhibit one or more of these difficulties, ELL students with disabilities are doubly challenged when they are also trying to learn English.

INCORPORATING TECHNOLOGY INTO READING INSTRUCTION

Since the 1990s, rapid advances in technology have provided many tools to support students with disabilities in learning to read. Computer software has been developed that provides students with disabilities instruction in certain aspects of reading or accommodates them in their areas of difficulty. Earobics,

What Can Special Education Teachers Do?

Yujeong Park, University of Florida

Becoming more knowledgeable about differences between students' native language and English is most helpful to special education teachers. The website of Ted Power, *English Language Learning and Teaching* (www.btinternet.com/~ted.power/phono.html), provides useful information about common mistakes in English pronunciation as well as a comparison of English sounds to those in other languages. Special education teachers can use this information to create extra practice with specific sounds.

When teaching vocabulary, special education teachers should become knowledgeable about similarities between students' native language and English because they can use these similarities to teach new vocabulary to students.[30] For example, there are several words in Spanish that look very similar to English (e.g., *banco* in Spanish for *bank* in English, *nombre* for *name*, *tigre* for *tiger*). Also, Spanish and English share many of the same root words. Teachers can ask students to predict the meaning of English words based on what they know in their native languages (e.g., *el elefante* in Spanish for an *elephant* in English). Additionally, picture cards can help these students to understand and remember common English words.

The language experience approach is another technique that special education teachers can use to improve ELL students' oral language and understanding of text.[31] The language experience approach uses students' personal experiences and home language and culture to support reading development.[32] In this approach, special education teachers accomplish the following:

- ► Encourage students to select a topic that is interesting to them
- ► Ask students to write about the topic in their own language
- ► Provide a peer to help students write the text in English
- ► Ask students to read the draft aloud
- ► Translate the text if it is in students' native language
- ► Ask questions about the text to extend student thinking and elaborate on ideas
- ► Identify sentences that are not complete and help students revise those sentences
- ► Read the text aloud first and ask students to read it aloud mimicking you
- ► Select words not easily recognized for the students' word banks for sight word practice

To improve fluency and comprehension, special education teachers can use many of the same strategies they use with students with reading disabilities. However, they should also consider using dual-language books, sometimes called bilingual books (e.g., Grimm's fairy tales in a side-by-side English-Spanish format). Dual language books include the original (native) language of students as well as an English translation. Teachers need to choose the books so that they match ELL students' abilities in vocabulary, fluency, and grammar. Additionally, before reading any text, special education teachers must be extra careful and help ELL students understand words used in the story that other students with reading disabilities might already know. To improve understanding, special education teachers can use pictures, diagrams, and actions.

WordMaker, READ 180, and Thinking Reader are all examples of software programs that provide computer-assisted instruction in key areas of reading. Two of these programs provide comprehensive instruction in reading, Earobics and Read 180. Earobics, commercially available at www.earobics.com, is a comprehensive program that teaches students grades K–3 skills in phonemic awareness, phonics, fluency, vocabulary, and comprehension. Read 180, available through Scholastic, provides comprehensive remedial reading and writing instruction to students in grades 4–12. The program involves a combination of teacher-directed instruction and computer-assisted instruction in phonics, vocabulary, fluency, spelling, comprehension, and writing.

WordMaker and Thinking Reader provide instruction in specific areas of reading. WordMaker (see www.donjohnston.com/resources/wordmaker_index.html) is a program designed to help students acquire the phonics skills necessary for reading and spelling words. In this program, students see, hear, and spell words through repeated practice opportunities, helping them to learn all the basic phonics patterns in monosyllabic words. Thinking Reader (www.tomsnyder.com) is a software program that teaches students using direct instruction to use comprehension strategies with digitized text (e.g., summarization, prediction, clarification, and visualizing). In addition to the outstanding instruction this program provides, Thinking Reader allows teachers to tailor the program so that students can continue to work on specific strategies if they cannot use them independently. Additionally, the digitized text can be read aloud to students who are disfluent and provide vocabulary support. Students can click on any word they do not know and hear a student-friendly definition.

Other technology applications can accommodate students who have decoding and oral reading fluency problems. Many commercially available texts can be digitized and read through text-to-speech software. Today, most computer programs have text-to-speech features that can be activated to read digitized text. Additionally, there are programs, such as Read&Write GOLD, that can provide text-to-speech support but can also be used for instructing students in strategies or writing reports. For instance, with Read&Write GOLD, teachers point out key ideas in the text by highlighting them. They can then show students how to use those key ideas to develop a summary of the text. Students can also highlight text and organize it into a file to use for studying texts or writing papers.

These are just a few of the assistive technologies available to teachers and their students with disabilities. Other examples of technologies can be found on the National Center on Accessible Instructional Materials website (NIMAS; see http://nimas.cast.org) and other websites mentioned in chapter 1 (e.g., LD OnLine). These technologies can provide important support to students with disabilities and other struggling learners who are identified through assessments.

TO SUM UP

▶ Use ongoing assessment to document student progress and identify students' needs.
▶ Collaboratively develop reading objectives and instructional plans with all professionals involved in your students' education.
▶ Use evidence-based strategies as the foundation for your instruction.
▶ Integrate the use of technology when appropriate to meet students' needs.
▶ Find ways to communicate students' ongoing progress with parents so that they can make good decisions about their child.

WHAT'S NEXT?

In this chapter, you learned numerous strategies for improving students' reading achievement. Teaching these strategies will lay the foundation for improving writing and the subskills of writing. In chapter 14, you will learn more strategies for improving the writing achievement of students with disabilities.

ADDITIONAL RESOURCES

▶ Reading Rockets: www.readingrockets.org

▶ Vaughn Gross Center Materials: www.meadowscenter.org/vgc/materials

▶ The Florida Center for Reading Research: www.fcrr.org

▶ The National Reading Panel: www.nationalreadingpanel.org/NRPAbout/about_nrp.htm

▶ Enchanted Reading: Storymap graphic organizers: www.enchantedlearning.com/graphicorganizers/storymap

▶ Center on Instruction: www.centeroninstruction.org

▶ International Dyslexia Association: www.interdys.org

▶ LD OnLine, sponsored by the National Center on Learning Disabilities: www.ldonline.org

▶ National Center on Response to Intervention: www.rti4success.org

▶ RTI Action Network: www.rtinetwork.org

CHAPTER FOURTEEN

Teaching Writing

✔ **In this chapter you will learn about:**

- The basic skills necessary for successful writing
- The process for generating text
- Strategies students will need to develop well-organized text
- Technological applications to support the development of written text

After learning strategies for teaching children to write, Sally, a second-year special educator, felt more confident helping her students generate ideas and organize them. "Before, my students would lay their heads down and refuse to write a word; now they're willing to try."

Writing is a complex skill that depends on students' knowledge of text structure and sentence structure, a rich vocabulary to capture one's ideas, strong background knowledge that provides the ideas needed for generating text, the ability to plan for and generate text, the ability to revise one's writing according to expected conventions, fluent skill in spelling, and fluent skill in handwriting or keyboarding.[1] Often students with high-incidence disabilities have problems in two or more of these areas, making writing an arduous and unpleasant process for them. Fortunately, there are strategies and technology applications that can help make writing a more pleasant process for students with disabilities.

BASIC SKILLS UNDERLYING PROFICIENT WRITING PERFORMANCE

In order to be able to generate ideas easily and transcribe those ideas into organized and well-developed text, students must be fluent in spelling, handwriting, and sentence construction. As a beginning special education teacher, you might be targeting instruction in one or more of these areas and will want your instruction to incorporate evidence-based practices.

Spelling Well

Spelling is a more difficult task for students with disabilities than decoding;[2] however, when combined with decoding instruction, systematic spelling instruction can better support students with disabilities in acquiring decoding. Systematic spelling instruction is just like phonics instruction. It involves helping students to learn to (1) segment words into syllables and syllables into individual letter and sounds,[3] (2) recognize morphological units in words and use them for decoding those words and spelling them (e.g., *please* is the base for *pleasing, pleasurable,* and *pleasant*),[4] and (3) use knowledge of spelling and decoding to read and spell sight words such as *because* or *where.* Thus, strategies we described in the reading chapter for promoting decoding and morphological awareness are quite effective in developing students' spelling abilities. In fact, spelling and decoding should be taught simultaneously using the principles of effective direct instruction because instruction in the one ability reinforces skills gains in the other.

Commercially available materials and computer-assisted instructional programs and games also exist to improve spelling. For example, the comprehensive Wilson Reading System is effective for teaching students with severe reading disabilities decoding and spelling skills (as well as fluency and comprehension skills).[5] Additionally, research studies show that *Spelling through Morphographs* helps students learn to spell multisyllabic words and maintain their learning over time.[6] There are also spelling games that can be downloaded from the Internet, such as VocabularySpellingCity (www.spellingcity.com). Special education teachers should take care to evaluate spelling programs in terms of the amount of systematic practice and review they provide for learning different spelling patterns. KidsSpell.com is great because teachers can either choose the words they want or create their own list. Additionally, teachers need to use the materials in ways that would follow an appropriate sequence of decoding and sight word instruction. For instance, students begin decoding and spelling instruction with the short vowel words and proceed to more difficult patterns such as vowel teams and multisyllabic words. Decoding and spelling sequences can be found in many instructional materials.

Handwriting or Keyboarding Fluency

When students generate text, they need to be able to write or keyboard easily.[7] If students are not fluent in either of these two areas, then they cannot take notes or generate text easily. Similar to spelling, too much attention is given to getting the words on paper rather than focusing on the ideas the student wants to take notes on or write about. Additionally, handwriting might be of such poor quality that neither the students nor their peers are able to decipher what they wrote. Such a situation leads to extreme frustration for students.

Handwriting programs, such as *Zaner-Bloser Handwriting*[8] and *Handwriting Without Tears,*[9] can be used to explicitly teach students how to form letters and do so fluently. The point of such instruction is not to help students develop attractive handwriting, but to be able to write fluently so that students can easily record their ideas or their teachers' ideas. Keyboarding games are also available for students to develop fluency in this area, and many of these games are free. For example, www.learninggamesforkids .com has multiple games that can be played at no cost. Although all students need keyboarding skills, for students with writing disabilities, skill in keyboarding is a must because these students may not be able to develop legible and fluent handwriting even with instruction. Keyboarding skills combined with instruction in spelling can help students develop the basic skills fluency they need and devote more attention to the content of their writing.

Knowledge of Sentence Structure

Decades of research on writing have demonstrated that direct grammar instruction is unlikely to have any impact on overall writing quality, and it can even hamper students' writing. However, teaching students who struggle to recognize different sentence types in their writing and combine sentences does seem to have some effect on the overall quality of students' writing, particularly those who struggle or those with disabilities. The sentence-writing strategy is one evidence-based strategy developed for students with learning disabilities that assists students in learning how to write different types of sentences. In this strategy, students learn the structure for different types of sentences.[10] First, they are taught how to identify a simple sentence by looking for the subject and verb. To identify the subject, they are taught to look for the who or what the sentence is about, and to identify the verb, they are taught to look for the action in the sentence. Once they learn how to identify a simple sentence, they are then taught, using cognitive strategy instruction principles, to use the PENS mnemonic to write a sentence. This mnemonic device directs students to do the following first:

▶ *P*ick a formula (one of the formulas used to characterize a particular type of sentence—in this case it would be subject + verb).

▶ *E*xplore the words to fit the formula.

▶ *N*ote the words by following the formula.

▶ *S*earch and check to ensure that the sentence is correct.

Second, they learn to combine simple sentences to form a compound sentence. Third, they learn what a dependent clause is and how it is different from a simple sentence. They then are taught how to combine dependent and independent clauses to form complex sentences, and complex and compound sentences to form compound complex sentences. Again, after they are taught to recognize each type of sentence, they are then taught that particular type of sentence using the PENS mnemonic.

Another strategy students can use to develop their ability to write increasingly sophisticated and intact sentences is the sentence-combining strategy.[11] In this strategy, students are first taught how to identify and write a complete sentence just as they were in the sentence-writing strategy. Once students can write a simple sentence, then they are taught to write more complex sentences using the steps found in table 14.1.

Direct instruction is used to help students learn the sentence-combining strategy. First, the teacher models how to write a simple sentence and then students practice writing simple sentences until they reach a certain level of fluency. Second, the teacher models combining sentences using coordinating conjunction cues. For instance, she might write the following two sentences and show students how they could be combined using *and* as the coordinating conjunction. First, "John ate his cake (and). Then, he went to the store. First, John ate his cake and then he went to the store." After teaching them to combine sentences using cues, she would omit the cue but underline key words, such as *first* and *then* in the previous example. As students gained proficiency, she would fade all cues.

A Rich Vocabulary and Background Knowledge

Students who have a strong command of the English language and sufficient background knowledge will provide more interesting and sophisticated text when asked to write. In the chapter on reading instruction, we emphasized multiple approaches for teaching vocabulary and we cannot stress enough the importance of using those approaches if you want to improve students' writing. Additionally, reading extensively to students, encouraging students to read many different types of texts, and engaging them in projects and experiments should help them to acquire the background and vocabulary knowledge

Table 14.1 Sentence-Combining Instruction

Instructional Skills	What Students Are Taught to Do
Combine smaller, simple sentences into complex sentences using a conjunction.	Students are taught first to combine simple sentences by using three common conjunctions (*and, but,* and *because*). For instance, they would be taught to combine "The boy ate the cake" and "The cake was delicious" to become "The boy ate the cake because it was delicious."
Insert adjectives or adverbs from one sentence into another sentence	Students are provided with two sentences that are related but one contains an adverb or adjective. Students are then taught to combine the two sentences into one. For example, "The boy ate the cake" and "The cake was delicious" becomes "The boy ate the delicious cake."
Insert adverbial or adjectival clauses from one sentence to another.	Students are provided with two sentences that are related and then taught to combine the two sentences to make a complex sentence with an adverbial or adjective clause. For example, "The boy stopped eating the cake" and "The boy was stuffed" becomes "The boy stopped eating the cake when he was stuffed." Or, "Terrance listened to his new CD" and "Terrance bought the CD at the Fireside Mall" becomes "Terrance listened to his new CD that he bought at the Fireside Mall."
Combine sentences, adjectives and adverbs, and adverbial and adjectival clauses into complex sentences.	Students are taught to develop complex sentences by using skills learned in previous units. For instance, they might be presented with the following sentences initially: "The boy ate the cake." "The boy was stuffed." "The boy ate a huge dinner." They are then taught to combine these sentences into one complex sentence: "The boy, who had just eaten a huge dinner, ate the cake but stopped when he was stuffed."

needed to generate text. Without this knowledge base, students will not be able to express themselves in interesting ways or elaborate on ideas in the text. Finally, teaching students to summarize text, a strategy described in the chapter on reading, is very powerful in helping students to improve their writing.

BECOMING AN INDEPENDENT WRITER

Many students with disabilities struggle to generate organized texts. Sometimes, these students do not have the background knowledge they need to write about a topic, and other times they are not able to organize their ideas prior to writing. Students with learning disabilities often simply write about everything they know related to a topic and sometimes about unrelated concepts without any obvious organizing framework. Additionally, students with disabilities often do not recognize how they can revise their text to improve its organization, coherence, or overall appearance. To help students with disabilities become more independent writers, you will have to teach them to set goals for writing, select and implement strategies, and monitor their progress.

Setting Goals

Prior to teaching students any strategies, you will want to help them understand why it is important to set goals for their writing. Students need to understand that all good writers have an overall goal and a set of subgoals for writing their papers.[12] For instance, a writer might want to convince readers that all children should get vaccines when they are babies. After setting this overall goal, the writer would have specific subgoals, which in this instance might include questions to be addressed in the paper, such as,

"Why are vaccinations important?" "What sorts of childhood diseases are prevented by vaccinations?" "How do the benefits of vaccinations outweigh the risks?" Finally, a writer would want to make a timeline for accomplishing the task. For instance, to support the development of the paper on childhood vaccinations, a student might write these goals: (1) I will find five articles about childhood vaccinations by the second week of class, (2) I will read each article and make notes about points related to the questions I want to answer by the fourth week of class, and (3) I will have a draft of each paragraph, except for the conclusion, by the fifth week of class. When developing goals, students initially will likely need strong support. The teacher might have to model how to set goals for a paper she would like to write, then work with students to set goals (such as those identified) for their papers. Additionally, it will be important to check in with students to discuss the progress they are making toward their goals and determine if any goals must be revised.

Teachers can also work with students to set goals for writing skills and strategies they would like to learn. One strategy developed by Karen Harris and Steven Graham that has been used to teach students how to set goals is called SCHEME. When using SCHEME, you engage students in the following steps:

▶ *Skills check:* In this step, you take stock of what a student does well and areas in which the student needs help.

▶ *Choose or construct goals:* At first, you will want to help students choose a goal for where to begin. For instance, your students may need to first work on the organizational skills just to start writing, such as finding a place to write without distractions, finding a good time of the day to write, or having available the tools needed to write. To get them started with this goal, you will talk with your students about how good writers organize themselves for the writing process and talk about why organizing yourself for the writing process is important. Once students become more adept at choosing their goals, then you can help them move to constructing their goals.

▶ *Hatch plans:* Now you want to help students put their goals into action. For instance, if you choose organizing for writing, you will help students generate a list of things they have to do to be organized, such as finding a place to write that is not distracting, having their computer or paper and pencil available, finding the resources they need for their paper, and finding a good time to write when they are not tired or hungry.

▶ *Execute the plan:* For this step, you tell students they will carry out the plans they developed.

▶ *Monitor results:* At this point, you want to help students examine how well they have been able to put their plan into action and if doing so has produced any positive results. For instance, you might want to help students look at the times they were writing outside of school and when those times helped them write the most. Then, you could help them examine why they were able to write more during those times. Such self-reflection will help students develop their own skills for evaluating their progress.

▶ *Edit:* Here you will help students make revisions to their plan to accomplish their goals. For example, students might find that doing their writing homework right after school is difficult. They find that they need a break and are distracted too easily. Thus, you encourage them to find a better time to write and evaluate their success when using that time.

Many students with disabilities have comprehensive problems and most young students are not self-regulated learners. To address this issue, you might want to provide them with a checklist of the different skills you want them to accomplish during the course of the year and suggest that you will be working with them to acquire each of the skills on the checklist. Then, you will work with them to select a skill to begin implementing. Exhibit 14.1 provides a checklist of skills developed by Steven Graham and Karen Harris.

Exhibit 14.1   Writing Process Checklist

Directions: Place a checkmark by each action that you did while writing this paper.

TIME AND PLACE

_____I made a schedule for when I would work on the paper.

_____I found a quiet place to write.

_____I got started working right away.

_____I kept track of how much time I spent working on the paper.

_____I always had the materials I needed each time I sat down to work.

UNDERSTANDING THE TASK

_____I read or listened to the teacher's directions carefully.

_____I asked the teacher to explain any part of the assignment that I did not understand.

_____I restated the directions in my own words.

PLANNING

_____I identified who would read my paper.

_____I identified what I wanted my paper to accomplish.

_____I started planning my paper before I started writing it.

_____I used a strategy to help me plan my paper.

SEEKING AND ORGANIZING INFORMATION

_____I tried to remember everything I already knew about this topic before I started to write.

_____I got all the information I needed before I started to write.

_____I organized all of the information I had gathered before I started to write.

WRITING

_____I thought about what I wanted my paper to accomplish as I wrote.

_____I thought about the reader as I wrote.

_____I continued to plan as I wrote.

_____I revised my paper as I wrote.

REVISING

_____I revised the first draft of my paper.

_____I checked to make sure that the reader would understand everything I had to say.

_____I checked to make sure that I accomplished my goals for the paper.

_____I made my paper better by adding, dropping, changing, or rearranging parts of my paper.

_____I corrected spelling, capitalization, and punctuation errors.

_____I used a strategy to help me revise.

_____I reread my paper before turning it in.

(Continued)

Exhibit 14.1   Continued

SEEKING ASSISTANCE

_____I asked other students for help when I needed it.

_____I asked my teacher for help when I needed it.

_____I asked my parents or other people for help when I needed it.

MOTIVATION

_____I told myself I was doing a good job while I worked on the paper.

_____I rewarded myself when I finished the paper.

Strategies for Planning and Generating Narrative and Expository Texts

Students with disabilities need strategies for planning the various types of texts they are likely to encounter when writing, including stories, explanatory texts, and persuasive texts.[13] Fortunately, researchers have developed several planning strategies that teachers can use to help students with disabilities in this arena.

Narrative Text

There are story grammar frameworks that can be used to help students learn to develop the major components of a story when writing. One such strategy that has been researched with students with disabilities is the story grammar strategy.[14] In the first step of this strategy, students are asked to think of a good story idea to share. Second, they are prompted to brainstorm as many ideas as possible by saying to themselves, "Let my mind be free." Third, they learn a series of prompts to remind themselves of each story part. The prompts are: W-W-W, WHAT = 2, HOW = 2.

- ▶ *Who* is the main character; who else is in the story?
- ▶ *When* does the story take place?
- ▶ *Where* does the story take place?
- ▶ *What* does the main character want to do; what do the other characters want to do?
- ▶ *What* happens when the main character tries to do it; what happens with the other characters?
- ▶ *How* does the story end?
- ▶ *How* does the main character feel; how do the other characters feel?

The students are then asked to brainstorm ideas for each of the story parts. For instance, they will be encouraged to write notes about the main character or what the main character wants to do.

Expository Text

Several planning strategies are available to help students with disabilities organize expository texts. One of these strategies incorporates a mnemonic for helping students write persuasive texts.[15] Prior to employing the strategy, students are encouraged to ask themselves two questions: Who will read my paper? Why am I writing this paper? Then, students are prompted to use the mnemonic TREE to prompt them to complete each step of the strategy:

▶ Note the *topic* sentence.

▶ Note *reasons*.

▶ *Examine* reasons—will my reader believe this?

▶ Note *ending*.

For each of the steps in the TREE strategy, students are encouraged to brainstorm or generate notes supporting the topic. When they are finished evaluating their notes, they can organize the points they want to introduce and use the mnemonic to guide the development of the essay.

Teachers can also show students how to use graphic organizers to develop expository texts. For instance, teachers can use a compare-and-contrast think sheet (see exhibit 14.2). When using such a sheet, teachers can help students see how concepts are similar and different. Students can be prompted to list the ways in which two concepts are similar or different and then expand on these. The categories of similarities and differences (along with the notes students take) can be used to develop their paper. Each category can become its own paragraph in the essay.

Graphic organizers can also be used for various types of expository tasks. In the following thinking and planning guide for writing a report, students are encouraged to consider their audience, their rationale for writing the text, ideas for the text they will draft, and ways of grouping their ideas. Exhibit 14.3, which was written by Yujeang Park, shows an example of how a graphic organizer is used to develop an outline for a report a student wrote about the battles of the Pacific in World War II.

Revising Texts

Once you have helped students to plan and generate text, the next step is to teach them how to revise their text. Students with disabilities often are unaware of what is needed to improve their text. They often do not recognize that details in a paragraph do not support the topic sentence. It is important to help them understand that their first draft is never their last draft. Good writers revise and revise at least two or more times. Plus, good writers have editors! Writing in the real world is rarely a solitary event.

Exhibit 14.2 Compare-and-Contrast Think Sheet[16]

Compare what?

On what?	Birds	Mammals
Skeleton system	Has a skeleton	Has a skeleton
Organ systems	Has circulatory, respiratory, nervous, and digestive systems	Has circulatory, respiratory, nervous, and digestive systems
Mode of transportation	Walks on two legs but mostly flies	Walks on four or two legs, some jump on two legs
Outside covering	Feathers	Hair or fur
Way of reproducing	Lays eggs	Gives birth to live young

Exhibit 14.3 Graphic Organizer Used to Write a Report

PLANNING THE FIRST DRAFT OF A REPORT

Name of the writer: *Colin Littlewood*

Topic: *Famous battles of the Pacific in World War II*

Who will the audience be? *My classmates*

What will be the purpose of my writing? *To let them know about the different battles and why they were important to the Allies*

Everything I already know about this topic—anything I can think of: *Pacific Theater, Iwo Jima, Midway, and Guadalcanal, capture land so can refuel plans, Ally victories, heroes in the battles, books written about the battles*

Possible ways to group my ideas (see figure 14.1):

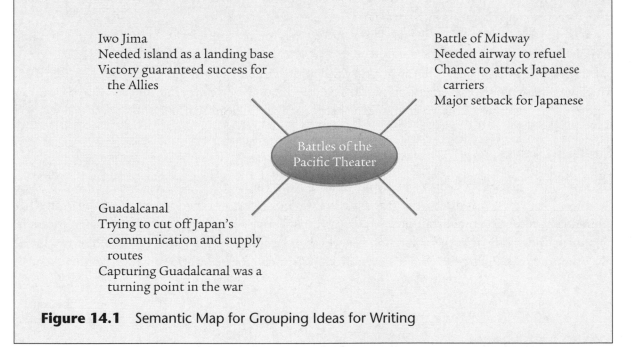

Figure 14.1 Semantic Map for Grouping Ideas for Writing

When teaching students to revise text, it is important to teach them evaluation criteria. Here is a list of self-evaluation criteria for persuasive writing developed by Charles MacArthur, a well-known writing researcher in special education:[17]

▶ Did I state my position clearly?

▶ Is my first reason clear and supported by details?

▶ Is my second reason clear and supported by details?

▶ Is my third reason clear and supported by details?

- ▶ Did I summarize my reasons at the end?
- ▶ Is my essay persuasive?
- ▶ How can I improve my next essay?

When teaching students to use these evaluation criteria, you will have to show them the difference between a clearly stated position and one that is not clearly stated. You will also have to help them see the difference between clear reasons and those that are unclear as well as the difference between reasons that are supported by details and those that are not. The best way to help them understand these differences is through the use of examples and nonexamples. Students can even help to critique essays that you have developed for the purpose of highlighting different problems.

Teachers can also help their students to revise each other's writing using the peer revising strategy.[18] In this strategy, a student's peer listens to him read the paper aloud. Once the writer has finished reading the paper, the listening peer summarizes what the paper was about and tells what he liked best. Then, the listening peer reads the paper aloud and asks himself two questions:

- ▶ Is everything clear?
- ▶ Can any details be added?

If he cannot understand a part of the text, the listener puts a question mark beside that part of the text. The listener then shares three suggestions for revising with the writer. The listener writes these suggestions in the text. At this point, the listener shares his feedback with the writer.

Once the feedback session is finished, the writer returns to edit the text. He only uses those suggestions that he believes will make the paper stronger. Before returning his paper to the listening peer, he edits it for errors by asking himself the following questions:

- ▶ Is each sentence complete?
- ▶ Are first letters of sentences capitalized? Are proper nouns capitalized?
- ▶ Is there punctuation at the end of each sentence?
- ▶ Circle words you are not sure of and correct with a spell-checker or dictionary.

The listening peer and writer then read the paper together while answering each of these questions and marking portions of the text that need to be changed.

SPECIAL CONSIDERATIONS FOR ELLs

Many ELLs develop text in their native language and then try to translate it into English. When translating text, they can easily make many errors, such as using inaccurate verb tenses and misusing articles. Their limited English vocabulary and facility with syntax affects their ability to generate text. Additionally, because they have limited English vocabulary, a problem that is compounded by a language-based disability, they will try to use words they know how to spell, making their writing even more simplistic. To help ELL students learn to write, it is important that special education teachers provide opportunities to develop oral language and adequate, structured writing instruction, particularly in cognitive strategies.[19]

When teaching ELL students writing, you must keep in mind that your initial goal is to help them use writing to create a bridge between spoken language and print, not to help them write without errors. You are using writing to promote their oral language and reading, so you will want to first focus on helping students record their ideas. In the following, we have listed some instructional strategies and tips you can use to help students with this bridging process:[20]

- ▶ Encourage students to choose and develop a topic based on their interest and background knowledge during the prewriting stage.
- ▶ Develop a topic board where you can use sticky notes to record topics students talk about during the day.
- ▶ Provide rich learning opportunities that include visuals and concrete experiences that will help students develop the language they need to write.
- ▶ Brainstorm ideas in class, particularly one-word ideas on a specific topic, such as hurricanes. The teacher then writes the one-word ideas on the board and students develop essays about them.
- ▶ Begin with nonfiction writing first and develop topics orally.
- ▶ Before asking students to write about a topic, review any relevant vocabulary that ELLs might not know or understand.
- ▶ Provide opportunities to practice spelling words used in their writing, particularly focusing on letter sound correspondences.
- ▶ Use word walls to support students' vocabulary learning and spelling.
- ▶ Teach students to use cognitive strategies for planning, generating, and revising text.
- ▶ Discuss the basic mechanics of writing (e.g., having spaces between words, using a capital letter at the start of a sentence, etc.) but do not overemphasize these.
- ▶ Have students use figures, story maps, and other types of graphic organizers to help organize and develop their ideas.
- ▶ Modify classroom tasks and materials so that they are appropriate for ELLs' literacy levels.
- ▶ Accept and praise all attempts at writing.
- ▶ Encourage students to share their writing with their peers and family.

Although many of these instructional tips apply to all students with writing disabilities, they are especially important for ELL students. For other instructional tips for teaching ELLs to write, go to everythingESL (www.everythingesl.net/inservices).

USING TECHNOLOGY TO SUPPORT WRITING

Technology can be used effectively to support students' basic writing skills, planning, and revision. Word processing software, such as Microsoft Word, can be used to assist students who exhibit spelling, handwriting, and grammar problems. These programs enable students to write legible text and check their text for spelling and grammar errors. Other programs, such as Co:Writer and Ginger software, developed by Don Johnston (www.donjohnston.com/products/cowriter/index.html) and Ginger (www.gingersoftware.com), respectively, enable teachers or parents to build word banks for students so that they may select the correctly spelled words when writing. Text-to-speech software, such as Dragon Dictate or Dragon Speak Naturally (www.nuance.com/dragon/index.htm), help students with extreme spelling problems because the student simply says what he or she wants to write and the computer translates those words into written text.

Other software programs can be used to assist students with the planning process. Kidspiration for elementary students and Inspiration for middle and high school students allow students to organize their ideas using semantic maps. If students struggle with using words to capture their ideas, they can use images instead and record ideas to accompany those images using speech-to-text software. Teachers can then show students how their semantic maps and the ideas represented in them can be translated into outlines.

To help students with the entire writing process, Don Johnston has developed SOLO 6 Literacy Suite (www.donjohnston.com/products/solo/index.html), which includes four software programs. Read:Outloud 6 is a print-to-speech software program that will help students access text to generate the knowledge they need for writing specific types of expository text. Draft:Builder 6 uses a three-step process to help students generate text. First, students develop an outline of their ideas using the outlining graphic that organizes ideas into topics and subtopics. Second, students use the notes feature to emphasize and expand ideas in the outline into complete sentences. The software is also set up so that students can only see the idea they are working on at that particular time, helping them to focus. After creating notes, students can reorganize parts of their outline as they see fit. Once the outline is organized, students can use the "draft it" template to generate text. Throughout the three-step process, students can use the read aloud and word prediction features of SOLO to listen to what they have written and secure support for spelling words.

TO SUM UP

▶ Use ongoing assessment to document student progress and identify student writing needs. Assessment can include examining student writing samples and determining student abilities to generate organized text, use appropriate sentence structure, use complex sentences, use rich vocabulary, and produce text that is free of spelling, punctuation, and grammatical errors.

▶ Set goals for improving writing. The generation and organization of ideas should always be the first goal. After all, writing is mostly about communicating ideas clearly.

▶ Use evidence-based strategies as the foundation for your instruction.

▶ Make sure to address all areas of writing, including handwriting, spelling, planning for writing, generating text, and revising text.

▶ Integrate the use of technology when appropriate to meet students' needs.

WHAT'S NEXT?

Now that you have a better understanding of teaching reading and writing, we will move on to teaching tools for mathematics instruction.

ADDITIONAL RESOURCES

▶ LD Online: www.ldonline.org

▶ Green, J. (2011). *The ultimate guide to assistive technology in special education: Resources for education, intervention, and rehabilitation.* Waco, TX: Pruford Press.

▶ Council for Exceptional Children: www.cec.sped.org

▶ The Access Center: www.k8accesscenter.org/training_resources/languagearts.asp

▶ Reading Rockets: www.readingrockets.org/article/22026

▶ Great Schools: www.greatschools.org/special-education/LD-ADHD/970-writing-instruction-students-with-learning-problems.gs

CHAPTER FIFTEEN

Teaching Mathematics

✔ In this chapter you will learn about:

- Characteristics of struggling learners in mathematics
- Ways to help students overcome math anxiety, learned helplessness, and passive learning
- The CCSS in mathematics and how these can be used to inform your teaching practices
- How to use evidence-based strategies to support struggling learners in mathematics
- Technologies that enhance mathematics learning

Ben, a new high school special educator, found that he needed a different attitude about math in order to be effective. "At the beginning of the year, I kept thinking, 'I didn't like math when I was a student. I only took one math-methods class when I was studying to be a teacher! Now, I'm supposed to co-teach in high school algebra!'" Fortunately he was paired up with a colleague who served as math coordinator for the district. She found resources, manipulatives, and software that Ben could use. "Slowly, I am gaining confidence in my ability to help my students succeed in algebra, though it's a long road."

Ask students whether they like mathematics and you will find many different reactions. Unfortunately, for many students, these reactions tend to become less and less positive as they progress through school. For students with disabilities, this negative reaction to mathematics often occurs earlier and is more striking. So, why is mathematics so difficult for many students with disabilities? And what can we do to help students become successful in learning and using mathematics?

WHAT MAKES MATH SO DIFFICULT FOR SO MANY STUDENTS?

Understanding mathematics involves understanding the concepts associated with mathematics and the procedures required to manipulate those concepts. Most mathematics educators will agree that gaining this deep understanding is complex and involves many different processes:[1]

▶ *Declarative knowledge:* This knowledge involves knowing the facts within mathematics. Examples include the relationship between $22 + 4 = 26$ and $26 - 22 = 4$ as well as the fact that a triangle has three sides. To be successful in mathematics, your students need to have a great deal of declarative knowledge that they can recall quickly and with little effort. The more automatic this factual knowledge is for students, the more they can concentrate on learning higher-order mathematical skills.

▶ *Procedural knowledge:* These are the algorithms, problem-solving procedures, and other rules that guide mathematics tasks, and involve two processes. The first is symbolic representation (knowing that $\div$ means *divide* and $\neq$ means *does not equal*). The second part of procedural knowledge involves knowing the steps necessary to solve mathematics problems. For example, the acronym PEMDAS provides the order of operations for solving complex arithmetic problems (*p*arentheses, *e*xponents, *m*ultiplication, *d*ivision, *a*ddition, and *s*ubtraction).

▶ *Conceptual knowledge:* This knowledge is the true understanding of mathematics, which goes beyond knowing facts and procedures. It involves understanding the relationship between declarative and procedural knowledge and how to use these to solve authentic mathematical problems. Conceptual knowledge is quite broad and requires making connections between concepts as part of doing mathematics. For example, although students should know how to use PEMDAS correctly to answer complex orders of operations in arithmetic problems, this is not enough. Having this procedural knowledge and knowing the rules are important, but so is using this knowledge to interpret real-world problems that make use of PEMDAS.

Many students with disabilities struggle across these three areas. They experience problems with math anxiety, short-term memory, the lack of strategies for solving multistep problems, and missing foundational knowledge. Because of this, you might hear your students say the following:

▶ "I have never been good at math." (Suzie, eleven-year-old girl)

▶ "I hate math. Every time I try, it feels like pressure." (Kate, nine-year-old girl)

▶ "My dad said that he couldn't do math either. I guess it's genetic." (Rob, twelve-year-old boy)

Because many students are so resistant to math, you face two connected challenges when supporting students with disabilities in mathematics:

▶ Helping students learn the procedures and strategies needed to succeed in math

▶ Helping students conquer their psychological aversion to mathematics

Students who struggle with mathematics or have a mathematical learning disability (MLD) have difficulty in one of the following areas:[2]

▶ Difficulty applying the procedures required for solving math problems.
- They might understand the concepts of using decimals to figure out how to calculate a 15 percent tip after eating a twelve-dollar meal, but they will have difficulty actually going through the steps to calculate it.

- ► Difficulty with remembering math facts or algorithmic procedures.
  - They might work on memorizing their multiplication facts and then forget them the next day.
- ► Difficulty understanding the abstract concepts represented in mathematics.
  - They may be able to remember the procedures required to solve particular problems but may not understand concepts such as why you get a smaller number when you multiply a fraction by another fraction.
- ► Difficulty understanding word problems and systematically applying what they know about the mathematical concepts within these problems. This is a major indication that the students do not have a strong conceptual understanding of the mathematical concepts being taught.
  - They might be able to follow a word problem you complete together and then not be able to independently apply the same concepts and processes to a slightly different word problem.

You may notice a tension in math education between giving students the procedures for mathematical problem solving and helping them develop a deeper understanding of what it means to do mathematics through developing and testing their own procedures. Depending on the teaching style of the math teachers with whom you work, you may need to have a conversation with them regarding how to best meet the needs of your students. Do not assume that because students have a disability related to mathematics, they cannot also develop a deep conceptual understanding.

Students with an MLD can have either one or more of these difficulties and will therefore struggle as they advance through increasingly more complex math concepts.

GOING BEYOND ARITHMETIC TO ALGEBRA

Some students may understand concepts and processes needed to solve basic arithmetic problems but may then struggle with more complex algebraic understanding.[3] Unfortunately, special education teachers sometimes focus only on the arithmetic fluency (such as learning multiplication facts) and ignore the more complex processes (such as using mathematical symbols to represent pattern relationships in written situations). Students do need to master basic arithmetic procedures to understand algebra and many aspects of geometry but they then need to learn new concepts that have foreign symbols and steps. For example, students can solve the problem $\frac{3}{4}x + \frac{2}{3}x$ with a fraction operation or with a calculator. What is most important is that the student understands the result conceptually. The student should be able to explain that the answer is a little less than $1\frac{1}{2}$ because two groups of $\frac{3}{4}$ equals $1\frac{1}{2}$ and $\frac{2}{3}$ is less than $\frac{3}{4}$, so the answer must be less than this amount.

Because much of what is learned in algebra has a foundation in arithmetic, it is extremely important for students to have this conceptual arithmetic understanding, even if their computational fluency is not completely developed. There are tools to help students with computations. However, these tools are not helpful if students do not have the basic understanding of concepts such as opposites, inverse, and equivalence. If arithmetic is approached with the goal of conceptual understanding, then moving to algebra is a transitional process of understanding how the new language fits and enriches the old concepts. If students do not have a conceptual understanding of arithmetic, however, they are going to have a very difficult time with algebra.

For students who struggle in math, algebraic instruction is critical because the stakes are incredibly high. In most states, students must pass high school algebra in order to graduate from high school. If students do not understand basic algebra, they cannot pass and therefore cannot graduate with a standard diploma.

CHARACTERISTICS OF STRUGGLING LEARNERS IN MATHEMATICS AND GENERAL STRATEGIES FOR SUPPORTING STUDENTS

Students who struggle with mathematics may display the following characteristics and behaviors:

▶ *Math anxiety:* Students with math anxiety experience negative emotions about doing mathematics, which interferes with their ability to learn new math concepts and procedures.

▶ *Learned helplessness:* When students believe that they cannot learn math, they ask for help prematurely, without trying to solve problems independently. Students who experience learned helplessness in mathematics do not believe they can learn mathematics and, therefore, request that others walk them through math problems.

▶ *Passive learning:* Students who have experienced failure or who have negative attitudes toward mathematics may back off from learning. They may sit through instruction but they will not actively participate.

The following eight tips help students overcome math anxiety, learned helplessness, and passive learning and should be used with evidence-based math instruction:

▶ Make math relevant and tied to the real world. Math does not exist in isolation from the world in which your students live. You can show them that math exists in their worlds in numerous ways:

- Highlight news stories that involve mathematics. For example, when studying exponents, you can find articles about human population growth.
- Tie concepts learned to problems they may face. Examples include calculating tips at restaurants, knowing the distance between home and school when taking different routes, and estimating how much a college education will cost at a local college given the increases in tuition over the past five years.
- Discuss the history of how mathematical concepts were developed. For example, your students can learn about the circumstances in which Pythagoras, Fibonacci, da Vinci, or Ben Franklin made their mathematical discoveries. You can also relate these to modern mathematics and scientific discoveries.

▶ Remind students that everyone makes mistakes and model how to react to making mistakes. Mistakes are a necessary part of the learning process. If you normalize making mistakes, it will take the pressure off the students to be perfect from the beginning. When you make mistakes (either purposefully or accidentally), use a think-aloud to problem solve. For example, when modeling how to check whether you have correctly computed a 20 percent tip for a meal, you state out loud that you put the decimal in the wrong place. This would mean that you initially computed a $40.00 tip instead of a $4.00 tip! Explicitly model how to correct your error without giving up or losing your confidence. You can say something like, "Hmm . . . $40 really doesn't make sense! I wonder what I did wrong? Let's see. I'm going to check my steps." In doing so, you can model positivity as well as strategic thinking in addressing the mistakes that you make. You also model the fact that the goal is to analyze the reasonableness of an answer or outcome rather than simply getting the answer correct.

▶ If you notice math anxiety or other symptoms of poor math self-concept, acknowledge that mathematics is difficult. By acknowledging the difficulty experienced by your students, you let them know that you understand their frustrations and fears about mathematics.

▶ Begin with concepts and procedures that the students already understand to build confidence. For example, when learning about Fibonacci numbers ($F_n = F_{n-1} + F_{n-2} = 0,1,1,2,3,5,8,13,21,34$, etc.), you can start by talking about occurrences in which the students can see Fibonacci patterns in nature such as the spirals of a sea nautilus. By doing so, you will bridge new concepts and procedures to something that the students already understand and reduce initial resistance or anxiety.

▶ Set realistic goals for learning new skills. Consider involving your students in this goal-setting process. For example, if learning about obtaining the surface area of a shape, the students can set goals for learning to do so for different objects such as a rectangular prism and a sphere. They can also decide how long they need to meet each goal. Goal setting will allow you and your students to make a plan for learning and then track progress toward those learning goals.

▶ Discuss with your students that math is a learning process rather than an innate ability. Many students who struggle with math believe that some people are born with the ability to do well in math and that people who do not have this natural math talent will always struggle with mathematics. This myth should be addressed by explaining that nobody is born knowing how to analyze data. Everybody has to learn it.

▶ Create a learning environment that offers choice in math learning and assessment. If appropriate for the students, students can choose the type of manipulatives they use (real versus virtual manipulatives), the types of technologies used for instruction, how they will demonstrate understanding of concepts, and so on.

   ● Be aware of gender biases in mathematics and highlight that females and males can both succeed in mathematics. Teachers, parents, and friends can perpetuate the stereotype that boys are good at math and girls are good at reading and writing. Strategies to counteract this include the following:

      ○ Create opportunities for students to interact with female and male mathematicians. Connect with your local college to find math majors who will volunteer to talk about their interest in mathematics.

      ○ Make sure that you have high expectations for your male and female students.

      ○ If you hear your students perpetuating negative stereotypes about females and mathematics, address it with them.

▶ Be patient. It can be frustrating when students struggle or forget concepts and procedures but do not let your students see this frustration.

Math Strategies for Students with More Complex Needs

Aleksandra Hollingshead, University of Cincinnati

VIGNETTE ONE: MOTIVATION FACTOR: MEET MARRIAH

Marriah is a third-grader participating in math instruction in her homeroom—a self-contained classroom for students with multiple disabilities. One of Marriah's IEP goals is to receptively and expressively label numbers from one to fifteen. She has been working on this goal for a long time and her teacher, Ms. Miller, seems to think she is not making any progress. Ms. Miller decided to consult with other teachers and a school psychologist. They came to a conclusion that maybe Marriah's instruction is not motivating enough in itself. Some strategies they come up with are as follows:

- ▶ Preference assessment
- ▶ Highly motivating tasks
- ▶ Frequent reinforcement
- ▶ Structured work task

Ms. Miller decided to conduct a preference assessment[4] to figure out Marriah's interests. First, she interviewed Marriah's parents, then observed Marriah during free play with unlimited access to many interesting toys, books, magazines, and so on, and finally she presented to Marriah multiple items to weigh which one would entice her most. It turned out that Marriah is mostly interested in magazines with teen celebrity pictures in it. Ms. Miller had an idea! She used her classroom computer to locate Google Images (www.google.com/images). In the browser she entered the names of multiple teen celebrities and printed out several pictures. She laminated the pictures for durability and placed a small piece of Velcro on their fronts. She also printed out small boxes with numbers from one to fifteen and laminated these as well. She placed an opposite part of the Velcro on the back of these numbers. Ms. Miller was ready to approach number teaching again! She placed the numbers one to five on the five pictures of celebrities by attaching the Velcro pieces to each other. Knowing the principles of structured teaching[5] and work systems, Ms. Miller began with the first five numbers and systematically taught receptive and expressive labeling of them to Marriah. Because the numbers were now associated with her favorite personalities, Marriah attended the instruction with increased motivation and quickly mastered the skill. Ms. Miller remembered to exchange the numbers and pictures every day to ensure actual skill mastery and generalization across the numbers and characters,[6] and not just visual memorization of the pictures.

INSTRUCTIONAL MATH STANDARDS

Instructional standards help us to understand what information students should know in order to successfully advance through school and into their postschool lives. In mathematics, the newly developed CCSS are quickly being adopted by most states. Although these standards do not prescribe a curriculum or a way of teaching mathematics, they do provide grade-specific blueprints for what and when students should learn critical content. In mathematics, the CCSS focus on making sure the students understand core concepts as well as the procedural skills needed to think mathematically. For grades prior to high school (K–8), the standards are provided for each grade level. At the high school level, they are provided by concept rather than by grade. Additionally, the CCSS include eight standards for mathematical practice for grades K–12 that provide the basic approaches to considering the teaching and learning of mathematics more globally (www.corestandards.org/the-standards/mathematics).

When thinking about how to design math instruction for students with disabilities, these eight practice standards are useful because they highlight the important math skills that students should have to be proficient in mathematics:[7]

> *Make sense of problems and persevere in solving them.* Students should be able to examine mathematical problems and have strategies to solve those problems strategically. This standard requires students to have a sophisticated understanding of data and be able to organize and represent data with words, tables, and graphs in a way that communicates their mathematical reasoning. For example, they should be able to interpret tables, graphs, and various mathematical expressions and apply these to unique problems such as understanding population density.

> *Reason abstractly and quantitatively.* Students should be able to understand abstractions related to mathematics and provide quantitative representations of those abstract concepts. In order to do so, students need to have a deep understanding of the concepts involved rather than a superficial idea of how to go through the steps to solve the problems. For example, students should not only be able to calculate the surface area of a sphere, but they should also be able to apply this skill to exploring how the surface area of a sphere and the surface area of a square with the same diameter would relate or how the change in the diameter of a planet would affect the surface area.

> *Construct arguments and critique the reasoning of others.* Students should be able to construct and defend arguments using data, logic, and reasoning. They should also be able to analyze others' mathematical arguments as well as justify their own mathematical reasoning based on their knowledge of mathematical concepts. For example, when learning about algebraic equations related to supply and demand, students should be able to explain the economic implications of their results.

> *Model with mathematics.* Students should be able to apply mathematics concepts to solve issues that arise in everyday life. For example, students should be able to represent information through diagrams, graphs, and formulas to help them understand the problems and steps toward solving them.

> *Use appropriate tools strategically.* Students should be able to assess which tools they need to solve mathematical problems and deepen their understanding of mathematics. These tools may include calculators, rulers, protractors, software, as well as digital content on websites.

> *Attend to precision.* Students should be able to communicate clearly about mathematics in a precise manner. They should understand that precision depends on the context. Students should be able to use mathematical notations consistently, label axes on graphs, and make accurate calculations. For example, when reporting world populations, students should know that they round to the nearest billion rather than to the nearest hundred and know that 100.25 is more precise than 100.2.

> *Look for and make use of structure.* Students should be able to recognize mathematical patterns and relationships. For example, students should be able to shift the perspective of geometric shapes and simplify complex equations by breaking them into component parts.

> *Look for and express regularity in repeated reasoning.* Students should be able to recognize repeated patterns or calculations. For example, they should be able to find shortcuts to solving problems and assess whether their results make sense.

The CCSS focus much more on deep understanding than on covering many areas within mathematics. This is good news for students with disabilities who have typically struggled with the breadth of content taught within curricula that focused on covering many areas of mathematics in little depth through spiral instruction. Spiraling curricula allocate short periods of time to new math concepts and then those concepts are revisited with increased sophistication as students progress through school. Unlike spiraling curricula, the CCSS focus more on deep understanding of a more limited number of topics in specific grade bands. The logic of spiral instruction was that even if students do not fully understand a concept, that concept will be revisited at a later date, and students will be able to gain further understanding at that time. If your school includes a spiral math curriculum, you will discover that the problem with this logic is that students who struggle in mathematics seemed to get further and further behind because they did not have the time to fully learn the math concepts before moving to new concepts.

HOW SHOULD I TEACH LEARNERS WHO HAVE DIFFICULTY KEEPING UP WITH THE CURRICULUM?

Most school districts will develop pacing guides, a suggested sequence of lessons aligned to the standards and standardized tests. Pacing guides have two major disadvantages: (1) students often need more time than is assigned to each concept and (2) students may lack important prerequisite concepts necessary for understanding current standards.

There are several strategies that have been found to support students with disabilities in becoming successful in learning mathematics. These fall within two broad categories:

▶ Provide more time for instruction and learning
▶ Emphasize strategies

The strategies provided in this chapter should be considered as part of a balanced math program that emphasizes conceptual understanding and procedural fluency as well as a balance between direct, explicit instruction and the use of metacognitive strategy instruction.

INSTRUCTION THAT SUPPORTS STUDENTS WITH DISABILITIES IN MATHEMATICS

In this section, you will learn strategies for supporting students with disabilities and other struggling learners in mathematics. These strategies include the concrete-representational-abstract (CRA) instructional method, the use of mnemonics to teach mathematical procedures, and the use of curriculum-based measures to inform your math instruction. Consider implementing these strategies as follows:

▶ *Teach the strategies explicitly.* There is a large body of research in mathematics that points to the importance of explicit instruction as part of math education. All of these strategies should explicitly be explained to the students so that they begin to feel ownership over their mathematics learning. For example, when teaching students to use the PEMDAS mnemonic, begin by explaining the purpose of this mnemonic and model its use in solving problems with multiple operations as well as engage students in activities that demonstrate why a specific order of operations is important for clear mathematics communications.

▶ *Use high-quality examples strategically.* When students are learning new math skills, begin with simple examples that allow students to learn the big ideas and then progress to more complex examples. Remember to model your own problem-solving processes through think-alouds. By modeling the steps of the strategies and your thinking processes, you are teaching the what and the how explicitly. The cognitive demand of the examples you choose should build from your students' current level of understanding. You do not want to overwhelm your students but you also want some level of productive struggling so that the students learn how to deal with struggle in mathematics incrementally. For example, when teaching students how to compute the percent of a number, you can start with a think-aloud such as, "Hmm . . . I need to find 20 percent of 200. I know several ways of solving this problem. I think I'm going to try to figure it out with mental math. I know that 10 percent of 100 is 10, and 20 percent of 100 must be 20. This means that 20 percent of 200 has to be 40! I better check my math on paper." This way, you use the examples and think-aloud to engage students in the mathematical challenges.

► *Encourage your students to use think-alouds as well.* This way, you can assess whether they understand the concepts and procedures and make corrections to misconceptions. After you have modeled think-alouds with your own strategic examples, your students can practice with you, with their peers, or on their own. You can then debrief with your students to question further their conceptual understanding and the processes that they used to solve the various problems they completed.

► *Assign homework that is similar to the modeled classroom examples.* The purpose of homework is to reinforce skills and procedures, not to expect students to make conceptual leaps. Often in textbooks, although examples are simple, homework is much more complicated. Make sure that you examine the homework problems to ensure that they are aligned with the classroom instruction. Do not expect students to make unnecessarily difficult leaps in understanding in order to successfully solve those problems.

The first strategy, CRA instruction, is teacher driven and helps students progress from understanding math concepts through a series of concrete to representational to abstract understandings. The second group of strategies is to teach students metacognitive strategies to help them tackle math problems independently. These should be explicitly taught step by step to the students so that they can internalize and generalize them. Finally, this section describes the use of assessment to help you track your students' progress and involve your students in being accountable for their own learning.

CRA Math Instruction

Students with disabilities often miss critical steps in understanding mathematical concepts. These gaps worsen as students progress through school and as math concepts become more and more complicated. What you will often find is that students who struggle in math do so because they have difficulty with the abstract concepts presented and, therefore, the procedures do not make any sense. For example, how could a student understand how to multiply fractions if they have difficulty understanding fractions in general!

One well-established strategy for supporting students with disabilities in mathematics is through transitioning students through CRA phases of mathematics understanding. You can use the CRA method to teach most mathematical concepts including basic arithmetic, place value, money skills, algebra, and geometry. Following are suggestions for implementing CRA in mathematics.[8]

Concrete Instruction

Introduce mathematical concepts at the concrete level. This often involves the use of manipulatives or real-world objects that the students can use to solve problems. For example, you can teach students basic arithmetic by using small wooden blocks or other counting manipulatives. Figure 15.1 shows a concrete

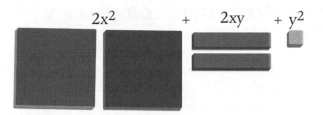

$$2x^2 \quad + \quad 2xy \quad + y^2$$

Figure 15.1 Concrete Example of Solving for an Unknown

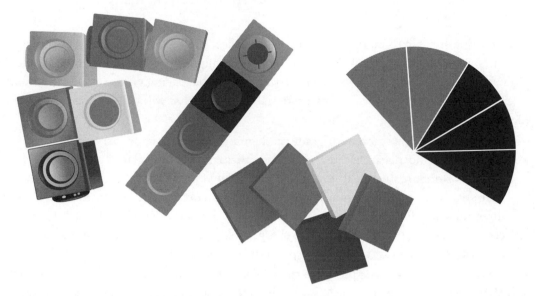

Figure 15.2 Examples of Common Math Manipulatives

example of solving for an unknown with algebra tiles as well as numerical notations and figure 15.2 shows examples of common math manipulatives.

Representational Instruction

Once the students can demonstrate understanding at the concrete level, you can transition to using visual representations of those concepts. For example, if you used small wooden blocks to help students understand basic addition, you would then transition to drawing those wooden blocks to help the students solve the arithmetic problems. By drawing the blocks rather than using the physical manipulatives, the students are moving toward a more abstract understanding of those concepts.

Abstract Instruction

When the students can create pictorial representations that represent mathematical processes, you can then transition them to using abstract notations such as numbers and symbols. At this stage, the students no longer need to rely on either concrete manipulatives or pictorial representations of those concrete objects. The students can understand the concepts and procedures symbolically.

Each student will get to abstract understanding at a different pace. Some students will easily gain abstract understanding in some areas of mathematics but may rely on pictorial representations for much longer with other concepts and procedures. Always try to remember the individual nature of learning mathematics.

WHAT IS THE BEST WAY TO INTEGRATE CRA INTO MATH INSTRUCTION?

Because most math curricula and textbooks are not arranged using the CRA method of instruction, you will most likely need to plan CRA methods on your own. This will be more straightforward for basic mathematical concepts and arithmetic computations than in more complex mathematics. One strategy that you can use to plan instruction CRA methods for basic arithmetic concepts and computations as well as for more complex mathematics is through a mnemonic called CRAMATH.[9] This strategy will help you think about how to implement CRA. CRAMATH stands for the following:

► Choose a math topic to be taught. You need to reflect the big idea you hope to convey to your students. Some math textbooks do a good job of highlighting these big ideas and some do not. However, your school district will likely provide you with a pacing guide or curriculum map tied to either the CCSS or other state instructional standards that will help you determine these big idea math topics.

- For example, if you teach sixth-grade mathematics, you may choose the topic of understanding positive and negative integers. The mathematics CCSS related to the number system includes standards in the following domain related to this concept: "6.NS.C5: Understand that positive and negative numbers are used together to describe quantities having opposite directions or values (e.g., temperature above or below zero, elevation above or below sea level, credits or debits, positive or negative charge); use positive and negative numbers to represent quantities in real-world contexts, explain the meaning of 0 in each situation."[10]

► Review the procedures needed to solve the problem. Once you know the big ideas of the lesson, you should consider the steps necessary to help the students gain conceptual understanding of those ideas and learn the procedural steps needed to solve the problems. This will help you plan how to teach the concepts and procedures to your students.

- For a conceptual understanding of positive and negative integers, students need to understand that whole numbers greater than zero are called *positive integers* and that whole numbers less than zero are called *negative integers*. You may consider how to introduce this concept, which will depend on your students' prior knowledge, interests, and so on. A concrete way of doing so is to use different colored beans to represent positive and negative integers or counting chips with different colored sides. If you are using different colored beans to represent positive and negative integers, you can have your students count a set of these objects by matching pairs of different beans and the color of positive objects remaining will represent the solution.

► Adjust the steps to eliminate notation or calculation tricks. In other words, simplify! It is better to teach students a strategy that can be generalized across many math problems than to teach shortcuts that sometimes work and sometimes do not work.

- For example, the mnemonic FOIL (*f*irst, *o*utside, *i*nside, *l*ast) is useful for multiplying two binomials $(a + b)(c + d)$ but it does not work for multiplying a binomial and a trinomial $(a + b)(c + d + e)$. It is better for students to think about polynomial multiplication as an application of the distributive property. However, the mnemonic PEMDAS is useful because it simply names a convention.

- In the positive and negative integer example, you can transition students toward moving their manipulatives to a number line, which is a consistent tool that will apply across contexts (temperature, elevation, credits or debits, etc.).

▶ *Match the abstract steps with appropriate concrete manipulatives.* The authors of CRAMATH emphasize the fact that you want to use manipulatives that the students can easily use in generalizing strategies.

- In the example related to understanding positive and negative integers, if students previously used wooden blocks as counters, and now you switch to a different manipulative (different colored beans), you will need to include instruction that explains the relationship between these manipulatives. It would have been better to begin with the same type of manipulative so that the students have consistency.

▶ *Arrange the concrete and representational lessons.* Your planning should purposefully ensure consistency between the concrete and representational phases of instruction. If students learn math concepts and procedures at the concrete level with specific concrete manipulatives, the pictorial representations must match those same concrete objects.

- For example, if your students are learning about positive and negative integers by matching different colored beans, they should then draw those same beans at the representational stage of learning. If they are using a number line along with their manipulatives, that number line should also be drawn as part of the representation.

- You will also want to be strategic in using consistent language across concrete and representational stages of instruction. Plan ahead to identify key vocabulary, procedures, and manipulatives so your instruction will be as effective as possible. In this example, vocabulary may include *integer, positive integer, negative integer, number line, less than,* and *greater than.*

▶ *Teach each concrete, representational, and abstract lesson to student mastery.* Teaching to mastery is key. Students should be able to demonstrate concrete understanding prior to being taught representations. For example, if students cannot solve the problem $6 - (-7)$ with concrete manipulatives or cannot represent this on a number line, continue working on this at the concrete stage prior to moving toward representational or abstract levels. Similarly, prior to entering the abstract instructional phase, students should consistently be able to draw representations of concepts and procedures. To do this effectively, you will need to set up a system of progress monitoring so that you and your students can track progress accurately. Exhibit 15.1 provides an example of a progress-monitoring checklist that you can use while implementing CRA with positive and negative integers.

▶ *Help students generalize what they learn through word problems.* The authors of CRAMATH acknowledged that students with disabilities often have difficulty with generalizing CRA across settings. You can help students generalize CRA by tying the math concepts and procedures you are teaching to real-world problems that are meaningful to the students.

Hints to using CRA effectively:

▶ Make sure that you explicitly show students the connections among the concrete, representational, and abstract levels of mathematical understanding. Otherwise, students will see them as unrelated. You can do this through the following actions:
- Use consistent language through all phases of instruction.
- Make connections among concrete and representational and abstract understanding. For example, for the representational phase, draw the exact manipulatives that the students used in the concrete phase. For the abstract phase, refer to those drawings and concrete manipulatives.

Exhibit 15.1 CRA Progress-Monitoring Checklist[11]

Student	Understanding positive and negative integers	Adding positive and negative integers	Applying positive and negative integers to real-world problems
Student A	C		
	R		
	A		
Student B	C		
	R		
	A		
Student C	C		
	R		
	A		

Adapted from Witzel, Riccomini, & Schneider (2008).

A Survival Guide for New Special Educators, by Billingsley, Brownell, Israel, and Kamman. Copyright © 2013 by John Wiley & Sons, Inc.

- If students get stuck at either the representational or abstract levels, go back to the earlier level. If the students struggle with more complete concrete problems, simplify the processes to make sure the students get the basic conceptual understanding.
- Tie CRA to real-world applications. You can create real-world problems out of any mathematical problem presented to the students. You can even have the students develop these problems.

METACOGNITIVE MATH STRATEGIES

Metacognitive strategies provide students with the step-by-step tools to help students progress toward independently solving problems. As a teacher, you should go through the processes required at each step of the strategy, model those steps, and then guide students through increasingly more complex problems as the students become more proficient with the strategies. Consider using a strategy-implementation process to help students progress toward using the strategies independently. One well-established process that you can use across instructional strategies and content areas involves the following steps:[12]

1. Pretest and introduce the students to the instructional strategy to elicit buy-in.
2. Describe the strategy for your students and when they may use the strategy to support their learning.
3. Model the strategy for the students with a think-aloud so that your students can understand the cognitive processes you are engaged in when using the strategy.
4. Engage in verbal practice of the strategy steps so that the students understand the steps and can then recall them when solving problems.
5. Provide guided, controlled practice with immediate feedback. When students become proficient in using the strategy, you should increase the complexity of the problems. This process goes hand in hand with progress monitoring.
6. Transition to independent practice with grade-appropriate materials when possible.
7. Posttest and create a plan for the student to generalize the strategy across settings.
8. Occasionally check to make sure that the student is maintaining the knowledge about the strategy and is using the strategy after it has been taught.

To learn more about general strategy instruction, visit the University of Kansas's Center for Research on Learning website (www.kucrl.org/sim).

First-level mnemonic strategies are often used to help students remember procedures needed to solve math problems. A simple mnemonic that you may have used for learning the order of operations in computing arithmetic problems is PEMDAS: *please excuse my dear Aunt Sally* (parentheses, exponents, multiplication, division, addition, and subtraction).

First-letter mnemonic strategies can be used to teach students more sophisticated procedures as well. Schema-based instruction[13] supports students in understanding the underlying processes involved in solving math problems through the use of metacognitive strategies. One example is the STAR strategy,[14] which provides students with a process for solving word problems:

S—*Search* the word problem.
- Read the problem carefully.
- Ask, "What do I know?" and "What do I need to find?"
- Write down what you know.

T—*Translate* the words into a picture and equation.

- Choose a variable.
- Identify the operations.
- Represent the problem (this can be at the concrete, representational, or abstract levels, depending on the student's level of understanding).

A—*Answer* the problem based on the picture and equation.

R—*Review* the solution to make sure it makes sense.

- Reread the problem.
- Ask, "Does my answer make sense? Why or why not?"
- Check the answer.

A similar strategy is called the FOPS schema-based strategy:[15]

▶ F—*Find* the problem type. In this step, you (or your students) should begin by reading the problem out loud and figuring out what type of problem it is. Students will learn how to find comparison statements such as "four times as much" or "half as many" within the problems to help cue them to the types of operations required to solve the problem.

▶ O—*Organize* the information in the problem by using a diagram. In this step, the students learn how to organize the information through schematic diagrams that show the relationships in the information provided by problem. You should use questioning strategically to help cue the students to the relevant information in the problem, the relationship between these pieces of information, and what information is unknown and necessary to solve the problem.

▶ P—*Plan* to solve the problem. In this step, you help the students translate the information from their schematic diagrams to an equation that will help them solve the problem.

▶ S—*Solve* the problem. In this last step, the students use the equation and diagram to solve the problem. They then check their answers to make sure that they make sense and are accurate.

ASSESSMENT AND FEEDBACK TO INFORM MATHEMATICS PRACTICE

As in all areas of teaching and learning, assessment should be closely tied to instruction. Providing ongoing feedback tied to learning plays an important role in teaching mathematics. When your students see the relationship between their learning and their performance, they can begin to take ownership of their learning. If they graph their performance and notice an upward trend, they realize that they are making progress. However, if they graph their performance and do not notice any improvements, you can explain to them that you will change the instruction because it is not effectively meeting their learning goals. In this way, you reinforce that learning math is a process rather than an inborn quality related to whether someone is either "good at" or "not good at" mathematics.

Curriculum-based measures (CBM) assess student progress on specific mathematics skills. Chapter 10 provides information about CBM in general. In mathematics, CBM can be used as follows:[16]

▶ Begin with the standards that the students are required to master and develop goals based on these standards and your students' areas of strength and weakness. Developing appropriate goals is very important because you then use these goals to provide feedback to the students.

Math Strategies for Students with More Complex Needs

Aleksandra Hollingshead, University of Cincinnati

VIGNETTE TWO: SCARY TESTING: MEET PETER

Peter is a fifth-grader with an emotional disorder who attends general education classes for most of his academic instruction. Peter is able to keep up with his classmates most of the time, especially if the classroom aide monitors his on-task behavior. The most problematic time for Peter is testing. He is very self-conscious and afraid of making mistakes, so whenever there is a test scheduled, Peter either tries to skip his classes or has a huge meltdown at home or school. Both his parents and teachers are concerned about his fear of tests and want to come up with a solution to accommodate Peter's anxiety. During her conversation with his parents, Ms. Miller, Peter's teacher, notices that he is completely involved in his video game on an iPad and does not even object to their talking about testing. She discovers a trick to helping Peter. For the next class, Ms. Miller brings in her iPad with a math game app she found that simulates the video game while testing the user's math skills. Systematically, Ms. Miller introduces the game to Peter and explains to him that from now on, during the tests, he can play this game instead. Initially, this strategy entices Peter to attend his classes even when there is testing. Eventually he realizes that Ms. Miller is able to check his score in the math game and grade him based on that result. He learns that testing can be fun!

▶ Conduct a task analysis to learn how well your students perform these standards. For example, in order for your students to be able to multiply fractions, they must be able to conceptually understand that fractions are part of a whole, recognize the relationship between the numerator and denominator, have fluency in basic multiplication, and so on. Each of these tasks should be considered as part of the CBM.

▶ Develop assessment items for each task within the skill sequence. These items should be of similar difficulty so that the student can demonstrate mastery specific to each task and difficulty level. For example, for addition of fractions, you want to start with fractions with the same denominators before moving to addition of fractions with different denominators. Likewise, you do not want to mix addition, subtraction, multiplication, and division problems in the same CBM. It is helpful to create multiple forms of the task-specific CBM because you will need to administer the same CBM until the student achieves a level of mastery.

▶ Administer and interpret the CBM. CBMs can be administered either in a large group or individually. It is helpful to administer math CBMs individually at least some of the time so ask probing questions as the students are working to see why they are solving problems in a particular way. Once you and your students score their CBM, chart their progress on a graph so that the student can see progress and you can see if the student is ready to move to a more complex skill achieving mastery or if instruction needs to be altered when the student does not make progress after several CBM cycles. It is important to help the students make connections between their performance on the CBMs and the instructional and personal goals that you set.

► If you get inconsistent or unclear results, ask students to explain their work, why they took certain steps, to explain their answers, or even to make connections between their math processes and real-world applications. This information will help you determine if you need to alter your instruction.

In addition to CBM, you should also administer or support mastery measures. These are related to the curriculum that is used in the general education curriculum. You may find that the math textbook provides good items to measure student mastery of curricular materials. If the assessment items in the book are not very strong, you can create your own items. Guidelines for using mastery-based assessments include the following:[17]

► Begin with the instructional objectives of the lesson. For example, an objective of a lesson might be to add fractions with different denominators.
► Develop items that measure performance toward this objective.
► Administer and interpret the assessment. You can consider mastery in several ways. One way is by looking at accuracy. Another way is by the amount of time students take to complete the task. For some objectives, you may be working on fluency. In this case, you will also want to note the amount of time it takes your students to complete the assessment. At other times, you may be looking at the problem-solving process that the students are using. In this case, you may consider using a rubric or a more qualitative measure of mastery.
► Reteach or continue to the next lesson and objectives.

In thinking about the use of assessment as an instructional strategy that supports student learning, you should keep in mind that it only works if the students are active participants in the assessment process. If, however, the students do not receive this feedback, it will not help improve their math abilities or confidence. Therefore, you should share assessment results with your students and collaboratively plan your next steps.

Task Analysis and Assessment

A task analysis is a breakdown of the smaller skills that a student may need to master in order to understand the full concept or skill. Some students will not require this level of instruction and some will. Task analysis is often associated with skills such as tying shoes, brushing teeth, and getting dressed but it can be useful for any task with component parts that are helpful to practice. Regardless of which strategies you use to support your students in learning math concepts and procedures, it may be helpful to consider how task analysis will fit within your practice. If you decide to use task analysis as part of math instruction, remember to individualize this to your students because they will each need different levels of skill breakdown to learn the math processes you are teaching. Table 15.1 provides an example of a task analysis for abstract-level subtraction.

All of these strategies can be used with students with diverse mathematics needs, regardless of disability category or level of functioning. It is sometimes difficult to think of how to apply these strategies with students with more significant disabilities.

Table 15.1 Task Analysis for Abstract-Level Solving of the Following: $70 - 55 = x$

Prerequisite skills	• Student should have conceptual and procedural understanding of concepts such as place value, zero, and regrouping. • Student should have demonstrated the concept of double-digit subtraction at the concrete and representational levels prior to the abstract level.
Task analysis steps	• Student identifies the problem as a subtraction problem. • Student starts by examining the ones column and recognizes that you cannot subtract five from zero. • Student borrows ten from the tens column. • Student subtracts the numbers in the ones column (10–5) and writes the answer (5) in the ones column. • Student goes to the tens column and subtracts (6–5) and writes the answer (1) in the tens column. • Student reads the answer (15). • Student checks the answer to make sure it makes sense.

FORMAL ASSESSMENT AND MATHEMATICS

In addition to informal assessments that closely relate to your instruction, your students are likely required to participate in the state mathematics assessments (with or without accommodations or modifications). These are intended to show evidence of students' learning the instructional standards in mathematics.

Another category of formal math assessments involves diagnostics to help you and the rest of the IEP team understand your students' areas of strength and weakness in mathematics. These standardized assessments provide information to help pinpoint areas where students will need additional supports. You may have access to assessment results from formal assessments that either include mathematics subtests as part of a more comprehensive assessment or from assessments specifically targeting mathematics as the primary focus of the assessments. Assessments that include mathematics as part of comprehensive formal assessments include IQ and performance assessments. These were listed and discussed in more detail in chapter 10.

Although there are numerous mathematics assessments, there are four popular individual assessments used to gather information about students' mathematics performance:

▶ *The BRIGANCE Comprehensive Inventory of Basic Skills II:* This is a criterion-referenced test that can be given as part of curriculum-based assessment. It is intended for students ages five through twelve.

▶ *The Comprehensive Mathematical Abilities Test:* This assessment is based on curriculum guides from several states and is intended for students ages seven through eighteen.

▶ *The KeyMath 3:* This is a diagnostic mathematics assessment for students ages five through twenty-two.

▶ *The Test of Early Mathematics Ability 3:* This assessment provides information about formal and informal math concepts for children ages three through nine.

These formal assessments in combination with informal assessments will provide you with the information you will need in order to inform your mathematics instruction.

Math Strategies for Students with More Complex Needs

Aleksandra Hollingshead, University of Cincinnati

VIGNETTE THREE: DAILY LIVING SKILLS: MEET MARK

Mark is a high school student diagnosed with Down syndrome. In recent years he has mastered simple addition and subtraction using various manipulatives and has learnt to label coins. His teacher, Ms. Smith, isn't sure how to combine these ideas and teach Mark addition and subtraction of money; she believes, though, that he is capable of acquiring this skill. Mark seems to be inconsistent with adding and subtracting coins and treats them as individual manipulatives, forgetting about their value. Ms. Smith finds out from Mark's mom that he loves shopping in grocery stores for deals on CDs and DVDs of his favorite cartoon character. Mark's mom also states during an IEP meeting that she would really like Mark to master money skills to be able to seek employment after he graduates from high school. Together they come up with a list of Mark's needs:

- ▶ In order to seek employment, Mark needs to acquire money skills.
- ▶ Mark needs to generalize addition and subtraction from manipulatives to coins.
- ▶ Mark is interested in CDs and DVDs and using a number line strategy[18] for addition and subtraction he has been successful so far.

Ms. Smith realizes that these last couple of years of Mark's education is critical for developing and mastering his daily living skills. Ms. Smith decides to use Mark's interest in CDs and DVDs to prime his money skills before an in-community application. She creates price labels and places them on a variety of old CDs and DVDs she found at Goodwill. Using a number line strategy she decides to start with full dollar amounts and then add the coins. Systematically she teaches Mark to count out the dollar amount needed for each CD or DVD. On mastering, she adds subtraction to this practice and teaches him to give change from a bigger dollar bill. After he masters that, she manipulates the prices to add the coins value. When Mark's skills are consistent at least 75 percent of the time, Ms. Smith decides he is ready for community practice. During their weekly community trips, Ms. Smith increases Mark's opportunities to purchase first CDs and DVDs and eventually other items actually needed for the classroom. Mark has multiple opportunities to deal with money exchange at the cash register. In the last year of Mark's education in high school, after knowing he has mastered the idea of money value, Ms. Smith in collaboration with Mark's family opens a checking account for him in a local bank and teaches him to use a debit card and check his balance as a daily living skill needed by most adults.

TECHNOLOGY-ENHANCED MATHEMATICS INSTRUCTION

In mathematics instruction, technology can be used to increase student engagement, help reinforce mathematics concepts and procedures with assessment, and help bring real-world applications to math teaching and learning. There are no universal technologies that school districts purchase to support mathematics learning but you will likely have access to some technologies for teaching mathematics either at your school or through your school district.

Technologies That Help Students Bypass Difficulties Associated with Their Disability

These technologies are individualized and are intended to meet the specific needs associated with mathematics difficulties. For example, calculators are a common accommodation provided on IEPs for students with disabilities that affect their math performance. Despite their popularity, there is much debate about the use of calculators in math instruction. Advocates of calculator use suggest that students can concentrate on learning higher-order math skills and using the calculators for simple computation. However, critics of calculators state that students need to gain a certain degree of fluency in mathematics and the use of calculators hinders students in gaining this quick recall of math facts. When considering whether to use calculators with your students, ask yourself the following questions:

> ▶ Does the calculator use support the learning objectives of your instruction?
> ▶ Are students overly focused on calculations rather than on the concepts addressed in instruction?
> ▶ Do your students understand the big idea concepts that underlie their calculator use?

If you answer "yes" to these questions, you should consider using calculators to support some instruction.

Technologies That Extend and Enhance Traditional Math Instruction

There are technologies that can provide real-world applications of math concepts, supplement the textbook, provide extension activities, and are intended for all learners, not just those who struggle with mathematics. For example, teachers may use an interactive whiteboard to allow students to interact with virtual manipulatives as they are learning new math concepts. Table 15.2 provides information about several popular technologies that support mathematical understanding.

Table 15.2 Technologies That Support Mathematics Teaching and Learning

Technology and Website	Information
The Geometer's Sketch Pad (Secondary) www.dynamicgeometry.com	This is software for visualizing and manipulating math concepts from basic arithmetic computations through sophisticated calculus. It is intended for grades 3 through college.
National Library of Virtual Manipulatives http://nlvm.usu.edu	This website provides a library of interactive, web-based virtual manipulatives that can be used across K–12 math instruction.
NCTM Illuminations http://illuminations.nctm.org	This website provides numerous standards-based virtual manipulatives, lessons, and links to other online resources.
TinkerPlots www.keycurriculum.com/products/tinkerplots	This software allows students to enter, manipulate, and graph their own data. It is designed for students in grades 4 to 9.
GeoGebra www.geogebra.org/cms	This free software includes numerous interactive activities in geometry, algebra, graphing, statistics, and so on. It is designed for students from elementary through college age.

TO SUM UP

▶ With your students, collaboratively develop instructional goals that are tied to the content standards.

▶ Monitor your students' progress toward meeting math benchmarks and goals.

▶ Teach your students to use math instructional strategies.

▶ Teach math content through a sequence of CRA understanding.

▶ Seek support from general education teachers, curriculum coordinators, and your students when you need to brainstorm, need resources, or need further suggestions.

WHAT'S NEXT?

Now that you have a basic understanding of how to support students with disabilities in mathematics, we are going to step back and look at ways that you can support students across the various content areas.

ADDITIONAL RESOURCES

▶ The Access Center: *Math:* www.k8accesscenter.org/index.php/category/math

▶ CAST math resources: www.cast.org/library/video/gr1_math

▶ IRIS Center math resources: http://iris.peabody.vanderbilt.edu/resources.html

▶ National Center for Learning Disabilities math resources: www.ncld.org/types-learning-disabilities/dyscalculia

▶ National Council for Teachers of Mathematics (NCTM): *Lessons and resources:* www.nctm.org/resources/default.aspx?id=230

CHAPTER SIXTEEN

Teaching Content

In this chapter you will learn about:

- How to help students access instructional content
- Instructional practices that support content knowledge
- Teaching content-specific vocabulary
- How to balance teacher-led and student-led learning activities

Angelica, a second-year special educator in a large urban district, felt overwhelmed by the many different content areas in which she was supporting her students. "I feel like I need to know all *the content for* all *my students' classes! It's like, how can I help them without knowing everything about everything?"*

As a special education teacher, you will likely spend a considerable amount of time helping your students understand and access instructional content. In teaching academic content, you will quickly realize that some students need minimal help to access the content in meaningful ways and other students will need considerable help or modification of content and assessment. Regardless of the degree of support students with disabilities require in learning content, one of your main roles is to coordinate with general education teachers to ensure that students with disabilities are meaningfully engaged in learning and can then demonstrate that understanding authentically.

WHAT CAN YOU DO TO SUPPORT STUDENTS WITH DISABILITIES IN LEARNING CONTENT?

You will probably spend a lot of time finding ways to teach content that bring about your students' academic success. An important point to remember when supporting students with and without disabilities is that learning content is more than learning facts. Each content area includes facts but also introduces a unique discipline-specific way of thinking. For example, a student reading the Declaration of Independence may be able to decode most of the words, yet not understand the important related events and jargon of that time, and without having the ability to use inferencing skills to extrapolate meaning, overall comprehension may be compromised or lost. Thus, simply learning facts about history, science, or mathematics will provide students with only a superficial understanding of the content. Consider working with your general education colleagues to identify the broader concepts, thinking processes, and skills associated with these content areas so that you ensure that students with disabilities develop as much depth of knowledge as possible. Ask them questions about what they believe are the most essential concepts and ideas in the content area and how those might be organized to best help students learn. The planning strategies in chapter 12 will help both of you decide on what to teach. Remember, how you co-plan and teach will be different, depending on your students' needs and the environments in which they are served. The following are some examples:

► Working in a collaborative environment where you co-teach with a content teacher
► Reinforcing instruction learned in an inclusive setting in small groups that may also contain individual instruction
► Being the content teacher of record in a self-contained instructional setting

Regardless of the instructional setting, you will work closely with content teachers on how to best support students with disabilities and therefore need to be aware of the strategies for collaborating outlined in chapter 3. Other suggestions to keep in mind include the following:

► Developing effective collaboration with your general education colleagues takes time. This is especially true if you do not have a strong foundational knowledge of the content. You may feel that you have little to contribute to the planning process and that your general education colleagues doubt your expertise. However, discussing the ways in which you can help and asking questions about what they believe is important to teach will enable you to be viewed as a credible partner. Over time, you will become more proficient in the content. As you do, clarity in your instructional role often naturally emerges.
► If you do not have a strong command of the instructional content, take the time to bolster your own content knowledge. You can do so by reviewing the instructional content ahead of time and asking questions of the content teacher, doing online research, and generally familiarizing yourself with the content area.
► Pay attention to your own attitude about the content area as you are learning. Sometimes you might experience anxiety and fear about learning new content successfully. These feelings are natural and are often shared by your students!
► Remember that you bring a specialized skill set that contributes to the learning of students with disabilities including the use of explicit learning strategies, comprehension strategies, and so on. Discuss your expertise with the content teachers so that they know what you bring to the table.

WHAT SPECIFIC THINGS CAN YOU DO TO HELP STUDENTS WITH DISABILITIES IN THE CONTENT AREAS?

There are several evidence-based strategies that you can use to support students with disabilities in the content areas. The following section explains three instructional practices that can help your students: scaffolding instruction, building students' background knowledge, and vocabulary instruction.

Scaffolding Instruction

The term *scaffolded instruction* is often used to describe how to gradually guide students to success in more and more complex concepts and procedures. As students gain the skills needed to independently learn a specific concept or task, guidance can be slowly withdrawn. In this way, your students receive just enough support to help them become successful and independent learners.

Although the concept of scaffolding appears simple, knowing how to scaffold instruction can be quite daunting. You begin by offering a great deal of support and, as your students begin to gain the skills and knowledge, you slowly phase out the supports. Several models exist for how to scaffold instruction effectively. One model by Diane Haagar and Jeanette Klingner suggest a six-step process.[1] Table 16.1 provides these six steps as well as examples of how one teacher used these steps to scaffold her students' strategy use.

Table 16.1   Scaffolding Instruction—Step by Step

Description of Scaffolding Process	THIEVES Strategy Example
1. Take total responsibility for the strategy, content, or process that you want your students to learn. It is important for you to provide all the guidance that students initially need as they are learning a new skill, strategy, or procedure. In this way, you can model, think aloud, and provide examples.	Mrs. Martin wants her struggling learners to use the strategy THIEVES[2] (*title*, *headings*, *introduction*, *every* first sentence, *visuals and vocabulary*, *end-of-chapter* questions, and *summary*) to use text features and prediction within expository texts. Before reading the social studies chapter, she says, "We are going to start learning about the pioneer days. Hmm . . . let's see. I notice the heading, 'Village Life.' I bet this section will explain how the pioneers lived." She models exploring the rest of the text features included within the section.
2. Invite the students to participate. Once you have demonstrated learning, your students can begin to work toward independence by joining you in the think-alouds, strategy steps, and examples.	Mrs. Martin asks Laura, "What did you notice that I did when I previewed this section?" Laura answers, "You paid attention to the things that popped out, like the bolded words and the pictures." Mrs. Martin then adds, "Did everyone notice how Laura used the THIEVES strategy to come to that conclusion?"
3. Cue the students to use the specific steps within the strategy, procedure, and so on. You will need to talk through the individual steps that the students should use until your students have internalized all the steps and processes required to use the strategy or procedure independently. Depending on your students, this may take a great deal of time. Internalizing the steps of a strategy may be quite challenging for some students. You can remind them of your think-alouds and the processes you used.	After Laura knows the steps of the strategy, Mrs. Martin asks her to use THIEVES with a partner for the next section in the chapter called, "Farming the Land." As Laura did her think-aloud with the THIEVES strategy, Mrs. Martin assesses if Laura understood the steps of the strategy. At one point, Mrs. Martin notices that Laura had difficulty gleaning information from the questions at the end of the section, so she asks Laura, "Can you put that question in your own words? What do you think you will learn about farming from this question?" Mrs. Martin expects Laura to learn the steps of THIEVES more quickly. In fact, she planned on introducing a new strategy by now. It looks like Laura is definitely improving but she still needs more practice.

(Continued)

Table 16.1 Continued

Description of Scaffolding Process	THIEVES Strategy Example
4. Cue the students generally to use the strategy or procedure. Once the students know the steps and processes, you may need to provide some general reminders and cues to help the students use the strategy or procedure independently.	After what seemed like a very long time of modeling and reinforcing the steps of the THIEVES strategy, Laura is finally able to use the strategy independently. However, when Mrs. Martin observes Laura in science, she notices that Laura is not using this strategy. Mrs. Martin thinks, "That's strange! Laura has been practicing using THIEVES in social studies but she doesn't even consider using it in science." Mrs. Martin walks over to Laura and whispers quietly to her, "You know, Laura, if you use THIEVES with this, I bet it will really help. What do you think?" Laura looks up and nods with agreement.
5. Reinforce the students' independence in using the strategy or procedure. When you notice the students using the strategy or procedure independently, offer specific feedback and praise.	The next day, Laura starts using the THIEVES strategy independently when given a reading assignment. Mrs. Martin provides specific praise and feedback to Laura. When she notices that Laura is looking through the chapter and scanning the first sentences of each section, Mrs. Martin is thrilled. She immediately tells Laura, "Look at you! Great job remembering THIEVES. I especially like how you are taking your time to read the first sentences of the major headings!"
6. Explicitly emphasize metacognitive awareness of why, when, and how to use the strategy or process. The goal of scaffolding is to move students to more and more independence in learning new skills and strategies. A major part of this involves creating opportunities for students to practice that independence. For the students to generalize what they are learning, they need to understand why and when the skills, procedures, and strategies are helpful. By clearly pointing out opportunities to use those skills and strategies and the students' successes, they will more likely use those strategies when you are not around. This step is critical. It may seem logical to you that your students should generalize strategies but many times students do not take knowledge learned in one area and apply it to another. You must help them make this leap so that they generalize the strategies that they have worked so hard to learn!	Since noticing that Laura was not using the strategy in science, Mrs. Martin has made many efforts to discuss with Laura how the THIEVES strategy can help with many of her expository texts. They brainstorm some opportunities to use this strategy. Mrs. Martin knows that Laura still needs many reminders to independently use the THIEVES strategy. They sit down together and write examples of when Laura could use the THIEVES strategy. They then create a plan for monitoring how well Laura uses THIEVES across the different areas they identifiy.

Basically, think about providing just enough support to help your students become independent learners. If you provide too many supports, your students can develop learned helplessness. If you do not provide enough supports, your students may be frustrated and unsuccessful. As you get to know your students, you will learn what level of scaffolding each of your students requires.

Building Background Knowledge

Your students will have varying amounts of background knowledge, which will affect how well they perform in their content classes. Students come to school with different cultural backgrounds, motivations, and life experiences. Being aware of these differences is important because knowing students' background knowledge will influence how you present new information to them.

Think about your own experiences. If you are a recent immigrant to Japan and are learning about World War II from their historical perspective, you may struggle with the concepts being taught because you do not have the cultural and historical background. Similarly, if you have not seen and touched a solar panel or have been exposed to the uses of solar energy, you may have a difficult time understanding how solar panels capture energy from the sun.

Students with disabilities may have gaps in their learning related to their disabilities or the type of instruction they previously received:

▶ In some schools, students with disabilities may receive individualized instruction during their content classes (e.g., science, social studies, geography, etc.). If students are not present for content instruction, over time, they will have significant gaps in their content knowledge.

▶ Students with disabilities may not be proficient readers so their limited reading skills (including limited vocabulary, ability to understand inferences or abstract concepts from texts, etc.) reduces their opportunities to learn from texts. When learning new content, these reading problems may become a barrier to their learning.

You should attempt to understand your students' basic skills as well as their academic content knowledge so that you can better assess the areas in which they will need support. There are many ways of assessing this knowledge including providing a pretest, asking the students to write or illustrate what they know and what they would like to learn about the topic, creating a KWL chart (*k*now, *w*ant to know, and afterward, what they have *l*earned), and so on. Once you have a general idea of your students' content understanding as well as the gaps in their knowledge, you can strategically work toward building their background knowledge. Table 16.2 provides tips for helping students access their background knowledge in the content areas.

Table 16.2 Accessing Background Knowledge

Accessing Background Knowledge	Examples
Tie new learning to information that is relevant to the students.	In teaching about electricity and circuits, Ms. Hodgins asked the students about what happens when they flip a light switch at the top of a staircase when the switch at the bottom of the staircase is on. She then reads a story to the students about Benjamin Franklin's electricity experiments.
Provide different ways for students to gain foundational understanding. As a word of caution, not all materials that you find online are good instructional materials or even accurate. Make sure that you preview all materials with a critical eye.	Prior to experimenting with building a circuit in class, Ms. Hodgins located various resources for her students who had little experience with electricity and circuits. These included TeacherTube videos about simple, parallel, and series circuits; iPad apps that allow students to either complete or break a circuit; and schematic diagrams of these circuits. These enabled her students to quickly get some background knowledge that helped them in learning about electricity and circuits.

(Continued)

Table 16.2 Continued

Accessing Background Knowledge	Examples
Use graphic organizers to tie new learning to previously learned information.	Ms. Hodgins noticed that the students had difficulty with the concept of conductors versus insulators. She created a graphic organizer that differentiated among good conductors, poor conductors, and insulators. The students then brainstormed what items would fall within each category. (Figure 16.1 shows Mrs. Hodgins's graphic organizer.) She then applied the concepts of conductors and insulators to different technologies available in the classroom and had the students point out different materials that make up those technologies, such as the rubber surrounding the wires in their classroom electric circuit kits.

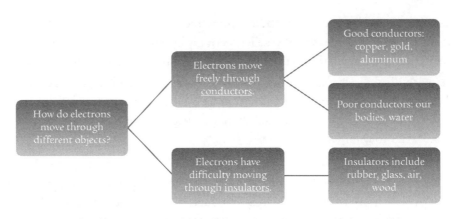

Figure 16.1 Mrs. Hodgins's Graphic Organizer

Building Content Vocabulary

In many of the content areas, vocabulary is a major barrier for students with disabilities. Because much content instruction relies on textbooks and reading comprehension is so closely tied to vocabulary knowledge,[3] understanding content-specific vocabulary is key to success in learning academic content. Consider the example of Ms. Hodgins who was teaching her students about electricity and circuits. This one unit included vocabulary such as *schematic diagram, parallel circuit, series circuit, simple circuit, conductor,* and *insulator.* Without understanding what these words mean, the students will have a very difficult time understanding associated concepts or demonstrating their understanding.

Before teaching your students the content-specific vocabulary, you need to decide which vocabulary words are critical for students to learn. In order to select vocabulary words strategically, you need to have criteria. There is no easy way of figuring out which words to teach. It may be helpful to consider categorizing words into one of three tiers, depending on their complexity as well as how frequently students encounter them.[4]

▶ Tier one words are terms or basic words that most students should already know. These words do not require a lot of instruction to learn because students will likely already have exposure to them. Tier one words are generic and are not tied to specific academic content. Examples include words such as *phone* and *talk.*

► Tier two words are those words that appear frequently in grade-level materials. Students must know these words in order to successfully understand the concepts being taught and the reading passages associated with the content area. These words also help students express their content understanding during assessments. Because of their importance, these words should be taught explicitly to the students. Tier two words at the middle school level might include *conflict, interdependence, investigation,* and *equality.*

► Tier three words are those words that the students will not encounter often and are content specific. They are often technical words associated with a specific academic content. You should teach these words as they arise in the content areas. In science, tier three words might include *amplitude, electromagnet,* and *polarization.* In social studies, tier three words may include *cartel, filibuster,* and *sovereignty.*

Once you decide which vocabulary words are critical for students to understand, there are many strategies that you can use to help your students understand the vocabulary tied to the content areas. Three strategies that you can use to help students understand tier three words are semantic mapping, Frayer's models, and mnemonic instruction.

Semantic Mapping

This strategy guides students through categorizing vocabulary words by similarities and differences with associated concepts. You may also sometimes hear people refer to this as *semantic webs* or *semantic networks.* All three terms essentially describe the same strategy. If used correctly, semantic maps help students draw on their own background knowledge to understand new words and concepts. To use semantic maps, you can use words, phrases, pictures, drawings, or a combination of these in order to show relationship between concepts and vocabulary words. An easy way to develop your first semantic map is to include the tier three word or phrase at the top of the map and then surround the web with examples, definitions, and pictures. Figure 16.2 provides an example of a semantic map with vocabulary words associated with food chains.

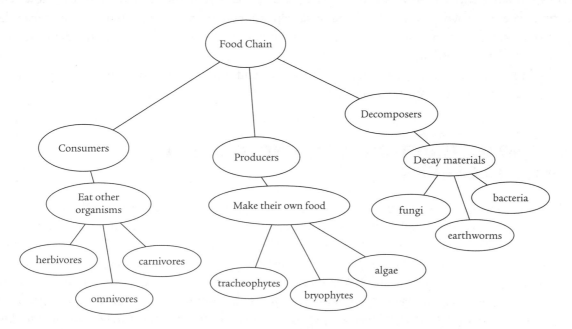

Figure 16.2 Semantic Map of Vocabulary Related to Food Chains

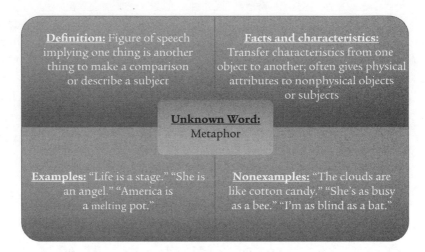

Figure 16.3 Frayer's Model Example for the Word *Metaphor*

Frayer's Models

Another helpful strategy for teaching students content vocabulary is the Frayer's model,[5] a strategy that employs a graphic organizer to help students understand the definition of words as well as examples and nonexamples. The graphic organizer can change, depending on the concept and vocabulary that is being taught, but generally it has the vocabulary word or phrase in the center of the diagram with four quadrants surrounding it: definition, facts and characteristics, examples, and nonexamples. An example of a Frayer's model is presented in figure 16.3.

Mnemonic Instruction

Mnemonic instruction involves using strategies to help students remember difficult vocabulary.[6] It works by linking the new word to words, images, or phrases that the students already know. There are three types of mnemonic strategies that can help students in learning content-specific vocabulary: keyword method, peg-word method, and letter-association method. Table 16.3 provides definitions and examples of each of these mnemonic strategies.

In addition to semantic mapping, Frayer's models, and mnemonic instruction, you can find other evidence-based vocabulary strategies in chapter 13.

UDL AND INSTRUCTIONAL TECHNOLOGIES IN CONTENT LEARNING

With all strategies described in this chapter, consider using the UDL framework as well as instructional technologies because these will support and enhance your use of strategies. Chapter 11 offers a framework that you can use in thinking about how to deliver content instruction. It is helpful to consider how to include multiple means of representation, action and expression, and engagement in content instruction. The chapter also discusses technologies that can be used to support content and vocabulary learning. For example, visual dictionaries can be used to support your students in learning and remembering critical vocabulary words. An example of a visual dictionary is the *Merriam-Webster Visual Dictionary Online* (http://visual.merriam-webster.com).

Table 16.3 Mnemonic Strategies

Mnemonic Strategy	Definition	Example
Key-word method	Use a word that sounds like the new vocabulary to remember the new word. Draw a picture of the association between the known term and the new vocabulary word.	To remember that prokaryotic cells are simpler, less complex than eukaryotic cells, the students associate prokaryotes with *prototype,* an early version, and imagine a prototype of a cell.
Peg-word method	Use rhyming words to represent numbers or an order of events and terms that your students need to remember. Have students begin by memorizing a set of rhyming words that are associated with steps in a procedure.	To remember the first ten amendments to our Constitution (the Bill of Rights), attach a visual image to each number. Examples of rhyming peg words: one = bun, two = shoe, three = tree The first amendment—freedom of speech, press, assembly, and religion—can be remembered by imagining someone biting into a bun with these freedoms within them, and so on.
Letter-association method	Use letters in a word to remember a series of terms.	To remember the order of the colors in the rainbow, ROY G BIV (red, orange, yellow, green, blue, indigo, violet)

TEACHING CONCEPTS WITH CONTENT ENHANCEMENTS

One of the first things you will do when planning how to support students with disabilities in the content areas is to identify the critical big ideas and major processes in an instructional unit. These big idea concepts and processes essentially are the most critical information and practices.

Chapter 12 contains strategies that can be used for planning content instruction including the SMARTER planning strategy, the unit organizer, and the lesson organizer.[7] These are planning tools that you and your general education colleagues can use to help students identify the critical information and concepts within the content areas and organize that knowledge in a strategic way. In doing so, you can meet the individual needs of your students and at the same time provide rigorous instruction on content area standards. These planning processes and strategies can be extremely helpful. Refer to chapter 12 for more information about how to plan effectively to support students with disabilities in the content areas.

Once you have identified the concepts and big ideas that you want to teach, you need to decide how to teach them. First, you must think about how complicated the concepts are that you would like to teach. Your instruction will be different, depending on the complexity of the concepts. This section provides strategies for teaching simple and more complex concepts within the content areas.

TEACHING SIMPLE CONCEPTS

Even concepts that you consider simple will require some level of instruction even if they are discussed only briefly. If the concepts are somewhat simple, you can teach them through concept attainment.[8] Concept attainment strategies help students differentiate between examples and nonexamples, define features of the concept, and apply their understanding of concepts to new situations. For example, if you are teaching students about democracy, students can identify countries that are or are not democracies, define democracies, and then evaluate the characteristics of their country against their definition. Once you believe that your students understand the concept of democracy, you can provide a country that does not fit clearly under the definition. A country that has recently become a democracy might be a perfect choice.

COMPLEX CONCEPTS

These are the big ideas and concepts that are typically difficult for students, especially those with disabilities. There are many reasons why a concept will be difficult for students. The concept is often abstract, described by complex vocabulary, and has many components or subconcepts. For example, totalitarianism is a complex concept often discussed using terms such as *authoritarian, regime, political repression, propaganda,* and *fascism.*

Content enhancement routines (CERs) provide clarity and organization to instructional content.[9] These were designed to support struggling learners in general education content learning by applying graphic devices and organization to instructional content. CERs provide a structured method for learning content in a manner that allows for questioning, describing, comparing, and other tasks associated with deep content understanding. An example of a CER is the concept of mastery routine,[10] which facilitates understanding of critical concepts by focusing on the most important characteristics of the concepts (always present, sometimes present, and never present characteristics) as well as using examples and nonexamples to promote understanding of those critical characteristics. As part of the concept mastery routine, you and your students will co-construct a graphic organizer called a *concept diagram.* This graphic organizer helps students develop a deep understanding of concepts by guiding them through the process of defining a concept. To help students define a concept, you use the cue-do-review process, which includes the following steps:

▶ *Cue phase:* You explain to students that you will co-construct the concept diagram in order to learn the concept. You discuss with your students the importance of the concepts to their learning within the content area as well as to real-world applications of the concept. Finally, it is important to discuss expectations that you have of student participation in the instruction.

▶ *Do phase:* You use the seven linking steps that are necessary to complete the concept diagram:

1. *Convey the concept:* In the first step, the teacher names the concept.

2. *Offer overall concept:* In the second step, the teacher either provides or elicits the larger concept in which the concept fits.

3. *Note the key words:* In the third step, the students brainstorm key words associated with the concept. Based on this students' brainstorm, the teacher can tell if it is necessary to provide further background knowledge. Then, together, teacher and students underline words that describe characteristics of the concept and circle words that are examples.

4. *Clarify characteristics:* In the fourth step, the students classify characteristics that are always, sometimes, or never present as part of the concept. This provides you an opportunity to learn what the students understand about the concept as well as what misconceptions they have.

5. *Explore examples:* In the fifth step, the teacher facilitates the students' exploration of examples and nonexamples of the concept. The students classify instances of the concept and decide if they are examples or nonexamples based on the characteristics of the concept (always, sometimes, and never present).

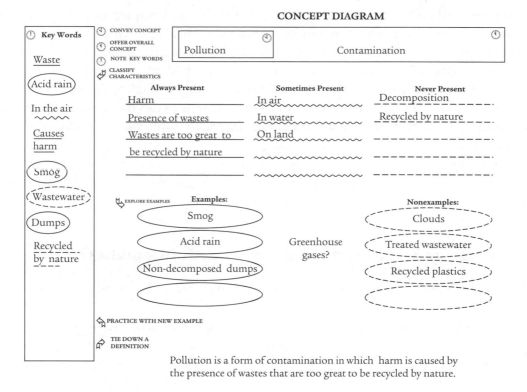

CONCEPT DIAGRAM

Figure 16.4   Concept Diagram[11]
© J. Bulgren.
Note: The instructor's manual for this routine is available in conjunction with professional development workshops. Go to www.edgeenterprisesinc.com for details as well as research results.

6. *Practice with the new examples:* In the sixth step, the students analyze new examples to decide whether they fit or do not fit within the concept. This can be done individually, as a group activity, and even as an assessment.

7. *Tie down a definition:* In the last step, the students and teacher use the information from the concept diagram to co-construct a definition that incorporates the concept and the characteristics that are always present.

After going through these steps, the teacher should review with the students the information as well as the process that the class underwent to co-construct the concept diagram.

▶ *Review phase:* You and the students review information in the concept diagram. Figure 16.4 provides an example of a completed concept diagram. You can learn more about these processes by visiting the University of Kansas Center for Research on Learning website (www.kucrl.org).

INQUIRY-BASED APPROACHES TO TEACHING AND LEARNING CONTENT

Many general education teachers have moved toward a more open, inquiry-based instructional approach. In science instruction, for example, the National Research Council defines inquiry as "a multifaceted activity that involves making observations; posing questions; examining books and other sources of information to see what is already known; planning investigations; reviewing what is already known in light of experimental evidence; using tools to gather, analyze, and interpret data; proposing answers, explanations, and predictions; and communicating results."[12] This approach puts students at the center of learning and gives them more leeway and open-endedness. Rather than having prescriptive labs or experiments in which the students follow a set of steps (much like a recipe in a cookbook), the students ask questions that are relevant to them and then are guided through a process in which they can decide how to answer those questions. Students are encouraged to use the tools associated with the specific content-area discipline to gather and analyze data and then interpret that information in order to explain and communicate what they are learning.

When working with students in the context of inquiry, remember that the purpose of inquiry is to allow students to explore, work collaboratively, and construct their own knowledge based on what they know about the world around them by using reasoning and data.

Why Can Inquiry Be Difficult for Students with Disabilities?

Students with disabilities may struggle with inquiry learning for several reasons:

▶ Inquiry learning is often open-ended with less guidance from teachers. Many interventions for students with disabilities rely heavily on either direct instruction or instruction that is more structured than inquiry. Because of this, many students with disabilities have not had a great deal of exposure to the skills needed to be successful within inquiry learning.

▶ Inquiry learning traditionally does not include strategic instruction. Some students, especially those with disabilities, may need help with the skills necessary for engaging in this process (e.g., making a plan and then following the plan, finding accessible resources, and working in a collaborative group). These skills are necessary to participate in the inquiry process and without support, students can struggle.

Teachers should be aware that many scholars use different labels to describe inquiry. In elementary and middle school science, for example, a popular inquiry method is the 5E model.[13] The following provides an example of how the 5E model can be used to help students learn about safe drinking water and water filtration. Please note that the teaching practices described can be adapted to other inquiry frameworks as well.

▶ *Engage*: Guide your students in thinking about the topic or concept using their prior knowledge. This step looks different for each inquiry and for different students because it depends on the prior knowledge of each student. Consider their home environments, their neighborhoods, music, local news, and interests when considering how to engage students in scientific inquiry.

  • *Example:* Find newspaper articles about water pollution either in your own area or in a country that has very poor water quality. The students can talk about where they get their water, how they know if their water is safe, and what they would do if their water were not safe.

  • This step is especially important for students with disabilities. Capturing their attention and tying the present inquiry to what they know will help motivate them to engage in learning. For many students with disabilities, this step provides an opportunity for success because they do not need much content knowledge to participate in this process; they can rely on their life experiences. In the case of learning about polluted water, almost every student will have had experiences of seeing contaminants in various water systems and will have an opinion about what it would be like to lack clean water.

▶ *Explore:* This phase involves hands-on activities or virtual simulations that allow students to answer questions that they develop or you create. You may decide to provide students questions prior to starting this phase, especially if they are new to inquiry or there are specific instructional goals you want them to meet.

- *Example:* If the testable question is, "How can a simple filtration system clean a contaminated water source?" the students can build simple water filters. Provide each group of students with a polluted water sample from a pond or use tap water and mix in pollutants such as sand, mud, salad dressing, or anything else that will contaminate the water source. You can then either provide the students with supplies for their water filter or have them find those supplies themselves. These can include a container for the filter (two-liter plastic soda bottle) and materials that will filter the water including sand, pebbles, activated carbon, cheese cloth, etc. The students then use these supplies to try to clean their water. Do the following for students with disabilities:
  - Engage in preteaching when necessary. For example, you can talk with them about the various materials that will be available during the exploration. If they have not heard of any of the materials or equipment (such as activated carbon), go over these items prior to the exploration.
  - Consider how to group students for the exploration. You may want to either preassign student roles or support your students in finding roles in which they can be successful. Once students have clarity about how to successfully navigate the group collaboration and begin working on their exploration, provide them with meaningful feedback about their progress.
  - In some cases, you may need to modify the question(s) that students with disabilities ask as part of their exploration. Students with very limited background knowledge or with intellectual impairments can still participate in inquiry learning with modification or adaptation.

▶ *Explain:* Once students have explored their question(s), provide an opportunity for them to reflect on their experimentation, describe what happened, and share their results.

- *Example:* The students share their postfiltration water. The groups compare the methods that they used to filter the water and the clarity of each group's water. This is a good opportunity for you to reinforce vocabulary and main concepts. As the groups share what they learned, you can also ask questions that address common misconceptions about water filtration. For example, you can ask whether water that looks clear can be assumed to be safe.
- Students with disabilities as well as those without disabilities often have misconceptions about what happened during their experiment, so attending to students' explanations is critical in assessing their content understanding.

▶ *Elaborate:* This step provides students with the opportunity to explain their findings further, based on other students' results and the subsequent discussion.

- *Example:* Each group can get together again to discuss their results in light of all groups' findings. They can think of ways to tweak their filter to make it more efficient.
- This step is often very difficult for students because it requires a critical analysis of what happened when students explored, how their results differed from other students' results, and how to change their exploration to get more positive results. Because this process can be difficult, consider how to scaffold this process for students. For example, you can provide guiding questions, a graphic organizer, or even conduct a think-aloud to help the students reflect on their inquiry process.

► *Evaluate:* In this step, the students reflect on their learning and extend their understanding to new situations. You can also provide an individual assessment at this point through a traditional test or a more authentic assessment. Another strategy is to have your students write an "exit ticket" that explains their understanding of the testable question.

- *Example:* After the students finished considering how to tweak their water filters, they talk about how water treatment plants filter the water in their city. In an exit ticket, the teacher asks the students to explain what they think people in third-world countries, who do not have good water treatment facilities, can do to ensure that they have safe drinking water.

- Consider providing students with options for demonstrating their understanding. For example, students with limited writing skills can illustrate their understanding and then narrate their illustration on an audio recorder.

Although the 5E inquiry method is rather prescribed, many teachers use pieces of this method or other methods. The big idea is that the students have the opportunity to direct their own learning. As in this example, you need to consider how to support students with disabilities in fully participating in inquiry learning.

Continuum of Student-Directed to Teacher-Directed Learning

So far in this chapter, we have talked about ways you can support students in better understanding and engaging in instructional content as well as in how to guide their own learning. Teaching practices such as cuing background knowledge and scaffolding instruction are actions you take in your instruction to support students. Thus, these practices are teacher directed. Traditional inquiry, however, is much more student directed. Typically, students should have a combination of teacher-directed and student-directed learning and most teaching and learning falls along a continuum between the two. Figure 16.5 provides a visual for considering instruction along this continuum.

The best way to balance the two approaches is to consider how you can embed explicit instruction that supports students with disabilities into an inquiry approach.[14] Neither approach on its own is sufficient.

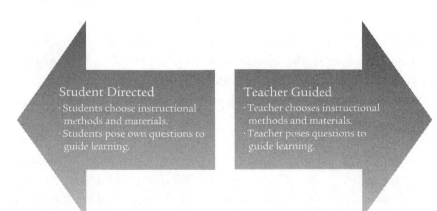

Figure 16.5 Student-Directed and Teacher-Directed Learning Continuum

How to Integrate Student-Directed and Teacher-Directed Learning

Mr. Perry is a special education teacher. He has three students in the social studies class that have transition goals related to working independently and with others. The current unit of instruction relates to World War II. He thought this would be an excellent opportunity to help the students with their instructional content and their transition IEP goals. His three students are the following:

► Monique has a specific learning disability in language processing that prevents her from reading efficiently. She often asks for help with assignments and does not like to work independently. When working with others, she takes a passive role and asks the other students to give her direction and answers.

► Robert has an autism spectrum disorder and struggles with organization and making inferences from texts. Additionally, he is a perfectionist and gets extremely anxious at the thought of "losing points" on any assignment. Consequently, it is difficult for him to work in collaborative groups because he frequently insists on "checking" his peers' work.

► Serge has a medical condition that prevents him from attending school regularly. When he does attend, he seems disengaged and does not have a strong peer group.

To meet the instructional and transition goals, Mr. Perry decided that all his students could benefit from more student-directed learning. He recognized, however, that the students needed a balance between an inquiry approach and instruction that is more teacher guided. Mr. Perry began his first lesson by having the students brainstorm questions to guide their learning. The students worked in groups to answer those questions, find their own resources, and select how they could demonstrate their understanding. Prior to beginning their research, Mr. Perry approved each group's question and made sure that students had a plan for finding answers to their questions. He reminded Monique to use her reading strategies, provided Robert with an organizational checklist, and made sure that there would be resources online for Serge so that he could continue to work from home.

Mr. Perry knew that some of his students would need further support. He made sure to create a resource list about World War II and guided some students who felt uncomfortable with the open-ended nature of this assignment. The groups decided how to demonstrate their understanding and could choose among creating a concept map, multimedia presentation, poster, or traditional essay. After the groups completed this assignment, they shared their products with the rest of the class.

WHAT IS THE RELATIONSHIP BETWEEN INQUIRY LEARNING AND PROBLEM-, PROJECT-, AND CHALLENGE-BASED LEARNING?

If you spend time in many K–12 schools, you will likely hear the terms *problem-based learning, project-based learning, and challenge-based learning*. Although these instructional approaches are different, they have a great deal in common. These instructional practices are typically student centered, require students to address real-world issues, and move students toward applying information to unique situations that are meaningful to students. Despite the similarities, there are distinct differences among these types of inquiry-based approaches. These differences result in different challenges for students with disabilities. Table 16.4 provides general definitions for the various instructional practices as well as some resources where you can get more information.

Table 16.4 Differences among Problem-Based, Project-Based, and Challenge-Based Learning

Inquiry	Definition	Example	Resources
Problem-based learning	Learning that attempts to solve a meaningful problem either individually or in collaborative groups	Students study how to clean up the polluted lake behind their school and present their findings to the city council.	PBLNetwork (http://pbln .imsa.edu)
Project-based learning	Learning that develops a product or project either individually or in collaborative groups	Students research how to create a sustainable moon colony. They then create a digital book with this information.	Buck Institute for Education (www.bie.org)
Challenge-based learning	Multidisciplinary learning that finds solutions to challenges	Students examine how their consumption of food affects the world around them and then provide ways to improve the food choices that they and their community make.	Challenge Based Learning (www.challengebasedlearning.org)

Teaching Content to Students with Moderate to Severe Disabilities: One Teacher's Use of Thematic Instruction

Aleksandra Hollingshead, University of Cincinnati

One approach to teaching academic content standards to students with more complex learning needs is to design themed instruction across content areas. This approach supports many students' need for routine and predictability, allows for generalization across content areas, and helps students see the relationship between knowledge in the different content areas. In the following vignette, Ms. Lee created a social studies and writing thematic unit around the concept of travel. She worked with six students in third through fifth grades. Five of her students were nonverbal and one student had limited verbal skills. Of her students, three used communication devices, one used picture symbols, and one had a system of pictures with sound imitation.

Social studies group: Ms. Lee wanted her students to work on recognizing a variety of vehicles and learning about the timeline of their inventions. Group instruction started with a short YouTube video to attract the students' interest. Ms. Lee found a song-based video presenting multiple types of vehicles. After the video was over, she referred to the schedule and explained to students that they would have to work with a SMART Board to learn about different types of transportation. Ms. Lee pulled up a menu of vehicles on the bottom of the SMART Board. She divided the screen into two parts. On one side, she wrote a name of a vehicle, and on the other side, she placed three pictures of vehicles with one representing the word. First, the students labeled pictures on their devices. Then she called one student to the board, and he dragged the correct picture to the word representation. This activity was repeated until all students had their turn to come up to the board and physically participate in the lesson.

Writing group: Ms. Lee wanted her students to work on sequencing events as well as writing complete sentences in their journals. She began by showing the students a timeline of travel inventions using event strips. All of the students were asked to build simple sentences and then write in their journals. The students wrote sentences such as, "First car, then plane." Throughout the thematic unit, the students would master recognizing the vehicles, demonstrate the ability to label them, match picture representations to written words, write complete sentences, and demonstrate the idea of a timeline with sequencing events.

TO SUM UP

▶ Familiarize yourself with the content standards. Even if you are modifying instruction, you need to always address these standards in your instruction.

▶ Consider the individual needs of your students in the content areas. You will see great variation in the needs of your students. This variability will result in different levels of scaffolding, supports, and modifications.

▶ Remember that supporting students in the content areas requires a great deal of collaboration with content-area teachers. Developing effective collaborative relationships with content teachers may take time.

▶ Encourage students to make connections between the content they are learning and their own life experiences and background knowledge.

▶ Reflect on the balance between explicit instruction and more open inquiry so that your students' instructional needs are being met.

WHAT'S NEXT?

Now that you have explored how to support students with disabilities in the content areas, we will look in more detail at strategies for supporting students with the most significant needs.

ADDITIONAL RESOURCES

▶ YouTube: Free cross-content video resources: www.youtube.com

▶ TeacherTube: Free cross-content, teacher-created video resources: http://teachertube.com

▶ Google Earth: Free cross-content resource including current and past geography: http://google.com/earth

▶ Brain POP: Free and fee-based cross content including US history, science, Internet safety, pop culture, science, and so on: http://brainpop.com

▶ WolframAlpha: Free cross-content data computation including mathematics, geographic, history, and scientific data computation: http://wolframalpha.com

▶ WayBack: Free US history content for elementary-aged students: http://pbskids.org/wayback

▶ The Library of Congress: Free US history website with digitized historical documents, photographs, sound recordings, and other resources from the Library of Congress: http://memory.loc.gov

▶ The JASON Project: Free and fee-based science inquiry-based education website from the National Geographic Society: http://jason.org

▶ NSDL Science Literacy Maps: Free science and mathematics education resources tied to the National Science Education Standards: http://strandmaps.nsdl.org

▶ AAAS Science Assessment website: Free online science assessment content related to conceptual understanding and common scientific misconceptions: http://assessment.aaas.org

CHAPTER SEVENTEEN

Teaching Students with Limited to Pervasive Intellectual Disability

Bree A. Jimenez

University of North Carolina at Greensboro

Pamela J. Mims

East Tennessee State University

In this chapter you will learn about:

- Definitions and characteristics of students with intellectual disability
- Assessments to guide curricular planning
- Instructional strategies
- Assessment of student learning

James is getting ready for the upcoming school year. He was prepared to teach students with high-incidence disabilities and will work with general education teachers to help these students achieve the standards for all learners. However, when James reviews his student caseload, he realizes that two of his students have a pervasive intellectual disability. Suddenly, James feels a little nervous about whether he has the background and skills necessary to help the general education teacher plan a classroom environment that is inclusive of all learners.

As a new teacher, you will be faced with many exciting challenges (we use the term *challenge* in a positive way!) in the next year or two. One challenge you may face is teaching students with multiple disabilities. Whether or not your preservice training prepared you to serve students with significant

303

support needs, this chapter will provide you with practical and evidence-based strategies that will benefit all students. The more you know about your students, the better you can serve them!

WHO ARE YOUR STUDENTS?

The American Association on Intellectual and Developmental Disabilities (AAIDD) has defined intellectual disability as a "disability characterized by significant limitations both in intellectual functioning and in adaptive behavior, which covers many everyday social and practical skills. This disability originates before the age of 18" (see appendix A).[1] Additionally, AAIDD describes levels of supports needed for intellectual disability and divides them up into the following: intermittent, limited, intensive, and pervasive. These levels of support are becoming a more common way to describe individuals with intellectual disability compared to terms such as *mild, moderate, severe,* and *profound.*

Individuals with intellectual disability may exhibit a variety of unique characteristics but generally speaking they exhibit significant delays in three major skill areas (see appendix A). First, individuals with intellectual disability have deficits in overall conceptual skills (e.g., language and literacy; time, number concepts, and money; self-direction). Second, social skills are often affected (e.g., social problem solving, rule following, interpersonal skills, self-esteem). Finally, delays may be exhibited in overall practical skills (e.g., daily living, health care, safety, occupational skills).

WHAT TO TEACH

When planning instruction for students with intellectual disability, it is important to review the specific legal mandates that drive current instruction in schools. Students with intellectual disability should follow the standard curriculum guidelines outlined by their local education agency (e.g., CCSS) with adaptations and accommodations. In chapter 4, special education law is addressed in detail; however, before we begin talking about the what and how of teaching students with intellectual disability, it is important to quickly review the why.

WHY TEACH BEYOND FUNCTIONAL SKILLS TO STUDENTS WITH INTELLECTUAL DISABILITIES

Curriculum and teaching for individuals with intellectual disability has changed focus over the last several decades. Most recently, a shift occurred in which the field has moved beyond just a functional curriculum. There are a couple of major reasons for this shift.

It Is the Law!

There are two major legislative acts that have affected the what and how of teaching students with moderate and severe disability since the 1990s:

▶ IDEA (1997): Ensures students with severe disability an education in their least restrictive environment
▶ No Child Left Behind (2001): Requires that students with "significant cognitive disability" participate in alternate assessments based on alternate achievement standards (same curriculum but progress can be measured at an alternate level of depth and knowledge)

Personal Relevance and "Least Dangerous Assumption"

Students with intellectual disability do have specific educational needs that differ from other students. When planning for this population of students, it is important to think about the curriculum and how it has personal meaning to the students. For many years, students with intellectual disability followed something called a *functional curriculum*. The term was originally used to define meaningful skills that students could use in school and their communities. Over time the term has taken on a new meaning and usually addresses life skills, such as toothbrushing, following a recipe, or safety skills in the community. Although all of these skills are important for students with intellectual disability to develop, it is important to plan instruction that aligns to the curriculum (e.g., CCSS) and continues to provide meaningful connections to the student's life today and in the future.

Our least dangerous assumption[2] [in teaching students with intellectual disability] is to presume competence.[3]

What do we know?

▶ We know that many students with intellectual disability have difficulties communicating and showing teachers what they know.

▶ We also know that many students with intellectual disability have not been taught academics and various skills needed to socialize and participate in learning with their peers without disability.

▶ Many students with intellectual disability have learned to read, access the curriculum with adaptations, and make lifelong social connections with age-appropriate peers.

▶ We know that even though not all students with intellectual disability will master all social and academic skills taught to them, the consequence of not presuming competence is far more detrimental. (We do not know unless we try!)

A personally relevant curriculum is the connection between the standards you teach and the way your students make connections with the content. Is not a personally relevant curriculum the goal for all students (see exhibit 17.1)?

Exhibit 17.1   Example of a Personally Relevant Curriculum

Common Core State Standard	Teaching Activity
Writing: Research to build and present knowledge Draw evidence from literary or informational texts to support analysis, reflection, and research.	Compare and contrast two or more characters, settings, or events in a story or a drama, drawing on specific details in the text (e.g., how characters interact).

Santiago is a student with a pervasive (severe) disability. He loves being read to, is able to identify some pictures of characters from familiar books. He is able to read familiar sight words (e.g., his name, *boy*, *girl*). Santiago's family enjoys reading books for leisure. In school, Santiago's class is reading the book *Because of Winn-Dixie* and comparing and contrasting the characters. At home, Santiago is now gaining skills to listen to books read by his siblings and participates in discussion about the characters. Although he may not be able to read the text on his own, Santiago is becoming a more active participant in a leisure activity that his entire family enjoys, which makes this English language arts standard personally relevant to his current and future life.

ASSESSMENTS TO GUIDE CURRICULAR PLANNING

When beginning the planning process for individuals with limited to pervasive intellectual disability, there are several common strategies often used to guide a team's efforts. Assessments such as ecological inventory, person-centered planning, adapted behavior assessments, and curriculum guides should be used to determine personal relevance of curriculum and individualized instructional needs. Each of these will be described in more detail in the following sections.

Ecological Inventory

An ecological inventory is a process in which skills are identified for current and future environments and then prioritized, task analyzed, and assessed. The team will use the results from the assessment to develop goals and objectives as well as individualized systematic instructional plans to support instruction (see exhibit 17.2).

Exhibit 17.2 Ecological Inventory of Teeth Brushing

Subenvironment and Activity: Bathroom and Teethbrushing	Performance Level			Component Skills			
				Check All That Apply			
	Check One						
Present Activities	Assistance on Most Steps	Assistance on Some Steps	Independent	Initiates Task	Asks for Help	Completes Task	Comments (Include Detailed Notes, Types of Prompts)
1. Get toothbrush from cabinet.			x	x			John performs steps one to five independently.
2. Get toothpaste from cabinet.			x	x			
3. Turn on water.			x	x			
4. Put water in drinking cup.			x	x			
5. Turn off water.			x	x			
6. Put toothpaste on toothbrush.		x				x	John's mother puts the toothpaste on the toothbrush.
7. Open mouth.			x	x			John opens his mouth and waits for his mother to brush his teeth.
8. Brush front teeth.	x						
9. Spit out toothpaste.			x	x			He spits out the toothpaste when verbally prompted.
10. Brush back teeth.	x						

Exhibit 17.2 Continued

Subenvironment and Activity: Bathroom and Teethbrushing	Performance Level			Component Skills			
	Check One			Check All That Apply			
Present Activities	Assistance on Most Steps	Assistance on Some Steps	Independent	Initiates Task	Asks for Help	Completes Task	Comments (Include Detailed Notes, Types of Prompts)
11. Spit out toothpaste.			x	x			
12. Rinse out mouth and toothbrush.			x	x			John rinses out his mouth independently. He also rinses off the toothbrush.
13. Get mouthwash from cabinet.			x	x			John gets out the mouthwash and hands it to his mother.
14. Pour mouthwash into cup.		x				x	His mother pours the mouthwash into the cup and hands it to him.
15. Sip and swish mouthwash.			x	x			
16. Spit out mouthwash into sink.			x	x			
17. Turn on water.			x	x			
18. Rinse out sink.			x	x			
19. Turn off water.			x	x			
20. Take flossing utensil from cabinet.			x	x			
21. Open mouth.			x	x			
22. Floss teeth.		x				x	John did this step independently under observation but his mother says that he usually does not do this. He did require a verbal prompt to keep flossing.
23. Put everything back in cabinet.	x						John's mother put everything back away in the cabinet.

Person-Centered Planning

Person-centered planning is a process involving a circle of friends that target improving the student's overall quality of life. It is typically conducted in a neutral environment in which all people relevant to the student will come together to discuss major hopes and concerns for the target student. The student should remain a major participant in this process because ultimately this process will lead to current priorities for goals and objectives as well as possible future options for goals and objectives. Some common ecological inventories used are MAPS[4] and True Directions.[5]

Adaptive Behavior Assessments

Another major approach to identifying student goals and objectives is through the use of adaptive behavior assessments. Some common adapted behavior assessments include the Vineland Adaptive Behavior Scales (VABS-II)[6] and Adaptive Behavior Assessment System (ABAS-II).[7] These assessments are designed to measure an individual's skills in the three domains described previously (i.e., conceptual skills, social skills, and practical skills).

Curriculum Guides

Finally, curriculum guides have long been used as an overall scope and sequence when planning for areas of instruction for an individual with intellectual disability. Curriculum guides, such as *Choosing Outcomes and Accommodations for Children*[8] and *The Syracuse Community-Referenced Curriculum Guide for Students with Moderate and Severe Disability,*[9] divide up curriculum into major life domains such as personal and home living, social skills, communication, and academics and provide a systematic approach to planning for the educational needs of students with disability.

HOW TO TEACH

After identifying what to teach, it is important to consider how to teach. With current legal mandates that require the use of research and evidence-based practices, teachers are no longer given the freedoms to use any intervention they would like. Rather, they must use practices supported by the research. This only makes sense . . . would you want a doctor testing out new medications on you or would you want medicines proven to work?

Research and Evidence-Based Practices

The notion of evidence-based practices to guide instruction of students with limited to pervasive intellectual disability is somewhat new to the field of special education. NCLB and IDEA require the use of evidence-based practices (strategies that have been proven to work with the population) in all schools and classrooms. For students with intellectual disability, specific instructional strategies have been proven effective (research to support them) across multiple disciplines (life skills, social skills, and academics). It is important when developing and implementing instruction to use the research-based practices for this population of students.

Systematic Instruction

Systematic instruction is an overarching term derived from the principles of applied behavior analysis (ABA) that use critical features such as prompting, fading, reinforcement, and error correction procedures. Research over the years has shown that systematic instructional strategies target functional, social, and academic skills for individuals with intellectual disability. Functional skills, such as using a task analysis and simultaneous prompting to teach individuals with an intellectual disability to wash their hands,[10] have been a major area supported by the research targeting systematic instruction. Additionally, many studies have supported the use of systematic instructional strategies such as time delay to teach social skills and initiating a greeting using a voice output device.[11] Most recently, systematic instructional procedures such as the system of least prompts

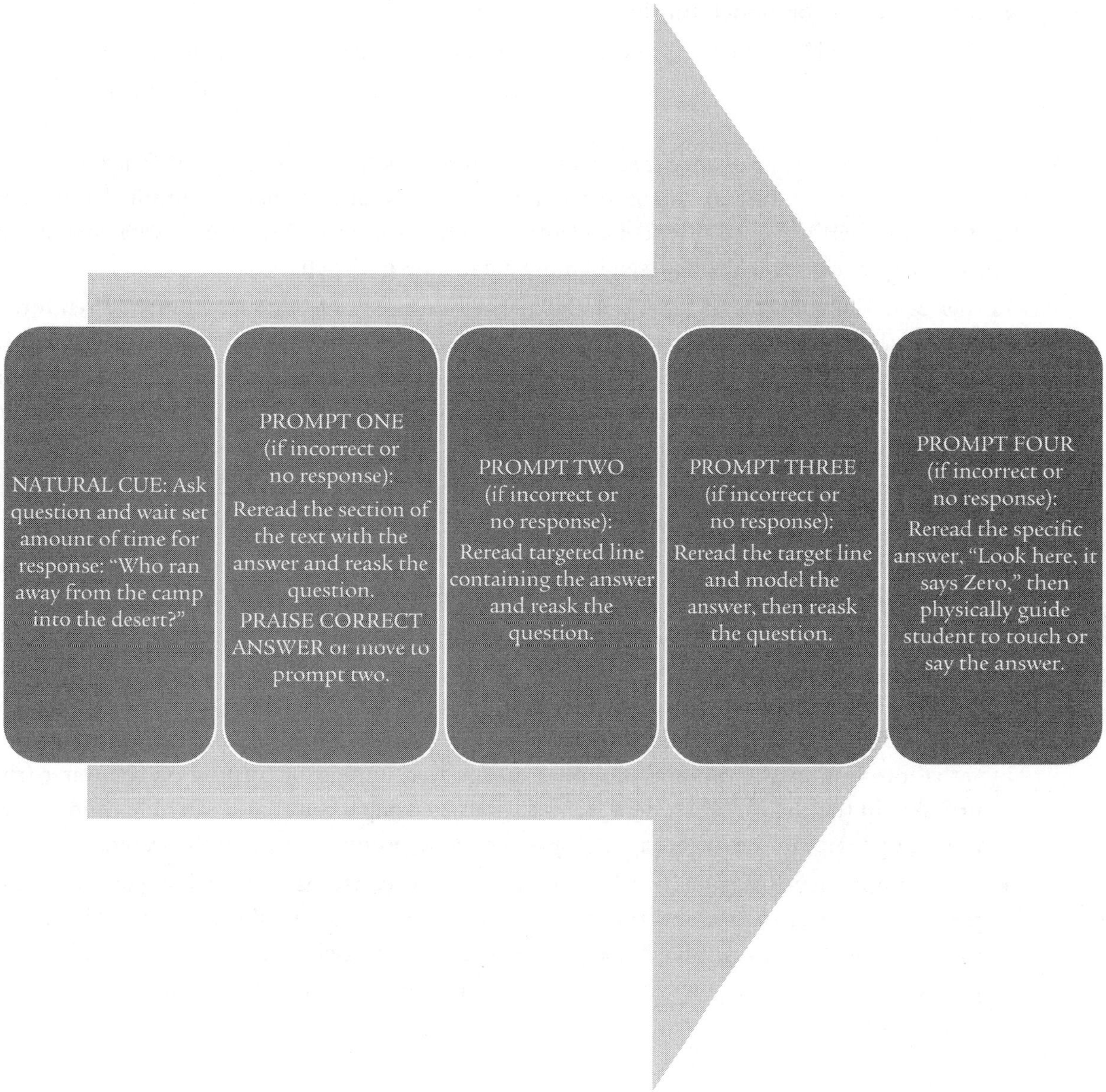

Figure 17.1 Example for Using Least Intrusive Prompts for Answering Comprehension Question with the novel *Holes* by Louis Sacher

have been used to teach comprehension of grade-level-adapted text to students with intellectual disability (see figure 17.1).[12]

As mentioned previously, systematic instruction contains some of the essential features of prompting, fading, reinforcement, and error correction.

▶ Prompts can be either delivered by the instructor or embedded into the stimulus and come in a variety of forms:

- Nonspecific verbal (e.g., "What do we do next?")
- Specific verbal (e.g., "Turn on the water.")
- Pictorial
- Gesture (instructor points to the sink handle)

- Model (instructor models turning on the water)
- Partial physical (instructor provides a slight physical nudge to the student's elbow)
- Full physical (instructor provides hand-over-hand assistance to help the student complete the skill)

▶ Prompts are a great way to support students in gaining a skill but they must be faded over time in order to transfer stimulus control to the target stimulus (discriminative stimulus) and allow the student to perform the skill independently (without prompts). There are several systematic fading strategies that will be discussed in more detail later in the chapter.

▶ Another essential component to systematic instruction is the systematic delivery of reinforcement. Instructors need to identify strong reinforcers before instruction occurs. When working on a new skill that is still in the acquisition phase, you may want to deliver reinforcement on a continuous schedule. Once the student starts responding with less prompting, it is important to systematically fade out continuous reinforcement.

▶ The final essential component to consider when implementing systematic instruction is to carefully plan for error correction procedures. There are different ways to provide an error correction when working on a skill with a student:

- It could be as simple as ignoring the error and highlighting the correct response.
- Another strategy for error correction is to move to a more intrusive prompt. This is commonly used with a prompting procedure such as least-to-most prompts or most-to-least prompts in which you provide a hierarchy of prompts. For example, if using least-to-most prompts to teach the chained skill of hand washing and using a prompt hierarchy of a verbal prompt, model prompt, and physical prompt, instead of turning on the water (the first skill in the chain), the student starts to grab for a paper towel, you can block and deliver the next prompt in the hierarchy (e.g., give the verbal prompt "Turn on the water.").
- When implementing sight word instruction using constant time delay, you show the target sight word *volcano* and the student says *waterfall*, you would say back, "This is the word *volcano*. You say, *volcano*." A key element of time delay is that the instructor does not pay attention to the incorrect response and immediately provides the student with the correct answer.

It is important also to consider partial participation when using systematic instruction. The principle of partial participation is that all students with intermittent to pervasive support needs can acquire many skills that allow them to function in the least restrictive environment (school and nonschool) through active versus passive responses to complete the task.

There are two major types of systematic instructional strategies:

▶ Stimulus and antecedent prompts, which occur within the presentation of the stimulus (e.g., when asked a comprehension question) or through the materials themselves

▶ Response prompts, which are delivered by the instructor after the presentation of the stimulus. The delivery is based on the student's incorrect or lack of response.

See exhibit 17.3 for a description of all prompting strategies.

Exhibit 17.3   Prompting Strategies

STIMULUS AND ANTECEDENT PROMPTS	RESPONSE PROMPTS
Two different prompting strategies that include the delivery of a prompt embedded in the teaching materials	*Five different prompting strategies that involve the delivery of a prompt after the presentation of the stimulus*

Stimulus Shaping
 	
Important features of the materials highlighted and systematically faded out over teaching trials
 	
EXAMPLE
 	
     *** Sam ***
     Sam *** ***
     *** *** Sam
     Sam T a
     M Sam x
     S b Sam
     put sit Sam
     Ask Sam did
     Bob dog Sam
     Sam Sue Am
     Sat Sam Mam
     Tam Sue Sam
	Time Delay (Constant and Progressive) uses Two Rounds of Instruction
	
	A zero delay round presentation of a target stimulus paired with a natural cue followed immediately by the controlling prompt
	
	A delay round presentation of a target stimulus paired with a natural cue followed by a set delay or latency period for the student to independently respond; if no response, a controlling prompt is delivered

Stimulus Fading
 	
Materials made more prominent and faded over time
 	
Volcano
 	
Volcano
 	
Volcano
	Least-to-Most Prompts
	
	Includes a hierarchy of prompts with a latency period between levels from least intrusive to more intrusive
	
	Learners have an opportunity to independently initiate the targeted step or skill on their own (after the presentation of the natural cue) before receiving a prompt in the hierarchy:
	
	  • Natural cue
	  • Verbal prompt
	  • Model prompt
	  • Physical prompt

	Most-to-Least Prompts Includes a hierarchy of prompts but these prompts are delivered from more intrusive to least intrusive The teacher starts out by providing the most-intrusive prompt in the hierarchy (e.g., a full physical prompt to turn on the water) for a predetermined criterion (e.g., four consecutive trials). After the student meets the predetermined criteria, the instructor then moves back to the delivery of the next prompt in the hierarchy (e.g., model prompt). This continues until the student responds to the natural cue and all of the prompts in the hierarchy have been delivered.

(Continued)

Exhibit 17.3   Continued

	Simultaneous Prompting
	Similar to constant or progressive time delay in that it includes instruction at a zero delay, but in this teaching procedure the instructor never provides a delay round
	The instructor includes a probe session to gather data on the learning that has occurred and this is followed by an instructional session that involves only a zero delay.

The use of systematic instruction to teach academics to students with intellectual disability is an evidence-based practice! [13]

With all of these systematic teaching strategies available, it is important that the instructor identify the best strategy to match the student and the skill. One way to ensure that there are no mistakes in the delivery of instruction by all involved (e.g., instructor, paraprofessionals, therapists, parents) is to create a systematic instruction plan (SIP) for every student goal. A SIP provides detailed guidelines for implementing instruction and is designed to keep instruction very consistent. The plan should include the following information: [14]

▶ The student objective

▶ The materials needed

▶ The setting and when instruction should occur

▶ Who is included in the delivery of instruction

▶ The specific prompts to be used

▶ The fading procedure to use (e.g., simultaneous prompting, time delay, graduated guidance, stimulus shaping)

▶ The defined plan to systematically fade out prompts

▶ The task analysis and chaining procedure if applicable

▶ The specific feedback to be given and the fading schedule for reinforcement

▶ Specific error correction procedures to be used

▶ Plans to promote generalization

▶ Plans to promote self-directed learning

Exhibit 17.4a shows the SIP for a student who is working on a goal to identify the main idea and two supporting details from a grade-appropriate fictional novel. Exhibit 17.4b shows the data collected and superimposed graph from the goal included in the SIP.

Exhibit 17.4a   Example SIP for a Seventh-Grade Student Working on an Objective in ELA

Content

(ELA)   MATH   SCIENCE   SOCIAL STUDIES

Specific strand(s): Reading for Understanding - Narrative Story

State standard: Grade 7: Competency Goal 2: The learner will synthesize and use information from a variety of sources. Objectives: 2.01–Respond to informational materials that are read, heard, and viewed by summarizing information

Alternate achievement: • The learner will explore and respond to a variety of print and nonprint texts (functional and literary). • Explore and analyze relationships among characters, ideas, concepts (including literary devices) and experiences. • Extend understanding by creating products that exemplify specific types of text.

Recommended priority skill: Identify and compare main idea and supporting details using complex strategies and complex age-appropriate text (such as across chapters or themes within texts).

Objective: Identify main idea from a chapter including at least two supporting details after repeated readings.

FORMAT

Unit description (what, from where): Unit on adversity (*Island of the Blue Dolphins*)

Materials: Graphic organizer with picture symbol representation of possible options, adapted seventh-grade chapter book

Adaptations needed (if any): Picture symbols of all responses and distracter pictures, adapted chapter book, voice output

Alternate materials (if any): Choice board with Velcro pieces

Setting and time: Embedded during lesson within the general education classroom for entire unit of instruction

Who will teach this target behavior: Special education teacher and peer mentor

INSTRUCTIONAL PROCEDURES

Prompting

Specific prompt(s) to be used: Nonspecific verbal (NSV), specific verbal (SV) , model (M), physical (P)

Fading (check one):

- ☐ None (simultaneous prompting)
- ☐ Time delay: progressive_____constant_____
- ☑ Least-intrusive prompts
- ☐ Most-to-least intrusive prompts
- ☐ Graduated guidance
- ☐ Stimulus fading and shaping
- ☐ Other (describe) _____

Define planned fading schedule: Wait five seconds for Leigh to respond. If no response, then give NSV prompt (e.g., "What do we need to do next?"); wait five seconds, if no or incorrect response then give SV prompt (e.g., "Is this the main idea or is this the main idea [while pointing to each])"; wait five seconds, if no or incorrect response then model (find the main idea and place back in array of options); if no or incorrect response then physically guide student to answer. Repeat for supporting detail.

(Continued)

Exhibit 17.4a   Continued

Feedback

Praise: Correct answers: "Nice job, you found the main idea (or supporting detail)." Incorrect answers: redirected–no praise

Fading schedule for praise: After three consecutive correct answers, start to praise every other correct response. After main idea and supporting detail are completed correctly, praise when task is complete rather than each individual response.

Error correction: If student starts to answer wrong, stop waiting for prompt and start next-intrusive level of prompting.

Generalization Procedures

Define plans for student to generalized learned target behavior: Different grade-appropriate text, different chapters, taught within unit (four to five lessons) with teacher and peers

Promotion of Self-Directed Learning

Define plans: Can choose which text to work on and select peer groups to work with in gen ed classroom

---

Exhibit 17.4b   Example Data Sheet with Superimposed Graph Reflecting Collected Data from the ELA SIP

Student name: Leigh

Target behavior: Identify main idea and supporting detail of grade-appropriate text

Criterion for mastery: Independently identify main idea from a chapter including at least three supporting details after repeated readings with 100 percent accuracy

Supporting detail 3	M	M	SV	NSV	NSV	SV	SV	NSV	I	I
Supporting detail 2	M	SV	SV		SV	SV	NSV	I	I	I
Supporting detail 1	M	SV	M	NSV	I	NSV	I	I	I	I
Main idea	M	M	SV	SV	NSV	NSV	I	I	I	I
%	0%	0%	0%	25%	25%	0%	50%	75%	100%	100%
DATE	9/8	9/9	9/10	9/12	9/13	9/14	9/17	9/21	9/24	9/25

I = independent response, M = model, NSV = nonspecific verbal, SV = specific verbal

Strategies for Teaching Students with Intellectual Disability and Hearing Loss to Participate in Story-Based Literacy Lessons

Megan Kemmery, University of North Carolina at Greensboro

Many students with intellectual disabilities participate in lessons with grade-appropriate literature, but for students with hearing loss and intellectual disability, additional strategies can be used to support universally designed lessons for all students.

► Sign key vocabulary several times within stories.

► Sequence pictures per page, per sentence or couple of sentences (chunking).

► Pull out three to four situations or scenes per chapter to act out with people and manipulatives to allow students to demonstrate comprehension.

► Decontextualize key vocabulary by explaining the meaning beyond the story.

► Provide opportunities for the student to interact with the word by having the student answer a question relating to the word. Remember to use lots of visuals and manipulatives to build meaning to the text.

Peer Supports

Students with intellectual disability often need additional support in the classroom to complete lessons and activities, and to participate in the social everyday aspects of school. Peer supports are a great way to help students in a natural way (without an adult following along with the student all day long!). When planning instructional support, teachers should think about two things:

► Layout: Is the classroom set up to allow all students to work together to support each other's learning (e.g., cooperative learning groups)?

► What skill(s) is being taught? Can a peer provide instructional support that is meaningful?

Peers can provide systematic instruction (e.g., embedded constant time delay of content vocabulary and concepts, task analytic instruction to complete a science experiment) to support their peers with intellectual disability. Remember, for peers to provide support for each other, they will need a little bit of training. Usually, one hour of training will be enough for students (as young as preschool age) to know what and how to support their peers with disability. Peer supports are a great way to create a learning community.

Research has shown that students who serve as peer supports typically maintain or increase their own academic progress![15]

Embedded Instruction

Systematic and explicit instruction can be delivered to students in all learning environments. One common concern about providing students with limited to pervasive intellectual disability support in inclusive settings is how to offer enough support during the ongoing fast-paced instructional lesson.

Embedded instruction is another research-based strategy that provides systematic instruction within the naturally occurring educational session.

Using systematic instruction, teachers, paraprofessionals, and peers can embed opportunities for students to learn new content during the ongoing lesson; for example, key vocabulary:

Step one: Identify the key vocabulary (e.g., *volcano, valley, mountain*).

Step two: Identify appropriate form of systematic instruction to teach the skill (e.g., time delay).

Step three: During the naturally occurring lesson, identify how many times you want to embed the learning trial (e.g., three trials per word, three trials to match the word to a picture to show comprehension).

Step four: During a science unit on landforms, the teacher or peer embeds trials for the student to identify the vocabulary word and match the word to the picture. Collect data on SIP to keep track of student progress.

Assistive Technology

Assistive technology (AT) is a common instructional strategy that, as defined by IDEA, "includes any item, piece of equipment, or product system, whether acquired commercially off the shelf, modified, or customized, that is used to increase, maintain, or improve functional capabilities of a child with a disability" (http://idea.ed.gov/explore/view/p/,root,statute,I,A,602,1,). AT can either be high tech or low tech. To be considered a high-tech device, it must have an electronic or battery-operated component (e.g., iTalk). To be considered a low-tech device, it must not require electronics or batteries for use (e.g., Picture Exchange Communication System [PECS][16]). AT can also be aided or unaided. To be considered aided, it requires some type of physical equipment that can either be high or low tech. To be considered unaided, there is no additional equipment; rather, it is something that can be demonstrated with the body (e.g., gestures, sign language).

When IDEA was amended in 1997 it required that AT be considered an option for every IEP. Additionally, technology should be included in the IEP whenever it is necessary to support the student in making reasonable education progress in the least-restrictive setting. There are three places in the IEP where AT may appear: annual goals and short-term objectives, necessary supplementary aids and services, and the list of necessary related services. IEP teams need to carefully consider each individual student's AT needs and make sure they are appropriately reflected in the IEP. Table 17.1 provides several examples of common low-tech and high-tech AT.

Self-Determination

Self-determination has been defined as "acting as the primary causal agent in one's life and making choices and decisions regarding one's quality of life free from undue external influence or interference."[18] It is important for teachers of individuals with intellectual disability always to be thinking about systematically teaching the components of self-determination in order for their students to become self-determined individuals. In fact, research has shown that students who are more self-determined tend to live more independently, have higher paying jobs, and perform better in school.[19] The components skills of self-determination are the following:[20]

- ▶ Choice making
- ▶ Decision making
- ▶ Goal setting
- ▶ Problem solving

- ▶ Self-regulation
- ▶ Self-efficacy
- ▶ Self-advocacy
- ▶ Self-awareness

Table 17.1 Examples of Assistive Technologies [17]

Low Tech	High Tech

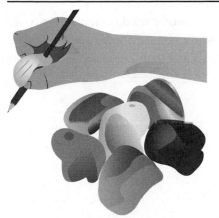

Pencil grips to assist in writing

Touch screen response board with voice output (available with one to more than one hundred options)

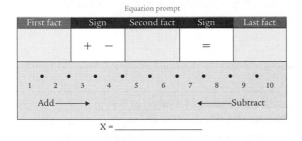

Adapted text and graphic organizers to assist in comprehension (e.g., solving an algebra equation)

iPad app to access and respond to curriculum

Goals should be developed in order for students to receive instruction in these component areas. Additionally, instruction in these component areas should occur during instructional activities using methods as described previously in systematic instruction.

Assessments

Assessments are a very important part of planning and teaching individuals with intellectual disability. It is necessary to assess what students already know in order to better plan instruction aligned to what students need to know. Formative and summative assessments give teachers the opportunity to inform and assess in order to measure student progress.

Formative Assessments

Formative assessments are those that are conducted to provide feedback to teachers and students during the course of instruction. For students with intellectual disability, a common formative assessment is data collection. Data collection is the objective and accurate measurement of a student's present level of performance on a targeted behavior.

Data should be collected daily and reviewed often in order to inform overall interventions. There are many types of data sheets for teachers to select from but it is important that your data sheet match the skills you are targeting. Table 17.2 shows different types of data sheets.

After a data collection system is in place, it is crucial that the data taken be used to make data-based decisions,[21] which are specifically informed decisions made for instruction based on the pattern of data graphed. There are five major data path options for teachers to consider when implementing data-based decisions:

▶ No progress
▶ Slow progress
▶ Adequate or steady progress
▶ Variable and inconsistent progress
▶ Mastery

When reviewing the data of at least two weeks collected a minimum of three times per week, a pattern should appear. Before analyzing the pattern it is important to draw an aim line (see exhibit 17.4b) on your graph, which is a line that is drawn from the current, baseline level of performance to the performance criterion

Table 17.2 Data Sheets

Kind of Data Sheet	How It Is Used
Repeated trial	A common data sheet that is used for delivery of a discrete skill in a set of teaching trials. For example, a teacher may have a goal for the student to identify eight out of ten sight words. The teacher would record the performance of the student on each individual word on the data sheet.
Repeated opportunity	Very similar to a repeated trial data sheet but this data sheet is for a skill that occurs throughout the day versus in one sitting at one time. For example, a teacher would use this data sheet for a goal in which the student needs to correctly identify time throughout the day. The data sheet has a place for each occurrence of the skill and also identifies where and with whom the skill occurs.
Frequency	Used to measure the number of times the student performs or does not perform a targeted skill. Teachers would use this data sheet for a behavior they are trying to increase or reduce by tallying and totaling the number of occurrences of the targeted behavior in a given time period. For example, if trying to get a count of the number of occurrences of hand raising after implementing a self-monitoring checklist, the teacher could use a frequency data sheet and tally and total the number of occurrences during math instruction.
Duration	Designed to measure the amount of time a targeted behavior occurs or a latency recording, the amount of time it takes the student to initiate a targeted response once the stimulus to respond is presented. For example, a teacher might use a latency recording sheet to time the amount of time it takes for the student to sit in his seat after the bell rings signaling class to begin.
Task analytic	Used for chained skills that make up a task analysis. For example, a task analytic data sheet could be used to record the steps for a student to independently complete a science experiment or the steps for a student to independently make a sandwich. The scorer would record the level of independence or performance on each individual step of the chained skill on the data sheet.

described in a behavioral objective. Once you have graphed your data (at least six data points) and drawn in the aim line, you need to look for one of the five data patterns:

▶ One pattern to look for is no progress. This means there is little to no improvement on the performance of the targeted skill (a flat line). If this is the case (and you did not just begin teaching the skill two weeks prior), you would simplify responding or shape responding. Some options include using assistive technology or teaching a subset of the targeted skill (Can the skill be broken down further?).

▶ When the data pattern has a slow improvement in comparison to the aim line, then it is likely a slow progress data pattern. In this case you need to improve antecedents. Some options for improving antecedents include providing stimulus prompts and then systematically fading these prompts over time or to use time delay to fade out prompts.

▶ When the data pattern demonstrates an adequate or steady progress in relation to the aim line, then it likely means your intervention is working. You should not change anything about instruction if this is the data pattern seen.

▶ When the data pattern appears variable or inconsistent over the days of data collection, then you likely have an issue with overall student motivation. They can do the skill some days but cannot on others. To improve motivation, two options are offering choices of materials to be used in instruction or varying reinforcers (e.g., do something novel as the reinforcer).

▶ The final data pattern to look for is mastery data pattern. This is when the student has met the performance criterion described in a behavioral objective for a sustained period of consecutive days. If this is the data pattern seen, you need to introduce a new skill but also work on maintenance of that current skill.

Table 17.3 provides an easy guide to data-based decisions.

Summative Assessments

All students should have the chance to show what they know. In the age of high accountability in education for students and teachers, it is important to develop assessments of learning that allow students with multiple and significant learning needs to demonstrate mastery and competence in specific skill and concept areas.

Table 17.3 Data-Based Decisions[22]

Data Pattern	Change Needed	Example Options
Inconsistent	Improve motivation	Vary reinforcers; offer choice of materials; have student self-monitor
Slow progress	Improve antecedents	Use time delay to fade prompts; use and fade stimulus cues
No progress	Simplify and reshape responding	Use AT; teach a subset of the skill
Adequate progress	Make no changes	
Mastery	Introduce new skill	Introduce new science terms; target a new daily living skill

Exhibit 17.5 Three Important Questions to Ask When Developing Summative Assessments[23]

Questions	Remember . . .	Example
Does the assessment highlight the big ideas learned in this unit or subject area?	You don't want to assess everything you have ever taught or talked about in class. The key concepts and skills should be taught systematically and assessed for growth and mastery.	*Content:* Science *Topic:* Forces of motion *Assessment item:* Student fills in blank with words or pictures to represent the following: <u>Kinetic energy</u> is the energy of motion. <u>Potential energy</u> is the energy at rest.
Is the assessment presented in a manner that allows the student to access the content?	Any modifications to the way the instructional material was presented during the lesson(s) should be available to the student during testing.	There are solutions in nature that help plants live. Text may be adapted to help students comprehend the main ideas of the chapter, science text, history event, or math story problem by adding picture cues to the key vocabulary and big ideas. Free public images on the Internet may be used to support the meaning of the vocabulary and provide access to the content being presented.
Does the student have a way to show what he or she knows?	Many students with limited to pervasive intellectual disability have significant communication needs. Students may communicate through various response modes (e.g., pointing, looking at a response option, vocalization, pressing a switch, circling an answer).	Why did the water change colors? A solute was added. / A book was added. / A solvent was added. Adapted text paired with a question and response options for students who cannot generate a verbal response

Examples of adapted text and response board to show comprehension are from Courtade, G., Jimenez, B., Trela, K., & Browder, D. M. (2008). *Teaching to science standards: An inquiry-based approach for middle and high school students with moderate and severe disabilities.* Verona, WI: Attainment Company.

All students are expected to demonstrate growth and mastery of learning objectives set forth by their grade level. Many students with limited to pervasive intellectual disability participate in alternate assessments based on alternate achievement standards. Whether the assessment is for a unit of instruction, or end-of-year assessment (e.g., state mandated), all students must be assessed. There are three important questions to ask when developing summative assessments for students with intellectual disability (see exhibit 17.5).

TO SUM UP

▶ General curriculum access for students with limited to pervasive intellectual disability is important! Legally all students are required to show progress on grade-level academic standards. More important, personally relevant curriculum should be developed for all students, including those with intellectual disability.

▶ When planning for the individualized needs of students, teachers should refer to ecological assessments, use person-centered planning, and adaptive behavior assessments. Curriculum guides can also provide guidance for instructional teams to plan for and meet students' individual academic and social needs.

▶ Students with limited to pervasive intellectual disability can learn academic skills aligned to grade-level standards. Systematic instruction is an evidence-based practice that should be used to support student learning. Specific and measurable goals should be set in order to monitor student progress toward curriculum and IEP goals and objectives.

▶ Planning for barriers that may impede students learning is a must! Assistive technology, peer supports, and embedded instruction are three possible ways to strengthen learning opportunities in a natural way. Successful inclusive learning environments use all of its members to support all learners.

WHAT'S NEXT?

Many students with limited to pervasive intellectual disability have multiple disabilities. When serving this population of student, the whole student must be planned for, including medical and physical needs. It is important to remember that a team approach when planning for this population is best!

ADDITIONAL RESOURCES

▶ Disability Assumptions: *Least dangerous assumption:* www.includingsamuel.com/Libraries /Resources_for_Teachers_and_Paraeducators/The_Least_Dangerous_Assumption_A_Challenge _to_Create_a_New_Paradigm.sflb.ashx

▶ Adapted grade-aligned text (including chapter books, such as *Because of Winn-Dixie, Holes, Call of the Wild*): http://coedpages.uncc.edu/access

▶ Collins, B. C. (2012). *Systematic instruction for students with moderate and severe disabilities.* Baltimore: Paul H. Brookes.

▶ Attainment Company provides curricular and assistive technology supports for serving students with intellectual disability: http://attainmentcompany.com

▶ Autism Internet modules (designed for educators and families to provide information and resources for serving students with autism and pervasive disorders): www.autisminternetmodules.org

▶ CAST: *Universal design for learning:* www.cast.org

▶ Free learning modules designed to address instruction for students with intellectual disability (e.g., systematic instruction, task analytic instruction, data-based decisions, teaching inquiry science, story-based mathematics, story-based lessons): http://mast.ecu.edu

PART FOUR

ADDITIONAL CONSIDERATIONS

CHAPTER EIGHTEEN

Managing Student Health Needs

Pamela W. Carter

University of North Carolina at Greensboro

✔ In this chapter you will learn about:

- Individualized health care plans (IHPs)
- Emergency care plans (ECPs)
- Specific health conditions of your students that require special attention
- Teacher tips for managing student needs pertinent to the described health conditions

It was a beautiful day. Miss James, a first-year K–2 pull-out resource teacher, decided to take her second-grade group outside to look for signs of spring as preparation for an upcoming writing assignment.

"I see daisies!" exclaimed Sara, running over to get a closer look at the flowers growing in the grass by the sidewalk to the school playground. Everyone eagerly followed. Suddenly, a buzzing sound could be heard.

"Ouch!" cried out Eric, slapping at his forearm. "A bee stung me!" Quickly, the rest of the children backed away from the daisy patch while Miss James hurried over. With alarm, she noticed that red hives were spreading from the site of the sting. Eric was anxiously crying and seemed to be having some trouble catching his breath as his lips began to swell. "Oh no!" thought Miss James, her mind racing. "What is happening? I've got to do something—but what?"

As a special education teacher, you are responsible for knowing all about your students' special needs. In addition to academic, behavioral, and social needs, some students have health issues that may affect their functioning at school.

INDIVIDUAL HEALTH CARE PLANS AND EMERGENCY CARE PLANS

In the past, many students with serious or chronic health conditions would have been institutionalized, hospitalized, or sent to special schools. Today, however, these students attend school alongside of their peers.[1] Because of advances in medical technology, many children are living with multiple and complex medical problems, childhood diseases, and chronic health conditions.[2] Teachers must be aware of the special health needs of all students as well as how these health conditions can affect students academically. If a student's health condition adversely affects his or her educational performance, the student may be eligible for special education and related services as "other health impaired" under IDEA. If the health condition requires only accommodations in the school setting, the student may then qualify for such service under Section 504 of the Vocational Rehabilitation Act.[3]

Many students with health conditions require management during the school day.[4] In most cases, school nurses lead the management of these needs and they will disseminate information about students' health concerns to school personnel through an individualized health care plan, known as an IHP (see exhibit 18.1 for a sample IHP addressing asthma). An IHP typically has up to five parts: assessment (including history and current status), nursing diagnosis, goals, nursing interventions, and expected outcomes. Periodically, the school nurse conducts an evaluation of the IHP, revising this document as needed. For some students, an emergency care plan (ECP) is included in the IHP to provide specific directions on what to do in a particular emergency situation.[5] (See exhibit 18.2 for a sample ECP addressing a severe allergic reaction.) School officials should obtain a medical release for any treatment done at school and should secure written parental consent to administer any needed medication to a student.[6]

In the process of developing an IHP or ECP for a student with a health need, school nurses interview the parents of the student and remain in contact with the family as long as the health need remains a concern.[9] There should also be precise two-way communication between teachers and the parents so that everyone involved with the student is aware of his or her current health status in terms of school functioning.

Although school nurses are certainly viewed as valuable assets to schools and are available to provide training for select school staff to monitor and manage some conditions, the amount of time nurses are assigned to schools varies across school districts, with some schools functioning without daily nurse availability.[10] Special educators thus need to stay abreast of basic student health management at all times and should be familiar with their students' IHPs and ECPs. Following is an overview of some of the possible student health conditions as well as practical teacher tips for managing these health needs in the classroom. Always consult with the school nurse about students' specific needs and adhere precisely to their IHPs and ECPs.

HEALTH CONDITIONS AND TEACHER TIPS

It is not enough to just be aware of what a particular health condition is or entails. As a special educator, you need to translate knowledge about a health condition into practical application in your classroom to be certain that the special needs of your student with a health condition are met. Following are teacher tips for managing the health needs of children with more common health conditions.

Exhibit 18.1 Sample Individualized Health Care Plan[7]

Effective dates _____
Student _____ Birthdate _____ School _____

Assessment Data	Nursing Diagnosis	Student Goals	Interventions for Asthma Management (NIC) Activities	Outcomes for Asthma Self-Management (NOC) Indicators
• Twelve-year-old diagnosed with asthma at age nine • Carries Proventil inhaler at all times • Independent in identifying symptoms and need for treatment • MD order normal PE program	Ineffective breathing pattern as characterized by shortness of breath, coughing, and wheezing related to asthma	• Student will demonstrate appropriate use of inhaler at the beginning of school year. • Student will initiate treatment when symptoms appear throughout the school year. • Student will keep record of peak flow meter readings if required throughout the school year. • Student will keep record of use of inhaler in the health office throughout the school year. • Student will avoid having an emergency asthma attack during this school year.	• Review use of inhaler with student at the beginning of the school year. (nurse) • At the beginning of the school year, review with teacher and appropriate staff the signs and symptoms of asthma exacerbation and when student should use his or her inhaler. (nurse) • Every two months, record student's inhaler use in health file. • Report increased use of inhaler to parents and physician. (nurse) **Emergency Care Plan** • See student asthma emergency protocol (in classroom, locker room, and nurse's office).	Never = 1 Rarely = 2 Sometimes = 3 Often = 4 Consistently = 5 Recognizes onset of asthma 1 2 3 4 5 Initiates action to manage personal triggers 1 2 3 4 5 Self-manages exacerbations 1 2 3 4 5 Reports asthma controlled 1 2 3 4 5

I have read and approve of the above plan for school health care.
Parent signature _____ School nurse signature _____

NIC = nursing interventions classifications, NOC = nursing outcomes classifications
From Sunrise River Press (2005). Reprinted with permission.

Exhibit 18.2 Emergency Care Plan[8]

ANAPHYLAXIS: SEVERE ALLERGIC REACTION

Date of plan development _____

Student _____ Birthdate _____ Student ID number _____

Address _____

Phone(s) _____ Fax number _____

Mother _____ Father _____

Parent designee _____

Physician _____ Phone _____

Preferred hospital _____

Medical condition:

   Severe allergic reaction to peanuts and peanut products

Location of medication and other supplies:

   EpiPen Jr. is kept in labeled drawer in locked medicine cabinet in health room.

Personnel that have access to key _____

Persons authorized to administer treatment:

School nurse _____ Nurse designee _____

Signs of emergency:

   Hives, itching, swelling, difficulty breathing, cyanosis (bluish discoloration of the skin caused by lack of oxygen in the blood), hypotension (low blood pressure), shock

Treatment for severe allergic reaction:

▶ Administer epinephrine injection or assist student with self-administration.

▶ Call 911 as needed, informing emergency personnel that student has severe allergic reaction to peanuts and that epinephrine injection has been given.

▶ Call parent or parent designee.

▶ Call student's physician to inform him or her of emergency situation.

▶ Record administration or self-administration of medication in student's health record (include date, time, source of exposure, treatment, if EMS was called, and signature).

▶ Emergency personnel are to transport to _____ or nearest emergency department.

From Sunrise River Press (2005). Reprinted with permission.

Allergies

Students who come to school with serious identified allergies need an IHP and ECP. Food allergies occur when a person's immune system overreacts to particular substances in food or drink such as wheat, egg products, milk products, nut products, shellfish, fish products, peanut products, or soy products.[11] Other students are allergic to bee, wasp, or hornet stings.[12] There are also students who are allergic to latex and products containing it, particularly students with spina bifida and those who have undergone multiple surgical procedures, especially from infancy.[13] Food allergies, insect sting allergies (bee, wasp, or hornet), and latex allergies are especially problematic because allergic responses can be serious at times. Rapid onset of life-threatening anaphylaxis is characterized by significant responses such as throat swelling, itchy rash, and low blood pressure. Students with these serious allergies may keep a personal epinephrine pen or anaphylaxis kit with them at all times to combat the effects of a possible allergic reaction.[14]

Some students (and their parents) may not know that they have a serious food or environmental allergy if they have not yet suffered such an allergic response. The first time an adverse reaction occurs could be at school. The American Academy of Pediatrics has recommended that schools maintain a schoolwide emergency care manual and ECP with at least two school personnel trained to manage emergency situations until the expertise of the school nurse or other emergency personnel can be employed.[15]

Other students may have IHPs for mild environmental allergies. School building dampness accompanied by mold can cause an allergic reaction in sensitive students, resulting in upper and lower respiratory symptoms, excess physician-diagnosed asthma, fatigue, headache, or eye and skin irritation.[16] Another environmental allergy that may affect students at school is allergic rhinitis, commonly known as *hay fever*. An allergic response (usually seasonal) to grass and tree pollen can cause repeated or continual sneezing, a blocked or runny nose, itchiness (eyes, nose, and throat), a general unwell feeling, headaches[17], and impaired concentration.[18] Hay fever can adversely affect school performance, especially if the student takes a sedating antihistamine to combat symptoms.[19] Students allergic to dust mites present with allergic responses similar to hay fever.[20]

TEACHER TIPS

▶ *Food, insect sting, and latex allergies.* Allergic reactions because of food, insect, or latex allergies can range from itching, hives, stomach pain, nausea, and diarrhea to life-threatening anaphylaxis that presents as sudden swelling, difficulty breathing, and shock. If you should observe anaphylaxis occurring, immediately follow the student's ECP precisely! To allay exposure to offending foods in the first place, be sure that the school cafeteria manager is aware of your students' allergies so that breakfast or lunch alternatives can be provided. When outdoors with a student allergic to insect stings, stay cognizant of bee, wasp, or hornet swarms, informing the school principal if you should see an active hive on school grounds. Strive to keep your classroom as latex free as possible.[21] See table 18.1 for a list of products that may contain latex and as well as a list of latex-free alternative products. Be sure to bring an anaphylaxis kit and your student's personal epinephrine pen on all field trips. Take a copy of your student's IHP and ECP with you as well.

▶ *Mold allergy.* Immediately report evidence of mold in your classroom space to the school principal so that action can be taken to remove it.

▶ *Hay fever.* Alert parents and the school nurse as needed if a student's chosen medication appears to be impairing his or her concentration in school.

▶ *Dust allergy.* Keep your classroom space well dusted and clean. When a student sensitive to dust encounters it, his or her nose will itch and often sneezing will begin, impeding focus on school activities and assignments.

Table 18.1 Latex in the Home and Community[22]

Products That May Contain Latex	Latex-Safe Alternatives
Art supplies, paints, glue, erasers, fabric paints	Elmer's, Faber-Castell erasers, Liquitex paints, acrylic paints, soap erasers, Crayola (except stamps, erasers), Play-Doh
Balloons	Mylar balloons, self-sealing Myloons
Balls: Koosh, tennis, bowling, ball pits	PVC (Hedstrom), Nerf foam balls
Carpet backing, gym floor, basement sealants	Provide barrier cloth or mat
Chewing gum	Wrigley gums, Bubblicious, Trident
Clothes: liquid appliqués on T-shirts, elastic on socks, underwear, sneakers, sandals	Cloth-covered elastic, neoprene, Buster Brown elastic-free socks
Condoms, diaphragms, contraceptive sponges	Polyurethane wide-seal silicone diaphragms, Trojan Supra condom, others
Crutch tips, hand grips, and axillary pads	Cover with cloth or tape
Diapers, rubber pants, incontinence pads	Huggies, Gold Seal, some Attends, Drypers, Always, Pampers, Luvs, others
Food handled with latex gloves	Synthetic gloves for food handling
Handles on rackets, tools, bicycles	Vinyl, leather handles or cover with cloth or tape
Kitchen-cleaning gloves	PVP, cotton liners
Latex paint	There is no natural rubber in latex paint.
Newsprint, ads, coupons	Provide barrier such as gloves.
Toys such as old Barbies, Stretch Armstrong	1992 Barbie, Mattel dolls, Kenner figures, toys by Fisher Price, Playskool, others
Rubber bands	String, plastic bands
Water toys, swimming equipment, bathing suits	Plastic, PVC, nylon, Suits Me swimwear
Wheelchair cushions, tires	Jay, ROHO, cover seat, use gloves
Zippered plastic storage bags	Waxed paper, plain plastic bags, Ziploc bags

Cotter, C., & Smith, M. (2005). Latex allergy. In C. K. Silkworth, M. J. Arnold, J. F. Harrigan, & D. S. Zaiger (Eds.), *Individualized healthcare plans for the school nurse* (p. 642). North Branch, MN: Sunrise River Press. Reprinted with permission.

Asthma

Asthma is a chronic disease in which airways overreact to various stimuli or triggers, making it hard for the affected individual to breathe.[23] It is the most common chronic childhood disease in the United States and the leading cause of school absences.[24] When an asthmatic student is exposed to a trigger (physical exercise, respiratory illnesses, allergens, environmental irritants, strong emotional reactions, or gastroesophageal reflux disease), chronic airway inflammation is furthered, the muscles surrounding the airways and lungs constrict, and excessive, thickened mucus is produced.[25] Long-term and short-term medications are available for individuals with asthma.[26] Medications that treat asthma fall into two broad categories: (1) long-term controller or maintenance medications and (2) quick-relief or rescue medications (inhaled or taken orally) that are designed to render fast relief in the event of an asthma attack.[27] Such quick-relief treatment in conjunction with rest is often effective in combatting asthmatic episodes but sometimes the student may need to be taken to a doctor's office or hospital for further medical management.[28]

TEACHER TIPS

▶ A student experiencing an asthma attack may have an anxious expression, wheeze and have tightness in chest, cough a lot, have shortness of breath and difficulty breathing, exhibit shaking chills with or without fever, or stop activity (not wanting to walk fast or far) while hunching over to breathe.[29] Immediately follow student's ECP precisely!

▶ Maintain familiarity of your asthmatic student's IHP because you may be trained to administer medication as needed on a nonemergency basis when the school nurse is not on campus.

▶ Bring your asthmatic student's medication as well as his or her IHP and ECP with you on all field trips for your student's protection.

▶ Clear your classroom of environmental irritants that may affect your student with asthma such as animal dander, dust, perfumes, scented powders, and hair sprays.[30]

▶ Use the following only in well-ventilated areas, replacing caps quickly: dry-erase markers, glue, paste, and natural cleaning agents.[31]

▶ Use only vinyl, leather, or wood furniture in your classroom space when possible.[32]

▶ Promote careful hand washing to allay contraction of illnesses.[33]

▶ Ensure that the heating, ventilation, and air-conditioning systems of your classroom are well maintained.[34]

▶ Report any evidence of mold in your classroom space to the school principal so that action can be taken to remove it.[35]

▶ Be sure your classroom space is free of cockroaches and other pests.[36]

▶ See that your student with asthma avoids exposure to idling buses.[37]

Attention Deficit Hyperactivity Disorder (ADHD)

ADHD is a neurobiological, developmental disability whose hallmark is a "persistent pattern of inattention and/or hyperactivity-impulsivity that is more frequent and severe than is typically observed in individuals at a comparable level of development." Some students with ADHD present with compliance and behavioral difficulties as well as social skills deficits and academic problems. The prevalence of ADHD is thought to range from 3 percent to 5 percent of the school-aged population with boys outnumbering girls by four to one to as much as nine to one, although there is some evidence that many girls with ADHD are simply never diagnosed.[38]

There are three types of ADHD: predominantly inattentive, predominantly hyperactive and impulsive, and combined type (also see appendix A).[39] Prescribed central nervous system (CNS) stimulant medications have been known to successfully treat ADHD symptoms. Common stimulant medications include Ritalin, Dexedrine, Adderall XR, and Cylert.[40]

TEACHER TIPS

▶ Some students taking stimulant medications to treat ADHD symptoms experience side effects depending on the particular medication prescribed. Possible side effects include insomnia, appetite loss, nausea, vomiting, abdominal pains, thirst, headaches, irritability, moodiness, and growth suppression.[41] You should promptly report any observed side effects to the school nurse and the student's parents.

▶ If your student with ADHD takes stimulant medication during the school day, be aware of the medication schedule on your student's IHP because you or a teacher assistant may be responsible for administering this medication if your school nurse is not present in your school each day.

▶ The combination of medication and behavioral and academic interventions can result in your student with ADHD exhibiting better classroom behavior and academic performance. Evidence-based behavioral interventions such as these may be helpful for individual students with ADHD:[42]

- *Token economy and response cost system:* system of reinforcement involving awarding or removing tokens or points contingent on behavior
- *Daily report card system:* contingency arrangement among the teacher, the student, and the parents in which parents reinforce at home documented good progress on target behaviors at school
- *Cognitive behavioral training system:* self-monitoring training to teach self-control (students learn to identify a problem, select a strategy, and think about the consequences of their actions)
- *Positive and negative reinforcement:* use of positive reinforcers with negative consequences such as loss of privileges (because the goal is to increase intrinsic motivation, positive reinforcements may be more powerful than negative consequences in the long run)

▶ You and the school counselor may wish to provide instruction to your student with ADHD on the recognition of social cues as well as calming and refocusing techniques.[43]

▶ Maintaining an organized classroom with clear routines and expectations in terms of academics as well as behavior will be very beneficial to your student with ADHD.

▶ Consider securing for your student with ADHD a freestanding study carrel or a small, portable study carrel (that can be placed on a desk) to aid focus and concentration in the classroom.

▶ Your student with ADHD may benefit from assignment modifications such as allowing him or her to complete work in small segments.

Cancer

Cancer occurs when abnormal cells grow in an uncontrolled way. Although cancer in children is much rarer than in adults, intensive research has been done to combat this pediatric illness, resulting in significant improvements in survival rates. More children confronting cancer are likely to be in school now as new technological therapies allay long hospital stays.[44]

Leukemia, a cancer of the blood-forming cells, is the most common type of childhood cancer with brain tumors being the second most common type. Cancer treatments include surgical intervention, cranial radiation therapy, CNS chemotherapy, bone-marrow transplantation, or some combination of these treatments. Unfortunately, common cancer therapies often result in adverse long-term CNS-related toxicities, commonly referred to as *neurocognitive late effects,* which may include declines in intellectual functioning or specific neurocognitive functions, delays in academic achievement, and school performance difficulties.[45]

▶ Per the ECP of your student with cancer, be observant of side effects of chemotherapy and radiation, which could include gastrointestinal problems, mouth sores, rashes, bruising or discoloration of skin, bleeding, headaches, lightheadedness, changes in energy or stamina, chest pain, hair loss, pain or difficulty with urination, fever, or changes in vision.[46] Precisely follow the ECP when side effects are seen and alert the school nurse or parents as needed.

▶ Children and youth with cancer are more vulnerable to the serious complications of chickenpox.[47] If your student with cancer is exposed to chickenpox, notify the school nurse and parents right away. They can check the immunization status of the student and observe for a possible outbreak that may occur despite vaccination.

▶ As needed, provide rest periods in the school nurse's office for your student with cancer.[48]

▶ Encourage your student with cancer to maintain fluid intake.[49]

▶ As needed, allow your student with cancer to complete mouth care (due to mouth sores) in the school nurse's office after meals.[50]

▶ Provide emotional support for your student with cancer and secure counseling from the school counselor as needed.[51]

▶ Promptly attend to any school performance difficulties exhibited by your student with cancer. Keep in mind that your student with cancer may have some absenteeism due to illness. In some cases, arrangements for a homebound teacher may be needed.

▶ Some students may be able to have continued instruction during hospitalization through a hospital school. Coordination with the hospital teacher can assist with transitions back to school.

Cardiovascular Disorders

Cardiovascular disorders involve the heart and blood vessels and can be categorized as congenital or acquired. Congenital conditions are present at birth and often involve other system abnormalities. These conditions commonly require palliative care (specialized care that is focused on providing patients with relief from symptoms, pain, and stress of a serious illness) or surgical repair, which may correct the presented problem. Acquired cardiovascular diseases are conditions that develop after birth and include heart rate and conduction problems, hypertension, atherosclerosis (hardening of the arteries), cardiomyopathy (a disease that weakens and enlarges the heart muscle), and chest pain. Treatments for acquired cardiovascular diseases include surgery, pacemaker implantation, oxygen therapy, medication, activity restrictions, and dietary restrictions.[52]

▶ Watch for signs of cardiac distress in your student with a cardiovascular disorder such as increasing fatigue or shortness of breath.[53] Immediately stop any activity at the onset of these symptoms and precisely follow your student's ECP!

▶ Your student's pediatric cardiologist or the school nurse may train your student with a cardiovascular disorder to alert you when his or her heart is racing or pounding (indication of cardiac dysrhythmia). Precisely follow his or her ECP in this instance as well.[54]

- Follow medically prescribed activity restrictions for your student with a cardiovascular disorder.[55]

- Be aware of any dietary restrictions for your student with a cardiovascular disorder and be sure that given guidelines are followed.[56]

- Secure school counseling services as needed to help your student with a cardiovascular disorder cope with his or her condition.[57]

- Adjust assignments or request homebound instruction to accommodate long-term absences of your student with a cardiovascular disorder.

- If your student with a cardiovascular disorder takes medication to address his or her condition, be aware of the possible side effects of the medication as outlined in your student's ECP.

Cystic Fibrosis (CF)

Students with cystic fibrosis (CF) have an inherited genetic condition that affects the digestive tract as well as the lungs.[58] It results in thickened mucus, causing obstruction in the small airways and subsequent respiratory and lung disease. CF treatments include chest physiotherapy (CPT) to clear clogged airways, various medications, inhaled antibiotics, dietary management, and counseling as needed.[59] A lung transplant from a donor followed by immunosuppressive medications and continuous monitoring of other organs affected by CF is a last resort course of action for those with CF whose lung functioning is significantly diminished.[60] Median survival age for persons with CF has increased to 33.4 years due to improved treatment and earlier diagnosis. Students with severe CF may experience declines in health status as early as during the middle school years.[61]

CF can affect students not only physically but also emotionally and socially. Students with CF may suffer body image problems in light of their short stature, slight builds, and clubbing of fingers. They have social challenges as well. Keeping pace with peers during recess or PE class is a struggle, time spent on chest physiotherapy and general fatigue may limit participation in extracurricular activities, and a feeling of isolation can result from needed hospital stays.[62]

TEACHER TIPS

- Signs that your student with CF is in respiratory distress (a medical emergency) include sudden increase in breathing difficulty as well as blood in the sputum (coughed-up mucus).[63] Precisely follow the ECP of your student with CF in this situation!

- You or a teacher assistant may receive training to operate and clean devices used for medication delivery as well as training to perform CPT for your student with CF on days the school nurse is not present at school.[64]

- Be sure that your student with CF increases his or her liquid intake during exercise.[65]

- If medically indicated, allow your student with CF to have nutritious snacks during the school day to increase needed caloric intake. Some students with CF experience gastroesophageal reflux symptoms following eating.[66]

- Research indicates that CF can adversely affect learning because this health condition is associated with depressed mood, anxiety, memory and concentration problems, fatigue, and absenteeism due to illness and hospitalization. Hence, you should closely monitor the school progress of your student with CF, providing academic help as needed.[67]

► If necessary, consider referring your student to the school counselor for help coping with CF.[68]

► When taking your class on a field trip, be sure to bring along any devices for medication delivery for your student with CF as well as this student's IHP and ECP.

Diabetes Mellitus

Diabetes mellitus is a group of metabolic diseases characterized by chronic hyperglycemia (high blood glucose) resulting in defects in insulin secretion, insulin action, or both.[69] Diabetes used to be classified per the treatment required to control the disorder (insulin-dependent versus non-insulin-dependent diabetes) or per the age of onset (juvenile diabetes or late-onset autoimmune diabetes of adulthood). The American Diabetes Association now recommends, however, that the classification of diabetes be based on the underlying disease mechanism. There are two types of diabetes that most often affect children and adolescents. Type 1 diabetes is caused by an absolute deficiency in insulin production by the pancreas. Type 2 diabetes involves insulin resistance and relative insulin deficiency.[70]

Students with diabetes may need daily blood glucose monitoring, management of food intake and exercise, and in some cases, oral medication or daily insulin administration.[71] Some students today use indwelling insulin injectors in lieu of individual dosing by injection.[72]

TEACHER TIPS

► All students who take insulin are at risk for hypoglycemia (low blood glucose) that can occur with an unusual amount of exercise, too much insulin, or skipped, delayed, or inadequate food intake. Hypoglycemia is one of the most immediate emergencies for a person with diabetes.[73] See table 18.2 for symptoms of mild, moderate, and severe hypoglycemia. Precisely follow your student's ECP if he or she should present with these symptoms!

Table 18.2 Reported Symptoms of Hypoglycemia[74]

Mild	Moderate	Severe
Sweating, headache	Aggressiveness	Altered states of consciousness, including coma or seizure
Tremors, palpitations	Drowsiness	
Pallor, behavior change	Confusion	

From Banion, C., & Valentine, V. (2011). Type 1 diabetes throughout the life span. In C. Mensing (Ed.), *The art and science of diabetes self-management education* (2nd ed., pp. 329–330). Chicago, IL: American Association of Diabetes Educators. Reprinted with permission.

► Students who take insulin are also at risk for hyperglycemia (high blood glucose) that can occur with missed insulin doses, inadequate insulin, overeating, intake of foods high in carbohydrates, certain illnesses, and ingestion of various medications. Symptoms of hyperglycemia include frequent urination, frequent thirst, blurred vision, fatigue, hunger, weight loss, abdominal pain, and numbness in the extremities.[75] Precisely follow your student's ECP if your student with diabetes presents with these symptoms as well! Some states require that schools develop a written diabetes management plan with the parents to further clarify what needs to be done in the school.

- ▶ The IHP for your student with diabetes should outline specifics about exercise and healthy foods. You may need to allow snacks during the school day if specified on the IHP.

- ▶ Students with diabetes sometimes exhibit fatigue and confusion in school, have problems with reading or visual scanning, present with slower response times, and have difficulty attending to task.[76] Adjust your expectations, instruction, and assignments accordingly.

- ▶ All materials for blood glucose monitoring and insulin administration must be brought on field trips for the protection of your student with diabetes.[77] Bring along a copy of your student's IHP and ECP as well.

- ▶ Keep in mind that school absences due to a chronic health condition such as diabetes can have adverse effects on educational progress.[78] Provide extra instruction as needed.

- ▶ A chronic health condition such as diabetes can also lead to social and emotional difficulties.[79] Secure the services of the school counselor as needed.

- ▶ An informative resource for educators can be found at the National Diabetes Education Program website (http://ndep.nih.gov).[80]

Dysfunctional Elimination Syndrome (DES)

Students with dysfunctional elimination syndrome (DES) may present with urinary urgency, urge incontinence, nocturnal enuresis (wetting the bed), encopresis (fecal soiling of clothing), urinary tract infections, and constipation. Their self-esteem tends to be lower (with learning adversely affected due to lack of self-confidence) than children who are continent (proficient with elimination).[81]

TEACHER TIPS

- ▶ It is important that you advocate at your school for clean student bathrooms with doors to the stalls. Research indicates that students with DES exacerbate their health condition when they choose not to use bathrooms at school that are dirty or lack doors to the stalls.[82]

- ▶ Allow your student with DES to use the restroom whenever needed, particularly because certain students could be on a laxative regimen due to a chronic health condition.[83]

- ▶ Monitor the fluid and fiber intake of your student with encopresis during the school day if such instructions are written in your student's IHP.[84]

- ▶ Arrange access to a private bathroom (such as in the school nurse's office) for your student with DES as needed.[85]

- ▶ Have the parents of your student with DES provide a change of clothing for their child as needed. Store this clothing in a private space such as in the school nurse's office.[86]

- ▶ Access the services of the school counselor for your student with DES as needed to address self-esteem issues and coping strategies.[87]

- ▶ Stay cognizant of possible self-esteem concerns in terms of your student with DES, keeping aware that your student may benefit from some extra attention academically due to lowered self-confidence.

- ▶ When taking the class on a field trip, discreetly bring a change of clothes for your student with DES to use as needed.

Epilepsy and Seizures

Epilepsy is a chronic disorder in which recurrent seizures occur within the brain.[88] Seizure activity happens when clusters of nerve cells or neurons in the brain exhibit abnormal or excessive electrical activity.[89]

There are two major categories of seizures: primary generalized and partial. Primary generalized seizures involve both cerebral hemispheres simultaneously at onset and include these seizure types: absence (episodes of prolonged staring—occasionally still referred to as *petit mal seizures*), atonic (loss of tone—known as *drop attacks* because loss of tone causes falls), clonic (rapid jerking of single or multiple extremities), myoclonic (quick, sudden, brief jerks), tonic (stiffening of single or multiple extremities), and tonic-clonic (loss of consciousness and intervals of symmetrical stiffness and jerking of all extremities—occasionally still referred to as *grand mal seizures* or *convulsions*). Partial seizures involve one cerebral hemisphere at onset and include these seizure types: simple partial (an aura, a particular sensation, occurs just prior to the seizure that presents as sensory or motor involvement usually confined to one side of the body without impairment in consciousness), complex partial (sensory and motor seizure with alteration in awareness—formerly referred to as *psychomotor* or *temporal lobe* seizures), and secondary generalized tonic-clonic (a partial seizure that evolves into tonic-clonic activity on both sides of the body).[90]

Several different anti-epileptic drugs (AEDs) are used to treat epilepsy.[91] When an individual with epilepsy is not responsive to medications, a vagus nerve stimulator (VNS) may be implanted by a surgeon in the left upper quadrant of the person's chest. This device works to deliver electrical stimulation to the vagus cranial nerve, providing an overall inhibitory effect on seizures. A vital component of VNS treatment is the availability of a hand-held magnet that can serve to give the individual or caregiver an external mode of control to abort or lessen the intensity of a seizure. The magnet is approximately the size of a large pencil eraser and comes encased in either a pager-type belt clip or a Velcro wristband. At the onset of a seizure, the magnet can be swiped over the location of the implanted VNS in the chest for two seconds to initiate additional stimulation. Epilepsy surgery is a treatment option for individuals who continue to experience chronic generalized seizures despite treatment with multiple medications.[92]

Not all seizures mean that a person has epilepsy because seizures can also be caused by high fever, alcohol or drug withdrawal, or an imbalance of body fluids or chemicals. Children with neurodevelopmental disorders such as autism, cerebral palsy, and intellectual disabilities as well as those who have suffered a stroke, head trauma, brain infection, or brain tumor may experience seizures.[93]

Seizures may be nonrecurrent (acute) or recurrent (chronic) and can be triggered by illness, sleep deprivation, fatigue, menses, bright and flashing lights, stress, or noncompliance with medication. Most seizures are self-limiting and spontaneously resolve within two to three minutes. However, some seizures can be prolonged or repetitive, constituting a medical emergency that warrants a call for an ambulance.[94]

Research indicates that students who suffer from primary generalized seizures are at higher risk for academic failure, specifically in the areas of reading and math. Furthermore, the longer the duration of the seizure activity (in number of years), the greater is the probability of the student having academic difficulties.[95]

Teacher Tips

▶ Students who present with a prolonged or repetitive primary generalized seizure involving convulsions and tonic-clonic jerking are having a medical emergency.[96] Precisely follow your student's ECP in this situation! See exhibit 18.3 for important first-aid suggestions.

Exhibit 18.3   First Aid for Seizures[97]

When a student is having a convulsive (generalized tonic-clonic) seizure, the following should be done:

1. Remove objects that may cause injury if hit during a seizure. Cushion head, remove glasses, loosen tight clothing.
2. Turn the student on his or her side (recovery position) and keep the airway clear.
3. Do not put anything in the student's mouth. (The student is unable to swallow his or her tongue. The recovery position will use gravity to keep the tongue from occluding the airway and prevent aspiration of saliva.)
4. Do not restrain the student during a seizure. This may cause more injury to extremities and is not necessary.
5. If the student has a VNS implant, use the VNS magnet as outlined in the ECP.
6. Observe the duration and characteristics of the seizure.
7. If the seizure does not stop within five minutes, administer rescue medication (Diastat), if ordered, as outlined in the ECP.
8. Initiate emergency medical services (EMS) according to the ECP.
9. If this is the student's first seizure, notify EMS.
10. Notify the student's parent as outlined in the ECP.

From Kiel, S., & Barclay, B. (2005) Seizures. In C. K. Silkworth, M. J. Arnold, J. F. Harrigan, & D. S. Zaiger (Eds.), *Individualized healthcare plans for the school nurse* (p. 828). North Branch, MN: Sunrise River Press. Reprinted with permission.

▶ If your student with epilepsy presents with a nonconvulsive partial seizure, keep the student in a safe environment (do not restrict the student's movement unless he or she is in danger), observe the duration and characteristics of the seizure, and if your student has one, use the VNS magnet as directed—see his or her ECP.[98]

▶ Make sure the school nurse trains you or a teacher assistant to administer AED medication on days when the school nurse is not at school to ensure employee competency. *When administering the medication, use only water to do this. Fruit juice can interact with the medicine.*[99]

▶ You may need to review academic material for students who tend to experience absence, simple partial, or complex partial seizures that cause them to momentarily miss out on part of a lesson. Closely monitor the comprehension of these students during instruction.

▶ Because research evidence exists purporting that students who experience primary generalized seizures are at higher risk for academic failure, stay cognizant of their educational progress, providing the necessary supports and making a referral to the school assistance team as needed.

▶ Students with epilepsy may find it hard to handle the pressure of their condition, developing a negative self-image (partially due to having little control over their seizures) as well as anxiety and depression.[100] Access the services of the school counselor as needed.

► If your student with seizures takes AED medication, bring this with you on field trips along with a copy of his or her IHP and ECP. If your student has a VNS implant, be sure he or she brings the accompanying VNS magnet device on field trips.

Gastrointestinal Disorders

The human gastrointestinal tract is divided into two sections: the upper gastrointestinal tract (including the mouth, esophagus, and stomach) and the lower gastrointestinal tract (including the small intestine, large intestine, and anus). Gastrointestinal problems can occur with or without associated developmental disabilities[101] and may result in school absenteeism at times.[102] There are a number of gastrointestinal disorders.

Eosinophils are a type of white blood cell. *Eosinophil-associated gastrointestinal disorders* (EGID) are defined by eosinophil-rich inflammation in the esophagus, stomach, small intestine, large intestine, or multiple intestinal segments. Sometimes EGID can manifest in severe symptoms such as vomiting, abdominal pain, diarrhea, difficulty swallowing, failure to thrive, and weight loss. Children and adolescents with EGID are often confronted with food hypersensitivity, sometimes resulting in the need of a feeding tube.[103]

Gastroesophageal reflux disease (GERD) is a chronic condition of the upper gastrointestinal tract resulting from a backward flow of gastric contents into the esophagus. Students with GERD typically experience chronic heartburn or acid indigestion. Another common symptom of this condition is difficulty swallowing.[104]

Inflammatory bowel disease (IBD) is a term used to describe the two most common chronic conditions of the lower gastroesophageal tract: ulcerative colitis and Crohn's disease. The exact cause of IBD is not known but research has proven that the immune system within the intestinal wall does not function properly in IBD.[105] Crohn's disease may be found in any part of the gastrointestinal tract but is usually located in the lower part of the small intestine and beginning of the large intestine. Intestinal obstruction is the most common complication of Crohn's disease. Ulcerative colitis manifests only in the innermost lining of the colon, resulting in inflammation and ulceration. Students with IBD can present with one or more of the following symptoms: abdominal pain, diarrhea, fever, fatigue, blood in the stool, weight loss, growth failure, and delayed puberty.[106]

Functional gastrointestinal disorders occur in the absence of underlying structural abnormalities and constitute the most common of all gastrointestinal conditions. Symptoms are nonspecific and can mimic those of organic disease such as IBD. Common symptoms include abdominal pain, diarrhea, constipation, and bloating.[107]

TEACHER TIPS

► Familiarize yourself with the IHP of your student with a gastrointestinal disorder so that you are aware of any noted dietary restrictions, physical restrictions, medications, or medical procedures (such as a feeding tube) your student may be confronted with.[108]

► In light of disease symptoms, allow your student with a gastrointestinal disorder immediate access to the school restroom or private bathroom (such as in the school nurse's office) as needed.[109]

► Be aware that your student with a gastrointestinal disorder may become fatigued at school. Alternate periods of activity with rest as needed.[110]

- ▶ Faced with the challenges of his or her condition, your student with a gastrointestinal disorder may be at increased risk for mood or behavioral difficulties.[111] Consultation with the school nurse and school counselor may be beneficial.[112]

- ▶ Keep in mind that your student with a gastrointestinal disorder may need to be absent from school due to his or her condition. Provide extra instruction and make academic adjustments to maintain the educational progress of your student.

HIV and AIDS

HIV stands for human immunodeficiency virus and AIDS stands for acquired immune deficiency syndrome.[113] HIV is not transmitted through daily casual contact but through unprotected sexual contact with individuals who have the disease, sharing needles with infected persons, or coming in contact with infected blood from mucous membranes or broken skin. The virus can also be passed from an infected mother to her child prenatally during labor and delivery or through breastfeeding.[114] The distinction between HIV and AIDS is a "marking in the progression of the disease."[115] AIDS is caused by the presence of HIV at the point of severe immunodeficiency. Confidentiality is an issue with HIV or AIDS because the disease involved can be viewed as stigmatizing; hence, parents may choose but are not required to share the HIV or AIDS status of their child with only certain school personnel. Infected students may need to take antiretroviral medications during school.[116]

TEACHER TIPS

- ▶ Universal precautions should be used when dealing with blood or bodily fluids from any student or staff member in school because the HIV or AIDS status of individuals may be unknown due to confidentiality. These precautions include wearing gloves when dealing with a bleeding injury and never sharing items such as toothbrushes because they have been in contact with bodily fluids.[117]

- ▶ Be aware of your student's medication schedule because missed dosages can lead to viral resistance.[118]

- ▶ Because infected students can become seriously fatigued, consider providing planned breaks and rest opportunities or restrictions on physical activities as needed.[119]

- ▶ Notify the parents of your student with HIV or AIDS if he or she should come into contact with anyone at school with an infectious disease such as influenza, pneumonia, or chickenpox.[120]

- ▶ Affected students may benefit from counseling.[121]

Sickle Cell Disease

Sickle cell disease is an inherited, chronic blood disorder that particularly affects African Americans in this country, causing inadequate oxygen delivery to various organs including the brain. Possible medical complications include episodes of pain and fatigue, bone damage, leg ulcers, infections, gallstones, blockages in the lungs, spleen, or liver, anemia, eye and kidney damage, jaundice, delayed growth, and silent strokes (strokes with no observable neurological signs but evidence of brain injury as indicated by brain lesions) or overt strokes.[122] Secondary hypertension can be another consequence of sickle cell disease. Careful monitoring and coordination of care are required for individuals with sickle cell disease because the symptoms can range from mild to life threatening.[123]

Research indicates that children with sickle cell disease who are considered to be high risk based on disease subtype tend to struggle with language deficits in terms of semantic, syntactic, and phonological processing. These deficits may have important implications for academic readiness, academic achievement, and school performance.[124]

Treatment of sickle cell disease varies. Some medications are being used with certain individuals to allay the effects of sickle cell disease.[125] Frequent blood transfusions have been documented to reduce stroke risk but such transfusions carry risks as well.[126] Additionally, bone marrow transplants have been reported to cure some persons of their sickle cell disease.[127]

TEACHER TIPS

▶ Warning signs that your student with sickle cell disease may need to immediately see his or her physician or be taken to the emergency room include a fever of 101 degrees or above, sudden change in vision, weakness or loss of feeling, shortness of breath, wheezing, coughing, swelling in the hands, joints, or feet, and pain in various parts of the body.[128] Precisely follow your student's ECP in this situation!

▶ On days your school nurse is not present, you or a teacher assistant may need to administer medication for intermittent episodes of pain.[129] Precisely follow instructions outlined in your student's IHP regarding pain medication.

▶ With help from the school nurse and school counselor, you may wish to consider teaching your student with sickle cell disease to use coping strategies during pain episodes. Students trained to use coping strategies such as relaxation with deep breathing, calming self-talk, and pleasant imagery not only lessen their pain response but are also more likely to be proactive in their own care.[130]

▶ Pace activities for your student with sickle cell disease and provide pleasant activities during pain episodes.[131]

▶ Allow your student to keep a water bottle with him or her and provide free access to the restroom as needed as adequate fluid is essential for students with sickle cell disease.[132]

▶ Because fatigue is associated with sickle cell disease, provide breaks for your student during the school day when he or she is tired and monitor his or her activity to prevent overexertion.[133]

▶ Help your student with sickle cell disease avoid very hot or very cold temperatures.[134]

▶ Consult with your school speech-language therapist if your student with sickle cell disease should exhibit language problems because he or she may benefit from speech-language therapy if found eligible for such services.

▶ Be sensitive to the fact that your student with sickle cell disease may have absences from school due to severe pain crises that require him or her to stay home or be hospitalized. Provide academic assistance and assignment modifications as needed.[135]

▶ If your student with sickle cell disease takes medication, bring it along on field trips as well as a copy of his or her IHP and ECP.

TOURETTE SYNDROME (TS)

According to the American Psychiatric Association, students with Tourette syndrome (TS) have a neurobiological disorder characterized by a wide range of involuntary motor and vocal movements and sounds known as *tics,* which usually begin to be observable around the age of six or seven. Tics may come and go or change in nature over time.[136] Table 18.3 describes the types of tics exhibited by students with TS. As a teacher, it is important that you are able to discern behaviors that are attributable to TS.

Table 18.3 Types of Tics[137]

Simple motor	Eye blinking, grimacing, neck jerking, shoulder jerking, tongue and mouth movements
Complex motor	Jumping, squatting, stamping the foot, thrusting out an arm, hitting or biting self, ritualistic movements (smelling an object, touching own or another's body, obsessive or compulsive patterns of behavior), grooming behaviors
Simple vocal	Throat clearing, sniffing, grunting, coughing, snorting, lip noises
Complex vocal	Echolalia (repeating last-heard sound, word, or phrase of another), palilalia (repeating own sounds or words), coprolalia (use of socially unacceptable sounds or words, often obscene), shouting words out of context

From Wong, D. L., et al., *Wong's nursing care of infants and children* (7th ed.). St. Louis: Elsevier Ltd. (2003). Reprinted with permission.

The cause of TS is unknown but there is mounting evidence that it is a genetic disorder. A medical diagnosis of this condition can be obtained only if prior to eighteen years of age and the following occurs: (1) multiple motor and one or more vocal tics have been documented as present, (2) the tics occur many times a day nearly every day or intermittently throughout a period of more than one year, and during this time, there was never a tic-free period of more than three consecutive months, (3) the tics cause marked distress or significant impairment in social, occupational, or other important areas of functioning, and (4) the tics are not due to a medication or some other medical condition. Treatments such as counseling, cognitive behavioral therapy, and psychotherapy are usually tried first to provide patient relief because available medications have various side effects.[138]

TS is four times more likely to occur in boys than girls, according to the American Psychiatric Association. Other conditions such as obsessive-compulsive disorder, ADHD, learning disabilities, behavioral problems, and sleep disorders may accompany TS.[139]

TEACHER TIPS

▶ Remember that tics are not purposeful behaviors. Keep in close contact with the parents of your student with TS so you are aware of new tics that may have emerged at home and could soon become evident at school.[140]

▶ Provide a private area outside of the classroom (such as the nurse's office) for your student with TS to express or release tics as needed (which can come in bouts). Have your student give you an agreed-on nonverbal cue to signal the need to go to this private area. Consider preferential seating (desk near door of classroom) so that your student can leave class as inconspicuously as possible.[141]

▶ Break down assignments into smaller sections for your student with TS and allow additional time for completion of tasks as needed.[142]

▶ Provide the modification of one-on-one testing in a separate room as needed because of vocal tics.[143]

▶ If your student with TS wishes, allow him or her to videotape required oral presentations at home to show later in class in lieu of having to stand up before classmates to speak.[144]

▶ Access the services of the school counselor for your student with TS as needed to address coping strategies, self-esteem issues, and self-advocacy strategies.[145]

▶ If your student with TS and his or her parents agree, strive to educate classmates and other school staff about TS to promote understanding of this particular health condition.[146]

► If your student with TS takes medication during the school day, be aware of the medication schedule on your student's IHP because you or a teacher assistant may be responsible for administering this medication if your school nurse is not present in your school each day.

TO SUM UP

► You are not alone in your effort to help manage the health needs of your students. The school nurse, school counselor, other teachers, teacher assistants, school therapist(s), school administrators, family physician(s), and parents are all part of the team to ensure the best possible school experience for your students with health needs.

► Make sure that you and others who work with the students understand the IHP and all emergency procedures outlined in the ECP.

► Take time to discuss the student's health needs with parents and the school nurse and be sure to ask questions if you have any concerns.

► Finally, remember that your students with health needs are not defined by their conditions. First and foremost, they long to be viewed simply as kids similar to their peers despite the health challenges they find themselves dealing with on a daily basis.

ADDITIONAL RESOURCES

► The primary source for this chapter is the following extensive handbook for school nurses: Silkworth, C., Arnold, M., Harrigan, J., & Zaiger, D. (Eds.) (2005). *Individualized healthcare plans for the school nurse.* North Branch, MN: Sunrise River Press.

► Here are some useful websites pertaining to the health conditions described in this chapter:
  - ADHD: www.adhd.com
  - Allergies: www.webmd.com/allergies/default.htm
  - Asthma: www.mayoclinic.com/health/childhood-asthma/DS00849
  - Cancer: www.cancer.gov/cancertopics/types/childhoodcancers
  - Cardiovascular disorders: www.chw.org/display/PPF/DocID/23020/router.asp
  - Cystic fibrosis: children.webmd.com/tc/cystic-fibrosis-topic-overview
  - Diabetes mellitus: www.diabetes.org
  - Dysfunctional elimination syndrome: www.webmd.com/mental-health/elimination-disorders-encopresis
  - Epilepsy and seizures: www.epilepsyfoundation.org
  - Gastrointestinal disorders: http://my.clevelandclinic.org/disorders/gastrointestinal_tract_disorders/hic_gastrointestinal_disorders.aspx
  - HIV and AIDS: kidshealth.org (search for HIV and AIDS)
  - Sickle cell disease: www.sicklecelldisease.org
  - Tourette syndrome: www.tsa-usa.org

PART FIVE

APPENDIXES

APPENDIX A

Definitions and Resources about Disability

From the National Dissemination Center for Children with Disabilities, nichcy.org (adapted with permission)

This appendix offers detailed information on the following disability categories:

- ▶ Attention deficit hyperactivity disorder (ADHD)[1]
- ▶ Autism spectrum disorders[2]
- ▶ Deafness and hearing loss[3]
- ▶ Developmental delay[4]
- ▶ Emotional disturbance[5]
- ▶ Intellectual disability[6]
- ▶ Other health impairment
- ▶ Specific learning disability[7]
- ▶ Speech and language disorders[8]
- ▶ Traumatic brain injury[9]
- ▶ Visual impairment including blindness[10]

The definitions provided at the beginning of each section largely come from IDEA.

ATTENTION DEFICIT HYPERACTIVITY DISORDER (ADHD)

Attention deficit hyperactivity disorder (ADHD) is one of the most common neurobehavioral disorders of childhood. It is sometimes referred to as attention deficit disorder (ADD). It is usually first diagnosed in childhood and often lasts into adulthood. Children with ADHD have trouble paying attention, controlling impulsive behaviors (may act without thinking about what the result will be), and, in some cases, are overly active.

What Are the Characteristics of ADHD?

It is normal for children to have trouble focusing and behaving at one time or another. However, children with ADHD do not just grow out of these behaviors. The symptoms continue and can cause difficulty at school, at home, or with friends.

A child with ADHD might exhibit the following characteristics:

▶ Have a hard time paying attention

▶ Daydream a lot

▶ Not seem to listen

▶ Be easily distracted from schoolwork or play

▶ Forget things

▶ Be in constant motion or unable to stay seated

▶ Squirm or fidget

▶ Talk too much

▶ Not be able to play quietly

▶ Act and speak without thinking

▶ Have trouble taking turns

▶ Interrupt others

What Are the *DSM-IV* Criteria and Symptoms for ADHD?

Either A or B:

▶ A. Six or more of the following symptoms of inattention have been present for at least six months to a point that is inappropriate for developmental level:

Inattention

- Often does not give close attention to details or makes careless mistakes in schoolwork, work, or other activities

- Often has trouble keeping attention on tasks or play activities

- Often does not seem to listen when spoken to directly

- Often does not follow through on instructions and fails to finish schoolwork, chores, or duties in the workplace (not due to oppositional behavior or failure to understand instructions)

- Often has trouble organizing activities

- Often avoids, dislikes, or doesn't want to do things that take a lot of mental effort for a long period of time (such as schoolwork or homework)

- Often loses things needed for tasks and activities (e.g., toys, school assignments, pencils, books, or tools)

- Is often easily distracted

- Is often forgetful in daily activities

▶ B. Six or more of the following symptoms of hyperactivity or impulsivity have been present for at least six months to an extent that is disruptive and inappropriate for developmental level:

HYPERACTIVITY

- Often fidgets with hands or feet or squirms in seat when sitting still is expected
- Often gets up from seat when remaining in seat is expected
- Often excessively runs about or climbs when and where it is not appropriate (adolescents or adults may feel very restless)
- Often has trouble playing or doing leisure activities quietly
- Is often on the go or often acts as if driven by a motor
- Often talks excessively

IMPULSIVITY

- Often blurts out answers before questions have been finished
- Often has trouble waiting one's turn
- Often interrupts or intrudes on others (e.g., butts into conversations or games)

▶ Some symptoms that cause impairment were present before age seven.

▶ Some impairment from the symptoms is present in two or more settings (e.g., at school, work, and at home).

▶ There must be clear evidence of clinically significant impairment in social, school, or work functioning.

▶ The symptoms do not happen only during the course of a pervasive developmental disorder, schizophrenia, or other psychotic disorder. The symptoms are not better accounted for by another mental disorder (e.g., mood disorder, anxiety disorder, dissociative disorder, or a personality disorder).

What Are the Subtypes of ADHD?

There are three different types of ADHD, depending on which symptoms are strongest in the individual:

▶ *Predominantly inattentive type:* It is hard for the individual to organize or finish a task, pay attention to details, or follow instructions or conversations. The person is easily distracted or forgets details of daily routines.

▶ *Predominantly hyperactive-impulsive type:* The person fidgets and talks a lot. It is hard to sit still for long (e.g., for a meal or while doing homework). Smaller children may run, jump, or climb constantly. The individual feels restless and has trouble with impulsivity. Someone who is impulsive may interrupt others a lot, grab things from people, or speak at inappropriate times. It is hard for the person to wait his or her turn or listen to directions. A person with impulsiveness may have more accidents and injuries than others.

▶ *Combined type:* Symptoms of these two types are equally present in the person.

Note: The term *ADD* is typically not used anymore. Those who might be diagnosed with ADD would now most likely be said to have *ADHD predominantly inattentive type* in today's terms.

Tips for Teachers

Just like parents, it is important for teachers to have the needed skills to help children manage their ADHD. However, because the majority of children with ADHD are not enrolled in special education classes, their teachers will most likely be regular education teachers who might know very little about ADHD and could benefit from assistance and guidance. Here are some tips to share with teachers for classroom success:

- ▶ Use a homework folder for parent–teacher communications.
- ▶ Make assignments clear.
- ▶ Give positive reinforcement.
- ▶ Be sensitive to self-esteem issues.
- ▶ Involve the school counselor or psychologist.

ORGANIZATIONS AND RESOURCES

ADD/ADHD and School: http://helpguide.org/mental/adhd_add_teaching_strategies.htm

ADD/ADHD in School: *ADHD in school: Classroom interventions for ADHD:* www.addinschool.com

Attention Deficit Disorder Association: info@add.org; www.add.org

Children and Adults with Attention Deficit/Hyperactivity Disorder (CHADD): www.chadd.org

Mayo Clinic: *Attention-deficit/hyperactivity disorder (ADHD) in children:* www.mayoclinic.com/health/adhd/DS00275

National Alliance on Mental Illness (NAMI): www.nami.org/Template.cfm?Section=By_Illness&Template=/TaggedPage/TaggedPageDisplay.cfm&TPLID=54&ContentID=23047

National Institute of Mental Health (NIMH): *Attention deficit hyperactivity disorder (ADHD):* www.nimh.nih.gov/health/topics/attention-deficit-hyperactivity-disorder-adhd/index.shtml

National Resource Center on ADHD: www.help4adhd.org

Network of Care for Behavioral Health: *All about ADHD in ASL:* http://chemung.ny.networkofcare.org/mh/nimh/video/signlanguage/2.cfm

AUTISM SPECTRUM DISORDERS

Autism means a developmental disability significantly affecting verbal and nonverbal communication and social interaction, generally evident before age three, which adversely affects a child's educational performance. Other characteristics often associated with autism are engaging in repetitive activities and stereotyped movements, resistance to environmental change or change in daily routines, and unusual responses to sensory experiences. The term *autism* does not apply if the child's educational performance is adversely affected primarily because the child has an emotional disturbance.

What Are the Characteristics of Autism Spectrum Disorders?

Each of the disorders on the autism spectrum is a neurological disorder that affects a child's ability to communicate, understand language, play, and relate to others. They share some or all of the following characteristics, which can vary from mild to severe:

► Communication problems (for example, with the use or comprehension of language)

► Difficulty relating to people, things, and events

► Playing with toys and objects in unusual ways

► Difficulty adjusting to changes in routine or to familiar surroundings

► Repetitive body movements or behaviors

Children with autism or one of the other disorders on the autism spectrum can differ considerably with respect to their abilities, intelligence, and behavior. Some children don't talk at all. Others use language in which phrases or conversations are repeated. Children with the most advanced language skills tend to talk about a limited range of topics and have a hard time understanding abstract concepts. Repetitive play and limited social skills are also evident. Other common symptoms of a disorder on the autism spectrum can include unusual and sometimes uncontrolled reactions to sensory information—for instance, to loud noises, bright lights, and certain textures of food or fabrics.

What Are the Specific Disorders on the Autism Spectrum?

There are five disorders classified under the umbrella category officially known as *pervasive developmental disorders,* or *PDD:*

► Autism

► Asperger syndrome

► Rett syndrome

► Childhood disintegrative disorder

► Pervasive developmental disorder not otherwise specified (often referred to as *PDDNOS*)

Although there are subtle differences and degrees of severity among these five conditions, the treatment and educational needs of a child with any of these disorders will be very similar. For that reason, the term *autism spectrum disorders*—or *ASDs,* as they are sometimes called—is used quite often now and is actually expected to become the official term to be used in the future.

The five conditions are defined in the *Diagnostic and Statistical Manual, Fourth Edition, Text Revision (DSM-IV-TR)* of the American Psychiatric Society (2000). This is also the manual used to diagnose autism and its associated disorders as well as a wide variety of other disabilities.

According to the 2000 edition of the *DSM-IV,* a diagnosis of autistic disorder (or *classic* autism) is made when a child displays six or more of twelve symptoms across three major areas:

► Social interaction (such as the inability to establish or maintain relationships with peers appropriate to the level of the child's development)

► Communication (such as the absence of language or delays in its development)

► Behavior (such as repetitive preoccupation with one or more areas of interest in a way that is abnormal in its intensity or focus)

When children display similar behaviors but do not meet the specific criteria for autistic disorder, they may be diagnosed as having one of the other disorders on the spectrum—Asperger's, Rett, childhood disintegrative disorder, or PDDNOS. PDDNOS is the least-specific diagnosis and typically means that a child has displayed the least specific of autistic-like symptoms or behaviors and has not met the criteria for any of the other disorders.

Terminology used with ASDs can be a bit confusing, especially the use of PDD and PDDNOS to refer to two different things that are similar and intertwined. Still, it's important to remember that, regardless of the specific diagnosis, treatments will be similar.

Tips for Teachers

▶ Learn more about the autism spectrum. Check out the research on effective instructional intervention and behavior on NICHCY's website (http://nichcy.org). The organizations listed at the bottom of this page can also help.

▶ Make sure directions are given step by step, verbally, visually, and by providing physical supports or prompts as needed by the student. Students with ASDs often have trouble interpreting facial expressions, body language, and tone of voice. Be as concrete and explicit as possible in your instructions and feedback to the student.

▶ Find out what the student's strengths and interests are and emphasize them. Tap into those avenues and create opportunities for success. Give positive feedback and lots of opportunities for practice.

▶ Build opportunities for the student to have social and collaborative interactions throughout the regular school day. Provide support, structure, and lots of feedback.

▶ If behavior is a significant issue for the student, seek help from expert professionals (including parents) to understand the meanings of the behaviors and to develop a unified, positive approach to resolving them.

▶ Have consistent routines and schedules. When you know a change in routine will occur (e.g., a field trip or assembly) prepare the student by telling him or her what is going to be different and what to expect or do.

▶ Work together with the student's parents and other school personnel to create and implement an educational plan tailored to meet the student's needs. Regularly share information about how the student is doing at school and at home.

ORGANIZATIONS AND RESOURCES

Autism Society of America: www.autism-society.org

Autism Speaks: www.autismspeaks.org

CDC (Centers for Disease Control and Prevention): Information in English and Spanish: www.cdc.gov/ncbddd/autism/index.html

Exploring Autism: Information in English and Spanish: www.exploringautism.org

First Signs: www.firstsigns.org

Global Autism Collaboration: www.autism.org

Interactive Autism Network: www.ianproject.org

National Autism Center: www.nationalautismcenter.org/index.php

OAR (Organization for Autism Research): www.researchautism.org

OASIS @ MAAP (Online Asperger Syndrome Information and Support [OASIS] and MAAP Services for Autism and Asperger Syndrome): www.aspergersyndrome.org

DEAFNESS AND HEARING LOSS

It's helpful to know that, although the terms *hearing impairment* and *hearing loss* are often used to describe a wide range of hearing losses, including deafness, IDEA actually defines the two terms separately. Hearing impairment is defined by IDEA as "an impairment in hearing, whether permanent or fluctuating, that adversely affects a child's educational performance." Deafness is defined as "a hearing impairment that is so severe that the child is impaired in processing linguistic information through hearing, with or without amplification."

Thus, deafness is viewed as a condition that prevents an individual from receiving sound in all or most of its forms. In contrast, a child with a hearing loss can generally respond to auditory stimuli, including speech.

What Are the Types of Hearing Loss?

Before we describe the types of hearing loss a person may have, it's useful to know that sound is measured by its loudness or intensity (measured in units called *decibels, dB*) and its frequency or pitch (measured in units called *hertz, Hz*).

Hearing loss is generally described as slight, mild, moderate, severe, or profound, depending on how well a person can hear the intensities or frequencies most strongly associated with speech. Impairments in hearing can occur in either or both areas and may exist in only one ear or in both ears. Generally, only children whose hearing loss is greater than 90 dB are considered deaf.

There are four types of hearing loss (http://ehealthmd.com/content/different-types-hearing-loss):

▶ *Conductive hearing losses* are caused by diseases or obstructions in the outer or middle ear (the pathways for sound to reach the inner ear). Conductive hearing losses usually affect all frequencies of hearing evenly and do not result in severe losses. A person with a conductive hearing loss usually is able to use a hearing aid well or can be helped medically or surgically.

▶ *Sensorineural hearing losses* result from damage to the delicate sensory hair cells of the inner ear or the nerves that supply it. These hearing losses can range from mild to profound. They often affect the person's ability to hear certain frequencies more than others. Thus, even with amplification to increase the sound level, a person with a sensorineural hearing loss may perceive distorted sounds, sometimes making the successful use of a hearing aid impossible.

▶ *A mixed hearing loss* refers to a combination of conductive and sensorineural loss and means that a problem occurs in the outer or middle and the inner ear.

▶ *A central hearing loss* results from damage or impairment to the nerves or nuclei of the central nervous system, either in the pathways to the brain or in the brain itself.

Tips for Teachers

Hearing loss or deafness does not affect a person's intellectual capacity or ability to learn. However, children who are hard of hearing or deaf generally require some form of special education services in order to receive an adequate education. Such services may include the following:

▶ Regular speech, language, and auditory training from a specialist
▶ Amplification systems
▶ Services of an interpreter for those students who use sign language

- ▶ Favorable seating in the class to facilitate lip reading
- ▶ Captioned films and videos
- ▶ Assistance of someone who takes notes for the student with a hearing loss so that the student can fully attend to instruction
- ▶ Instruction for the teacher and peers in alternate communication methods, such as sign language counseling

Children who are hard of hearing will find it much more difficult than children who have normal hearing to learn vocabulary, grammar, word order, idiomatic expressions, and other aspects of verbal communication. For children who are deaf or have severe hearing losses, early, consistent, and conscious use of visible communication modes (such as sign language, finger spelling, and cued speech), amplification, and aural or oral training can help reduce language delay.

By age four or five, most children who are deaf are enrolled in school on a full-day basis and do special work on communication and language development. Parents work with school personnel to develop an IEP that details the child's special needs and the services and supports that will be provided to meet those needs. IDEA requires that the IEP team address the communication needs of a child who is deaf or hard of hearing.

It is important for teachers and audiologists to work together to teach the child to use his or her residual hearing to the maximum extent possible, even if the preferred means of communication is manual. Because the great majority of deaf children (over 90 percent) are born to hearing parents, programs should provide instruction for parents on implications of deafness within the family.

People with hearing loss use oral or manual means of communication or a combination of the two. Oral communication includes speech, lip reading, and the use of residual hearing. Manual communication involves signs and finger spelling. Total communication, as a method of instruction, is a combination of the oral method plus signing and finger spelling.

ORGANIZATIONS AND RESOURCES

Alexander Graham Bell Association for the Deaf and Hard of Hearing: www.agbell.org

American Hearing Research Foundation: www.american-hearing.org

American Society for Deaf Children: www.deafchildren.org

ASHA (American Speech-Language-Hearing Association): www.asha.org

Beginnings (For parents of children who are deaf or hard of hearing): www.ncbegin.org/index.php

Better Hearing Institute: www.betterhearing.org

CDC (Centers for Disease Control and Prevention): *Hearing loss in children:* www.cdc.gov/ncbddd/dd/ddhi.htm

Deaf Culture Online: www.deaf-culture-online.com/index.html

Hands and Voices: www.handsandvoices.org

Hearing Loss Association of America: www.hearingloss.org

How's Your Hearing? Ask an Audiologist: www.howsyourhearing.com

Laurent Clerc National Deaf Education Center: *Info to go:* http://clerccenter.gallaudet.edu/Clerc_Center/Information_and_Resources/Info_To_Go.html

Listen Up!: www.listen-up.org

Medline Plus: *Hearing disorders and deafness:* www.nlm.nih.gov/medlineplus/hearingdisordersanddeafness.html

National Association of the Deaf: www.nad.org

National Center for Hearing Assessment and Management: www.infanthearing.org

NICHCY (National Dissemination Center for Children with Disabilities): Communication needs as one of IDEA's special factors: www.nichcy.org/schoolage/iep/meetings/special-factors#deaf; checklist for IEP teams: www.nichcy.org/schoolage/iep/meetings/special-factors/considering-hearingloss

NIDCD (National Institute on Deafness and Other Communication Disorders): www.nidcd.nih.gov/health/hearing

Pepnet2: Regional postsecondary education centers to increase access to postsecondary education for persons who are deaf: www.pepnet.org

DEVELOPMENTAL DELAY

For children from birth to age three (under IDEA Part C) and children from ages three through nine (under IDEA Part B), the term *developmental delay,* as defined by each state, means a delay in one or more of the following areas: physical development, cognitive development, communication, social or emotional development, or adaptive (behavioral) development. Through IDEA, early intervention services and special education services are made available to our nation's children.

It's a good idea to find out if your state has added details to this definition of developmental delay. States are allowed to do so, if they choose. They also decide on the age range of children with whom the term may be used (three through five, three through nine, or any subset between three and nine). Your local school or early intervention program should be able to tell you the definition of developmental delay that's used in your area. You can also visit NECTAC (www.nectac.org/~pdfs/pubs/nnotes21.pdf) to find out how your state defines developmental delay as well as the criteria of eligibility for services to young children, birth through two years of age, and their families.

Under IDEA, your state may not require that your local school district also adopt and use the term *developmental delay* in working with children. If your local school district decides to use the term, it must use the same definition and age range as the state does. Your local school district may not use the term at all if your state has chosen not to use the term.

Types of Developmental Delays and the Developmental Evaluation

The developmental evaluation should be conducted by a highly trained professional who can use the results to create a profile of your child's strengths and weaknesses. The evaluation needs to look at five developmental areas:

▶ Physical development (fine motor skills, gross motor skills)

▶ Cognitive development (intellectual abilities)

▶ Communication development (speech and language)

▶ Social or emotional development (social skills, emotional control)

▶ Adaptive development (self-care skills)

The results of the developmental evaluation will be used to decide if your child needs early intervention services and a treatment plan. Early intervention services are tailored to meet a child's individual needs and, as such, are a very important resource to children experiencing developmental delays. Early intervention services can include the following:

▶ Assistive technology (devices a child might need)
▶ Audiology or hearing services
▶ Speech and language services
▶ Counseling and training for a family
▶ Medical services
▶ Nursing services
▶ Nutrition services
▶ Occupational therapy
▶ Physical therapy
▶ Psychological services

ORGANIZATIONS AND RESOURCES

CDC: *Child development:* www.cdc.gov/ncbddd/child

CDC: *Developmental monitoring and screening:* www.cdc.gov/NCBDDD/childdevelopment/screening.html

Encyclopedia of Children's Health: *Developmental delay:* www.healthofchildren.com/D/Developmental-Delay.html

First Signs: All about early detection of developmental delays and disabilities, especially autism: www.firstsigns.org

How Kids Develop: *What is developmental delay and what services are available if I think my child might be delayed?:* www.howkidsdevelop.com/developDevDelay.html

IDEA: State eligibility definitions for infants and toddlers with disabilities: www.nectac.org/pdfs/pubs/nnotes21.pdf

Keep Kids Healthy: *Developmental delays:* www.keepkidshealthy.com/welcome/conditions/developmentaldelays.html

NICHCY: Connect with the disability community and parent expertise: www.nichy.org

NICHCY: *Developmental milestones:* www.nichcy.org/disability/milestones

Parent to Parent USA: Interested in talking to other parents whose children have developmental delays? P2P USA will connect you with other parents for support and exchange: www.p2pusa.org

Every state has a parent training and information center, known as the PTI. Some states have several. If you are looking to connect with state and local resources or have questions about services and parent rights, talk to your PTI. Find the PTI for your state by visiting http://nichcy.org/state-organization-search-by-state. One of the "quick select" choices includes "parent training centers." Click that option, then your state. The PTI will be listed in your results.

EMOTIONAL DISTURBANCE

Emotional disturbance means a condition exhibiting one or more of the following characteristics over a long period of time and to a marked degree that adversely affects a child's educational performance:

- ▶ An inability to learn that cannot be explained by intellectual, sensory, or health factors
- ▶ An inability to build or maintain satisfactory interpersonal relationships with peers and teachers
- ▶ Inappropriate types of behavior or feelings under normal circumstances
- ▶ A general pervasive mood of unhappiness or depression
- ▶ A tendency to develop physical symptoms or fears associated with personal or school problems

The term includes schizophrenia. The term does not apply to children who are socially maladjusted, unless it is determined that they have an emotional disturbance.

What Are the Characteristics of Emotional Disturbance?

As is evident in IDEA's definition, emotional disturbances can affect an individual in areas beyond the emotional. Depending on the specific mental disorder involved, a person's physical, social, or cognitive skills may also be affected. The National Alliance on Mental Illness (NAMI) puts this very well:

> Mental illnesses are medical conditions that disrupt a person's thinking, feeling, mood, ability to relate to others, and daily functioning. Just as diabetes is a disorder of the pancreas, mental illnesses are medical conditions that often result in a diminished capacity for coping with the ordinary demands of life.

Some of the characteristics and behaviors seen in children who have an emotional disturbance include:

- ▶ Hyperactivity (short attention span, impulsiveness)
- ▶ Aggression or self-injurious behavior (acting out, fighting)
- ▶ Withdrawal (not interacting socially with others, excessive fear or anxiety)
- ▶ Immaturity (inappropriate crying, temper tantrums, poor coping skills)
- ▶ Learning difficulties (academically performing below grade level)

Children with the most serious emotional disturbances may exhibit distorted thinking, excessive anxiety, bizarre motor acts, and abnormal mood swings. Many children who do not have emotional disturbance may display some of these same behaviors at various times during their development. However, when children have an emotional disturbance, these behaviors continue over long periods of time. Their behavior signals that they are not coping with their environment or peers.

What Are Some Specific Types of Emotional Disturbances?

As mentioned, *emotional disturbance* is a commonly used umbrella term for a number of different mental disorders. Let's take a brief look at some of the most common of these.

Anxiety Disorders

We all experience anxiety from time to time, but for many people, including children, anxiety can be excessive, persistent, seemingly uncontrollable, and overwhelming. An irrational fear of everyday situations may be involved. This high level of anxiety is a definite warning sign that a person may have an anxiety disorder.

As with the term emotional disturbance, *anxiety disorder* is an umbrella term that actually refers to several distinct disabilities that share the core characteristic of irrational fear: generalized anxiety disorder, obsessive-compulsive disorder (OCD), panic disorder, posttraumatic stress disorder, social anxiety disorder (also called *social phobia*), and specific phobias.

According to the Anxiety and Depression Association of America, anxiety disorders are the most common psychiatric illnesses affecting children and adults. They are also highly treatable. Unfortunately, only about one-third of those affected receive treatment.

Bipolar Disorder

Also known as manic-depressive illness, bipolar disorder is a serious medical condition that causes dramatic mood swings from overly high and irritable to sad and hopeless, and then back again, often with periods of normal mood in between. Severe changes in energy and behavior go along with these changes in mood.

For most people with bipolar disorder, these mood swings and related symptoms can be stabilized over time using an approach that combines medication and psychosocial treatment.

Conduct Disorder

Conduct disorder refers to a group of behavioral and emotional problems in youngsters. Children and adolescents with this disorder have great difficulty following rules and behaving in a socially acceptable way. This may include some of the following behaviors:

▶ Aggression to people and animals
▶ Destruction of property
▶ Deceitfulness, lying, or stealing
▶ Truancy or other serious violations of rules

Although conduct disorder is one of the most difficult behavior disorders to treat, young people often benefit from a range of services that include the following:

▶ Training for parents on how to handle child or adolescent behavior
▶ Family therapy
▶ Training in problem-solving skills for children or adolescents
▶ Community-based services that focus on the young person within the context of family and community influences

Eating Disorders

Eating disorders are characterized by extremes in eating behavior—either too much or too little—or feelings of extreme distress or concern about body weight or shape. Females are much more likely than males to develop an eating disorder.

Anorexia nervosa and *bulimia nervosa* are the two most common types of eating disorders. Anorexia nervosa is characterized by self-starvation and dramatic loss of weight. Bulimia nervosa involves a cycle of binge eating, then self-induced vomiting or purging. Both of these disorders are potentially life threatening.

Binge eating is also considered an eating disorder. It's characterized by eating excessive amounts of food while feeling unable to control how much or what is eaten. Unlike with bulimia, people who binge eat usually do not purge afterward by vomiting or using laxatives.

According to the National Eating Disorders Association, "the most effective and long-lasting treatment for an eating disorder is some form of psychotherapy or counseling, coupled with careful attention to medical and nutritional needs. Some medications have been shown to be helpful. Ideally, whatever treatment is offered should be tailored to the individual, and this will vary according to both the severity of the disorder and the patient's individual problems, needs, and strengths."[11]

Obsessive-Compulsive Disorder

Often referred to as OCD, obsessive-compulsive disorder is actually considered an anxiety disorder. OCD is characterized by recurrent, unwanted thoughts (obsessions) and repetitive behaviors (compulsions). Repetitive behaviors (hand washing, counting, checking, or cleaning) are often performed with the hope of preventing obsessive thoughts or making them go away. Performing these rituals, however, provides only temporary relief, and not performing them markedly increases anxiety.

A large body of scientific evidence suggests that OCD results from a chemical imbalance in the brain. Treatment for most people with OCD should include one or more of the following:

▶ Work with a therapist trained in behavior therapy
▶ Cognitive behavior therapy (CBT)
▶ Medication (usually an antidepressant)

Psychotic Disorders

Psychotic disorders is another umbrella term used to refer to severe mental disorders that cause abnormal thinking and perceptions. Two of the main symptoms are delusions and hallucinations. Delusions are false beliefs, such as thinking that someone is plotting against you. Hallucinations are false perceptions, such as hearing, seeing, or feeling something that is not there. Schizophrenia is one type of psychotic disorder. There are others as well.

Treatment for psychotic disorders will differ from person to person, depending on the specific disorder involved. Most are treated with a combination of medications and psychotherapy (a type of counseling).

Tips for Teachers

Typically, educational programs for children with an emotional disturbance need to include attention to providing emotional and behavioral support as well as helping them to master academics, develop social skills, and increase self-awareness, self-control, and self-esteem. A large body of research exists regarding methods of providing students with positive behavioral support in the school environment so that problem behaviors are minimized and positive, appropriate behaviors are fostered. It is also important to know that, within the school setting, the following should be considered:

▶ For a child whose behavior impedes learning (including the learning of others), the team developing the child's IEP needs to consider strategies to address that behavior, including positive behavioral interventions, strategies, and supports.

▶ Students eligible for special education services under the category of emotional disturbance may have IEPs that include psychological or counseling services. These are important related services available under IDEA and are to be provided by a qualified social worker, psychologist, guidance counselor, or other qualified personnel.

ORGANIZATIONS AND RESOURCES

AACAP (American Academy of Child and Adolescent Psychiatry): *Facts for families,* a series in English (www.aacap.org/cs/root/facts_for_families/facts_for_families_keyword_alphabetical) and Spanish (www.aacap.org/cs/root/facts_for_families/informacion_para_la_familia) that includes many briefs on specific mental disorders. AACAP also operates different resource centers, which offer consumer-friendly definitions, answers to frequently asked questions, clinical resources, expert videos, facts for families, and much more. Visit the resource center home page (www.aacap.org/cs/resource.centers) if you are concerned with one of the following:

- Anxiety disorders
- Autism
- Bipolar disorder
- Conduct disorder
- Depression
- Oppositional defiant disorder

American Psychological Association (APA): English: www.apa.org/index.aspx; Spanish: www.centro deapoyoapa.org

NAMI (National Alliance on Mental Illness): English: www.nami.org; Spanish: http://tinyurl .com/28rweba

NIMH (National Institute of Mental Health): English: www.nimh.nih.gov/health/index.shtml; Spanish: www.nimh.nih.gov/health/publications/espanol/index.shtml

SAMHSA (Substance Abuse and Mental Health Services Administration): http://mentalhealth .samhsa.gov; Substance abuse and mental health treatment referral line: www.samhsa.gov/treat ment/index.aspx

Detailed information on specific emotional disturbances or related issues such as positive behavior supports is also available from these sources:

Anxiety and Depression Association of America: www.adaa.org

Conduct Disorders: A soft place to land for battle-weary parents: www.conductdisorders.com

Encyclopedia of Mental Disorders: www.minddisorders.com/index.html

National Eating Disorders Association: www.nationaleatingdisorders.org

OSEP Technical Assistance Center on Positive Behavioral Interventions and Supports: The PBIS Center provides research-based information on how to provide behavioral supports to children who need them: www.pbis.org

Something Fishy (eating disorders): www.something-fishy.org

INTELLECTUAL DISABILITY

Intellectual disability refers to significantly subaverage general intellectual functioning that exists concurrently with deficits in adaptive behavior, is manifested during the developmental period, and adversely affects a child's educational performance. Until October 2010, IDEA used the term *mental retardation*. At that point, Rosa's Law was signed by President Obama. Rosa's Law changed the term to be used in future to *intellectual disability*. The definition of the term itself did not change.

What Are the Characteristics of an Intellectual Disability and How Is It Diagnosed?

Intellectual disability is a term used to describe when a person has certain limitations in mental functioning and in skills such as communicating, taking care of him- or herself, and social skills. These limitations cause these students to need more intensive supports and may cause a child to learn and develop more slowly than typical.

Children with intellectual disabilities (sometimes called *cognitive disabilities*) may take longer to learn to speak, walk, and take care of their personal needs such as dressing or eating. They are likely to have trouble learning complex concepts in school and may take longer to learn basic academic skills. Some students may need additional adaptations or modifications in order to learn specific content or concepts.

There are many signs of an intellectual disability:

- ▶ Sit up, crawl, or walk later than other children
- ▶ Learn to talk later or have trouble speaking
- ▶ Find it hard to remember things
- ▶ Not understand how to pay for things
- ▶ Have trouble understanding social rules
- ▶ Have trouble seeing the consequences of their actions
- ▶ Have trouble solving problems
- ▶ Have trouble thinking logically

Intellectual disabilities are diagnosed by looking at two main criteria:

- ▶ The ability of a person's brain to learn, think, solve problems, and make sense of the world (called *IQ* or *intellectual functioning*)
- ▶ Whether the person has the skills he or she needs to live independently (called *adaptive behavior* or *adaptive functioning*)

Intellectual functioning, or IQ, is usually measured by a test called an IQ test. The average score is 100. People scoring below 70 to 75 are thought to have an intellectual disability. To measure adaptive behavior, professionals look at what a child can do in comparison to other children of his or her age. Certain skills are important to adaptive behavior:

- ▶ Daily living skills, such as getting dressed, going to the bathroom, and feeding one's self
- ▶ Communication skills, such as understanding what is said and being able to answer
- ▶ Social skills with peers, family members, adults, and others

To diagnose an intellectual disability, professionals look at the person's IQ and his or her adaptive skills. Both of these are highlighted in the definition of this disability within our nation's special education law, IDEA.

Tips for Teachers

▶ Learn as much as you can about intellectual disability. The organizations listed in the following section will help you identify techniques and strategies to support the student educationally.

▶ Be as concrete as possible. Demonstrate what you mean rather than only giving verbal directions. Instead of just relating new information verbally, show a picture. Provide the student with hands-on materials and experiences and the opportunity to try things out.

▶ Break longer, new tasks into small steps. Demonstrate the steps. Have the student do each step, one at a time. Provide assistance as necessary.

▶ Give the student immediate feedback. Provide prompts only as necessary to allow students to become independent with new skills over time.

▶ Teach students life skills such as academics, daily living, social skills, and occupational awareness and exploration, as appropriate. Involve the student in group activities or clubs. Provide opportunities for peers with and without disabilities to work together to build a learning community.

▶ Work together with the student's parents and other school personnel to create and implement an IEP tailored to meet the student's needs. Regularly share information about how the student is doing at school and at home.

ORGANIZATIONS AND RESOURCES

American Association on Intellectual and Developmental Disabilities: The AAIDD definition manual contains the world's most current and authoritative information on intellectual disability, including best-practice guidelines on diagnosing and classifying intellectual disability and developing a system of supports for people living with an intellectual disability: www.aaidd.org

The Arc: info@thearc.org; www.thearc.org; find a local chapter near you: www.thearc.org/page .aspx?pid=2437

Division on Autism and Developmental Disabilities (DADD): A division of the Council for Exceptional Children, DADD offers many publications and journals for professionals: http:// daddcec.org/Home.aspx

OTHER HEALTH IMPAIRMENT

Other health impairment means having limited strength, vitality, or alertness, including a heightened alertness to environmental stimuli, that results in limited alertness with respect to the educational environment that is due to chronic or acute health problems such as asthma, attention deficit disorder or attention hyperactivity disorder, diabetes, epilepsy, a heart condition, hemophilia, lead poisoning, leukemia, nephritis, rheumatic fever, sickle cell anemia, and Tourette syndrome; and that adversely affects a child's educational performance. Eight of the twelve health conditions noted in IDEA's definition are included in chapter 18 of this book. Following is information on the four conditions that are not included in chapter 18.

Hemophilia

Hemophilia is a rare and inherited disorder in which your blood doesn't clot properly. As a result, people with hemophilia may bleed after an injury for a longer time than those without the disorder. Bleeding can also be internal, especially in the knees, ankles, and elbows.

The disorder occurs when a person is born without the protein (or with too little of it) that causes blood to clot. With very few exceptions, this disorder usually occurs only in males. However, it's a myth that persons with bleeding disorders such as hemophilia bleed to death from even minor injuries. In truth, the condition ranges from mild to severe. Symptoms include the following:

- ▶ Excessive bleeding
- ▶ Excessive bruising
- ▶ Easy bleeding
- ▶ Nose bleeds

Each year, about four hundred children are born with hemophilia. It's estimated that approximately eighteen thousand people in the United States have hemophilia.

ORGANIZATION AND RESOURCE

National Hemophilia Foundation: www.hemophilia.org

Lead Poisoning

Lead can build up in the body over a period of months or years. Even a small amount of lead in the body can cause serious problems—hence the term *lead poisoning*. Children under the age of six are especially vulnerable because their mental and physical abilities are still developing.

Exposure to lead-based paint or paint dust is the most common avenue to lead poisoning. This exists in older buildings and poses a serious health hazard. That is why the paint we use today does not contain lead. It's also why there has been a public awareness and prevention campaign since the 1990s to alert people to the dangers of being exposed to lead.

Unfortunately, the signs that a child may have lead poisoning are rather nonspecific, sometimes making diagnosis more difficult. Symptoms can include the following:

- ▶ Irritability
- ▶ Loss of appetite
- ▶ Weight loss
- ▶ Sluggishness
- ▶ Abdominal pain
- ▶ Vomiting
- ▶ Constipation
- ▶ Unusual paleness (pallor) from anemia
- ▶ Learning difficulties

National Lead Information Center (NLIC): www.epa.gov/lead/; EPA site in Spanish: www.epa.gov/espanol/

Nephritis

Nephritis means that one or both of a person's kidneys are inflamed. The kidneys are very important organs in the body because they clean the blood by filtering out excess water, salt, and waste products from the food we eat. Healthy kidneys keep protein in the blood, which in turn helps our bodies soak up water from the tissue inside. Damaged kidneys, however, can leak protein into the urine, which affects the ability of the body to absorb water from our tissues. This causes the tissues to swell.

Nephritis may be due to infection but it's more commonly associated with autoimmune disorders that affect the major organs of the body. Individuals with lupus, for example, are at much higher risk for developing nephritis. When associated with lupus, nephritis cannot be cured but it can be treated and often goes into remission. Antibiotics are the primary treatment for nephritis. With lupus, steroids may also be used.

You may also hear the term *nephrotic syndrome* used. Children and adults can have nephrotic syndrome. In itself, it is not a disease but may be the first signs of kidney disease that impairs the body's ability to produce urine. In children, nephrotic syndrome is most common between the ages of one and a half and five years and seems to affect boys more often than girls. Symptoms in children include the following:

▶ High levels of protein in the blood or, paradoxically, low levels
▶ Swelling when salt and water build up in the tissues
▶ Less frequent urination
▶ Weight gain from water retention

Diagnosing childhood nephrotic syndrome involves taking a urine sample to test for protein.

ORGANIZATION AND RESOURCE

American Society of Pediatric Nephrology: www.aspneph.com

Rheumatic Fever

Rheumatic fever can develop as a complication of untreated or poorly treated strep throat or scarlet fever in about twenty days. Although it is most often seen in children from five to fifteen, younger children and adults can also contract rheumatic fever. It's not very common in the United States, although it is fairly common worldwide. Symptoms include the following:

▶ Fever
▶ Pain in one joint that migrates to another joint
▶ Red, hot, or swollen joints
▶ Small, painless nodules beneath the skin
▶ Rapid, fluttering, or pounding heartbeats (palpitations)

- Fatigue
- Shortness of breath
- A painless rash with a ragged edge
- Jerky, uncontrollable body movements, most often in the hands, feet, and face
- Unusual behavior, such as crying or inappropriate laughing

It's very important to treat rheumatic fever because it can cause permanent damage to the heart, especially the valves. Diagnosing the condition usually involves a physical exam by the doctor, who will look for signs of tender or swollen joints, the tell-tale rash, and abnormal heart rhythm. Typically, a blood test for strep throat is also done.

Antibiotics are the usual treatment for rheumatic fever to eliminate the strep bacteria from the system. Depending on the severity of the infection, treatment may also include anti-inflammatory drugs to bring down the swelling in the joints. It's also not unusual for a person to have to take low-dose antibiotics continuously for years (especially the first three to five years after the first episode) to prevent rheumatic fever from coming back.

ORGANIZATION AND RESOURCE

Mayo Clinic: *Rheumatic fever:* www.mayoclinic.com/health/rheumatic-fever/DS00250

We'd also like to point out that IDEA's definition uses the phrase "such as . . ." That's significant. It means that the disabilities listed are not the only ones that may be considered when a child's eligibility for special services under IDEA is decided. A child with a health impairment not listed in IDEA's definition may be found eligible for special services and assistance. What's central to all the disabilities falling under "other health impairment" is that the child must have the following:

- Limited strength, vitality, or alertness due to chronic health problems
- An educational performance that is negatively affected as a result

SPECIFIC LEARNING DISABILITY

Specific learning disability refers to a disorder in one or more of the basic psychological processes involved in understanding or in using language, spoken or written, that may manifest itself in the imperfect ability to listen, think, speak, read, write, spell, or to do mathematical calculations. The term includes conditions such as perceptual disabilities, brain injury, minimal brain dysfunction, dyslexia, and developmental aphasia. The term does not include learning problems that are primarily the result of visual, hearing, or motor disabilities; of intellectual disability; of emotional disturbance; or of environmental, cultural, or economic disadvantage.

What Are Some Characteristics of Specific Learning Disabilities?

Learning disabilities (LD) vary from person to person. One person with LD may not have the same kind of learning problems as another person with LD. Sara, in our example online, has trouble with reading and writing. Another person with LD may have problems with understanding math. Still another person may have trouble in both of these areas as well as with understanding what people are saying.

Whereas there is no one sign that a person has a learning disability, there are certain clues. Most relate to elementary school tasks because learning disabilities tend to be identified in elementary school. This is because school focuses on the very things that may be difficult for the child—reading, writing, math, listening, speaking, and reasoning. A child probably won't show all of these signs or even most of them. However, if a child shows a number of these problems, then parents and the teacher should consider the possibility that the child has a learning disability.

▶ Trouble learning the alphabet, rhyming words, or connecting letters to their sounds
▶ Make many mistakes when reading aloud and repeat and pause often
▶ Not understand what he or she reads
▶ Have real trouble with spelling
▶ Have very messy handwriting or hold a pencil awkwardly
▶ Struggle to express ideas in writing
▶ Learn language late and have a limited vocabulary
▶ Have trouble remembering the sounds that letters make or hearing slight differences between words
▶ Have trouble understanding jokes, comic strips, and sarcasm
▶ Have trouble following directions
▶ Mispronounce words or use a wrong word that sounds similar
▶ Have trouble organizing what he or she wants to say or not be able to think of the word he or she needs for writing or conversation
▶ Not follow the social rules of conversation, such as taking turns, and may stand too close to the listener
▶ Confuse math symbols and misread numbers
▶ Not be able to retell a story in order (what happened first, second, third)
▶ Not know how to begin a task or how to go on from there

If a child has unexpected problems is struggling learning to read, write, listen, speak, or do math, then teachers and parents may want to investigate more. The child may need to be evaluated to see if he or she has a learning disability.

Tips for Teachers

▶ Break tasks into smaller steps and give directions verbally and in writing.
▶ Give the student more time to finish schoolwork or take tests.
▶ Let the student with reading problems use instructional materials that are accessible to those with print disabilities.
▶ Let the student with listening difficulties borrow notes from a classmate or use a tape recorder.
▶ Let the student with writing difficulties use a computer with specialized software that checks spelling and grammar or recognizes speech.
▶ Learn about the different testing modifications that can really help a student with LD show what he or she has learned.
▶ Teach organizational skills, study skills, and learning strategies; these help all students but are particularly helpful to those with LD.

- ► Work with the student's parents to create an IEP tailored to meet the student's needs.
- ► Establish a positive working relationship with the student's parents. Through regular communication, exchange information about the student's progress at school.

Organizations and Resources

LD OnLine: For educators: www.ldonline.org/educators; teaching and instruction: www.ldonline.org/indepth/teaching

Learning Disabilities Association of America: *For teachers:* www.ldanatl.org/aboutld/teachers/index.asp

National Center for Accessible Instructional Materials (AIM): http://aim.cast.org

National Center for Learning Disabilities: Especially for teachers: www.ncld.org/students-disabilities/ld-education-teachers

Reading Rockets: For teachers: www.readingrockets.org/audience/teachers

TeachingLD: A service of the Division for Learning Disabilities (DLD) of the Council for Exceptional Children: www.dldcec.org

SPEECH AND LANGUAGE DISORDERS

Speech or language impairment refers to a communication disorder such as stuttering, impaired articulation, a language impairment, or a voice impairment that adversely affects a child's educational performance.

What Are the Characteristics and Different Types of Speech or Language Impairments?

The characteristics of speech or language impairments will vary depending on the type of impairment involved. There may also be a combination of several problems. With an articulation disorder, a child has difficulty making certain sounds. These sounds may be left off, added, changed, or distorted, which makes it hard for people to understand the child.

Leaving out or changing certain sounds is common when young children are learning to talk, of course. A good example of this is saying *wabbit* for *rabbit*. The incorrect articulation isn't necessarily a cause for concern unless it continues past the age when children are expected to produce such sounds correctly.

Fluency refers to the flow of speech. A fluency disorder means that something is disrupting the rhythmic and forward flow of speech—usually, a stutter. As a result, the child's speech contains an abnormal number of repetitions, hesitations, prolongations, or disturbances. Tension may also be seen in the face, neck, shoulders, or fists.

Voice is the sound that's produced when air from the lungs pushes through the voice box in the throat (also called the *larynx*) making the vocal folds within vibrate. From there, the sound generated travels up through the spaces of the throat, nose, and mouth and emerges as our voice.

A voice disorder involves problems with the pitch, loudness, resonance, or quality of the voice. The voice may be hoarse, raspy, or harsh. For some, it may sound quite nasal; others might seem as if they are stuffed up. People with voice problems often notice changes in pitch, loss of voice, loss of endurance, and sometimes a sharp or dull pain associated with voice use.

Language has to do with meanings rather than sounds. A language disorder refers to an impaired ability to understand and use words in context. A child may have an expressive language disorder (difficulty in expressing ideas or needs), a receptive language disorder (difficulty in understanding what others are saying), or a mixed language disorder (which involves both).

Some characteristics of language disorders include the following:

- ▶ Improper use of words and their meanings
- ▶ Inability to express ideas
- ▶ Inappropriate grammatical patterns
- ▶ Reduced vocabulary
- ▶ Inability to follow directions

Children may hear or see a word but not be able to understand its meaning. They may have trouble getting others to understand what they are trying to communicate. These symptoms can easily be mistaken for other disabilities such as autism or learning disabilities so it's very important to ensure that the child receives a thorough evaluation by a certified speech-language pathologist.

Tips for Teachers

- ▶ Learn as much as you can about the student's specific disability. Speech-language impairments differ considerably from one another so it's important to know the specific impairment and how it affects the student's communication abilities.
- ▶ Make sure that needed accommodations are provided for classwork, homework, and testing. These will help the student learn successfully.
- ▶ Consult with others (e.g., the speech-language pathologist) who can help you identify strategies for teaching and supporting this student, and ways to adapt the curriculum.
- ▶ Find out if your state or school district has materials or resources available to help educators address the learning needs of children with speech or language impairments.
- ▶ Communicate with the student's parents. Regularly share information about how the student is doing at school and at home.

ORGANIZATIONS AND RESOURCES

ASHA (American Speech-Language-Hearing Association): actioncenter@asha.org; www.asha.org

Cleft Palate Foundation: www.cleftline.org

National Stuttering Foundation: info@WeStutter.org; www.nsastutter.org

New York Online Access to Health (NOAH): *Speech and language (communication) disorders:* www.noah -health.org/en/bns/disorders/speech

NIDCD (National Institute on Deafness and Other Communication Disorders): nidcdinfo@nidcd .nih.gov; www.nidcd.nih.gov

Prelock, P. A., Hutchins, T., & Glascoe, F. P. (2008). How to identify the most common and least diagnosed disability of childhood. *The Medscape Journal of Medicine, 10*(6), 136. Retrieved from www.ncbi.nlm.nih.gov/pmc/articles/PMC2491683

The Childhood Apraxia of Speech Association of North America (CASANA): www.apraxia-kids.org

The Stuttering Foundation: info@stutteringhelp.org; www.stuttersfa.org

TRAUMATIC BRAIN INJURY

Traumatic brain injury (TBI) refers to an acquired injury to the brain caused by an external physical force, resulting in total or partial functional disability, psychosocial impairment, or both, and which adversely affects a child's educational performance. The term applies to open or closed head injuries resulting in impairments in one or more areas, such as cognition; language; memory; attention; reasoning; abstract thinking; judgment; problem solving; sensory, perceptual, and motor abilities; psychosocial behavior; physical functions; information processing; and speech. The term does not apply to brain injuries that are congenital or degenerative or to brain injuries induced by birth trauma.

What Are Some Characteristics of Traumatic Brain Injury?

A TBI can change how a person acts, moves, and thinks and can also change how a student learns and acts in school. The term *TBI* is used for head injuries that can cause changes in one or more areas:

- ► Thinking and reasoning
- ► Understanding words
- ► Remembering things
- ► Paying attention
- ► Solving problems
- ► Thinking abstractly
- ► Talking
- ► Behaving
- ► Walking and other physical activities
- ► Seeing and hearing
- ► Learning

The signs of brain injury can be very different depending on where the brain is injured and how severely. Children with TBI may have one or more manifestations in the following areas:

- ► *Physical disabilities:* Individuals with TBI may have problems speaking, seeing, hearing, and using their other senses. They may have headaches and feel tired a lot. They may also have trouble with skills such as writing or drawing. Their muscles may suddenly contract or tighten (this is called *spasticity*). They may also have seizures. Their balance and walking may also be affected. They may be partly or completely paralyzed on one side of the body or both sides.
- ► *Difficulties with thinking:* Because the brain has been injured, it is common that the person's ability to use the brain changes. For example, children with TBI may have trouble with short-term memory (being able to remember something from one minute to the next, such as what the teacher just said). They may also have trouble with their long-term memory (being able to remember information from a while ago, such as facts learned last month). People with TBI may have trouble concentrating and only be able to focus their attention for a short time. They may think slowly. They may have trouble talking and listening to others. They may also have difficulty with reading and writing, planning, understanding the order in which events happen (called *sequencing*), and judgment.

► *Social, behavioral, or emotional problems:* These difficulties may include sudden changes in mood, anxiety, and depression. Children with TBI may have trouble relating to others. They may be restless and may laugh or cry a lot. They may not have much motivation or much control over their emotions.

A child with TBI may not have all of these difficulties. Brain injuries can range from mild to severe, and so can the changes that result from the injury. This means that it's hard to predict how an individual will recover from the injury. Early and ongoing help can make a big difference in how the child recovers. This help can include physical or occupational therapy, counseling, and special education.

It's also important to know that, as the child grows and develops, parents and teachers may notice new problems. This is because students are expected to use their brains in new and different ways as they grow. The damage to the brain from the earlier injury can make it hard for the student to learn new skills that come with getting older. Sometimes parents and educators may not even realize that the student's difficulty comes from an earlier injury.

Tips for Teachers

► Find out as much as you can about the child's injury and his or her present needs. Find out more about TBI through the resources and organizations listed in the next section. These can help you identify specific techniques and strategies to support the student educationally.

► Give the student more time to finish schoolwork and tests.

► Give directions one step at a time. For tasks with many steps, it helps to give the student written directions.

► Show the student how to perform new tasks. Give examples to go with new ideas and concepts.

► Have consistent routines. This helps the student know what to expect. If the routine is going to change, let the student know ahead of time.

► Check to make sure that the student has actually learned the new skill. Give the student lots of opportunities to practice the new skill.

► Show the student how to use an assignment book and a daily schedule. This helps the student get organized.

► Realize that the student may get tired quickly. Let the student rest as needed.

► Reduce distractions.

► Keep in touch with the student's parents. Share information about how the student is doing at home and at school.

► Be flexible about expectations. Be patient. Maximize the student's chances for success.

ORGANIZATIONS AND RESOURCES

American Academy of Family Physicians. (2010). *Traumatic brain injury.* Retrieved from http://family doctor.org/online/famdocen/home/common/brain/head/1058.html

Brain Injury Association of America (BIA): www.biausa.org; find your state BIA affiliate: www.biausa .org/state-affiliates.htm

Brainline: Information available in English and Spanish: info@BrainLine.org; www.brainline.org

CDC. (2010). *Traumatic brain injury.* Retrieved from www.cdc.gov/TraumaticBrainInjury

Family Caregiver Alliance: Information in English, Spanish, and Chinese: www.caregiver.org/caregiver/jsp/home.jsp

National Institute of Neurological Disorders and Stroke. (2011, January). *NINDS traumatic brain injury information.* Retrieved from www.ninds.nih.gov/disorders/tbi/tbi.htm

National Resource Center for Traumatic Brain Injury (NRCTBI): www.neuro.pmr.vcu.edu

TBI Recovery Center: www.tbirecoverycenter.org

The Perspectives Network, Inc.: TPN@tbi.org; www.tbi.org

VISUAL IMPAIRMENT INCLUDING BLINDNESS

Visual impairment refers to an impairment in vision that even with correction adversely affects a child's educational performance. The term includes partial sight and blindness.

What Are the Characteristics of Visual Impairment Including Blindness?

The effect of visual problems on a child's development depends on the severity, type of loss, age at which the condition appears, and overall functioning level of the child. Many children who have multiple disabilities may also have visual impairments resulting in motor, cognitive, and social developmental delays.

A young child with visual impairments has little reason to explore interesting objects in the environment and thus may miss opportunities to gain know-how and to learn. This lack of exploration may continue until learning becomes motivating or until intervention begins.

Because the child cannot see parents or peers, he or she may be unable to imitate social behavior or understand nonverbal cues. Visual handicaps can create obstacles to a growing child's independence.

What Are Some Different Types of Visual Impairments?

The terms *partially sighted, low vision, legally blind,* and *totally blind* are used in the educational context to describe students with visual impairments. They are defined as follows:

Partially sighted indicates that some type of visual problem has resulted in a need for special education.

Low vision generally refers to a severe visual impairment, not necessarily limited to distance vision. Low vision applies to all individuals with sight who are unable to read the newspaper at a normal viewing distance, even with the aid of eyeglasses or contact lenses. They use a combination of vision and other senses to learn, although they may require adaptations in lighting or the size of print and, sometimes, Braille.

Legally blind indicates that a person has less than 20/200 vision in the better eye or a very limited field of vision (20 degrees at its widest point).

Totally blind students learn via Braille or other nonvisual media.

Visual impairment is the consequence of a functional loss of vision rather than the eye disorder itself. Eye disorders that can lead to visual impairments include retinal degeneration, albinism, cataracts, glaucoma, muscular problems, corneal disorders, diabetic retinopathy, congenital disorders, and infection.

Organizations and Resources

American Council of the Blind: info@acb.org; www.acb.org

American Foundation for the Blind (AFB): afbinfo@afb.net; www.afb.org/default.asp; AFB's service center, where you can search and identify services for blind and visually impaired persons in the United States and Canada: www.afb.org/services.asp

Blind Childrens Center: www.blindchildrenscenter.org

IRIS Center: *Accommodations to the physical environment: Setting up a classroom for students with visual disabilities:* http://iris.peabody.vanderbilt.edu/v01_clearview/chalcycle.htm

IRIS Center: *Instructional accommodations: Making the learning environment accessible to students with visual disabilities:* http://iris.peabody.vanderbilt.edu/v02_successsight/chalcycle.htm

IRIS Center: *Serving students with visual impairments: The importance of collaboration.* This module underscores the importance of the general education teacher's collaborating with professionals and other individuals knowledgeable about the needs of students with visual disabilities: http://iris.peabody.vanderbilt.edu/v03_focusplay/chalcycle.htm

Lighthouse International: http://lighthouse.org

National Association for Parents of the Visually Impaired (NAPVI): napvi@perkins.org; www.napvi.org

National Braille Association (NBA): www.nationalbraille.org

National Braille Press: contact@nbp.org; www.nbp.org

National Eye Institute, National Institutes of Health: US Department of Health and Human Services: 2020@nei.nih.gov; www.nei.nih.gov

National Federation of the Blind: www.nfb.org

National Library Service for the Blind and Physically Handicapped: Library of Congress: nls@loc.gov; www.loc.gov/nls

NICHCY: *Connect with the expertise of special education:* www.nichcy.org/schoolage/effective-practices/speced#visual

NICHCY: For information on accessible instructional materials—what they are, who's eligible to receive them, and what the law requires schools to do—visit the special topic section of the October 2010 *News You Can Use:* www.nichcy.org/newsletters/oct2010

Prevent Blindness America: www.preventblindness.org

The Foundation Fighting Blindness (formerly the National Retinitis Pigmentosa Foundation): info@blindness.org; www.blindness.org

Key Special Education Cases

Case Name	Decision	Implications for Special Education
Board of Education of Hendrick Hudson Central School District v. *Rowley* 458 US 176 (1982)	• Determined that the term *appropriate* aims to meet individual needs of students, not maximize potential • Defined *free and appropriate public education* (FAPE)	• Improved the process of IEP, ensuring that the plans were more tailored to each child's individual needs • Opened up public education to more children who could benefit from it
Irving Independent School District v. *Amber Tatro* 468 US 883 (1984)	• Determined under what circumstances a medical treatment is a related service under EAHCA and must be provided by the school	• Helped ensure that children with special medical needs were covered under special education law • Helped make public education available to more children
Honig, California Superintendent of Public Instruction v. *Doe et al.* 484 US 305 (1988)	• Determined that emotional disturbance fell under the provisions of EAHCA and that a child could not be denied an education because of it	• Helped more children with emotional disturbances stay in the classroom • Determined that if a parent disagrees with a decision to move a child from his or her current placement, the child cannot be moved until an administrative or judicial review is completed
Florence County School District Four et al. Petitioners v. *Shannon Carter* 510 US 7 (1993)	• Determined that a school can be required to reimburse parents for tuition if they unilaterally pull their child out of school because the school is not meeting the educational needs of the child appropriately	• Helped provide more opportunities for children with disabilities to acquire an appropriate education • Takes away some of the financial burden some parents may experience as a result of privately educating a child with special needs
Jacob Winkelman v. *Parma City School District* (2007)	• Determined that parents could act as legal counsel in a court case regarding the implementation of IDEA	• Gives parents more leverage to advocate for their children's educational needs in a courtroom

APPENDIX C

Assessment Vocabulary and Concepts

In norm-referenced tests, we assume that all people's scores will fall within a range of scores referred to as a *normal distribution*. In a normal distribution, most people fall in mid-range with fewer people performing in either the extremely high or extremely low ranges. This distribution is often characterized as a *bell curve* with a peak in the number of people scoring in the mid-range and tapering on either side with fewer people performing above or below the mid-range.

One of the best and most common measures of describing how the average number of people perform on any assessment is referred to as the *mean*. Essentially, the mean is calculated by adding all the scores of the students who participated in an assessment and then dividing that score by the number of participants. Two other common ways of calculating average performance involves either determining the *mode* (examining the scores of all the people who participated in any assessment and determining the score that occurred the most frequently) or the *median* (the score occurring in the middle if all scores were lined up from lowest to highest scores). When looking at a diagram of any normal distribution, the mean, median, and mode are equal. In this way, the normal distribution is symmetrical and is shaped like a bell.

In describing how students perform along the entire normal distribution, we are interested in how they do compared with their peers. Therefore, we must have a precise way of describing the distance of their scores from the mean. The most common way of doing so is by describing the number of *standard deviations (SD)* from the mean of any particular score. A standard deviation describes the variability in the scores in relationship to the mean. For example, approximately 68 percent of all participants will score within one SD from the mean. Similarly, approximately 95 percent of all participants will score within two SD from the mean and approximately 99 percent of all participants will score within three SD from the mean. This is a valuable tool in describing a student's performance compared with a peer group.

An example of a norm-referenced assessment that you have likely encountered is an *intelligence quotient*, or *IQ test*. Because of the prevalence of RTI in many school systems, IQ tests are used less and less. For the purpose of this appendix, however, IQ tests can illustrate many of the concepts described thus far. Let's assume that our example IQ test has a mean score of 100 with a standard deviation of 10. As a person scores further away from 100, he or she moves further away from average. In interpreting this IQ test, therefore, you can assume the following:

Very superior: > 130 (three SD above the mean)
Superior: 120–129 (two SD above the mean)
High average: 111–119 (one SD above the mean)
Average: 90–110 (the mean range)
Low average: 80–89 (one SD below the mean)
Borderline: 70–79 (two SD below the mean)
Mild delay: 55–69 (three SD below the mean)
Moderate   delay: 40–54 (four SD below the mean)

Another way to report norm-referenced scores involves the use of *percentiles,* which provides the scores below which a set percentage of people score. For example, if someone receives a percentile score of fifty, 50 percent of people scored below or above that person. Thus, the fiftieth percentile indicates the testing average. If, however, a person scores in the seventieth percentile, that person scored better than 70 percent of all test takers.

VALIDITY AND RELIABILITY

Before being able to interpret assessment scores, you must make sure that the assessments provide you with the information you are seeking about your students. If you are not confident in the assessment, you cannot accurately interpret their results. In making such determinations, it is important to understand the concepts of validity and reliability. Although these concepts seem simple on face value, validity and reliability can be quite tricky, especially in light of all the different assessments given to students with disabilities.

Validity

For an assessment to be valid, you must have confidence that it measures what you want it to measure. At its simplest, a valid assessment measures what it is supposed to measure.[1] Within the broad area of assessment validity, there are specific types of validity. One of the main ones that you will likely need to understand is *predictive validity,* which refers to whether the assessment results accurately predict the student's future behavior. For example, you may be familiar with college entrance exams. You may wonder whether such entrance exams predict how well students perform in college. Another area of validity is *content validity,* which addresses whether items on an assessment actually measure the areas that you are attempting to assess. For example, some people inaccurately assess students' reading fluency (the rate at which a student reads) as a measure of reading comprehension. Although there is a relationship between the rate at which someone reads and his or her comprehension, a test of fluency does not directly assess reading comprehension. Finally, *construct validity* refers to whether the assessment measures a theoretical construct as intended, such as motivation, creativity, and intelligence. Establishing construct validity can be tricky because the constructs are often abstract.

Reliability

In order for an assessment to be reliable, you must have confidence that if you give a student an assessment repeatedly, the results consistently will be the same or very similar and that the skills measured in the assessment are measured consistently throughout the instrument. Similar to validity, there are several areas of reliability with which you should become familiar. One such area is *test-retest reliability,* which is a measure of whether students will receive a similar score if they retake the assessment at a later time. For example, if students take an IQ test in the third grade, it is assumed that the IQ test is reliable and people will receive similar scores when retaking the test in the fourth grade. Another form of reliability that you should consider is *interrater reliability.* This form of reliability addresses whether there is consistency between people who administer and score the assessments. For example, if you and another teacher score an assessment given to the same student, you should both score the student similarly and be able to draw the same conclusions. A third type of reliability is *alternate form reliability,* which asserts that when there are multiple versions of the assessment (such as a form A and a form B), both will have similar items of equal difficulty so that the scores from one form could correspond to scores from other forms.

Together validity and reliability allow you to be confident that, if an assessment is given as described in a manner consistent with good assessment practices, the resulting scores will be accurate. However, although we hope that all of the assessments that we give to students (both with and without disabilities) will be valid and reliable, no assessment is 100 percent accurate. We assume that there is always room for error in an assessment. This is one of the main reasons why a nondiscriminatory evaluation *must* include multiple measures!

There is much more to validity and reliability than this appendix can provide. In general, on formal assessments, you can find information about the validity and reliability of the assessment in the testing manual. On curriculum-based measures and other teacher-made tests, consider the general principles in designing, grading, and interpreting the assessments.

APPENDIX D

Tips for Preparing for Observations and Evaluations

Today teacher evaluation systems are changing across the United States. Some states and districts are putting in place new evaluation systems that combine student growth scores and teacher observations to determine teacher effectiveness. In addition, states may use other forms of evaluation, such as teacher portfolios, parent surveys, and teacher collaboration and professionalism.

Evaluations are usually designed to address one of two purposes: (1) formative evaluation, feedback, and assistance designed to help teachers become more effective, and (2) summative evaluation, which is used to make decisions related to continuation or termination. The latter may cause you anxiety; however, it is important to keep in mind that relatively few teachers are discontinued due to problems in performance. As much as possible, try to focus on the formative aspects of evaluation and work throughout your career to continue to improve your effectiveness and to become an accomplished special educator.

The following tips are designed to help you understand and prepare for your evaluations.

Learn about the teacher evaluation system. Teacher evaluation systems vary substantially across states and districts. Learn about the teacher evaluation system in your district. We hope that teacher evaluation purposes and procedures will be addressed during the orientation to your district. If not, be sure to look for information on the district website. In addition, ask your principal and mentor(s) to help you understand and prepare for evaluation.

Prepare for the pre-observation conferences and the observation. Districts may have unannounced or announced observations and some have a combination of the two types. These evaluation systems may be based on a specific system of observation. For example, Charlotte Danielson's framework for teaching (www.danielsongroup.org) is one of the most widely used frameworks for teacher evaluation in the United States. This framework includes four areas (planning and preparation, classroom environment, instruction, and professional responsibilities), although environment and instruction will usually be the focus of the observation. Some districts have systems designed specifically for special education teachers, and others are evaluated on the systems used for all teachers. In some districts, you may be asked to provide evaluators with material prior to the conference. For example, typical requests include a written lesson plan, specific goals and objectives for the unit or lesson being taught, or areas in which you would like evaluators to focus on during the observation. Sometimes conferences are held prior to the observation to discuss the lesson to be taught and to identify specific behaviors for the evaluator to observe. This may be particularly helpful if the evaluator does not have a background in special education. To prepare for the pre-observation conference, do the following:

▶ Review any written guidelines for pre-observation or conference planning and address each aspect of the guidelines (e.g., provide a lesson plan).

▶ Learn about the observation system being used and pay attention to the specific behaviors that will be included in the observation.

▶ If there is a specific form or checklist used in the evaluation system, become familiar with it and discuss it with your mentor or principal.

▶ Identify any specific things you think the observer needs to know about the situation in which you are teaching (e.g., how the material is being modified in a co-taught class or the behavior plan for a student who may act out).

▶ Identify any questions you have for the observer, such as if he or she plans to focus on specific teaching behaviors during the evaluation.

▶ Listen carefully to what the observer says and note any points that are important in preparing for the observation (e.g., what the observer is looking to observe).

In preparing for the observation, consider the following:

▶ The best way to address observations is to be consistently prepared for teaching and to do your best on a daily basis. If announced, provide the observer with a copy of the lesson plan in advance of the lesson.

▶ If the observer asks where you would like them to sit, consider the area that will be the least distracting to you and the students.

▶ Remember that all teachers are likely to encounter some challenges during the observation—don't expect everything to go perfectly.

Preparing for and participating in the post-observation conference. Post-observation conferences are usually designed to discuss the lesson and identify teaching strengths and areas for development. These conferences may also be used to pinpoint areas of focus for a subsequent observation.

▶ After the observation, take a few minutes to jot down anything you would like to discuss with the evaluators (e.g., things you felt went well, unanticipated problems, areas in which you would like advice).

▶ Allow the observer to take the lead in the post-observation conference because there may be specific things that he or she is required to consider.

▶ It is important to remember that evaluation systems are designed to help teachers improve—listen carefully to any suggestions for improvement without getting defensive.

▶ Do share anything that happened during the observation that you feel the evaluator needs to know (e.g., material part of IEP, student behavior).

▶ If you feel you need professional development in some area of need, this is a good time to discuss possibilities for additional learning.

▶ During the conference, write down suggestions and any ideas for future development.

Your annual evaluation conference. Your final evaluation conference is likely to include data about your performance across the year (e.g., observations, informal evaluations) and possibly student growth scores. These evaluations may seem perfunctory or they may be extensive, depending on local policies and practices. You may also be asked to identify areas in which you need assistance. Please do ask questions if there is any part of the evaluation process that you do not understand.

APPENDIX E

Bonus Web Content

You can access free downloadable versions of a number of the tools found in this book on our publisher's website. Just go to www.josseybass.com/go/specialeducator and you'll be able to download a zip file containing the following materials:

Exhibit 1.2: Job Interview Questions

Exhibit 3.1: Sample: Beginning-of-Year Letter from Special Education Teacher

Exhibit 3.2: Encouraging Note to Parents about Their Child

Exhibit 3.3: Teacher–Parent Communication Log

Exhibit 3.4: Paraeducator Schedule Form

Table 3.2: Tips for Planning and Leading an Effective Professional Meeting

Table 4.2: Select Federal Laws Affecting Students with Disabilities

Chapter 5, unnumbered table: Supplementary Aids and Services - chart

Exhibit 5.2: IEP at a Glance (Elementary Level)

Exhibit 6.1: Roles and Responsibilities Organizational Table

Table 6.2: Emily's Goals

Chapter 6, unnumbered : Keeping Student Data Organized template (contributor textbox)

Exhibit 6.2: First-Day Checklist

Table 7.1: Surface-Responding Techniques

Table 7.2: Whole-Class Responding Techniques

Table 7.3: Mixed-Responding Techniques

Exhibit 7.2: Behavior Contract

Exhibit 7.3: Check-in, Check-out table

Exhibit 7.4: Common Behavioral Functions - Function Matrix

Exhibit 7.5: Sample Point Sheet

Exhibit 7.6: Sample Point Sheet

Please feel free to use each tool as is or customize for your own classroom. We hope you find these materials useful.

Notes

CHAPTER ONE

1. Mastropieri, M. A. (2001). Is the glass half full or half empty? Challenges encountered by first-year special education teachers. *The Journal of Special Education, 35*(2), 66–74.
2. Fall, A. M. (2010). Recruiting and retaining highly qualified special education teachers for high poverty districts and schools: Seven recommendations for educational leaders. *Journal of Special Education Leadership, 23*(2), 76–83.
3. Adapted from Billingsley, B. (2005). *Cultivating and keeping committed special education teachers.* Thousand Oaks, CA: Corwin Press.

CHAPTER TWO

1. Whitaker, S. D. (2000). What do first year special education teachers need? Implications for induction programs. *Teaching Exceptional Children, 33*(1), 28–36.
2. White, M., & Mason, C. Y. (2006). Components of a successful mentoring program for beginning special education teachers: Perspectives from new teachers and mentors. *Teacher Education and Special Education, 29*(3), 191–201.
3. Stein, E. (2010). Teaching secrets: Advice for a new special ed. teacher. *Education Week Teacher.* Retrieved from www.edweek.org/tm/articles/2010/06/30/tln_stein_speced.html
4. Blue-Banning, M., Summers, J. A., Frankland, H. C., Nelson, L. L., & Beegle, G. (2004). Dimensions of family and professional partnerships: Constructive guidelines for collaboration. *Council for Exceptional Children, 70*(2), 167–184.
5. Council for Exceptional Children. (2010, January). *CEC ethical principles for special education professionals.* Retrieved from www.cec.sped.org/AM/Template.cfm?Section=Ethics_and_Practice_Standards
6. Howatt, W. A. (2001). *Creating wellness at home and in school.* Bloomington, IN: Phi Delta Kappa Educational Foundation.
7. Common Core State Standards Initiative. (2012). *About the standards.* Retrieved from www.corestandards.org/about-the-standards
8. Shah, N. (2012). States adapting best practices from special ed. for standards. *Education Week, 31*(29), S32–S33.
9. Ibid.

10. Ehren, B. J., Blosser, J., Rother, F. P., Paul, D. R., & Nelson, N. W. (2012). Core commitment: The common core state standards are here, and school-based SLPs are in a prime position to help students. *ASHA Leader, 17*(4), 10–13.

11. Holbrook, M. D. (2007). A seven-step process to creating standards-based IEPs. Retrieved from www.project forum.org.

12. Samuels, C. A. (2011, January 12). Special educators look to align IEPs to common-core standards. *Education Week, 30*(15), 8–9.

13. Ibid.

14. Kardos, S. M., & Johnson, S. M. (2010). New teachers' experiences of mentoring: The good, the bad, and the inequity. *Journal of Educational Change, 11*(1), 23–44.

15. House, J. S. (1981). *Work stress and social support.* Reading, MA: Addison-Wesley.

16. Littrell, P., Billingsley, B., & Cross, L. (1994). The effects of principal support on general and special educators' stress, job satisfaction, health, school commitment, and intent to stay in teaching. *Remedial and Special Education, 15*(5), 297–310.

17. Danielson, C. (2007). *Framework for teaching: Enhancing professional practice* (2nd ed.). Alexandria, VA: Association for Supervision and Curriculum Development.

18. Kardos & Johnson (2010).

19. Smith, T. M., & Ingersoll, R. M. (2004). What are the effects of induction and mentoring on beginning teacher turnover? *American Educational Research Journal, 41*(3), 681–714.

20. Billingsley, B., Israel, M., & Smith, S. (2011). Supporting new teachers: How online resources and web 2.0 technologies can help. *Teaching Exceptional Children, 43*(5), 20–29.

21. Billingsley, B. (2005). *Cultivating and keeping committed special education teachers.* Thousand Oaks, CA: Corwin Press.

CHAPTER THREE

1. Billingsley, B., Griffin, C., Smith, S. J., Kamman, M., & Israel, M. (2009). *A review of teacher induction in special education: Research, practice, and technology solutions.* Gainesville: National Center to Inform Policy and Practice in Special Education Professional Development (NCIPP), University of Florida.

2. Cross, R., & Parker, A. (2004). *The hidden power of social networks: Understanding how work really gets done in organizations* (pp. 65–66). Boston: Harvard Business School Press.

3. Covey, S. (2004). *The 7 habits of highly effective people: Powerful lessons in personal change.* New York: Simon & Schuster.

4. Billingsley, Griffin, Smith, Kamman, & Israel (2009).

5. Blue-Banning, M., Summers, J. A., Frankland, H. C., Nelson, L. L., & Beegle, G. (2004). Dimensions of family and professional partnerships: Constructive guidelines for collaboration. *Exceptional Children, 70*(2), 167–184.

6. Ibid.

7. Brown, M. (2009). A new multicultural population: Creating effective partnerships with multiracial families. *Intervention in School and Clinic, 45*(2), 124–136.

8. Billingsley, Griffin, Smith, Kamman, & Israel (2009).

9. Trautman, M. L. (2004). Preparing and managing paraprofessionals. *Intervention in School and Clinic, 39*(3), 131–138.

10. Riggs, C. G. (2004). To teachers: What paraeducators want to know. *The Council for Exceptional Children, 36,* 8–12.

11. Ashbaker, B., & Morgan, J. (2006). *Paraprofessionals in the classroom.* Boston: Pearson/Allyn & Bacon.

12. Hauge, J. M., & Babkie, A. M. (2006). Develop collaborative special educator-paraprofessional teams: One para's view. *Intervention in School and Clinic, 42*(1), 51–53.

13. Ibid.

14. Devlin, P. (2008). Create effective teacher-paraprofessional teams. *Intervention in School and Clinic, 44*(1), 41–44.

15. Trautman, M. L. (2004). Preparing and managing paraprofessionals. *Intervention in School and Clinic, 39*(3), 131–138.

CHAPTER FOUR

1. Individuals with Disabilities Education Improvement Act of 2004, 20 U.S.C. §1415 300.39.
2. Education for All Handicapped Children Act of 1975, Public Law 94–142 (1975).
3. Northwest Regional Education Service District. (2012). *Determining least restrictive environment.* Retrieved from www.nwresd.k12.or.us/specialed/pdf/19.DeterminingLRE.pdf
4. NICHCY. (2010). *Parent rights under IDEA.* Reprinted with permission from http://nichcy.org/schoolage/parental-rights
5. Individuals with Disabilities Education Improvement Act of 2004, 20 U.S.C. §1400 (2004).
6. NICHCY. (2010). *10 basic steps in special education.* Retrieved from http://nichcy.org/schoolage/steps
7. Rehabilitation Act of 1973, 29 U.S.C. §504. Amended as 29 U.S.C. §794 (1973).
8. Americans with Disabilities Act of 2008, Public Law 110–325 (2008).
9. Family Educational Rights and Privacy Act of 1974, 20 U.S.C. §1232g (1974).
10. Stevens, E., & Snell, M. E. (1995). The special educator as expert witness. *Teacher Education and Special Education, 18,* 124–132.

CHAPTER FIVE

1. Rebhorn, T. (2009, April). Developing your child's IEP. *Parent Guide 12,* 1–28. Quote from page 10. Retrieved from http://nichcy.org/publications/pa12
2. NICHCY. (2010, September). *Benchmarks or short-term objectives.* Retrieved from http://nichcy.org/schoolage/iep/iepcontents/benchmarks
3. Ibid.
4. NICHCY. (2010, September). *Special education.* Retrieved from http://nichcy.org/schoolage/iep/iepcontents/specialeducation
5. Ibid.
6. Holbrook, M. D. (2007, August). *Standards-based individualized education program examples.* Alexandria, VA: Project Forum. Retrieved from http://projectforum.org/docs/standards-basediepexamples.pdf
7. Gierach, J. (2009). *Assessing students' needs for assistive technology (ASNAT): A resource manual for school district teams* (5th ed., p. 7). Milton: Wisconsin Assistive Technology Initiative. Retrieved from www.wati.org/content/supports/free/pdf/ASNAT5thEditionJun09.pdf
8. Ibid.
9. The IRIS Center. (nd). *Assistive technology: An overview.* Vanderbilt University. Retrieved from http://iris.peabody.vanderbilt.edu/at/at_04_trans_reed.html
10. Meaden, H., Sheldon, D. L., Appel, K., & DeGrazia, R. L. (2010). Developing a long-term vision: A road map for students' future. *Teaching Exceptional Children, 43*(2), 8–14.
11. Henrico County Public Schools, Exceptional Education and Support Services. *Facilitating an effective IEP meeting.* Reprinted with permission.
12. Meaden, Sheldon, Appel, & DeGrazia (2010).

CHAPTER SIX

1. Billingsley, B., Griffin, C., Smith, S. J., Kamman, M., & Israel, M. (2009). *A review of teacher induction in special education: Research, practice, and technology solutions.* Gainesville: National Center to Inform Policy and Practice in Special Education Professional Development (NCIPP), University of Florida.
2. Chicago Public Schools. (2010). *Roles and responsibilities.* Office of Special Education and Supports. Retrieved from www.cpsspecialeducation.org/index.php?option=com_content&view=article&id=1924&Itemid=819

3. MizTeacher. (2008, July 7). *Help! The first day of school in special ed.!* Proteacher discussion thread. Retrieved from www.proteacher.net/discussions/showthread.php?t=89927

4. Remember the Milk. www.rememberthemilk.com

5. HiTask. http://hitask.com

6. Toodledo. www.toodledo.com

7. Simplenote. simplenoteapp.com

8. Google Tasks. http://mail.google.com/mail/help/tasks

9. Powers, D. (2012). Untitled photograph of teacher's desk. Used with permission. Retrieved from http://mspowers1.blogspot.com

CHAPTER SEVEN

1. Gresham, F. M. (2004). Current status and future directions of school-based behavioral interventions. *School Psychology Review, 33,* 326–343. Hawken, L. S., Vincent, C. G., & Schumman, J. (2008). Response to intervention for school behavior: Challenges and opportunities. *Journal of Emotional and Behavioral Disorders, 16,* 213–225. Sugai, G., & Horner, R. H. (2002). Introduction to the special series on positive behavior support in schools. *Journal of Emotional and Behavioral Disorders, 10,* 130–135.

2. Simonsen, B., Fairbanks, S., Briesch, A., Myers, D., & Sugai, G. (2008). Evidence-based practices in classroom management: Considerations for research to practice. *Education and Treatment of Children, 31,* 351–380.

3. Ibid.

4. Ibid.

5. Sayeski, K. L., & Brown, M. R. (2011). Developing a classroom management plan using a tiered approach. *Teaching Exceptional Children, 44,* 8–17.

6. Hyman, I. A., & Snook, P. A. (1999). *Dangerous schools: What we can do about the physical and emotional abuse of our children.* San Francisco: Jossey-Bass.

7. Ryan, J. B., Sanders, S., Katsiyannis, A., & Yell, M. Y. (2007). Using time-out effectively in the classroom. *Teaching Exceptional Children, 39,* 60–67.

8. Jordan, A., Glenn, C., & McGhie-Richmond, D. (2010). The supporting effective teaching (SET) project: The relationship of inclusive teaching practices to teachers' beliefs about disability and ability, and about the roles as teachers. *Teaching and Teacher Education, 26,* 259–266.

9. Emmer, E. T., & Stough, L. M. (2001). Classroom management: A critical part of educational psychology, with implications for teacher education. *Educational Psychologist, 36,* 103–112.

10. Epstein, M., Atkins, M., Cullinan, D., Kutash, K., & Weaver, R. (2008). *Reducing behavior problems in the elementary school classroom: A practice guide* (NCEE #2008-012). Washington, DC: National Center for Educational Evaluation and Regional Assistance, Institute of Education Sciences, US Department of Education. Retrieved from http://ies.ed.gov/ncee/wwc/PracticeGuide.aspx?sid=4

11. Wentzel, K. R. (1996). Social and academic motivation in middle school: Concurrent and long-term relations to academic effort. *The Journal of Early Adolescence, 16,* 390–406. Ryan, A. M., & Patrick, H. (2001). The classroom social environment and changes in adolescents' motivation and engagement during middle school. *American Educational Research Journal, 38,* 437–460.

12. Beaty-O'Ferrall, M. E., Green, A., & Hanna, F. (2010). Classroom management strategies for difficult students: Promoting change through relationships. *Middle School Journal, 41,* 4–11.

13. Brophy, J., & McCaslin, M. (1992). Teachers' reports of how they perceive and cope with problem students. *The Elementary School Journal, 93,* 3–68.

14. Zion, S., & Blanchett, W. (2011). [Re]conceptualizing inclusion: Can critical race theory and interest convergence be utilized to achieve inclusion and equity for African American students? *Teachers College Record, 113,* 2186–2205. Skiba, R. J., Simmons, A. B., Ritter, S., Gibb, A. C., Rausch, M. K., Cuadrado, J., et al. (2008). Achieving equity in special education: History, status, and current challenges. *Exceptional Children, 74,* 264–288.

15. Neal, L. R., McCray, A. D., Webb-Johnson, G., & Bridgest, S. T. (2003). The effects of African American movement styles on teachers' perceptions and reactions. *The Journal of Special Education, 37,* 49–57.

16. Feldlaufer, H., Midgley, C., & Eccles, J. S. (1988). Student, teacher, and observer perceptions of the classroom environment before and after the transition to junior high school. *The Journal of Early Adolescence, 8,* 133–156.

17. Scott, T. M., Nelson, C. M., & Liaupsin, C. J. (2001). Effective instruction: The forgotten component in preventing school violence. *Education and Treatment of Children, 24,* 309–322.

18. Ibid.

19. Tincani, M., Ernsbarger, S., Harrison, T. J., & Heward, W. L. (2005). Effects of two instructional paces on pre-K children's participation rate, accuracy, and off-task behavior in the "Language for Learning" program. *Journal of Direct Instruction, 5,* 97 109.

20. Brophy, J. (1986). Teacher influences on student achievement. *American Psychologist, 41,* 1069–1077.

21. Heward, W. L. (2003). Ten faulty notions about teaching and learning that hinder the effectiveness of special education. *The Journal of Special Education, 36,* 186–205.

22. Haydon, T., Conroy, M. A., Scott, T. M., Sindelar, P. T., Barber, B. R., & Orlando, A. M. (2010). A comparison of three types of opportunities to respond on student academic and social behaviors. *Journal of Emotional and Behavioral Disorders, 18,* 27–40.

23. Sugai & Horner (2002).

24. McIntosh, K., Campbell, A. L., Carter, D. R., & Dickey, C. R. (2009). Differential effects of a tier two behavior intervention based on function of problem behavior. *Journal of Positive Behavior Interventions, 11,* 82–93.

25. Gresham, F. M., Watson, T. S., & Skinner, C. H. (2001). Functional behavioral assessment: Principles, procedures, and future directions. *School Psychology Review, 30,* 156–172.

26. Ibid.

27. Ibid.

28. Ibid.

29. Ibid.

30. Adapted from Umbreit, J., Ferro, J., Liaupsin, C., & Lane, K. (2007). *Functional behavioral assessment and function-based intervention: An effective, practical approach.* Upper Saddle River, NJ: Prentice Hall.

31. Filter, K. J., & Horner, R. H. (2009). Function-based academic interventions for problem behavior. *Education and Treatment of Children, 32,* 193–210. Ingram, K., Lewis-Palmer, T., & Sugai, G. (2005). Function-based intervention planning: Comparing the effectiveness of FBA function-based and non-function-based intervention plans. *Journal of Positive Behavior Interventions, 7,* 224–236. Newcomer, L. L., & Lewis, T. J. (2004). Functional behavioral assessment: An investigation of assessment reliability and effectiveness of function-based interventions. *Journal of Emotional and Behavioral Disorders, 12,* 168–181.

32. Umbreit, Ferro, Liaupsin, & Lane (2007).

33. Robinson, T. R., Smith, S. W., Miller, D. M., & Brownell, M. T. (1999). Cognitive behavior modification of hyperactivity-impulsivity and aggression: A meta-analysis of school-based studies. *Journal of Educational Psychology, 91,* 195–203.

34. Robinson, T. R. (2007). Cognitive behavioral interventions: Strategies to help students make wise behavioral choices. *Beyond Behavior, 17,* 7–13.

35. Briere, D., & Simonsen, B. (2011). Self-monitoring interventions for at-risk middle school students: The importance of considering function. *Behavioral Disorders, 36,* 129–140.

36. Peterson, R., Albrecht, S., & Johns, B. (2009). CCBD's position summary on the use of physical restraint procedures in school settings. *Behavioral Disorders, 34,* 223–234.

CHAPTER EIGHT

1. Brownell, M., & Walther-Thomas, C. (2002, March). An interview with Dr. Marilyn Friend. *Intervention of School and Clinic, 37,* 223–228.

2. Friend, M., & Cook, L. (2007). *Interactions: Collaboration skills for school professionals* (5th ed.). Boston: Allyn & Bacon.

3. Enren, B., Laster, B., & Watts-Taffe, S. (2012). *Creating shared language for collaboration in RTI.* RTI Action Network. Retrieved from www.rtinetwork.org/getstarted/buildsupport/creating-shared-language-for-collaboration-in-rti

4. Kochhar-Bryant, C. (2008). *Collaboration and systems coordination for students with special needs.* Upper Saddle River, NJ: Merrill/Pearson Education.

5. Friend & Cook (2007).

6. Bondy, E., & Brownell, M. (1997). Overcoming barriers to collaboration among partners-in-teaching. *Intervention in School and Clinic, 33(2),* 112–115.

7. Theresa. (2011, September 30). *Too much of a good thing?* Reality 101: CEC's Blog for New Teachers. Retrieved from www.cecreality101.org/2011/09/theresa-too-much-of-a-good-thing.html

8. Ibid.

9. Thousand, J., Villa, R., & Nevin, A. (2006). The many faces of collaborative planning and teaching. *Theory Into Practice, 45*(3), 239–248.

10. Solis, M., Vaugn, S., Swanson, E., & McCulley, L. (2012). Collaborative models of instruction: The empirical foundations of inclusion and co-teaching. *Psychology in the Schools, 49*(5), 498–510.

11. Mancillas, A., Cook, L., Hurley, D., & Murawski, W. (2007). *Interactions collaboration skills for school professionals.* Boston: Pearson.

12. Adapted from Cook, L., & Friend, M. (1995). Co-teaching: Guidelines for creating effective practices. *Focus on Exceptional Children, 28*(3), 1–16.

13. Milik, D. (2007). *Experiences of co-teaching: Crafting the relationship.* Doctoral dissertation. Retrieved from UF Online Dissertations (UF003874751).

CHAPTER NINE

1. Roorda, D., Kooman, H., Spilt, J., & Oort, F. (2011). The influence of affective teacher-student relationships on students' school engagement and achievement. *Review of Educational Research, 81*(4), 493–529.

2. Wang, M., Brinkworth, M., & Eccles, J. (2012). Moderating effects of teacher-student relationship in adolescent trajectories of emotional and behavioral adjustment. *Developmental Psychology.* doi: 10.1037/a 0027916.

3. Arbeau, K., Coplan, R., & Weeks, M. (2010). Shyness, teacher-child relationships, and socio-emotional adjustment in grade 1. *International Journal of Behavioral Development, 34* (3), 259–269.

4. Hamre, B., & Pianta, R. C. (2006). Student-teacher relationships. In G. G. Bear & K. M. Minke (Eds.), *Children's needs III: Development, prevention, and intervention* (pp. 59–72). Bethesda, MD: National Association of School Psychologists.

5. Chartier, T. (2012, September 6). Frustrated with math? Try Angry Birds! *Huff Post, Science.* Retrieved from www.huffingtonpost.com/tim-chartier/frustrated-with-math-try-_b_1581042.html

6. Izzo, M., & Lamb, P. (2002). *Self-determination and career development: Skills for successful transition to postsecondary education and employment.* White paper written in collaboration with Ohio State University, the Center on Disability Studies at the University of Hawaii at Manoa, and the National Center on Secondary Education and Transition. Retrieved from www.ncset.hawaii.edu/publications/pdf/self_determination.pdf

7. Alberta Learning. (2002). *Unlocking potential: Key components of programming for student with learning disabilities.* Edmonton: Crown in Right of Alberta.

8. Test, D., Fowler, C., Wood, W., Brewer, D., & Eddy, S. (2005). A conceptual framework of self-advocacy for students with disabilities. *Remedial and Special Education, 26*(1), 43–54.

9. Rychly, L., & Graves, E. (2012). Teacher characteristics for culturally responsive pedagogy. *Multicultural Perspectives, 14,* 44–49. Richards, H., Brown, A., & Forde, T. (2007). Addressing diversity in schools: Culturally responsive pedagogy. *Teaching Exceptional Children, 39*(3), 64–68.

10. Nieto, S. (2001, June 18). *Sonia Nieto's reply.* Retrieved from http://knowledgeloom.org/forum_read.jsp?t=1&messageid=1475&forumid=1022&location=8&tool=2&bpinterid=1110&spotlightid=1110&testflag=yes

CHAPTER TEN

1. Common Core State Standards. (2010). *The standards.* Retrieved from www.corestandards.org
2. Fuchs, L. S., & Fuchs, D. (2007). A model for implementing responsiveness to intervention. *Teaching Exceptional Children, 39*(5), 14–20.
3. Ibid.
4. Stecker, P. M., Lembke, E. S., & Foegen, A. (2008). Using progress-monitoring data to improve instructional decision making. *Presenting School Failure, 52*(20), 48–58.
5. Deno, S. L. (1985). Curriculum-based measurement: The emerging alternative. *Exceptional Children, 52,* 219–232.
6. Stecker, Lembke, & Foegen (2008).
7. Silva, M., Munk, D. D., & Bursuck, W. D. (2005). Grading adaptations for students with disabilities. *Intervention in School and Clinic, 41*(2), 87–98.
8. Jung, L. A., & Guskey, T. R. (2010). Grading exceptional learners. *Educational Leadership, 67*(5), 31–35.
9. Munk, D. D., & Bursuck, W. D. (2004). Personalized grading plans: A systematic approach to making the grades of included students more accurate and meaningful. *Focus on Exceptional Children, 36*(9), 1–11.
10. Friend, M., & Bursuck, W. D. (2012). *Including students with special needs: A practical guide for classroom teachers* (6th ed.) Upper Saddle River, NJ: Pearson Education.
11. Ibid.
12. Munk & Bursuck (2004).
13. Gaumer-Erickson, A. S., Kleinhammer-Tramill, J., & Thurlow, M. (2007). An analysis of the relationship between high school exit exams and diploma options and the impact on students with disabilities. *Journal of Disability Policy Studies, 18*(2), 117–128.
14. Office of Special Education Programs. (2008). *Twenty-seventh annual report to Congress on the implementation of the Individuals with Disabilities Education Act, 2005.* Washington, DC: Department of Education.
15. Gaumer-Erickson, A. S., & Morningstar, M. E. (2009). The impact of alternate high school exit certificates on access to postsecondary education. *Exceptionality, 17*(3), 150–163.
16. Council for Exceptional Children. (1997). *Policies for delivery of services: Ethnic and multicultural groups* (section 3, part 1, pp. 20–21). Arlington, VA: Author.
17. Salvia, J., Ysseldyke, J. E., & Bolt, S. (2010). *Assessment in special and inclusive education* (11th ed.). Belmont, CA: Wadsworth, Cengage Learning.

CHAPTER ELEVEN

1. Center for Applied Special Technology. (2007). *Teaching every student: Getting to know you the UDL way.* Retrieved from www.cast.org/teachingeverystudent/tools/main.cfm?t_id=12
2. Center for Applied Special Technology (CAST). (2011). *Universal design for learning guidelines, version 2.0.* Wakefield, MA: Author. Used with permission.
3. UDL-IRN. (2011). *UDL in the instructional process, version 1.0.* Lawrence, KS: Author.
4. Quintana, C., Reiser, B. J., Davis, E. A., Krajic, J., Fretz, E., Duncan, G. D., et al. (2004). A scaffolding design framework for software to support science inquiry. *The Journal of the Learning Sciences, 13,* 337–386.
5. Individuals with Disabilities Education Act of 2004, 20 U.S.C., §1401(25) (2004).
6. Individuals with Disabilities Education Act of 2004, 20 U.S.C., §1401(26) (2004).
7. Zabala, J. S. (2005). *Joy Zabala's resources for assistive technology in education.* Retrieved from www.JoyZabala.html

CHAPTER TWELVE

1. Lenz, K., & Deshler, D. D. (2004). *Teaching content to all: Evidence-based inclusive practices in middle and secondary schools.* Boston: Pearson.

2. Ibid.

3. Lenz, K. (2006). Creating school-wide conditions for high-quality learning strategy classroom instruction. *Intervention in School and Clinic, 41,* 261–266.

4. Lenz, B. K., Bulgren, J. A., Schumaker, J. B., Deshler, D. D., & Boudah, D. A. (2006). *The unit organizer routine.* Lawrence, KS: Edge Enterprises, Inc.

5. Lenz, B. K., Marrs, R. W., Schumaker, J. B., & Deshler, D. D. (1993). *The lesson organizer routine.* Lawrence, KS: Edge Enterprises, Inc.

6. Ibid.

7. Weiner, B. (1979). A theory of motivation for some classroom experiences. *Journal of Educational Psychology, 71,* 3–25.

8. Borkowski, J. G., Weyhing, R. S., & Carr, M. (1988). Effects of attributional retraining on strategy-based reading comprehension in learning-disabled students. *Journal of Educational Psychology, 80,* 46–53.

9. Reid, R., & Lienemann, T. O. (2006). *Strategy instruction for students with learning disabilities.* New York: Guilford.

10. Scruggs, T., Mastropieri, M., & Okolo, C. (2008). Science and social studies for students with disabilities. *Focus on Exceptional Children, 41,* 1–24.

11. Ibid.

12. Spaulding, L. S., & Flanagan, J. S. (2012). DIS$_2$ECT: A framework for effective inclusive science instruction. *Teaching Exceptional Children, 44,* 6–14.

13. Okolo, C. M., Ferretti, R. P., & MacArthur, C. (2007). Talking about history: Discussions in a middle school inclusive classroom. *Journal of Learning Disabilities, 40,* 154–165. Ferretti, R. P., MacArthur, C. M., & Okolo, C. (2002). Teaching effectively about historical things. *Teaching Exceptional Children, 34,* 66–69.

14. Vaughn, S., & Bos, C. (2009). *Strategies for teaching students with learning and behavior problems* (2nd ed.). Upper Saddle River, NJ: Pearson Education.

15. Greenwood, C. R., Delquadri, J. C., & Hall, R. V. (1989). Longitudinal effects of classwide peer tutoring. *Journal of Educational Psychology, 81,* 371–383. Delquadri, J. C., Greenwood, C. R., & Whorton, D. (1986). Classwide peer tutoring, *Exceptional Children, 52,* 535–561.

16. Fuchs, D., & Fuchs, L. S. (1997). Peer-assisted learning strategies: Making classrooms more responsive to diversity. *American Educational Research Journal, 34,* 174–206.

17. Calhoon, M. B., & Fuchs, L. (2003). The effects of peer-assisted learning strategies and curriculum-based measurement on the mathematics performance of secondary students with learning disabilities. *Remedial and Special Education, 24,* 235–245.

18. Fuchs, L., Fuchs, D., Yazdian, L., & Powell, S. (2002). Enhancing first grade children's mathematical development with peer-assisted learning strategies. *School Psychology Review, 31,* 569–583.

19. Klingner, J. K., Vaughn, S., & Boardman, A. (2007). *Teaching reading comprehension to students with learning difficulties.* New York: Guilford.

20. Aronson, E. (2005). *Jigsaw in 10 easy steps.* Middletown, CT: Social Psychology Network. Retrieved from www.jigsaw.org/steps.htm

21. Maheady, L., Michielli-Pendl, J., Harper, G. F., & Mallette, B. (2006). The effects of Numbered Heads Together with and without an incentive package on the science test performance of a diverse group of sixth graders. *Journal of Behavioral Education, 15,* 25–39.

CHAPTER THIRTEEN

1. National Institute of Child Health and Human Development. (2000). *Report of the National Reading Panel. Teaching children to read: An evidence-based assessment of the scientific research literature on reading and its implications for reading instruction* (NIH Publication No. 00-4769). Washington, DC: US Government Printing Office.

2. Troia, G. (2004). Phonological processing and its influence on literacy learning. In C. A. Stone, E. R. Silliman, B. J. Ehren, & K. Apel (Eds.), *Handbook of language and literacy* (pp. 271–301). New York: Guilford.

3. O'Connor, R., & Jenkins, J. J. (1995). Improving the generalization of sound/symbol knowledge: Teaching spelling to kindergarten students with disabilities. *The Journal of Special Education, 29,* 255–275.

4. O'Connor, R. (2007). *Teaching word recognition.* New York: Guilford.

5. Gaskins, I. W. (2005). *Success with struggling readers: The Benchmark School approach.* New York: Guilford.

6. Knight-Mckenna, M. (2008). Syllable types: A strategy for reading multisyllabic words. *Teaching Exceptional Children, 40,* 18–24.

7. Ibid.

8. Henry, M. K. (2003). *Unlocking literacy: Effective decoding and spelling instruction.* Baltimore: Paul H. Brookes.

9. Ibid.

10. O'Connor, R., Fulmer, D., Harty, K. R., & Bell, K. M. (2005). Layers of reading intervention in kindergarten through third grade: Changes in teaching and student outcomes. *Journal of Learning Disabilities, 38,* 440–455.

11. Reutzel, D. R., & Cooter, B. (2012). *Teaching children to read: The teacher makes the difference* (6th ed.). Boston: Pearson. Henry (2003).

12. Beck, I., McKeown, M. G., & Kucan, L. (2002). *Bringing words to life: Robust vocabulary instruction.* New York: Guilford.

13. Ibid.

14. *Vocabulary in Context.* Retrieved from www.mc.cc.md.us/faculty/~steuben/public_html/vocabularycontext.htm

15. Ehri, L. C., Sallow, E., & Gaskins, I. (2009). Grapho-phonemic enrichment strengthens keyword analogy instruction for struggling young readers. *Reading and Writing Quarterly, 25,* 162–191.

16. Hudson, R. F., Pullen, P. C., Lane, H. B., & Torgeson, J. K. (2009). The complex nature of reading fluency: A multidimensional view. *Reading and Writing Quarterly, 25,* 4–32.

17. Hudson, R. F., Isakson, C., Richman, T., Lane, H. B., & Arriaza-Allen, S. (2011). An examination of small group decoding intervention for struggling readers: Comparing accuracy and automaticity criteria. *Learning Disabilities Research and Practice, 26,* 15–27.

18. O'Connor (2007).

19. Reutzel & Cooter (2012).

20. Zeno, S. M., Ivens, S. H., Millard, R. T., & Duvvuri, R. (1995). *The educator's word frequency guide.* Brewster, NY: Touchstone Applied Science Associates. Reprinted by permission of Touchstone Applied Science Associates, Inc.

21. Ibid.

22. Kuhn, M. R., & Schwanenflugel, P. J. (2008). *Fluency in the classroom.* New York: Guilford.

23. Brownell, M. T., Smith, S., Crockett, J. B., & Griffin, C. C. (2012). *Inclusive instruction: Evidence-based practices for teaching students with disabilities.* New York: Guilford.

24. Ibid.

25. Schumaker, J. B., Denton, P. H., & Deshler, D. D. (1984). *The paraphrasing strategy.* Lawrence, KS: The University of Kansas.

26. Brownell, Smith, Crockett, & Griffin (2012).

27. Englert, C. S., & Mariage, T. V. (1991). Making students partners in the comprehension process: Organizing the reading "POSSE." *Learning Disability Quarterly, 14,* 123–138.

28. Ibid.

29. Deno, S. L. (1985). Curriculum-based measurement: The emerging alternative. *Exceptional Children, 52,* 219–232.

30. Hammer, C. S., Lawrence, F. R., & Miccio, A. W. (2003). Exposure to English before and after entry into HS: Bilingual children's receptive language growth in Spanish and English. *International Journal of Bilingual Education and Bilingualism.* doi: 10.2167/beb376.0. Retrieved from www.cls.psu.edu/pubs/faculty/hammer/Hammer,%20Lawrence,%20Miccio%20BEB%202008.pdf

31. Helman, L. A. (2009). Opening doors to texts: Planning effective phonics instruction with English learners. In L. A. Helman (Ed.), *Literacy development with English learners: Research-based instruction in grades K–6* (pp. 138–155). New York: Guilford.

32. Montero, M. K., & Kuhn, M. R. (2009). English language learners and fluency development: More than speed and accuracy. In L. A. Helman (Eds.), *Literacy development with English learners: Research-based instruction in grades K–6* (pp. 156–177). New York: Guilford.

CHAPTER FOURTEEN

1. Graham, S., Harris, K. R., & Chorzempa, B. F. (2002). Contribution of spelling instruction to the spelling, writing, and reading of poor spellers. *Journal of Educational Psychology, 94,* 669–686. Reid, R., & Lienemann, T. O. (2006). *Strategy instruction for students with learning disabilities.* New York: Guilford.
2. Ehri, L. C., & Wilce, L. S. (1987). Cipher versus cue reading: An experiment in decoding acquisition. *Journal of Educational Psychology, 79,* 3–13.
3. Berninger, V. W., Abbott, R. D., Brooksher, R., Lemos, Z., Ogier, S., Zook, D., & Mostafapour, E. (2000). A connectionist approach to making the predictability of English orthography explicit to at-risk beginning readers: Evidence for alternative, effective strategies. *Developmental Neuropsychology, 17,* 241–271.
4. Bowers, P. N., Kirby, J. R., & Deacon, S. H. (2010). The effects of morphological awareness instruction on literacy skills: A systematic review of the literature. *Review of Educational Research, 80,* 144–179.
5. Wilson, B. A. (1988). *Wilson reading system.* Wilson Language Training. Retrieved from www.wilsonlanguage.com
6. Hesse, K. D., Robinson, J. W., & Rankin, R. (1983). Retention and transfer from a morphemically based direct instruction spelling program in junior high. *Journal of Educational Research, 76,* 276–279.
7. Graham, S., & Harris, K. (2005). Improving the writing performance of young struggling writers: Theoretical and programmatic research from the Center on Accelerating Student Learning. *Journal of Special Education, 39,* 19–33.
8. Zaner-Bloser. (2012). *Zaner-Bloser handwriting.* Retrieved from www.zaner-bloser.com/zaner-bloser-handwriting/zaner-bloser-handwriting-overview
9. Handwriting Without Tears. (2011). *Handwriting without tears.* Retrieved from www.hwtears.com/hwt
10. Schumaker, J. B., & Sheldon, J. (1985). *The sentence writing strategy.* Lawrence: University of Kansas.
11. Saddler, B., & Graham, S. (2005). The effects of peer-assisted sentence combining instruction on the writing performance of more and less skilled young writers. *Journal of Educational Psychology, 97,* 43–54.
12. Graham, S., & Harris, K. (2005). *Writing better: Effective strategies for teaching students with learning difficulties.* Baltimore: Paul H. Brookes.
13. Ibid.
14. Ibid.
15. Ibid.
16. MacArthur, C. (nd). *Strategy instruction in writing.* Retrieved from www.k8accesscenter.org/sharing/documents/MacArthur_Write.ppt
17. MacArthur (nd).
18. MacArthur, C., Graham, S., & Schwartz, S. (1991). Knowledge of revision and revising behavior among students with learning disabilities. *Learning Disability Quarterly, 14,* 61–74.
19. Olson, C. B., & Land, R. (2007). A cognitive strategies approach to reading and writing instruction for English language learners in secondary school. *Research in the Teaching of English, 41,* 269–303.
20. Cartledge, G., Gardner, R., & Ford, D. Y. (2009). *Diverse learners with exceptionalities: Culturally responsive teaching in the inclusive classroom.* Upper Saddle River, NJ: Pearson.

CHAPTER FIFTEEN

1. Goldman, S., & Hasselbring, T. (1997). Achieving meaningful mathematics literacy for students with learning disabilities. *Journal of Learning Disabilities, 30*(2), 198–208.

2. Johnson, E. S., Humphrey, M., Mellard, D. F., Woods, K., & Swanson, H. L. (2010). Cognitive processing deficits and students with specific learning disabilities: A selective meta-analysis of the literature. *Learning Disability Quarterly, 33,* 3–18.

3. Witzel, B., Smith, S. W., & Brownell, M. T. (2001). How can I help students with learning disabilities in algebra? *Intervention in School and Clinic, 37*(2), 101–104.

4. Cooper, J., Heron, T., & Heward, W., (2007). *Applied behavior analysis.* Columbus, OH: Pearson Merrill Prentice Hall.

5. Carnahan, C., Hume, K., Clarke, L., & Borders, C. (2009). Using structured work systems to promote independence and engagement for students with autism spectrum disorders. *Teaching Exceptional Children, 41*(4), 6–14.

6. Westling, D., & Fox, L. (2009). *Teaching students with severe disabilities.* Columbus, OH: Pearson Merrill.

7. Common Core State Standards. (2010). *The standards.* Retrieved from http://corestandards.org/the-standards

8. Witzel, B. S., Riccomini, P. J., & Schneider, E. (2008). Implementing CRA with secondary students with learning disabilities in mathematics. *Intervention in School and Clinic, 43*(5), 270–276.

9. Witzel, Riccomini, & Schneider (2008).

10. Common Core State Standards. *Grade 6: The number system.* Retrieved from www.corestandards.org/Math/Content/6/NS

11. Witzel, Riccomini, & Schneider (2008).

12. Lenz, B. K., Deshler, D. D., & Kissam, B. R. (2004). *Teaching content to all: Evidence-based inclusive practices in middle and secondary schools.* New York: Allyn & Bacon.

13. Montague, M., & Jitendra, A. (2012). Research-based mathematics instruction for students with learning disabilities. In H. Fograsz & F. Rivera (Eds.), *Towards equity in mathematics education: Gender, culture, & diversity* (pp. 481–502). Heidelberg: Springer. doi: 10.1007/978-3-642-27702-3_44.

14. Maccini, P., & Hughes, C. A. (2000). Effects of a problem-solving strategy on the introductory algebra performance of secondary students with learning disabilities. *Learning Disabilities Research & Practice, 15,* 10–21.

15. Montague & Jitendra (2012).

16. Gurganus, S. P. (2007). *Math instruction for students with learning problems.* Boston: Allyn & Bacon.

17. Ibid.

18. Westling, D., & Fox, L. (2009). *Teaching students with severe disabilities.* Columbus, OH: Pearson Merrill.

CHAPTER SIXTEEN

1. Haagar, D., & Klingner, J. K. (2005). *Differentiating instruction in inclusive classrooms: The special educators' guide.* Boston: Allyn & Bacon.

2. Manz, S. L. (2002). A strategy for previewing textbooks: Teaching readers to become THIEVES. *The Reading Teacher, 55,* 434–435.

3. Gersten, R., Fuchs, L. S., Williams, J. P., & Baker, S. (2001). Teaching reading comprehension strategies to students with learning disabilities: A review of research. *Educational Research, 71*(2), 279–320.

4. Beck, I. L., McKeown, M. G., & Omanson, R. C. (1987). The effects and uses of diverse vocabulary instructional techniques. In M. G. McKeown & M. E. Curtis (Eds.), *The nature of vocabulary acquisition* (pp. 147–163). Hillsdale, NJ: Erlbaum.

5. Frayer, D. A., Fredrick, W. C., & Klausmeier, H. J. (1969). *A schema for testing the level of concept mastery.* Working paper no. 16. Madison: Wisconsin Research and Development Center for Cognitive Learning.

6. Scruggs, T. E., & Mastropieri, M. A. (2007). Science learning in special education: The case for constructed versus instructed learning. *Exceptionality, 15*(2), 57–74.

7. Lenz, K., & Deshler, D. D. (2004). *Teaching content to all: Evidence-based inclusive practices in middle and secondary schools.* Boston: Pearson.

8. Joyce, B. R., Weil, M., & Calhoun, E. (2004). *Models of teaching* (7th ed.). Boston: Allyn & Bacon.

9. Bulgren, J. A., Deshler, D. D., & Lenz, B. K. (2007). Engaging adolescents with LD in higher order thinking about history concepts using integrated content enhancement routines. *Journal of Learning Disabilities, 40,* 121–133.

10. Bulgren, J., & Scanlon, D. (1998). Instructional routines and learning strategies that promote understanding of content area concepts. *Journal of Adolescent & Adult Literacy, 41*(4), 292–302.

11. Bulgren, J. A., Schumaker, J. B., & Deshler, D. D. (1993). *The concept mastery routine.* Lawrence, KS: Edge Enterprises, Inc.

12. National Research Council. (1996). *National science education standards.* Washington, DC: National Academies Press.

13. Bybee, R. W., Powell, J. C., & Trowbridge, L. W. (2008). *Teaching secondary school science: Strategies for developing scientific literacy* (9th ed.). Columbus, OH: Pearson.

14. Israel, M., Maynard, K., & Williamson, P. (in press). Promoting literacy-embedded authentic STEM instruction for students with disabilities and other struggling learners. *Teaching Exceptional Children.*

CHAPTER SEVENTEEN

1. American Association on Intellectual and Developmental Disabilities (2012). *Definition of intellectual disability.* Retrieved from www.aaidd.org/content_100.cfm?navID=21

2. Donnellan, A. M. (1984). The criterion of the least dangerous assumption. *Behavioral Disorders, 9,* 141–150.

3. Jorgensen, C. (2005). The least dangerous assumption: A challenge to create a new paradigm. *Disability Solutions, 6*(3), 1, 5–9.

4. Artesani, J. A., & Mallar, L. (1998). Positive behavior supports in general education settings: Combining person-centered planning and functional analysis. *Intervention in School and Clinic, 38,* 33–38.

5. Chambers, C. R., & Childre, A. L. (2005). Fostering family-professional collaboration through person-centered IEP meetings: The True Directions model. *Young Exceptional Children, 8*(3), 20–29.

6. Sparrow, S. S., Cicchetti, D., & Balla, D. A. (2005). *Vineland adaptive behavior scales* (2nd ed.). Minneapolis: NCS Pearson.

7. Harrison, P. L., & Oakland, T. (2003). *Adaptive behavior assessment system* (2nd ed.). San Antonio: The Psychological Corporation.

8. Giangreco, M. F., Cloninger, C. J., & Iverson, V. S. (1998). *Choosing outcomes and accommodations for children: A guide to educational planning for students with disability* (3rd ed.). Baltimore: Paul H. Brookes.

9. Ford, A., Schnorr, R., Meyer, L., Davern, L., Black, J., & Dempsey, P. (1989). *The Syracuse community-referenced curriculum guide for students with moderate and severe disability.* Baltimore: Paul H. Brookes.

10. Parrott, K. A., Schuster, J. W., Collins, B. C., & Gassaway, L. J. (1996). Simultaneous prompting and instructive feedback when teaching chained tasks. *Journal of Behavioral Education, 10,* 3–19.

11. Snell, M. E., Chen, L.-Y., & Hoover, K. (2006). Teaching augmentative and alternative communication to students with severe disability: A review of intervention research 1997–2003. *Research & Practice for Persons with Severe Disability, 31,* 203–214.

12. Browder, D. M., Trela, K. C., & Jimenez, B. A. (2007). Increasing participation of middle school students with significant cognitive disability. *Focus on Autism and Other Developmental Disability, 22,* 206–219. Mims, P. J., Hudson, M., & Browder, D. M. (2012). The effects of systematic instruction on teaching comprehension skills during a biography to students with significant intellectual disability. *Focus on Autism and Other Developmental Disability, 27,* 67–80.

13. Spooner, F., Knight, V. F., Browder, D. M., & Smith, B. R. (2011). Evidence-based practices for teaching academic skills to students with severe developmental disabilities. *Remedial and Special Education.* doi: 10.1177/0741932511421634.

14. Spooner, F., Browder, D., & Mims, P. (2011). Using evidence-based instructional strategies. In D. Browder & F. Spooner (Eds.), *Curriculum and instruction for students with moderate and severe disability.* New York: Guilford.

15. Staub, D., & Peck, C. (1995). What are the outcomes for non-disabled students? *Educational Leadership, 52*(4), 36–41.

16. Bondy, A. S., & Frost, L. A. (1994). The picture exchange communication system. *Focus on Autism and Other Developmental Disability, 9*(3), 1–19.

17. Courtade, G., Jimenez, B., Trela, K., & Browder, D. M. (2008). *Teaching to science standards: An inquiry-based approach for middle and high school students with moderate and severe disabilities.* Verona, WI: Attainment Company.

18. Wehmeyer, M. L. (1996). Self-determination as an educational outcome: Why is it important to children, youth and adults with disability? In D. J. Sands & M. L. Wehmeyer (Eds.), *Self-determination across the life span: Independence and choice for people with disability* (p. 22). Baltimore: Paul H. Brookes.

19. Wehmeyer, M. L., & Palmer, S. B. (2003). Adult outcomes for students with cognitive disability three-years after high school: The impact of self-determination. *Education and Training in Developmental Disability, 38,* 131–144.

20. Wehmeyer, M. L., & Schwartz, M. (1997). Self-determination and positive adult outcomes: A follow-up study of youth with mental retardation and learning disability. *Exceptional Children, 63,* 245–255.

21. Browder, D., Spooner, F., & Jimenez, B. (2011). *Standards-based individualized education plans and progress monitoring.* In D. Browder & F. Spooner (Eds.), *Teaching students with moderate and severe disabilities.* New York: Guilford

22. Jimenez, B., Mims, P. J., & Browder, D. M. (in press). Data-based decisions guidelines for teachers of students with severe intellectual and developmental disability. *Evidence and Training in Autism and Developmental Disability.*

23. Courtade, Jimenez, Trela, & Browder (2008).

CHAPTER EIGHTEEN

1. Lowe, J. (2005). Using individualized healthcare plans in the special education process. In C. Silkworth, M. Arnold, J. Harrigan, & D. Zaiger (Eds.), *Individualized healthcare plans for the school nurse* (pp. 45–57). North Branch, MN: Sunrise River Press.

2. Brandstaetter, P., Leifgren, M., & Silkworth, C. (2005). Special education: Other health impairment. In C. Silkworth, M. Arnold, J. Harrigan, & D. Zaiger (Eds.), *Individualized healthcare plans for the school nurse* (pp. 59–68). North Branch, MN: Sunrise River Press.

3. DePaepe, P., Garrison-Kane, L., & Doelling, J. (2002). Supporting students with health needs in schools: An overview of selected health conditions. *Focus on Exceptional Children, 35*(1), 1–22.

4. Heller, K., & Tumlin, J. (2004). Using expanded individualized health care plans to assist teachers of students with complex health care needs. *The Journal of School Nursing, 20*(3), 150–160.

5. Herrmann, D. (2005). Individualized healthcare plans. In C. Silkworth, M. Arnold, J. Harrigan, & D. Zaiger (Eds.), *Individualized healthcare plans for the school nurse* (pp. 1–5). North Branch, MN: Sunrise River Press.

6. DePaepe, Garrison-Kane, & Doelling (2002).

7. Poulton, S., & Denehy, J. (2005). Integrating NANDA, NIC, and NOC into individualized healthcare plans. In C. K. Silkworth, M. J. Arnold, J. F. Harrigan, & D. S. Zaiger (Eds.), *Individualized healthcare plans for the school nurse* (p. 35). North Branch, MN: Sunrise River Press. Reprinted with permission.

8. Smith, M. (2005). Anaphylaxis: Severe allergic reaction. In C. K. Silkworth, M. J. Arnold, J. F. Harrigan, & D. S. Zaiger (Eds.), *Individualized healthcare plans for the school nurse* (p. 201). North Branch, MN: Sunrise River Press. Reprinted with permission.

9. Herrmann (2005).

10. Winland, J., & Shannon, A. (2004). School staff's satisfaction with school health services. *The Journal of School Nursing, 20*(2), 101–106.

11. DePaepe, Garrison-Kane, & Doelling (2002).

12. Laskowski-Jones, L. (2006). Bee, wasp, & hornet sting. *Nursing, 36*(7), 58–59.

13. Cotter, C., & Smith, M. (2005). Individualized healthcare plans. In C. Silkworth, M. Arnold, J. Harrigan, & D. Zaiger (Eds.), *Latex allergy* (pp. 663–642). North Branch, MN: Sunrise River Press.

14. DePaepe, Garrison-Kane, & Doelling (2002).

15. Ibid.

16. Sahakian, N., White, S., Park, J., Cox-Ganser, J., & Kreiss, K. (2008). Identification of mold and dampness-associated respiratory morbidity in two schools: Comparison of questionnaire survey responses to national data. *Journal of School Health, 78*(1), 32–37.

17. Dixon, L., & Smith, S. (2009). Immunotherapy for hay fever: An introduction. *Practice Nurse, 20*(4), 188–191.

18. Walker, S. (2011). Management of hay fever. *Primary Health Care, 21*(5), 25.

19. Lepkowska, D. (2011). Hay fever can have a devastating impact on school achievement. *British Journal of School Nursing, 6*(4), 167–168.

20. Bostock-Cox, B. (2010). Hay fever and perennial rhinitis. *Practice Nurse, 39*(5), 1–6.

21. Smith, M. (2005). Individualized healthcare plans. In C. Silkworth, M. Arnold, J. Harrigan, & D. Zaiger (Eds.), *Individualized healthcare plans for the school nurse* (pp. 195–203). North Branch, MN: Sunrise River Press.

22. Cotter, C., & Smith, M. (2005). Latex allergy. In C. K. Silkworth, M. J. Arnold, J. F. Harrigan, & D. S. Zaiger (Eds.), *Individualized healthcare plans for the school nurse* (p. 642). North Branch, MN: Sunrise River Press. Reprinted with permission.

23. Dougherty, J. (2005). Asthma. In C. Silkworth, M. Arnold, J. Harrigan, & D. Zaiger (Eds.), *Individualized healthcare plans for the school nurse* (p. 255). North Branch, MN: Sunrise River Press.

24. Stingone, J., & Claudio, L. (2006). Asthma and enrollment in special education among urban schoolchildren. *American Journal of Public Health, 96*(9), 1593–1598.

25. Dougherty (2005).

26. DePaepe, Garrison-Kane, & Doelling (2002).

27. Dougherty (2005).

28. DePaepe, Garrison-Kane, & Doelling (2002).

29. Dougherty (2005).

30. Ibid.

31. Ibid.

32. Ibid.

33. Ibid.

34. Ibid.

35. Ibid.

36. Ibid.

37. Ibid.

38. Morisoli, K., & McLauglin, T. F. (2004). Medication and school interventions for elementary students with attention deficit hyperactivity disorder. *International Journal of Special Education, 19*(1), 97.

39. Vereb, R., & DiPerna, J. (2004). Teachers' knowledge of ADHD, treatments for ADHD, and treatment acceptability: An initial investigation. *School Psychology, 33*(3), 421–428.

40. Morisoli & McLauglin (2004).

41. Ibid.

42. Ibid.

43. Duffy, C. (2005). Attention deficit hyperactivity disorder. In C. Silkworth, M. Arnold, J. Harrigan, & D. Zaiger (Eds.), *Individualized healthcare plans for the school nurse* (pp. 181–193). North Branch, MN: Sunrise River Press.

44. Dahlheimer, T. (2005). Cancer. In C. Silkworth, M. Arnold, J. Harrigan, & D. Zaiger (Eds.), *Individualized healthcare plans for the school nurse* (pp. 349–366). North Branch, MN: Sunrise River Press.

45. Daly, B., Kral, M., & Brown, R. (2008). Cognitive and academic problems associated with childhood cancers and sickle cell disease. *School Psychology Quarterly, 23*(2), 230–242.

46. Dahlheimer (2005).

47. Ibid.

48. Ibid.

49. Ibid.

50. Ibid.

51. Ibid.

52. Posey, A., & Hudson, E. (2005). Cardiovascular disorders. In C. Silkworth, M. Arnold, J. Harrigan, & D. Zaiger (Eds.), *Individualized healthcare plan for the school nurse* (pp. 391–400). North Branch, MN: Sunrise River Press.

53. Ibid.

54. Ibid.

55. Ibid.

56. Ibid.

57. Ibid.

58. DePaepe, Garrison-Kane, & Doelling (2002).

59. Strawhacker, M. (2005). Cystic fibrosis. In C. Silkworth, M. Arnold, J. Harrigan, & D. Zaiger (Eds.), *Individualized healthcare plans for the school nurse* (pp. 401–415). North Branch, MN: Sunrise River Press.

60. DePaepe, Garrison-Kane, & Doelling (2002).

61. Strawhacker (2005). Cystic fibrosis.

62. Ibid.

63. Ibid.

64. DePaepe, Garrison-Kane, & Doelling (2002).

65. Ibid.

66. Strawhacker (2005). Cystic fibrosis.

67. DePaepe, Garrison-Kane, & Doelling (2002).

68. Strawhacker (2005). Cystic fibrosis.

69. Craig, M., Hattersley, A., & Donaghue, K. (2009). Definition, epidemiology and classification of diabetes in children and adolescents. *Pediatric Diabetes, 10*(Suppl. 12), 3–12.

70. Fowler, M. (2010). Diagnosis, classification, and lifestyle treatment of diabetes, *Clinical Diabetes, 28*(2), 79–86.

71. DePaepe, Garrison-Kane, & Doelling (2002).

72. Kaup, T., & Chatterton, J. (2005). Diabetes. In C. Silkworth, M. Arnold, J. Harrigan, & D. Zaiger (Eds.), *Individualized healthcare plans for the school nurse* (pp. 431–459). North Branch, MN: Sunrise River Press.

73. Ibid.

74. Banion, C., & Valentine, V. (2011). Type 1 diabetes throughout the life span. In C. Mensing (Ed.), *The art and science of diabetes self-management education* (2nd ed., pp. 329–330). Chicago: American Association of Diabetes Educators. Reprinted with permission.

75. Kaup & Chatterton (2005).

76. DePaepe, Garrison-Kane, & Doelling (2002).

77. Ibid.

78. Ibid.

79. Ibid.

80. Mandali, S., & Gordon, T. (2009). Management of type 1 diabetes in schools: Whose responsibility? *Journal of School, 79*(12), 599–601.

81. Boisclair-Fahey, A. (2009). Can individualized health care plans help increase continence in children with dysfunctional elimination syndrome? *The Journal of School Nursing, 25*(5), 333–341.

82. Ibid.

83. Ibid.

84. Mosca, M., & Haren, K. (2005). Encopresis. In C. Silkworth, M. Arnold, J. Harrigan, & D. Zaiger (Eds.), *Individualized healthcare plans for the school nurse* (pp. 497–509). North Branch, MN: Sunrise River Press.

85. Ibid.

86. Ibid.

87. Ibid.

88. Austin, J., Kakacek, J., & Carr, D. (2010). Impact of training program on school nurses' confidence levels in managing and supporting students with epilepsy and seizures. *Journal of School Nursing, 26*(6), 420–429.

89. DePaepe, Garrison-Kane, & Doelling (2002).

90. Kiel, S., & Barclay, E. (2005). Seizures. In C. Silkworth, M. Arnold, J. Harrigan, & D. Zaiger (Eds.), *Individualized healthcare plans for the school nurse* (pp. 823–844). North Branch, MN: Sunrise River Press.

91. DePaepe, Garrison-Kane, & Doelling (2002).

92. Kiel & Barclay (2005).

93. Ibid.

94. Ibid.

95. DePaepe, Garrison-Kane, & Doelling (2002).

96. Kiel & Barclay (2005).

97. Kiel, S., & Barclay, B. (2005). Seizures. In C. K. Silkworth, M. J. Arnold, J. F. Harrigan, & D. S. Zaiger (Eds.), *Individualized healthcare plans for the school nurse* (p. 828). North Branch, MN: Sunrise River Press. Reprinted with permission.

98. Kiel & Barclay (2005).

99. DePaepe, Garrison-Kane, & Doelling (2002).

100. Austin, Kakacek, & Carr (2010).

101. Sullivan, P. (2008). Gastrointestinal disorders in children with neurodevelopmental disabilities. *Developmental Disabilities Research Reviews, 14,* 128–136.

102. Strawhacker, M. (2005). Inflammatory bowel disease. In C. Silkworth, M. Arnold, J. Harrigan, & D. Zaiger (Eds.), *Individualized healthcare plans for the school nurse* (pp. 617–631). North Branch, MN: Sunrise River Press.

103. Cortina, S., McGraw, K., deAlarcon, A., Ahrens, A., Rothenberg, M., & Drotar, D. (2010). Psychological functioning of children and adolescents with eosinophil-associated gastrointestinal disorders. *Children's Health Care, 39,* 266–278.

104. Makuchal, P. (2005). Gastroesophageal reflux disease. In C. Silkworth, M. Arnold, J. Harrigan, & D. Zaiger (Eds.), *Individualized healthcare plans for the school nurse* (pp. 517–525). North Branch, MN: Sunrise River Press.

105. Strawhacker (2005). Inflammatory bowel disease.

106. Ibid.

107. Collins, S. (2007). Translating symptoms into mechanisms: Functional GI disorders. *Advances in Physiology Education, 31*(4), 329–331.

108. Strawhacker (2005). Inflammatory bowel disease.

109. Ibid.

110. Ibid.

111. Cortina, McGraw, deAlarcon, Ahrens, Rothenberg, & Drotar (2010).

112. Strawhacker (2005). Inflammatory bowel disease.

113. Spears, E. (2006). Students with HIV/AIDS and school consideration. *Teacher Education and Special Education, 29*(4), 213–234.

114. DePaepe, Garrison-Kane, & Doelling (2002).

115. Spears (2006).

116. DePaepe, Garrison-Kane, & Doelling (2002).

117. Ibid.

118. Ibid.

119. Ibid.

120. Newell, M. (2005). HIV/AIDS. In C. Silkworth, M. Arnold, J. Harrigan, & D. Zaiger (Eds.), *Individualized healthcare plans for the school nurse* (pp. 571–583). North Branch, MN: Sunrise River Press.

121. DePaepe, Garrison-Kane, & Doelling (2002).

122. Ibid.

123. Holman, C. (2005). Sickle cell disease. In C. Silkworth, M. Arnold, J. Harrigan, & D. Zaiger (Eds.), *Individualized healthcare plans for the school nurse* (pp. 845–864). North Branch, MN: Sunrise River Press.

124. Puffer, E., Sanchez, C., Stancil, M., & Roberts, C. (2009). Language processing deficits in sickle cell disease in young school-age children. *Developmental Neuropsychology, 34*(1), 122–136.

125. Holman (2005).

126. DePaepe, Garrison-Kane, & Doelling (2002).

127. Holman (2005).

128. DePaepe, Garrison-Kane, & Doelling (2002).

129. Ibid.

130. Ibid.

131. Ibid.

132. Holman (2005).

133. DePaepe, Garrison-Kane, & Doelling (2002).

134. Ibid.

135. Ibid.

136. Christner, B., & Dicker, L. (2008). Tourette syndrome—a collaborative approach focused on empowering students, families, and teachers. *Teaching Exceptional Children, 40*(5), 44–51.

137. Wong, D. L., Hockenberry, M. J., Wilson, D., Winkelstein, M. J., & Klein, N. E. (2003). *Wong's nursing care of infants and children* (7th ed.). St. Louis: Elsevier Ltd. Reprinted with permission.

138. Gray, L. (2005). Tourette syndrome. In C. Silkworth, M. Arnold, J. Harrigan, & D. Zaiger (Eds.), *Individualized healthcare plans for the school nurse* (pp. 947–959). North Branch, MN: Sunrise River Press.

139. Ibid.

140. Christner & Dicker (2008).

141. Ibid.

142. Ibid.

143. Ibid.

144. Ibid.

145. Gray (2005).

146. Ibid.

APPENDIX A

1. Centers for Disease Control and Prevention. (2010). *Attention-deficit/hyperactivity disorder.* Retrieved from http://www.cdc.gov/ncbddd/adhd/index.html

2. National Dissemination Center for Children with Disabilities. (2010, June). *Autism.* Retrieved from http://nichcy.org/disability/specific/autism

3. National Dissemination Center for Children with Disabilities. (2010, June). *Deafness and hearing loss.* Retrieved from http://nichcy.org/disability/specific/hearingloss

4. National Dissemination Center for Children with Disabilities. (2012, March; 2009, August). *Developmental delay.* Retrieved from http://nichcy.org/disability/specific/dd

5. National Dissemination Center for Children with Disabilities. (2010, June). *Emotional disturbance.* Retrieved from http://nichcy.org/disability/specific/emotionaldisturbance

6. National Dissemination Center for Children with Disabilities. (2011, January). *Intellectual disability.* Retrieved from http://nichcy.org/disability/specific/intellectual

7. National Dissemination Center for Children with Disabilities. (2011, January). *Learning disabilities.* Retrieved from http://nichcy.org/disability/specific/ld

8. National Dissemination Center for Children with Disabilities. (2011, January). *Speech and language impairments.* Retrieved from http://nichcy.org/disability/specific/speechlanguage

9. National Dissemination Center for Children with Disabilities. (2011, March). *Traumatic brain injury.* Retrieved from http://nichcy.org/disability/specific/tbi

10. National Dissemination Center for Children with Disabilities. (2004). *Blindness/visual impairment.* Retrieved from http://nichcy.org/disability/specific/visualimpairment

11. National Eating Disorders Association. (2004). *Treatment of eating disorders.* Retrieved from www.nationaleatingdisorders.org/uploads/file/information-resources/Treatment%20of%20Eating%20Disorders.pdf

APPENDIX C

1. Overton, T. *Assessing learners with special needs.* Upper Saddle River, NJ: Pearson Education.

Index

e represents exercise or exhibit; *f* represents figure; *t* represents table.

5E model, 296–298

504 plan. *See* Section 504 of the Rehabilitation Act of 1973

Flanagan, J. S., 228

Flesner, D. M., 145–146

Flexibility, 144

Flipboard (app), 202

Flipcam (software), 201

Florence County School District Four et al. Petitioners v. *Shannon Carter* (1993), 373

Flow charts, 201

Fluency: in arithmetic, 266; of speech, 367

Fluency, reading: benefits of, 243; definition of, 235; of ELLs, 249; note taking and, 253; strategies for promoting, 243–245

Fluid intake, 341

Foegen, A., 176

FOIL mnemonic, 274

Folders, student, 103

Food allergies, 328–329

FOPS strategy, 278

Formal assessment, 281

Formative assessments, 317–320

Forte, T., 100–101

4Teachers.org (website), 23*t*

Frayer's model, 292*f*, 293*t*

Free and appropriate education (FAPE) provision, 49

Frequency data sheet, 318*t*

Friend, M., 140

Fuchs, D., 230

Fuchs, L., 230

Function based interventions (FBIs), 129–134

Function matrix, 129*e*

Functional behavioral assessments (FBAs), 127–129

Functional curriculum, 305

Functional skills, 308

G

Gardiner-Walsh, S., 107–109

Gas stations, 109

Gastroesophageal reflux disease (GERD), 339

Gastrointestinal disorders, 339–340

Gender bias, 268

General education teachers: building relationships with, 42–43; as facilitators, 204; in instructional planning, 216, 217; matching students to, 143; perspectives of, on co-teaching, 153–154; positive feedback for, 147; providing assistance to, 146, 147–149; reducing resistance from, 145–146; UDL and, 198–199

Generalization: in cognitive strategy instruction, 226*t*; in direct instruction, 225*t*; of new vocabulary, 242

GeoGebra software, 283*t*

Geometer's Sketch Pad (website), 283*t*

GERD. *See* Gastroesophageal reflux disease

Getting-to-know-you activities, 106

Ginger software, 262

Gizmos, 195

Glucose monitoring, 335, 336

Goal setting, of students: in cooperative learning, 229; for fluency, 245; lesson planning and, 221; for mathematics, 268; worksheets for, 201; for writing, 255–256

Goal setting, of teachers: for collaboration, 140, 142; for co-teaching, 151; examples of, 94*t*; for organizational success, 93–94; to reduce resistance, 146

Goals, instructional: CBMs and, 176; UDL and, 197

Google Docs, 101, 193

GPS, 107

Grade-level chairs, 108

Grading work, 183–186

Graduation exit exams, 186

Graham, S., 256

Grammar-checking applications, 203

Grand mal seizures, 337

Graphic organizers, 195*t*, 200; for content area instruction, 290*f*, 290*t*, 295; to promote reading comprehension, 246; for writing tasks, 259–260*e*. *See also specific types*

Graphing data, 176–177

Gratitude, expressions of, 29–30

Greenwood, C., 230

Group processing, 229

Group responses, 232

Grudges, 160

Guided imagery approaches, 228

Guided practice, 226*t*

Guskey, T., 183

H

Haagar, D., 287

Handwriting, 253

Handwriting Without Tears, 253

Harris, K., 256

Hay fever, 329

Health conditions, 325–326. *See also specific conditions*

Hearing impairment, 315, 353–355

Hemophilia, 363

Heterogeneous groups. *See* Cooperative learning strategies

High school classrooms: assessment considerations for, 186–188; design of, 98–101; first-day activities for, 106; tips for motivation in, 162–163

High school diploma: algebra and, 267; alternatives to, 186–187

High school dropouts, 77

High-achieving students, 230

High-frequency behaviors, 134–136

High-frequency words, 243, 244*t*

High-stakes exams, 186

High-tech assistive technology, 208, 317*t*

Hi-lo books, 200

HIV/AIDS, 340

Holden, K. B., 28

Hollingshead, A., 269, 279, 283, 300–301

Homebound instruction, 333, 334

Homework. *See* Student work

Honig, California Superintendent of Public Instruction v. *Doe et al.* (1988), 373

Hospital school, 333

Humor, 163

Hyperactivity, 349

Hyperglycemia, 335

Hypertension, 333, 340

Hypoglycemia, 335

I

IAES. *See* Interim alternative education setting

IBD. *See* Inflammatory bowel disease

Idealism, of new teachers, 12

Identifying students with disabilities, 55

IEP meetings: case manager's role in, 92*t*; dealing with conflict during, 80*e*; etiquette for, 79–80*e*; ground rules for, 79*e*; notifying parents of, 76–77, 78*e*; parent participation in, 77; planning for, 78*e*; purpose of, 66; required participants in, 74, 78*e*; time management during, 80*e*; tips for facilitating, 78–81*e*

IEPs: aligning standards with, 173; alternative assessments and, 181; assistive technology and, 75–76, 208, 316; challenges of, 65;

classroom organization and, 97; collaborative logs and, 155; components of, 67–74, 67f; conflicts regarding, 30; examples of, 71; forms for, 84–85e; free and appropriate education provision and, 49; grading adaptations and, 184–186; grading myths and, 183; IDEA provisions and, 52; least restrictive environment and, 50; organizing the process of, 83, 85; overview of, 66; paraeducator's contribution to, 41; providing assistance with, 147–149; self-advocacy and, 165–166; suggestions for successful writing of, 66–67, 86; summary forms for, 83; testing accommodations and, 179, 180

Ignoring errors, 310

Ignoring inappropriate behavior, 133–134

IHPs. *See* Individualized health care plans

Immediate assistance, 146

Impulsivity, 349

Inattention, 348

Inclusive settings: collaboration in, 142–146; for content area instruction, 286; grading adaptations in, 184–186; resistance in, 145–146

Incontinence, 336

Independent practice, 226t

Individualized health care plans (IHPs), 326, 327e

Individuals with Disabilities Education Act (IDEA): assessment and, 58; assistive technology and, 75, 207, 208, 316; collaboration and, 18; confidentiality and, 16; developmental delays and, 355; intellectual disability and, 304; other health impairments and, 365; overview of, 48t, 51; provisions of, 51–53; special educators' tasks related to, 53

Induction, for new teachers, 22

Infection, 340

Inflammatory bowel disease (IBD), 339

Inflected endings, 237t, 239, 240t

Inquiry approaches: for content area instruction, 295–300; description of, 227; versus problem-, project-, and challenge-based learning, 299, 300t; students' challenges with, 296–298

Inquiry, definition of, 295–296

Insect stings, 329

Inspiration (software), 196t, 262–263

Instructional activities: behavior management and, 122–124; evaluation of, 177; for first day of school, 106; providing engaging types of, 122–124; to teach about instructional technology, 204; UDL and, 197–198

Instructional approaches, general types of, 223–232

Instructional planning: assessments and, 216–217; benefits of, 223; in content areas, 293; for co-teachers, 104, 150, 154; guidelines for, 216–223; importance of, 215–216; for intellectual disability, 306–308; resistance-reducing strategies and, 145; for students with intellectual disabilities, 304; UDL and, 196

Instructional strategies. *See specific strategies*

Instructional supports, multitiered: description of, 175; UDL and, 199

Instructional technologies: concerns about, 191–192; for content area instruction, 206–207; definition of, 191; examples of, 203; getting started with, 203–204; teaching students about, 204; types of, 205–206

Instructional time, 18

Insulin, 335, 336

Intellectual disability: assessments and, 306–308, 317–321; assistive technology and, 316; characteristics of students with, 304, 361; definition of, 304, 360; diagnosis of, 361–362; evidence-based practice and, 308; instructional planning for, 304, 306–308; instructional standards and, 305; legal issues regarding, 304, 308; personal relevance and, 305; self-determination and, 316–317; tips and resources for, 362

Intelligence quotient (IQ), 361, 374–375

Intelligence tests, 178t, 374

Interactive whiteboards, 204–205

Interdependence, 229

Interest: in student work, 117t; in students' lives, 159–160

Interim alternative education setting (IAES), 54

Interpreters: for IEP meetings, 77; for parent communication, 34

Interrater reliability, 376

Intervention Central (website), 23t

Interviews, for data collection, 128

Interviews, job, 5, 7, 8–9e

iPods, 196t, 201

IQ, 361, 374–375

IRIS (website), 22, 23t

Irving Independent School District v. Amber Tatro (1984), 373

Isolated phonological awareness instruction, 235

Itinerant teachers, 107–109

J

Jacob Winkelman v. Parma City School District (2007), 373

Jargon, 188

Jigsaw strategy, 232

Jimenez, B. A., 303

Job description, 4

Job offers, 10

Job search: challenges in, 4; geographical areas for, 4; importance of, 3; interviews in, 5, 7, 8–9e; steps in, 4–5; websites for, 5

Johnston, D., 262, 263

Jones, A., 162–163

Journals, of teachers, 106

Judgments, making: about parents, 34; conflict resolution and, 31; of students' cultures, 120

Jung, L. A., 183

Juvenile diabetes, 335

K

Kemmery, M., 315

Key words, 294

Keyboarding, 253

KeyMath 3, 281

Keynote (software), 196t

Key-word method, 293t

Kidspiration (software), 196t, 262–263

KidsSpell.com, 253

Klingner, J., 231, 287

Knowledge review, 222

Kucan, L., 241

L

Labeling students, 174

Language disorders, 367–368

Language problems, 341

Latex allergies, 329, 330t

Latino students, 120

Laughter, 163

Laws: intellectual disability and, 304, 308; learning about, 16; listing of, pertaining to special education, 373; overview of, 48t; purpose of, 47; regarding assessment, 173–175; regarding FBAs, 127. *See also specific laws*

LD Online (website), 24t

Lead poisoning, 353–354

Learned helplessness, 267–268, 288

Learner needs, 197

Learning disability, 365–367

Learning environment, 268

Learning Suffixes (website), 200

purpose of, 13–14; organizational challenges of, 93; professional standards of, 14–15; realities of, 11–13; required knowledge of, 16–17, 19–20; stress management of, 18–19; support network for, 20–22, 23–24*t*; time management of, 18. *See also* Special education teachers

No Child Left Behind (NCLB) Act: assessment and, 58; case related to, 60; content standards and, 17; intellectual disability and, 304, 308; reading instruction and, 234

No-name folders, 99

Nondiscriminatory evaluation, 174

Nonexamples, 292

Nonverbal communication, 28

Nonverbal redirection, 117*t*

Norm-referenced assessments: description of, 178; statistical concepts related to, 374–375

Note taking: fluency and, 253; to organize work, 94–95

Numbered heads together strategy, 232

Nurses, 326

O

Objectives, mathematics, 280

Observation: in FBA process, 128; for teacher evaluations, 377–379

Obsessive-compulsive disorder (OCD), 359–360

Office staff, 110

Okolo, C., 227, 229

Online learning resources: description of, 22; listing of, 23–24*t*

Open Office (software), 196*t*

Open syllables, 238

Order of operations, 265, 277

Organizational skills, of students, 169–171

Organizing work: classroom design and, 98–104; for co-teachers, 103–104; for first-day tasks, 104–106; importance of, 90; as itinerant teachers, 107–110; paperwork tips for, 95; routines for, 95; table for, 94; time management and, 95, 96–97; volunteering and, 96

Other health impaired, 326, 362–365

Outcomes, 198

"Overcoming Barriers to Collaboration among Partners-in-Teaching" (Bondy and Brownell), 145

Overhead projectors, 204

P

Pacing, of instruction: behavior management and, 122; in mathematics, 271

PALS. *See* Peer-assisted learning strategies

Panther rule, 239

Paperwork, organizing, 95, 100–102

Paraeducators: data collection by, 41; evaluation of, 42; feedback for, 39, 42; getting input from, 41; inclusion of, in IEPs, 41; initial work with, 39, 41–42; policies related to, 41; professional learning for, 41; schedule for, 40*e*; successful communication with, 29–30

Parent notification: about disciplinary action, 54; about IEP meetings, 76–77, 78*e*; about legal rights, 60

Parent participation: Education for All Handicapped Children Act and, 49, 51*e*; in IEP meetings, 77; in transition planning, 82–83

Parents: appreciation of, 34; communication log for, 36*e*; confidentiality of, 35; cultures and needs of, 37; as experts on children, 34; legal rights of, 34, 51*e*, 55, 60; letters to, 33*e*; managing conflicts with, 30–31; non-English-speaking, 34; online communication with, 35; positive notes to, 33–34; promoting positive relationships with, 31–35; providing assessment results to, 187–188; regular communication with, 35; self-advocacy and, 166; sharing resources with, 35; successful communication with, 29; support groups for, 29

Parity, 140

Partial participation, 310

Partial seizures, 337, 338

Partially sighted students, 371

Park, Y., 249

Partner reading, 244–245

Passive learning, 267–268

Patience, 268

Patterns, 270

PDD. *See* Pervasive developmental disorders

Peer attention, 134

Peer pressure, positive: to build motivation, 161; purpose of, 116; to reinforce positive behaviors, 134

Peer revising strategy, 261

Peer supports, 315–316

Peer training, 316

Peer tutoring, 230

Peer-assisted learning strategies (PALS), 230–231, 245

Peer-reviewed research (PRR), 66

Peg-word method, 293*t*

PEMDAS strategy, 277

PENS strategy, 254

Percentiles, 187

Personal connections, 165

Personal information, 159–160

Personally relevant curriculum, 305

Person-centered planning, 307

Perspectives, individual, 144

Pervasive developmental disorders (PDD), 351

Petit mal seizures, 337

PhET, 195

Phone calls, 96

Phonics: definition of, 235; description of, 235; versus spelling, 253; teaching strategies for, 235–238

Phonological awareness: definition of, 235; description of, 235; teaching strategies for, 235–238

Physical disabilities, 369

Planning. *See* Instructional planning

PLOP. *See* Present levels of performance

Podcasts, 196*t*

Point systems: examples of, 135*e*; purpose of, 134

Poisoning, 363–364

Policies: learning about, 16; parent partnerships and, 32; related to paraeducators, 41

Pollutants, 331

Positive attribution style, 225, 227

Positive integers, 274

Positive reinforcement, 332

POSSE strategy, 246, 247*f*

Post-observation conferences, 378

Power, T., 249

PowerPoint (software), 196*t*

Powers, D., 102

Praise: description of, 117*t*; effective use of, 118; motivation and, 162

Precorrection, 117*t*

Predictions, making, 245*t*

Predictive validity, 375

Predominantly hyperactive-impulsive ADHD, 349

Predominantly inattentive ADHD, 349

Prefixes, 239, 240*t*

Present levels of performance (PLOP): example statements of, 68–69; overview of, 68; writing tips for, 68

Presentation accommodations, 179

Previewing text, 231

Prezi (software), 196*t*

Primary generalized seizures, 337, 338

Primary sources, 229

Self-contained classrooms, 140–142

Self-determination, 316–317

Self-esteem: dysfunctional elimination syndrome and, 336; grading myths regarding, 183

Self-monitoring, of behaviors, 136

Self-questioning, 245t

Self-reflection, 168

Semantic maps, 218, 260e, 291

Sensorineural hearing losses, 353

Sentence structure, 254

Sentence-combining strategy, 254, 255t

Serious video games, 206

SETT process, 209

Setting accommodations, 180

The 7 Habits of Highly Effective People (Covey), 27

Severe disability. *See* Intellectual disability

Shared purpose, 121

Shared responsibility, 140

Short-term objectives. *See* Benchmark objectives

Sickle cell disease, 340–341

Sight words, 243, 310

Signal and share response, 124t

Signaling response, 123t

Simple motor tics, 342t

Simple partial seizures, 337

Simple vocal tics, 342t

Simulations, 195

Simultaneous prompting, 312e

SIP. *See* Systematic instruction plan

Skill assessment, of paraeducators, 39

SMART Inclusion (wiki), 205

SMARTER planning process, 217–218, 219t

Smartphones, 94, 107

Social difficulties, 358, 370

Social networking, 35

Social phobia, 358

Social skills instruction, 125, 132

SOLO 6 Literacy Suite, 263

Sound manipulation, 236t

Spanish language, 249

Spaulding, L., 228

Special Connections (website), 22, 24t

Special education, definition of, 47

Special education services: diagnosis required for, 174; evaluation to receive, 174; IEP development and, 71, 73

Special education teachers: as advocates, 14; areas of need of, 12t; content-area instruction and, 285–286; desk organization of, 102; as facilitators, 204; keys to success of, 13; matching students to, 143; most challenging task of, 65; roles and responsibilities of, 91, 92, 93e, 158–159, 164. *See also* New teachers

Specific learning disability, 365–367

Specific praise, 118

Speech/language disorders, 367–368

Speech-language therapist, 341

Spell-checking applications, 203

Spelling, 236t, 238, 253

Spelling through Morphographs, 253

Spiral instruction, 271

Spivak, W., 199–202

Stable final consonants, 238

Standard deviations, 374

Standardized assessments: accommodations and adaptations for, 179–181; in mathematics, 281; types of, 178

Standards: aligning assessment with, 173; becoming knowledgeable about, 14–15; description of, 20; grading adaptations and, 184;

intellectual disability and, 305; in mathematics, 269–271, 278; of professionalism, 20–21; for teacher evaluations, 20. *See also* *specific standards*

STAR strategy, 277–278

State assessments, 281

State teaching standards, 14; aligning IEPs with, 173; description of, 173; instructional planning guidelines and, 216

Stecker, P., 176

Stereotypes, 268

Stimulant medications, 331–332

Stimulus fading, 311e

Stimulus prompts, 310, 311e

Storage spaces, 101

Story grammar strategy, 258

Story maps, 246

Story-based literacy lessons, 315

Strategy-implementation processes, 277–278

Stress management: respectful communication and, 28; tips for, 18–19

STTAR strategy, 132–133

Student collaborative logs, 157e

Student dictionaries, 241–242

Student records: privacy and, 16; reviewing, in FBA process, 128

Student responsibilities, 169–171

Student seating: for behavior management, 114; design for, 98

Student work: classroom design and, 99; feedback on, 183; in mathematics, 272

Student-directed inquiry, 298–299

Students: becoming knowledgeable about, 17–18; building cooperative relationships among, 121–122; first-day tasks for, 104–105; matching teachers to, 143; as participants in IEP meetings, 78e; as participants in transition planning, 82–83

Student–teacher relationships. *See* Relationships, student–teacher

Stylus markers, 204

Success: celebrating, 163; motivation and, 162; providing opportunities for, 122

Suffixes, 239, 240t

Summarization, 245t

Summative assessments, 319–321

Supervisors, 36, 38

Supplementary aids/services: examples of, 74; IEP development and, 74; purpose of, 74

Support groups, for parents, 29

Support network, for new teachers: challenges to, 20; creation of, 20–22, 23–24t

Surface-responding techniques: purpose of, 116; types of, 117t

Syllables, 238–241

Symbolic representation, 265

Syracuse Community-Referenced Curriculum Guide for Students with Moderate and Severe Disability, 308

Systematic instruction, 308–312

Systematic instruction plan (SIP), 312, 313–314e

T

Task analysis, 279, 280, 281t

Task analytic data sheet, 318t

Task management programs, 94

TBI. *See* Traumatic brain injury

Teacher bags, 109

Teacher evaluation process: learning about, 38; preparing for, 377–379

Teacher-directed inquiry, 298–299

Teachers. *See* General education teachers; Special education teachers